Fro[m ...]
to Hollywood

To Lisa and Gary —
with warmest good
wishes —
[signature]
Vancouver
2007

To Lisa &
Gary
It's a book about
family!
[signature] 19 January 2007

Contemporary Cinema 3

Series Editors
Ernest Mathijs &
Steven Jay Schneider

Editorial Advisory Board:
Martin Barker (University of Wales-Aberystwyth)
Wanda Bershen (Founder, Red Diaper Productions)
Mark Betz (University of London, King's College)
David Bordwell (University of Wisconsin-Madison)
Sean Cubitt (University of Waikato, New Zealand)
Roger Garcia (Former Director, Hong Kong International Film Festival)
Joke Hermes (University of Amsterdam)
Jim Hillier (University of Reading)
Mark Jancovich (University of Nottingham)
Douglas Kellner (University of California-Los Angeles)
Soyoung Kim (Korean National University of Arts)
Amy Kronish (Consultant in Jewish & Israeli Film)
Barney Oldfield (General Manager, Angelika Entertainment)
Murray Pomerance (Ryerson University, Canada)
Michael Renov (University of Southern California)
David Schwartz (Chief Curator of Film, American Museum of the Moving Image)
M.M. Serra (Executive Director, Film-Makers Cooperative)
J. David Slocum (New York University)
Christina Stojanova (Wilfrid Laurier University, Canada)
Kristin Thompson (University of Wisconsin-Madison)

Contemporary Cinema is a series of edited volumes and single-authored texts focusing on the latest in film culture, theory, reception and interpretation. There is a concentration on films released in the past fifteen years, and the aim is to reflect important current issues while pointing to others that to date have not been given sufficient attention.

From Hobbits to Hollywood

Essays on Peter Jackson's
Lord of the Rings

Edited by
Ernest Mathijs and Murray Pomerance

Rodopi

Amsterdam - New York, NY 2006

Institutional support:
The Department of Theatre, Film and Television Studies at the
University of Wales-Aberystwyth

The paper on which this book is printed meets the requirements
of "ISO 9706:1994, Information and documentation - Paper for
documents - Requirements for permanence".

ISBN-10: 90-420-2062-8
ISBN-13: 978-90-420-2062-7
ISSN: 1572-3070
©Editions Rodopi B.V., Amsterdam - New York, NY 2006
Printed in the Netherlands

To Hedwig,

And to Nellie and Ariel,

Our first guides on this journey

*If there's no pleasure for me in it,
I feel no obligation to a work of art.*

Orson Welles to Peter Bogdanovich

CONTENTS

List of Illustrations   v
Dramatis Personae   ix
Acknowledgments   xiii
Contributors   xv

Introduction: There and Back Again: An Editors' Tale   1
Ernest Mathijs and Murray Pomerance

The Lord of the Rings as Allegory: A Multiperspectivist Reading   17
Douglas Kellner

The Lord of the Rings and Family: A View on Text and Reception   41
Ernest Mathijs

The Fading of the Elves: Eco-Catastrophe, Technopoly, and Bio-Security   65
Sean Cubitt

On Being a 1960s Tolkien Reader   81
Martin Barker

Epic Fantasy and Global Terrorism   101
Ken Gelder

A Land of Make Believe: Merchandising and Consumption of *The Lord of the Rings*   119
Ian Conrich

Fic Frodo Slash Frodo: Fandoms and *The Lord of the Rings*   137
Jennifer Brayton

The Lord of the Rings as Melodrama   155
Sarah Kozloff

Masculinity, Whiteness, and Social Class in *The Lord of the Rings*   173
Lianne McLarty

Urban Legend: Architecture in *The Lord of the Rings* 189
Steven Woodward and Kostis Kourelis

The Lord of the Rings and The Fellowship of the Map 215
Tom Conley

Enchantments of *The Lord of the Rings*: Soundtrack, Myth, Language, and Modernity 231
James Buhler

"Wicked, tricksy, false": Race, Myth, and Gollum 249
Cynthia Fuchs

"What does the Eye Demand": Sexuality, Forbidden Vision and Embodiment in *The Lord of the Rings* 265
Ruth Goldberg and Krin Gabbard

Scale, Spectacle and Movement: Massive Software and Digital Special Effects in *The Lord of The Rings* 283
Kirsten Moana Thompson

Morphing Sean Astin: "Playing Fat" in the Age of Digital Animation 301
Jerry Mosher

Gollum and Golem: Special Effects and the Technology of Artificial Bodies 319
Tom Gunning

The Laddy Vanishes 351
Murray Pomerance

Works Cited and Consulted 373

Index 393

List of Illustrations

Image 1:	A transformation of transformations: Peter Jackson and Ian McKellen go over the shooting script based on the screenplay based on the trilogy of books for the trilogy of films this collection studies (© New Line Cinema, Yahoo Movies.com)	15
Image 2:	Fractured family lines and failure to destroy the ring. (Courtesy of Dr. Kristine Larsen, Central Connecticut State University).	47
Image 3:	Elrond's father figure hands Aragorn the sword Andúril re-establishing an allegiance. Digital frame enlargement (© New Line Cinema).	51
Image 4:	Family in the Extended DVD edition: Faramir and Boromir (Courtesy: www.theonering.net)	52
Image 5:	The new alliance between Rohan and Gondor: Eowyn and Faramir. (© Yahoo Movies.com)	58
Image 6:	Point-to-point technology: Saruman using the Palantír (Copyright © Quintessential Lord of the Rings Movie Shots – www.warofthering.net)	73
Image 7:	Frodo Has Failed. (www.myirony.com, 2/02/2003)	104
Image 8:	The Burger King "Ring of Power" of figurines. (www.fastfoodtoys.net)	124
Image 9:	Air New Zealand's flying billboard for *The Lord of the Rings*. (Copyright © Brinkley Wings Collection, www.brinkley.cc)	136
Images 10/11:	A new breed of fan being identified through their consumer practices. (Photographs by Katherine Zion)	145

Image 12:	Paying homage to virtue, the Hobbits at Minas Tirith. Digital frame enlargement. (© New Line Cinema)	162
Images 13/14:	Fine features, large eyes. Elijah Wood before *The Lord of the Rings*	163
Image 15:	pastoral view of the Shire of Alan Lee and John Howe. (www.tlotr.com)	194
Image 16:	The miniature comforts and warm whites of Hobbit houses. (http://img-fan.theonering.net)	200
Image 17:	The gothic fashion of Isengard and Barad Dûr (from the poster of The Two Towers)	203
Image 18:	The map of Middle Earth according to Jackson. Digital frame enlargement. (© New Line Cinema)	222
Image 19:	From the map to the world inside it. Digital frame enlargement. (© New Line Cinema)	224
Image 20:	Bilbo's map of The Lonely Mountain. Digital frame enlargement. (© New Line Cinema)	227
Image 21:	Sauron's eye as a giant flaming vaginal slit. (directxscreensavers.com).	273
Image 22:	The Pillars of the King Digital frame enlargement. (© New Line Cinema)	287
Images 23/24:	Massive's digital agent, and agents in action at Pelennor Fields (Copyright © Massive Industries)	293
Images 25/26:	Sean Astin displays his lean physique as star of the 1993 football film *Rudy* (left) and his pot belly after gaining thirty-five pounds to play Samwise Gamgee in *The Lord of the Rings* (right). Courtesy TriStar Pictures (left), New Line Cinema (right).	307

Image 27:	Sam and Gollum discuss how rabbits ("coneys") should be prepared. (© New Line Cinema)	316
Image 28:	"It's the only way. Go in... or go back." The body of the Andy Serkis/CGI creation, Gollum. Digital frame enlargement. (© New Line Cinema)	335
Images 29/30:	In *The Fellowship of the Rings* we see the Witch King through *Frodo's* invisibility but at the climax of *The Return of the King*, when Frodo is in the grasp of Gollum, the screen is filled with *our* vision of the invisible "boy." Digital frame enlargements (© New Line Cinema)	365

Dramatis Personae

The Fellowship
Frodo Baggins:	Elijah Wood
Samwise "Sam" Gamgee:	Sean Astin
Meriadoc 'Merry' Brandybuck:	Dominic Monaghan
Peregrin "Pippin" Took:	Billy Boyd
Strider, Ranger of the North/	
Aragorn, son of Arathorn, heir to Gondor's throne:	Viggo Mortensen
Legolas Greenleaf of Mirkwood:	Orlando Bloom
Gimli of Lonely Mountain, son of Gloin:	John Rhys-Davies
Boromir of Gondor, son of Denethor:	Sean Bean

Hobbits
Bilbo Baggins:	Ian Holm
Gollum/Sméagol:	Andy Serkis
Deagol, friend of Sméagol:	Thomas Robins
Everard Proudfoot:	Noel Appleby
Mrs. Everard Proudfoot:	Megan Edwards
Rosie Cotton, wife of Sam Gamgee:	Sarah McLeod
Elanor Gamgee, daughter of Sam Gamgee:	Alexandra Astin
Farmer Maggot:	Cameron Rhodes

Wizards
Gandalf the Grey, later Gandalf the White:	Ian McKellen
Saruman the White of Isengard:	Christopher Lee

Elves
Galadriel of Lothlorien, Lady of the Golden Wood:	Cate Blanchett
Celeborn, Lord of the Golden Wood:	Marton Czokas
Elrond, Lord of Rivendell:	Hugo Weaving
Arwen, daughter of Elrond:	Liv Tyler
Haldir, Elf of Lorien:	Craig Parker
Gil-Galad, an Elven King:	Mark Ferguson

Men of Bree
Harry Goatleaf, the Gatekeeper of Bree:	Martyn Sanderson
Barliman Butterbur, proprietor of the Prancing Pony:	David Weatherley

Men of Gondor

Isildur, son of Elendil:	Harry Sinclair
Elendil, King of Gondor:	Peter McKenzie
Faramir, son of Denethor, brother of Boromir:	David Wenham
Madril, Lieutenant of Faramir:	John Bach
Damrod, Ranger of Ithilien:	Alistair Browning
Denethor, Steward of Gondor/Minas Tirith:	John Noble
Irolas [Beregond in Tolkien's book], soldier:	Ian Hughes

Men of Rohan

Eomer, brother of Eowyn:	Karl Urban
Gamling, Lieutenant of Théoden:	Bruce Hopkins
Théodred, Prince of Rohan:	Paris Howe Strewe
Háma, doorwarden of Théoden:	John Leigh
Eowyn, sister of Eomer:	Miranda Otto
Theoden, King of Rohan:	Bernard Hill
Grima Wormtongue:	Brad Dourif
Éothain, son of Morwen:	Sam Comery
Freda, daughter of Morwen:	Olivia Tennet
Morwen, mother of Theoden:	Robyn Malcolm
Haleth, son of Háma:	Calem Gittins
Aldor, soldier at Helm's Deep:	Bruce Allpress
Grimbold, rider of Rohan:	Bruce Phillips

Agents of Mordor and Isengard

Sauron, The Dark Lord:	Sala Baker
The mouth of Sauron:	Bruce Spence
The Witch-King of Angmar, Lord of the Nazgûl:	Shane Rangi
	Brent McIntyre
Gothmog, Lieutenant of Morgul:	Lawrence Makoare
Grishnákh, orc, would-be slayer of Merry and Pippin:	Stephen Ure
Gorbag, Captain of the Orcs at Minas Morgul:	Stephen Ure
Shagrat, Captain of the Orcs at Cirith Ungol:	Peter Tait
Lurtz, Uruk-hai warrior of Saruman:	Lawrence Makoare
Uglúk, Uruk-hai commander of Isengard:	Nathaniel Lees
Maúhur, Uruk-hai commander at Helm's Deep:	Robbie Magasiva

Other orcs, Uruk-hai and Ringwraiths variously played by... Victoria Beynon-Cole, Lee Hartley, Sam La Hood, Chris Streeter, Jonathan Jordan, Semi Kuresa, Clinton Ulyatt, Paul Bryson, Lance Fabian Kemp, Jono Manks, Ben Price, Philip Grieve, Paul Holmes, Piripi Waretini, Robert Pollock, Ross Duncan, Pete Smith, Jed Brophy, Joel Tobeck, and Sala Baker

Other Creatures

King of the Dead:	Paul Norell
Treebeard the Ent:	voice by John-Rhys Davies
The Voice of the Ring:	Alan Howard

Acknowledgments

We extend our sincere thanks to a number of persons, wizards, sages, and assorted humble folk without whose very generous assistance we would never have been able to realize this project at all, let alone so relatively swiftly after the release of the Peter Jackson films. To Martin Barker and Kate Egan (Aberystwyth) for being such wonderful fellow travelers on the *Lord of the Rings* Audience project, our gratitude; and the same to Nathan Holmes (Chicago), for buoyancy of spirit; Taija and Matthew Queen (Vancouver), for testing us on factual knowledge; Steven Jay Schneider (Los Angeles), for being at the cradle of this endeavour with such a warm and enthusiastic good humor, and for his support as we worked. A special "bedankt" to Hedwig Mathijs (Brussels) for feedback and advice on images, and to Howard and Ron Mandelbaum at PhotoFest (New York) for their canny and precise photographic help.

David Kerr (Toronto) has been a hard-working research assistant, sometimes abandoned in the dank caves of the Index Monster for days and nights too long.

We are indebted to the Dean of Arts at Ryerson University, and to the Department of Theatre, Film, and Television Studies, University of Wales, Aberystwyth.

Our colleagues at Editions Rodopi have been special partners and we wish especially to thank Christa Stevens, Fred Van der Zee, and Pier Post.

Ernest sends his warmest thanks to Emily Perkins, for careful editing, love, and for being there in Brussels on that spring night; and Murray his to Nellie Perret and Ariel Pomerance for their unbounded interest, knowledge, and excitement, the deepest inspiration of all.

Ernest Mathijs (Aberystwyth)
Murray Pomerance (Toronto)
February 2006

Contributors

Martin Barker is Professor of Film & Television Studies at the University of Wales, Aberystwyth, where he directs the Centre for Audience & Reception Studies. He has researched racism, comic books, methods of film analysis, and film audiences. He is the (co-)author of *The Crash Controversy* (2001), *From Antz to Titanic* (2000), *The Lasting of the Mohicans* (1998), *Knowing Audiences* (1997), and *Comics: Ideology, Power and the Critics* (1989), and numerous essays in edited books and journals. He directed the Lord of the Rings international audience project.

Jennifer Brayton is Assistant Professor in the Department of Sociology at Ryerson University. Her research includes popular culture and media, cyberculture studies, and sexual identity. She is a member of Canadian Women's Studies Association, and the Canadian Sociology and Anthology Society. One of her recent essays appears in *Popping Culture* (2005). She is planning social research on Canadian female DJs and writing a textbook on Canadian popular cultural industries.

James Buhler is associate professor of music theory at The University of Texas at Austin. He is co-editor of *Music and Cinema* and has written extensively on music and film sound. He is currently at work on *Auditory Culture and the American Cinema, 1895-1933*.

Tom Conley, author of *The Self-Made Map: Cartographic Writing in Early Modern France* (1996) and *A Map in a Movie* (forthcoming 2006), has translated works of Marc Augé, Michel de Certeau, Gilles Deleuze, Louis Marin, and other writers. He teaches in the Departments of Romance Languages and Visual & Environmental Studies at Harvard University.

Ian Conrich is Senior Lecturer in Film Studies at Roehampton University, and Editor of *Journal of British Cinema and Television*. He is Chair of the New Zealand Studies Association. He was a Guest Editor of a special issue of *Post Script* on Australian and New Zealand cinema, he is the author of *New Zealand Cinema* , and (co-)editor of seven books, including *New Zealand Fictions: Literature and Film* (2005), *New Zealand - A Pastoral Paradise?* (2000), and *Contemporary New Zealand Cinema* and *New Zealand Filmmakers*.

Sean Cubitt is Professor of Screen and Media Studies at the University of Waikato, New Zealand. His most recent publications include *EcoMedia*

(2005), *The Cinema Effect* (2004), *Simulation and Social Theory* (2001), and *Digital Aesthetics* (1998). He is currently writing on the history of light.

Cynthia Fuchs is Director of George Mason University's Film & Media Studies Program, as well as film-tv-dvd editor for *PopMatters.com*, and film reviewer for Philadelphia Citypaper (citypaper.net) and Screenit.com. She has published articles on hiphop, Prince, Michael Jackson, the Spice Girls, queer punks, "bad" kids in *Bully* and *George Washington*, and media coverage of the war against Iraq. She edited *Spike Lee: Interviews* (2002), and co-edited *Between the Sheets, In the Streets: Queer, Lesbian, and Gay Documentary* (1997).

Krin Gabbard is Professor of Comparative Literature and English at the State University of New York at Stony Brook. He is the author of *Black Magic: White Hollywood and African American Culture* (2004) and *Jammin' at the Margins: Jazz and the American Cinema* (1996) and the co-author of *Psychiatry and the Cinema* (2nd ed., 1999). He is the editor of *Jazz Among the Discourses* and *Representing Jazz* (1995). He is currently writing a cultural history of the trumpet.

Ken Gelder is Professor in English and Cultural Studies at the University of Melbourne, Australia. His books include *Popular Fiction: The Logics and Practices of a Literary Field* (2004), *Uncanny Australia: Sacredness and Identity in a Postcolonial Nation* (with Jane M. Jacobs, 1998), and *Reading the Vampire* (1994). He is also editor of *The Horror Reader* (2000) and has recently edited the second edition of *The Subcultures Reader* (2005).

Ruth Goldberg has a maniacal teaching schedule, at SUNY/Empire State College, New York University School of Continuing and Professional Studies and the Escuela Internacional de Cine y TV in San Antonio de los Baños, Cuba. Her work has been included in the revised edition of *Planks of Reason: Essays on the Horror Film*, *Fear Without Frontiers*, and *Japanese Horror Cinema*. She is a contributor to the Cuban film journal *Miradas*, and has also contributed to the journals *Kino-eye* and *Limen*.

Tom Gunning is Edwin A. and Betty L. Bergman Distinguished Service Professor of the Humanities at The University of Chicago. He is author of two books, *The Films of Fritz Lang* (2000) and *D. W. Griffith and the Origins of America Narrative Film* (1991), as well as over a hundred articles on early cinema, the avant-garde, film genres, and issues in film theory and history. His publications have appeared in a dozen languages. He is currently writing on the theory and history of motion in cinema.

Douglas Kellner is Professor of Education and holds the George F. Kneller Philosophy of Education Chair at the University of California Los Angeles. He is author of *Camera Politica: The Politics and Ideology of Contemporary Hollywood Film* (with Michael Ryan), *Critical Theory, Marxism, and Modernity*, *Media Culture* and *Media Spectacle*, a trilogy of books on postmodern theory with Steve Best, a trilogy of books on the Bush administration incl. *Grand Theft 2000* and *Media Spectacle and the Crisis of Democracy*. His website: www.gseis.ucla.edu/faculty/kellner/kellner.html

Kostis Kourelis is an archaeologist and art historian specializing in the medieval Mediterranean. He has excavated and surveyed ancient and medieval sites in Greece, Italy, Tunisia, and Ukraine. He is currently assistant professor of Art History at Clemson University. Dr. Kourelis has published on rural archaeology, domestic architecture, and topics of historiography. He is excavating an Islamic/Norman village in Sicily, a Crusader port in the Peloponnesos and a Byzantine city on the Black Sea.

Sarah Kozloff, Professor of Film at Vassar College, is the author of two books, *Invisible Storytellers: Voice-over Narration in American Fiction Film* and *Overhearing Film Dialogue*, as well as numerous articles and chapters. She specializes in American cinema, especially in questions related to sound, genre, and narrative.

Ernest Mathijs is Assistant Professor Film and Theatre at the University of British Columbia. He researches the reception of alternative cinema, and published in a.o. *Screen* and *Cinema Journal*. He (co-)edited *The Cinema of the Low Countries*, *Big Brother International*, and *Alternative Europe*, and co-directs the book series *Contemporary Cinema* and *Cultographies*. He was part of the international *Lord of the Rings* research, and is finishing a book on David Cronenberg.

Lianne McLarty is Professor of Film Theory and Criticism and Director of the Department of Film Studies, University of Victoria (BC). Her areas of interest include the politics of popular culture, feminism, cultural theory, avant-garde cinema (particularly Canadian), and horror and science fiction films. Her publications have appeared in *The Dread of Difference: Gender and the Horror Film* (YR), *Mythologies of Violence in Postmodern Media* (YR), *The Canadian Journal of Communication*, and *Take Two: Defining the Sequel*, (YR).

Jerry Mosher teaches film studies at California State University-Long Beach and is a doctoral candidate in the Department of Film, Television and Digital Media at UCLA. His dissertation examines how the American film industry has represented the fat body. He has published essays on fat and culture in the anthologies *Bodies Out of Bounds: Fatness and Transgression* (2001), *The End of Cinema As We Know It: American Film in the Nineties* (2001), and *Where the Boys Are: Cinemas of Masculinity and Youth* (2005).

Murray Pomerance is Professor of Sociology at Ryerson University. He is the author of *Savage Time* (2006), *Johnny Depp Starts Here* (2005), *An Eye for Hitchcock* (2004), and *Magia d'Amore* (1999), and (co-)editor of *Cinema and Modernity* (2006), *Where the Boys Are* (2005), *BAD: Infamy, Darkness, Evil, and Slime on Screen* (2004), and *Ladies and Gentlemen, Boys and Girls* (2001). He is editor of the "Horizons of Cinema" series at SUNY Press and, with Lester D. Friedman, co-editor of the "Screen Decades" series at Rutgers University Press.

Kirsten Moana Thompson is an Assistant Professor of Film Studies at Wayne State University in Detroit. She specializes in blockbusters and contemporary American cinema, animation, and German and New Zealand cinema. She is co-editor of *Perspectives on German Cinema* (with Terri Ginsberg, 1996) and has published in *Adaptations* (2004); *Blockbusters* (2003), *New Zealand Filmmakers* (YR), and *Reading The Rabbit; Explorations in Warner Bros. Animation* (1998).

Steven Woodward is a scholar of film and literature who currently teaches popular culture, children's literature, film, and screenwriting courses at Clemson University in South Carolina. He has published a number of essays on film, most recently "The Arch Archenemies of James Bond," and is now editing a book about the influence of the Polish filmmaker Krzysztof Kieslowski and revising a book manuscript about British poet Walter de la Mare.

There and Back Again: An Editors' Tale

Ernest Mathijs and Murray Pomerance

Here is a book about a trio of films made from a trio of books! At the very least, a transformation of transformations! Can there be anything left to say, to think, or to dream about Gandalf and Frodo, Samwise Gamgee, Merry, Pippin, Aragorn, Legolas, Gollum, Gimli, Boromir and Faramir, Theoden, Eowyn, Arwen, Elrond, and their many advisors, friends, foes, and family who come almost to breathe through the pages of J.R.R. Tolkien's and Peter Jackson's trilogies? Or, to put this more sharply: given the plethora of carping and alternately adulatory lay criticism, the bubbling worldwide fan discourse, and the widespread conviction not only that Jackson has accomplished something magnificent and important with his films but also that we already know what that is, have already understood and digested it, is there really anything of substance that can further be said, written, conceived about *The Lord of the Rings* that is worth reading? Our conviction in making this book, shared with our collaborators in many disciplines and countries, is that from the point of view of critical and scholarly analysis, the "Ring" of these films has not yet come out of the streambed of popular culture. For ardent fans of Tolkien, for ardent followers of Jackson, even for those whose fixation lies upon Elijah Wood or Liv Tyler or Orlando Bloom or Ian McKellen, as well as for those who yearn for a deeper appreciation of cinema and its relation to culture, the essays contained in these pages promise to open a new vista of interrogation and light.

That of all directors it should have been Peter Jackson who made these films is by no means obvious, even though he had long been an admirer of Tolkien's books and had come to regard *The Lord of the Rings* as "the holy grail of cinema" (quoted in Grant *Assault*, 27). The director of *Bad Taste* and *Braindead*, and a boyhood fan of Cooper and Schoedsack's *King Kong* (1933) who proceeded to use an 8 mm camera for shooting dinosaurs, Jackson first read the Tolkien books "as a teenage apprentice photo-engraver, and he boldly claims his goal is to make Middle Earth look like it was shot on location" (27). But before this film, virtually all of his work exploited a comic vision to some degree, and indulged in one or another version of the grotesque; he had established himself as a filmmaker who could be counted on to produce what Barry Grant calls "a deft synthesis of comedy and splatter" (*Assault*, 14). At the same time, he had a bold ambition, "to compete with Hollywood but with the resources to do so" (27). His devotion to New Zealand filmmaking, which has led him to shoot all his pictures there and even to form WETA, an indigenous special effects company that rivals George Lucas's Industrial Light and Magic, is certainly, as Grant suggests, an explicit address to the American domination of cinema (2); this to such a degree that Jackson, even before *The Lord of the Rings*, was well on the way to establishing the prowess of New Zealand cinema. On the other hand, whether with this trilogy, and with *King Kong* (2005), it is true, as Costa Botes suggests, that Jackson has proven "it is possible for New Zealanders to make ambitious, and thoroughly entertaining genre films for the rest of the world, *which aren't necessarily tainted by commercial compromise*" (quoted in Grant, 2; emphasis added), is perhaps less clear. At this writing, the *Rings* trilogy has realized some $US 3 billion worldwide; and we cannot overlook the fact that the principal cast was not composed of New Zealanders.

Yet, as adventures, as spectacles, as adaptations, as cultural statements, as evidence of globalization, the Jackson *Rings* films constitute a prodigious achievement, not to mention the facts of their commercial viability and ideological force. It seemed entirely appropriate, therefore, to bring together scholars from many disciplines who would wish to address a broad array of features of these films. They are lively cultural product, they are in the air, they are on the lips of millions around the world, and they have not systematically and rigorously been studied to a depth as they are in these pages.

Any film has two conditions of existence: an aesthetic one and a political. Like other cultural artifacts, a film leads a double life as *objet d'art* and public statement about the world. This double life is at the core of studies of art ever since criticism began to look beyond the work and into the world in which it appears, not just as a means of finding evidence for composition and symbol, but also to find art's function, goals, implications, and inferences. And since the advent of film at the break of the twentieth century, film criticism has been increasingly living up to the same credo. As Walter Benjamin points out in his famous essay on the work of art in the age of mechanical reproduction (a comment seen as an originating point for visual culture studies, film studies, and the sociology of art), the aesthetics and the politics of cinema are never separate entities, they are inextricable, so that nothing is ever just cinematically beautiful or tasteful, and nothing in a film is ever just a message or an opinion (Benjamin, *Illuminations*).

Not surprisingly then, when Peter Jackson's film version of *The Lord of the Rings* trilogy went on release between December 2001 and December 2003, it was often linked to topical and social concerns. *The Two Towers*, was reviewed in the British tabloid *Daily Mail*, as an "epic film for epic times," a tautological but nonetheless characteristic attempt to make a connection between the film and world events. So is Elvis Mitchell's claim in *The New York Times* that this is a film about the price of triumph characteristic, or National Geographic's attempt to link *The Lord of the Rings* to American frontier mythology and to presidents like Franklin Delano Roosevelt. In the weeks preceding and following the release of *The Return of the King*, the academic cultstud-l list, a discussion list of cultural studies scholars, saw a big debate of all things gendered (sexist), ethnic (racist), classed (bourgeois), religious (catholic, intolerant), ideological (conservative), and methodological (the text as source of knowledge) in reading the trilogy. Certainly style, symbols, narrative, and structure were discussed too, but always already together with politics, usually contemporary. As much as Middle Earth and its battles and quests was remote, elusive, and insubstantial as a ficional construct, then, it was also and simultaneously apparently present, embodied, and alive in the culture where the films were shown.

Poor old John Ronald Reuel Tolkien! No matter how hard he protested in the introduction to the second edition of *The Lord of the Rings* that there was no allegorical or topical undercurrent to his story, that it was a tale and nothing more, ephemeral for all its enchantment, the many, *many,* wide-ranging interpretations it received persisted in setting it up as pregnant with cultural relevance and social urgency beyond any aesthetic achievement. Several of the essays in this book mention this resistance of Tolkien to any political interpretation, so that for some critics at least it has become a central pillar in the architecture of our interpretation of the material. Tolkien wrote, in response to some early political interpretations of *The Hobbit* and the first edition of *The Lord of the Rings*, this proclamation:

> As for any inner meaning or "message," it has in the intention of the author none. It is neither allegorical nor topical . . . I cordially dislike allegory in all its manifestations, and always have done so since I grew old and wary enough to detect its presence. I much prefer history, true or feigned, with its varied applicability to the thought and experience of readers. I think that many confuse "applicability" with "allegory"; but the one resides in the freedom of the reader, and the other in the purposed domination of the author (*Fellowship*, "Foreword," xvii-xviii)

Tolkien emphatically denies any influence from World War I and II upon his work ("nothing in it was modified by the war that began in 1939 or its sequels . . . the real war does not resemble the legendary war in its process or its conclusion" [xvii]) or from social surroundings ("it has been supposed by some that 'the scouring of the Shire' reflects the situation in England at the time when I was finishing my tale. It does not" [xviii]).

Tolkien's insistence on narrative, structure, and style, on aesthetics, as dominant concerns for meaning and value, and on a purely literary and linguistic lineage, of course fits the image of the ivory-tower Oxford don that he was. It also fits that of his colleague, the scholar C.S. Lewis, who defended him saying, "Tolkien's book is not an allegory" (*Letters*). But coming from the pre-eminent American fantasy critic Lin Carter a claim like this raises eyebrows. Carter, who stated in 1969 that *The Lord of the Rings* is "neither satire nor allegory," was the most important spokesperson for the fantasy genre of the time. Why would he miss the chance to inject *The Lord of the Rings* with cultural relevance? Because, like Tolkien, he wanted the genre to become more respectable in its own right – not for its politics, but for its aesthetics. Carter was not just backing a writer he greatly admired but also attempting to carve out a non-political canon for the genre that writer's masterpiece belongs to, establishing a link with the greats of literature. Carter believed he needed to counter what he thought were all-too-easy links with contemporary politics, especially "the similarity which some readers or critics have noticed between the war of Gondor against Mordor and the 1960s cold-war East-West confrontation" (*A Look Behind*, 70). Note how Carter uses *another* war and another, more contemporary era in his example. His dispute is with those who read the book as especially relevant to the times they live in. For Carter this is a sin of people new to reading, exactly what, for him, "a very large number of Tolkien's most enthusiastic admirers appear to be" (*A Look Behind*, 66; those experienced in reading, one assumes, would more likely read the book in line with the history of literature itself). True, Carter admits, the *Lord of the Rings* story could be seen as allegorical because "it presents the War Between Good and Evil (or Light and Darkness) when the plot is reduced to the very simplest of terms . . . with the all-important, incredibly dangerous Ring as a symbol for today's nuclear weaponry." But, he continues, since that would mirror the plot of every movie ("any action yarn"), it would reduce the argument to "nonsense" (67).

Why, after all this, would anyone still insist on trying to make any political interpretation of *The Lord of the Rings*? This is where Peter Jackson's version comes in. It is, first and foremost, a movie trilogy, and as such it adheres to different critical standards than writing, no matter how popular both may be in their specific appearances. Following Carter, one could say it is because film viewers and critics, like inexperienced readers, are not capable of looking beyond their immediate frame of reference ("the times they live in") and do not have recourse to the history of aesthetics (of the genre or of film in general). But following film studies, and tying this back to Benjamin, one could also say that the frame of reference of film criticism insists on a different balance between aesthetics and politics, one, perhaps, in which politics play a more significant and accepted role. That is why this book covers both the aesthetics and politics of the *Lord of the Rings* film trilogy. But the mix of these approaches, both in the chapters and in the book as a whole, is not random. The general thread moves from emphasizing the political condition to highlighting the aesthetic one, from the most obviously political concerns to the most strictly aesthetic. But throughout, all chapters maintain the balance between the two conditions.

The first chapter, "The Lord of the Rings as Allegory: A Multiperspectivist Reading" by Douglas Kellner, is unapologetically political, insisting on offering exactly what Tolkien, Lewis, and Carter refuted: a reading that treats the film cycle as a sociopolitical and moral-existential allegory articulating a neoconservative ideology. For Kellner, the films mirror the position of the German Bildungsroman, with its portrayals of Gemeinschaften, cosy communities that need protection from outside evil. Pointing to the remarkable similarities between, for instance, Treebeard's motivation for the March of the Ents in *The Two Towers* and connecting it to the war cries and rallies for intervention in Iraq, or to the bloody (and manly) celebration of military valor and heroism, Kellner comes to the conclusion that *The Lord of the Rings*, in its appearance as well as in its topical presence, fits the hysteria of the War on Terror, a triumph of anxious conservatism.

The representation of communities in wartime, and the implications of lineage and family bonds on social cohesion are also at the centre of Ernest Mathijs's "*The Lord of the Rings* and Family: A View on Text and Reception." But where Kellner treated the *Lord of the Rings* story world in its entirety, Mathijs concentrates on individual and close blood- and love ties. Relying on both textual and reception materials, and focusing on the difficulty of determining which version of *The Lord of the Rings* films should, in fact, be seen as the proper text, Mathijs argues that the way in which family lineages are represented in the Extended DVD editions gives the story a fundamentally different theme, one that holds that only established, traditional family bands (and values), especially those consecrated through (future) marriage (Aragorn/Arwen, Faramir/Eowyn, Sam/Rose), and individuals who, by allowing mother figures to approach, break patriarchal patterns, are able to resist the evil corruption of war and social disruption.

A third chapter using an association with community politics is Sean Cubitt's "The Fading of the Elves: Eco-Catastrophe, Technopoly, and Bio-Security." Employing a comparison between Tolkien and Heidegger as a point of convergence, Cubitt outlines how *The Lord of the Rings* portrays a departure from a world based on craftsmanship and apprenticeships, an ecologically balanced world close to nature, to a world based on new divisions of labour, high-technology protocols (the Palantir), industrial pollution, and government by class divisions. Cubitt draws a parallel with the location for the trilogy and juxtaposes the native view of New Zealand (Aotearoa in Maori) that the film crew needed for recreating Middle-Earth against the modern view that facilitated the production of that fantasy world.

These three chapters make direct links between the film texts and contemporary political concerns, such as totalitarianism, family, ecology, technology, patriarchy, and war and terror, asserting the political meaning of the films, and indeed their pressing topical relevance, not just culturally but personally as well (the personal is always political). The next two essays sustain that focus on cultural politics but take a more distanced position in trying to explain the conditions under which political interpretations of film come into being. In "On Being a 1960s Tolkien Reader," Martin Barker starts by observing dissimilarities between *Lord of the Rings* books and films. Incongruities in the film adaptations, such as the Ents being tricked into war by Pippin's leading them the wrong way in their own forest, might lead, suggests Barker, to different meanings (a motive of persuasion in the novels being dropped in favour of deception in the films), and to wondering how such interpretations are evidence of certain positions towards the work. Barker then traces the origins of the interpretive communities of Tolkien's work to the 1960s, to suggest that these sprung from within groups for whom progressive, radical politics (and life styles) was a key common feature. Four decades later, Barker argues, radical interpretations of the films may have to rely on interpretive communities and fan groups who share common grounds (and readings, and objections) without meeting each other, but who, in their presumed private reading positions, nevertheless demonstrate a "belief" that there are others "out there."

Ken Gelder's chapter "Epic Fantasy and Global Terrorism" concentrates on readings of *The Lord of the Rings* that explicitly use the topical arsenal of anxieties towards the war on terror (and its figurehead George W. Bush). Gelder describes the range of common languages and metaphors used by those writing about the politics of fantasy and those involved in the war on terror, and notes how the curious overlaps create cultural (excess) baggage for the *Lord of the Rings* text. He focuses on the conceptualizations of evil as monolithic and neverending that are used in epic fantasy, showing how the religiously inspired, organic nation-state's backbone of "good" in epic fantasy is drenched with nostalgia for lost traditions and dying cultures, resisting the modern world. On the basis of this he concludes that fantasy itself may be seen as terroristic on a global scale.

While the politics of *The Lord of the Rings* are central in the first five chapters, all of them also show what the implications and opportunities of those politics are for the aesthetics. Gelder's discussion of epic fantasy lays out some of the structural format – a clearcut antagonism; Barker's argument on the differences between book and film calls attention to formal ways in which action films usually resolve debate or tension (by violence or deception, not by winning the argument); Cubitt's dichotomy between a naturalist and an industrial world extends to the visual template for portrayal of good and bad; Mathijs's analysis of family bonds and patriarchy demonstrates how relations between characters act out in dialogue, posture, and gender; and Kellner's discussion of valor, heroism, and Gemeinschaft lays out the core moral values for characters and story world, and how they inform all actions in the film.

The next chapters tie politics and aesthetics together by making both subject to the economical conditions of production and consumption; they use a political-economic approach for explorations of the economic existence of *The Lord of the Rings* and its impact as a cultural phenomenon. In "A Land of Make Believe: Merchandising and Consumption of *The Lord of the Rings*," Ian Conrich examines the promotional campaigns and tie-ins accompanying the release of the trilogy, and shows how its preset frame of reference as a fantasy story about unspoiled good and corrupt evil allowed a network of associations from which companies, institutions, and even governments tried to benefit. Conrich concentrates on those elements of public presence that can be seen as meaningful to the reputation of the *Lord of the Rings* text, such as collectibles and prestige merchandising, and the cultural appropriation of New Zealand, at least in terms of commercial culture; and contrasts these with the mass merchandising expected of a twenty-first century blockbuster. He thus establishes a set of terms to which *The Lord of the Rings* relates, not just economically and politically, but aesthetically as well (the New Zealand landscape being a prime example).

Moving from corporate imperative to socially organized private experience, Jennifer Brayton's chapter "Fic Frodo Slash Frodo: Fandoms and *The Lord of the Rings*" asks to what extent conditions of consumption can be seen to have impact on either the text itself or on its readings. She compares original *Lord of the Rings* fandom, from the 1960s onwards, with specific fan concerns surrounding the preparation and release of the film trilogy. Using examples such as worries over Arwen's role, or the relationship between Eowyn and Faramir, Brayton charts the features of the trilogy's fandom and that fandom's sophisticated use of (and reliance upon) interactive new technologies such as the Internet (websites, chat rooms, fan discussion lists), computer games, and digitally produced fan fiction. She thus shows how the line becomes thin between the political implications of these technologies and their implications for the aesthetics of textual reading, between the effort of production and the enjoyment present for fans as they consume.

Of all things aesthetic, genre is perhaps the most overtly political way of classifying and evaluating films, especially with the lowbrow politics attached to genres like science-fiction and fantasy (crude in their conservatism or liberalism). Most fans of *The Lord of the Rings* see it as a fantasy tale, and most critics described it as an epic. But, even in passing, many also seem to note its allegiance to other genres often also looked down upon. Two chapters in this book explore these allegiances. In "The Lord of the Rings as Melodrama," Sarah Kozloff argues how, curiously, the generic rules of another often disdained genre, the melodrama, apply to *The Lord of the Rings*. The moral compass, so essential to melodrama, is at the core of the Fellowship's quest (it's not just about the Ring but about saving the hearts and minds of Middle Earth). Kozloff explains how the story uses spectacle and realism to heighten emotional effects, and suspense and delay for pathos – as shown by the frequent rescues in the nick of time. Fittingly, Kozloff also stresses how the film starts and ends in a place of innocence; the refusal to include the scouring of the Shire in the film reaffirms it as some sort of Eden to which the heroes can safely return. Even the final farewell(s) in the film, teary as they are, confirm the melodramatic tenor of the trilogy.

In her chapter "Masculinity, Whiteness, and Social Class in *The Lord of the Rings*," Lianne McLarty discusses the implications of representations of race, gender, and class in the film trilogy through concentration upon the horror genre, a genre whose critical treatment since the 1970s relies upon such political treats. By discussing the bodies of Middle Earth inhabitants as sites of horror (especially with regard to Orcs and Uruk-Hai, but also contrasting them with the angelic Elves or the sage Wizards, not just in terms of skin color but also in their masculine presence). By putting the aesthetic qualities of the characters in a political frame of reference, McLarty highlights the binary oppositions between good and evil in *The Lord of the Rings* as cemented in cultural stereotyping.

Less subject to formulaic repetition than genre, and hence usually more prone to escaping such political frameworks (though certainly not immune to them) are issues of narrative and style. Such considerations are at the nexus of the next five chapters. All start with the observation of a particular narratively or stylistically salient element which is then connected to other parts of the films' structures, and whose political inferences are explored. Steven Woodward and Kostis Kourelis's chapter "Urban Legend: Architecture in *The Lord of the Rings*" focuses on the sources of inspiration underlying the designs and settings of the films. Noting how the architecture's European lineage clashes with the indigenous landscape (there is no Polynesian architecture used, nor any reference to the British colonial past), Woodward and Kourelis concentrate on graphic designer Alan Lee's work for the books and, later, films and his use of psychedelic imagery, and on German expressionist examples. On the basis of this, they distinguish between four basic types of designs: the vernacular, the naturalistic, the grotesque, and the archaeological (which they tie with heroism), explaining how this typology gives the films a historicity, authority, and vintage.

In similar fashion, Tom Conley's chapter "*The Lord of the Rings* and the Fellowship of the Map" recounts the inspirations for the all-telling map that structures the conflicts, meetings, and travels in Middle Earth (even if some of the travels actually undertaken seem to flout the laws of speed and time). As Conley points out, the role of the map in the trilogy is not just to lay out a logic of time and space, but also, and more importantly, to inaugurate the narrative and set boundaries for good and evil. Such an all-telling map has to occur in the opening scenes of course, and that is why Conley's analysis concentrates on the maps (in their different appearances) in the first moments of the film, even before the title appears). Conley notes the political aspect of the maps by demonstrating the link between the voice-off narrative (and its use of the word "power"), visual aids (erupting flames), and the appearance and structural importance of that first map that establishes our spatial relation to the narrative world of the films.

Shifting from visual to audio style, "Enchantments of *The Lord of the Rings*: Soundtrack, Myth, Language, and Modernity" by James Buhler also foregrounds the beginning of the trilogy, deliberating its use of sounds and music. Drawing upon Tolkien's musings about the place of music and song in his Middle Earth mythology, Buhler considers the ways in which language disenchants (in the Weberian understanding of the term) and modernizes the story world of Middle Earth. Which is why, before all else, there has to be music, Elven music, and the voice of

Galadriel to initiate the sense of history and premodernity in the prologue (not present in the original books, but tellingly crucial to the BBC Radio versions from the early 1980s) that precedes the proper story.

The subsequent two chapters emphasize characterization and performance, two elements of film style at the crux of (at least) popular aesthetics of cinema, be it in the portrayal of stardom and celebrity (notoriously absent in Jackson's Hollywood production, with even Liv Tyler's image subdued) or in the more sober depiction of actual performance crafts (which in the case of *The Lord of the Rings* often boiled down to stressing camaraderie during a year-long shoot and endurance of harsh conditions). Arguably the biggest star in *The Lord of the Rings*, definitely one which can lay claim to endurance and harsh conditions, and certainly one of the most surprisingly popular, is Gollum/Andy Serkis. "'Wicked, Tricksy, False': Race, Myth, and Gollum" by Cynthia Fuchs singles out race as the key factor that determines Gollum; yet it also seems to be his main lack. For Fuchs, Gollum remains ultimately unraced or, more precisely, is "racializing," stuck in a neverending process of becoming a race. He is not just half this/half that, as in those most famous "schizophrenic" scenes where Gollum/Sméagol decides on the boundaries of his loyalty to Frodo, because his bond with other Hobbits (he is somewhat of a Hobbit himself) and other creatures in Middle Earth is constantly under renegotiation. His shifting allegiances set him up as both unique and disposable ("to be pitied," as Frodo puts it) and give his presence and the performance by Serkis a political dimension, that of the ultimate outsider to proper enculturation.

Ruth Goldberg and Krin Gabbard, in their chapter "'What does the Eye Demand': Sexuality, Forbidden Vision and Embodiment in *The Lord of the Rings*," also zoom in on Hobbits, especially their peculiar gender identities. Using a psychoanalytical perspective on the relationship between the Hobbits (Sam and Frodo mostly, but also Merry and Pippin), they observe a range of gay and homo-erotic overtones in Jackson's version of the story. Goldberg and Gabbard analyze several of these aesthetic motives and tropes (the vulva-like Eye of Sauron, the multiple father figures the Hobbits are offered, the metaphor of the burden of the

Ring, the sting of Shelob – a "she" with a sting), combining them into a view on the cinematic representation of the supposed innocence of Hobbits. They arrive at the – unmistakenly political – conclusion that, as in *The Wizard of Oz*, the Ringbearer and his Fellowship have to conquer above all a topography of desire before they can go back to that place like no other, home.

We now arrive at the core of aesthetics: its *techné*, as Aristotle has it. The final four essays in this book discuss medium-specific aesthetics, techniques at the front of contemporary filmmaking, calling their political implications into question. More than recent science-fiction cinema, *The Lord of the Rings* has pushed the application and verisimilitude of special effects. The world depicted may not be real, but it looks as real as any fan or viewer could have imagined it – in fact the "realness" of the screened is mentioned by so many that it is a sign of how clear-cut a picture audiences had of a never before fully represented Middle Earth; something the inspirations and inferences mentioned by Woodward and Kourelis and Conley offer evidence for, and a point Barker traces back to the 1960s imagining of Middle Earth and its politics. Kirsten Moana Thompson's essay "Scale, Spectacle and Movement: Massive Software and Digital Special Effects in *The Lord of The Rings*" lays out how special effects achieved this believability in shapes, movement, and action. She puts particular emphasis on representations of shock and awe – raw violence (special effects to depict suffering) as well as dazzlement and grandeur (special effects to impress), and on the combination of both in choreographed battle-scenes with their structured (or not so structured) group behavior of (military) bodies and masses (marching, battling, dying or surviving). Central to her discussion is a detailed analysis of the role of the Massive software program in producing crowd imagery for these films.

As far as mass and body are concerned, in contemporary cinema the look and shape of the actor are as much a special effect as any other, and "Morphing Sean Astin: "Playing Fat" in the Age of Digital Animation," Jerry Mosher's detailed analysis of how actor Sean Astin prepared and executed his role as "fatty" Hobbit Samwise Gamgee, sheds light on the increasingly important technique of literally shaping the performance (especially in times of the celebration of perfect body control). In an era when losing or gaining weight often seems equal to performative excellence (and winning awards) it is essential to discuss the cult of the body in acting. Mosher's emphasis on the requirement that Astin maintain an uncomfortable and for him atypical body shape for an extended period of time puts the politics of body representation in a new perspective.

Moving from the general to the particular, Tom Gunning's essay "Gollum and Golem: Special Effects and the Technology of Artificial Bodies" also focuses on special effects and bodies, but draws inspiration from the mythology of the giant clay avenger of the Golem, linking it to Gollum, the full-fledged CGI character of *The Lord of the Rings*. Gunning probes the implications of having digital-only characters for film practices of acting and representations of behavior to explore whether the techniques employed to create "new screen life" solely through ADR, Motion Capture, and animation bear any danger, or if the skills that created the body of Gollum are perhaps no less other-worldly than good old clay (or the cinematic equivalents of frame animation and human voice recording).

Finally, if film has sometimes been called the most visual of arts because of its ability to travel (one recalls the popularity of so called "travelling" films in the late nineteenth century), it has now, thanks to special effects and what is accepted in science-fiction, horror, and fantasy narratives, also embraced the representation of the invisible. Murray Pomerance's essay "The Laddy Vanishes" queries the aesthetic possibilities of depicting the present/absent: the invisible body. Pomerance demonstrates how the effect of Frodo's Ring-wearing is not just a clever stylistic device offering opportunities for changing perspectives, camera-tricks, and the introduction of dream-like interludes, but has an important narrative function as well, one which it shares with only a small group of (film) stories (making *The Lord of the Rings* representative of (yet) another subgenre: the film of invisibility). Crucially, the Ring-wearing also has political significance: it questions the connection between what we see and what we believe, a connection so evident to a visual medium like film, and one so meshed with issues of perception and reception that it has huge theoretical potential – film, said Bazin, is about what we don't see as much as about what we do.

Image 1: A transformation of transformations: Peter Jackson and Ian McKellen go over the shooting script based on the screenplay based on the trilogy of books for the trilogy of films this collection studies (Copyright © New Line Cinema, available at Yahoo Movies.com)

So, from a focus on politics that inevitably includes aesthetics to discussions of medium specific aesthetics that cannot ignore the political connotations they contain, this book offers, through one trilogy, a look at what one part of cinema is today, and what it means. Perhaps these essays can also be understood more broadly, as being about not only *The Lord of the Rings* but cinema itself.

Now, unwearied but out of bread crumbs, we need a good ending, or at least a new start. No chain of long farewells as Jackson made. We just say, dear reader: read on.

•

The Lord of the Rings as Allegory: A Multiperspectivist Reading

Douglas Kellner

Since the 1970s, Hollywood film has been feeding on a rich tradition of fantasy literature and stories, myths, and legends that resurrect heroes of a long-forgotten past for entertainment and moral guidance in a degraded and confused present world. Following the trauma of Vietnam, the *Star Wars* cycle nourished fantasies of adventure and redemption in a mythic world where the distinction between Good and Evil was clear, heroes were paragons of virtue and villains embodiments of malevolence. *Superman*, *Batman*, *Conan*, *Hulk*, and other cycles of superhero films nourished fantasies that powerful figures would triumph over evil and maintain order and stability. But it is perhaps Peter Jackson and his colleagues' *The Lord of the Rings* cycle that goes furthest in providing a fully-developed alternative fantasy world that provides moral instruction, compelling mythical narratives, and epic transcendence of the horrors of the contemporary world.

Certainly, *The Lord of the Rings* trilogy has been the most popular, acclaimed, and fetishized film cycle of the Third Millennium and has intensified and expanded Tolkien readership for the novels that are the basis of the cinematic epic, while generating a devoted following for the films. In this study, I counter the reading that *The Lord of the Rings* is mere escapist fantasy and argue that it reproduces the dominant conservative and patriarchal militarist ideology manifest in the United States and elsewhere during the past years and that, if we are to grasp its power and effects as well as decode its ideological subtexts, it should be read in the light of the epochal Terror War now raging. Although Tolkien scorned allegorical readings of his *The Lord of the Rings* cycle, I assert that the novels and film cycle can be read as socio-political and moral-existential allegory that articulates conservative ideology.[1] Of course, the text is highly polysemic, subject to multiple readings, and has been widely read as religious allegory, a reading whose popularity I will take as symptomatic of its conservative ideological underpinnings.

As a moral-existential allegory, *The Lord of the Rings* relates to the German *Bildungsroman* theme of maturity and development (Marcuse *Kunstlerroman*; Kellner *Marcuse*). Like the figures in Joseph Campbell's hero myth, the young heroes of *The Lord of the Rings* have adventures, undergo challenges, and grow and mature into exemplary moral figures, and their relationships and fellowship convey specific social values, a range of which I engage in this study (Campbell *Hero*; Lawrence and Jewett *Myth*). As a political allegory, both the novels and films are clearly conservative attacks on industrial and technological modernity, yearning for an idealized past of stable communities, social hierarchy, and romantic attachment to the soil and earth. These thematics, as I will highlight, have profound similarities to Nazi ideology and articulate in the present with the patriarchal conservativism and crusading militarism of the George W. Bush administration. Indeed, I will argue that despite its contradictions, complexities, and positive aspects, *The Lord of the Rings*

---

[1] On allegory, see Benjamin (*Origins*) and Jameson (*Unconscious*). I am not offering one privileged allegorical reading for *The Lord of the Rings*, but am arguing that a plurality of allegorical readings are possible of the novels and film cycle. While some critics scorn allegorical interpretations because they allegedly build on one-to-one schematic readings of texts, I am using a model of allegory, based on a reconstruction of the positions of Walter Benjamin and Jameson cited above, that posits different levels of allegory in texts ranging from existential and moral to political and philosophical. I am also interpreting *The Lord of the Rings* as a polysemic text that has multiple readings and effects so that numerous allegorical dimensions and readings are possible; hence, I am articulating certain possible readings that can claimed to be well grounded in the text, reception, and historical context of the films and am not reducing the *Lord of the Rings* phenomenon to a single reading or dimension.

provides ideological sustenance for Bushian rightwing conservativism and militarism.[2]

Tolkien's *The Lord of the Rings* cycle was written during an epoch of world war when totalitarian systems arose that threatened democratic countries like England who were forced to enter into alliances to defend themselves against fascism. Although the film cycle was largely conceived and produced before the September 11, 2001 terrorist attacks on the United States, its release and reception followed those events; and the context of its reception has been within a Terror War that has been raging since the September 11 spectacle of terror. In this context, the film cycle can be seen as projecting a crusading militarism that celebrates social hierarchy, patriarchal masculinism, and a deeply conservative vision and critique of the modern world. By interrogating the narrative, discourses, cinematic spectacle, and specific film stories, sequences, and scenes, I will unfold the "political unconscious" of the cinematic epic and its allegorical articulations of highly conservative notions of gender, sexuality, race, class, and politics. Utilizing a multiperspectivist approach, I will also be interested in articulating some of the ambiguities and contradictions of the film, the tensions with Tolkien's novel, and its reception and response with critics and audiences. My main interest in the film cycle and its reception is to use the material to provide a diagnostic critique of the present age (see Kellner and Ryan *Camera Politica*; Kellner *Media Culture*; Kellner *Dangers*).

From the perspective of diagnostic critique, popular films provide important insights into the psychological, socio-political, and ideological make-up of a society or culture at a given point in history. Reading films diagnostically allows one to gain insights into social problems and conflicts, and to appraise the dominant ideologies and emergent oppositional forces. Moreover, diagnostic critique enables one to perceive the limitations and pathologies of both mainstream conservative and liberal political ideologies and oppositional ones (see Kellner *Media*

---

[2] For my views of the Bush administration and account of the contemporary socio-political system that provides a background to the release and reception of *The Lord of the Rings* films, see Kellner (*Grant Theft*; *Spectacle*; *Dangers*; and *Crisis*). I should probably note here that I am not arguing that *The Lord of the Rings* cycle are fascist films, but that they have fascist motifs.

Culture, 116-117). This interpretive approach involves a dialectic of text and context, using texts to read social realities and context to help situate and interpret key films of the epoch.

The Lord of the Rings films were illustrative of a global fantasy-production machine with a creative team drawn from all over the (especially) English-speaking world. The novel cycle that inspired the films was penned by English writer J.R.R. Tolkien; the film was funded by American corporations like Miramax and Time Warner; the director, writers, and production crew were largely from New Zealand where the film was shot; and actors came from throughout the English-speaking world. The global popularity of *The Lord of the Rings* films was related to a deep need for fantasy, escapism into alternative worlds, and distractions from the turbulent and distressing conflicts of the contemporary era, as well to the enticements of a technologically dazzling cinematic epic machine generating a fully articulated fantasy universe. Yet the "escape" led precisely into the tentacles of the conservative ideology that has been a major source of the present world disorder.

Shire, *Gemeinschaft*, and the Fellowship of the Ring

The film trilogy opens with a Prologue announcing that "the world has changed" and the old ways have been lost forever, a conservative lament that pervades the cycle. A narrator tells the story of the magical Rings that were forged to give leaders of respective human, dwarf, and elf worlds the power and wisdom to govern successfully. But a Master Ring, the One Ring, was produced by the Dark Lord Sauron to give him power over all domains. His attempt to control the world led to an alliance of threatened peoples and nations and to a war against him, in which Sauron was defeated and the Ring passed into the hands of a human, Isildur, the ruler of Gondor. The Prologue takes place in a long past prehistory, evoking a mythic time that is being destroyed by the advent of modernity. Tolkien's project, in part, was to create a specifically English mythology to compete with German and other European mythologies, although, curiously, his story of the Ring and how it was produced and corrupted was remarkably similar to Wagner's reworking of the Nibelungen Saga in his operatic Ring cycle. Jackson and his crew are faithful to the mythic and epic scale of Tolkien's saga, as was Fritz Lang in his two-part cinematic rendition of the Nibelungen tales (1924) – a high cinematic level to which Jackson and company aspire.

Isildur is corrupted and destroyed by the Ring and it is lost in a lake. Much later, it is found by a Hobbit, Gollum, who is also corrupted. After years of exile, he loses it in an isolated mountain where it is found by yet another Hobbit, Bilbo Baggins. Baggins, seemingly oblivious to its corruptive force, takes the Ring and returns to his home in the Shire, a land in Tolkien's imaginary Middle Earth which most scholars and fans recognize as a fantasy vision of Merry Olde England. The Shire is a *Gemeinschaft*, or organic community of the sort valorized by conservatives against the intrusion of *Gesellschaft*, the encroaching industrial society (see Tönnies *Community*). I will argue that Jackson's *The Lord of the Rings* shares this conservative, ideological, *gemeinschaftlich* vision and that the trilogy as a whole can be read as a critique of industrial and technological modernity--a somewhat ironic critical vision in view of the astonishingly complex cinematic technology that went into the work's creation. Indeed, Tolkien's narrative and Jackson's adaptation provide a vision of a Fall from harmony, community, peace, and stable values into an anarchic, violent, and hostile world--exactly the vision of modernity projected by conservatives since the 18th century or earlier (Hughes *Consciousness*).

The Hobbits are introduced as diminutive, good-natured folk who love hearth and home, a good smoke, and good brew. Baggins returns to pen "A Hobbit's Tale" and his nephew Frodo is excited by the visit of the old wizard Gandalf who arrives to celebrate Baggins' 111th birthday. Baggins seeks adventure and leaves the Shire, giving his house and the Ring to Frodo, after which an uneasy Gandalf travels to read the account of Isildur which conveys the story of Sauron's Ring and its dangers. Gandalf intuits the return of Sauron and tells Frodo that the Ring is dangerous and that they must take it from the Shire and hide it until Gandalf receives further instruction concerning how to deal with the problem. Another Hobbit, the gardener Sam overhears the story of the

Ring, and Gandalf decrees that Sam and Frodo together leave the Shire to hide the Ring from Sauron.

On their way to an inn, The Prancing Pony, where they are to meet Gandalf, Sam and Frodo are pursued by nine faceless riders, the Ringwraiths or Nazgûl, who represent the nine Kings who lost the power of their original Rings when Sauron gained the one Ring. They are now his slaves and are on a mission to retrieve the Ring for him. Running from the faceless men in black riding black horses, Sam and Frodo encounter fellow young Hobbits Merry and Pippin stealing food; they are chased together by the farmer and the Nazgûl. In a frightening scene, the black-clad Riders suddenly attack the Hobbits on their jet black horses, hissing ferociously and chasing the terrorized Hobbits through the woods. Seen through the eyes of the little Hobbits, the Black Riders appear as dangerous forces of violence and evil.

At the Inn, some of the Hobbits fill up on excessive amounts of brew while a mysterious cloaked man called "Strider" smokes and watches over the proceedings. He reveals himself to be a friend and when the Men in Black come for the Hobbits, he tries to help them. A frightened Frodo puts on the Ring to become invisible and telepathically connects with Sauron who has psychic access to those who put on the Ring. Seeing Sauron's Eye, shaped like a flaming vagina, Frodo learns the fearful power of the Ring but also the danger that threatens them if Sauron is to get the Ring.

In a parallel story, Gandalf goes to his old friend, the wizard Saruman the White, to help get advice concerning what to do about the dangers of the Ring. Saruman, however, has gone over to Sauron's side and warns Gandalf that their only chance of survival and maintaining power is to merge with Sauron and get hold of the Ring. Resurrecting Cold War imagery, Saruman looks like the evil Russian Rasputin with his tall, emaciated stick-beard, maniacal eyes, and overall aura of Evil. Saruman and Gandalf fight and Gandalf barely escapes alive. We also see that Saruman is breeding a monstrous race of fighters by cross-breeding Orcs and Goblins. They appear as the horrible and bestial Uruk-hai, with extremely bad teeth, dark swarthy skin with awful complexion, and violent and barbarian behavior. Both the Orcs, whom Sauron created by

The Lord of the Rings *as Allegory*

torturing and mutilating humans, and the Uruk-hai whom Saruman has bred, represent fears of eugenics and genetic engineering, such as were visualized by the Nazis and are taking form in the cloning laboratories of the present. The beasts are extremely ugly and menacing killing machines and can serve to represent a threat from massified non-Western peoples of color, a fear that haunted the Nazis and a variety of conservatives and liberals.

Sensing the dangers of Sauron's hordes, Gandalf, the four Hobbits, and Strider travel to the Elf Kingdom Rivendell where they meet up with the Elf Legolas, the Dwarf Gimli, and the human Boromir (Sean Bean). The mysterious Strider, who is soon revealed as Aragorn, the relative of Isildur and rightful heir to Gondor, meets up with the Elf-princess Arwen, who has chosen to sacrifice her immortality to be with the human she loves. While Arwen will appear occasionally throughout the epic, it is basically a male adventure with little space for women.

Aragorn must overcome his fear and hesitancy and assume the sword of his father and prove himself in war. In the Elf Kingdom, the group congregates in the Council of King Elrond where they debate what to do with the Ring. While the Council bickers over who will take the Ring to destroy it in the fires of Mount Doom in the heart of Sauron's Kingdom of Mordor, where it was forged, Frodo assumes responsibility and Elrond declares the rest of the crew "Nine Companions, the Fellowship of the Ring." Elrond gives Aragorn and the Hobbits Merry and Pippin daggers; their ascent to masculinity will involve using the dagger to successfully kill villains, hardly a healthy model of male socialization and maturation.

At first the Fellowship is divided into squabbling races with Elves and Dwarves hostile toward each other and the Hobbits suspicious of all. Tolkien is extremely racialist, creating races and different species that have specifically delineated features and that are often hostile to other groups, and these species worlds are replicated in Jackson's film. Dwarves are somewhat shorter and rougher than humans and the Hobbits are utterly childlike, while the Elves are tall, alabastrine, immortal beings. Humans and others contemptuously refer to Hobbits as "Halflings," and groups like Elves and Dwarves exhibit intense distrust and hostility toward each other. The squabbling groups in the Fellowship must overcome their differences and bond together to fight Sauron and his monsters, whose armies are ruthless killers devoid of any moral scruples.

The Fellowship, and positive figures in Jackson's trilogy, are largely white, often with blonde hair and/or blue eyes, signifying distinctly Aryan configurations, while the villains are invariably dark in complexion or soul, setting up a deeply racist problematic. While Gandalf appeared at first to be the wise leader, he is often uncertain; as the Fellowship begins the long trek to Mordor to destroy the Ring, they get lost, almost die in snowy mountainous trails, become entangled in the Caves of Moria, and encounter numerous enemies. In the Caves of Moria, Gandalf is pursued by a fire-monster, Balrog, who appears to kill him in a fiery blast as he hurtles into the pits of a mountain, seemingly consumed by flames. Another human member of the Fellowship, Boromir, is shown to be overly attracted to the Ring, wanting to use it to defeat Sauron and protect his Kingdom. Indeed, Boromir is so attracted to its power that he is corrupted, trying to steal it from Frodo to use for himself. Boromir is shot in battle and his death represents another cautionary warning of how the Ring as a sign of absolute power corrupts and destroys those who want it for questionable purposes.

Through their travels and battles, the group is bonded together into a true Fellowship, where it is All for One, and One for All. Each member achieves heroic deeds and is recognized by others in the group as a valuable member. While the Council of Elrond appeared to be democratic and allow the Fellowship to debate and make choices, as they bond in battle natural leaders come to the fore and in the succeeding episodes democracy disappears, as if it were a conflicted, ineffectual way of dealing with problems and making decisions. The novel and film cycle suggests that only a few individuals are strong and moral enough to resist the temptations of power (i.e. the Ring) and that superior individuals will rise to leadership and eventually produce a King and stable social structure.

The politics are thus on the whole highly antidemocratic and conservative. A white-clad and ethereal Elf-Queen, Galadriel, warns Frodo of the great dangers of the Ring and herself appears monstrous when she gets too close to it, dramatizing the self-transforming and corruptive power of the Ring. Curiously, the two major female characters in the novel and film cycle are Elves, presented as idealized embodiments of female virtue, although in the brief scene where she is attracted by the Ring Galadriel presents the dangerous side of women. Later images will present extremely sexist spectacles of female castration in the spider Shelob. Thus, on the whole, the patriarchal cycle exhibits extremely problematical representations of women.

The narrative projects dangers of a total destruction of established societies, and as the story proceeds it produces an aura of unease and fear, uncannily like the mood in the United States and other Western countries threatened by terrorism in the post-9/11 environment. Like Bush, *The Lord of the Rings* promotes a bifurcated metaphysical division between Good and Evil and advances a notion of Absolute Evil. Like the Bush administration, *The Lord of the Rings* films could help generate paranoia and anxiety about dire threats from the East and from Evil Ones, as Osama bin Laden, Al Qaeda, and assorted terrorist groups proclaimed Jihad against the United States and the West. Jackson's film cycle thus resonated with the mood of the time, perhaps increasing fear and the need for authoritarian leadership, while embodying notions of a "clash of civilizations" and privileging military action as the most effective mode of fighting "evil."

As the Fellowship leaves the Elf Kingdom to weave toward Mordor, undergoing more battles with Sauron's legions, the members are separated from each other, with Merry and Pippin captured by the Uruk-hai and Frodo and Sam cut off and soldiering on alone. Yet the essential bonding has taken place through common suffering and military action and henceforth the Fellowship is a Bruderbund, a Band of Brothers, tightly bound together to fight the forces of Evil and complete their mission (see Theweleit *Male Fantasies*, Vols. 1 and 2).

Mountains, the *Bruderbund*, and the Two Towers

The Two Towers opens in media res with gorgeous panoramic shots of mountains. Much of the action in the film will take place in high cliffs, valleys, elevated towers, hillside fortresses, and caves. A popular genre of Nazi cinema unfolded in mountains, which filmmakers like Leni Riefenstahl presented as transcendent sites of glorious nature where *volkish* Aryans could be free and united in a *Gemeinschaft* with like-minded people. Threatening forces would emerge to disturb this idyll, but good Aryan heroes would triumph and restore the community to peace, order, and fascist bliss. Riefenstahl's 1932 film *Das Blaue Licht* (*The Blue Light*), for instance, shows a beautiful young woman, played by Riefenstahl herself, saving an idyllic mountain town from a mysterious blue light that led men to death, a film that so inspired Hitler he asked her to lead his film industry.

The Two Towers opens with the main characters of the *Gemeinschaft* and Fellowship already expelled from paradise and separated on their perilous quest to defeat the forces of evil. Eschewing narrative preamble, the opening montage quickly cuts to a replay of Gandalf's battle with the fire-breathing monster Balrog in the first film. The exploding flames that appear to consume Gandalf evoke images of fiery and hellish industrial forges that produce iron and thus destroy preindustrial modernity and threaten the earth itself. This visual and thematic attack on industrial production and modernity stands at the center of *The Two Towers* and Jackson's entire trilogy, in a faithful reprise of Tolkien's vision.

Appearing to be consumed in fire in the first film of the trilogy, Gandalf the Grey is now magically resurrected as Gandalf the White, reborn as an even greater symbol of Good, his metamorphosis signaled by the religious glow of light and white halo that bathe his transformed face. Jackson is here drawing on religious iconography to present the very white and patriarchal symbol of Good. Eschewing the visual racism that plagued *Star Wars* with its all-too-black Darth Vader, *The Two Towers* pits Gandalf against a very White Lord Saruman, although it's clear from the narrative that Saruman is a very Dark Lord and Force of Evil who has gone over to the Dark Side, serving Sauron, the Lord of Darkness himself and the very embodiment of absolute evil.

After a sequence showing Sam and Frodo wandering through the mountains – two lost souls in quest of a route to Mordor where they can

The Lord of the Rings *as Allegory*

throw the Ring into a pit of fire – the scene cuts to Merry and Pippin, now captives of the Uruk-hai. Close-ups of the menacing beasts portray them as ugly and sadistic figures of darkness and evil, tormenting the young Hobbits. The Uruk-hai are extremely monstrous, with scaly faces, bad teeth, and glaring eyes, presenting a caricature of evil savages and barbarians of color, a frightening evocation of a clash between forces of Good and Evil, Civilization and Barbarism, coded into the opposition of White and Black. Some of the monsters seem to have iron masks burnt into their faces, and the masks become even more striking and developed as the trilogy develops, perhaps projecting a visual warning of the dangerous fusion of technology and humanity in its dramatization of how the industrial and the technological take over and drain away the human. The Uruk-hai also represent the fusion of the human and the technological in modern warfare, illustrating how war was becoming a technological mode of combat. Technological combat is a form of fighting devalued in the Tolkien novels and Jackson's cinematic trilogy in favor of individual heroism, valor, and medieval warfare.

The peril and ensuing adventures will draw Merry and Pippin closer together, bonded through extreme experiences and surviving grave dangers together. Homoeroticism will indeed emerge as the emotional center of the film as Frodo and Sam, Merry and Pippin, and the other Brothers of the Fellowship bond ever closer together in the mode of the German Bruderbund that extolled the intimacies of male friendship and brotherly valor that provided a front for homoeroticism (see Theweleit *Male Fantasies* Vols. 1 and 2). Yet a distance between Sam and Frodo is established in scenes where Sam persistently refers to his social superior as "Mr. Frodo," although at the end Sam will be awarded for his faithful service and allowed to emerge as a hero himself, suggesting that Everyman can achieve acclaim and validation by following orders and staying in his place.

Women have little part in the Fellowship/Bruderbund. Aragorn, who will emerge as a major figure in the trilogy, is separated in this episode from the Hobbits and is portrayed as the romantic love interest of the Rohan King's daughter Eowyn. However, flashbacks establish that Aragorn's true love is the Elf princess Arwen who has renounced elvish immortality to be with him. The unreciprocated love of Eowyn will enable her in the following film to become a warrior heroine, but the second installment of the film sacrifices focus on romance for the more masculine pursuits of valor and military heroism.

In fact, neither Tolkien's novels nor Jackson's films have any complex heterosexual relationships, sexuality, or even erotic desire and conflict. While novelists like Jane Austin and Henry James eschew portraying sexual relations, their work teems with sexual desire, tensions, conflicts, and ambiguities – exactly like in life. In *The Lord of the Rings*, however, there is no overt sexuality or heterosexual relationship besides chaste and extremely conventional roles and depictions (until, perhaps, the third film that provides a powerful visual assault on female sexuality in the figure of the Spider monster Shelob).

Frodo and Sam, still journeying towards Mordor, are pursued by the mysterious Gollum who provides much of the narrative tension of the film. The story will reveal that Gollum was formerly a Hobbit named Sméagol who got possession of the Ring and was corrupted by its power. He has become hideously deformed by the interaction, appearing like an emaciated and barely human survivor of the German concentration camps. Yet beneath the monster is a benign Hobbit, wishing to do good, and the conflict between his good and bad side becomes a major focus of the narrative.

In general, Gollum provides a cautionary warning as to what obsession with the Ring and addiction to power can do to someone. In deprivation, he craves his "precious" talisman of power, although he knows its destructive force. The film presents a parable of addiction, as Gollum is torn apart by his need for the destructive substance. Captured by the two Hobbits, Gollum agrees to lead them to Mordor if they will release him. During the course of *The Two Towers*, Frodo himself undergoes a Gollumesque conflict, torn between wanting to carry out his mission and destroy the Ring and yet seeking its power for himself. The conflicted and increasingly despondent Frodo is kept on target by the steady and solid friendship of Sam, who shows that ordinary fellows can rise to the occasion and become heroes if they loyally serve their master and follow orders.

Meanwhile, freed from the Orcs, Merry and Pippin wander through a mysterious forest where they are captured by the benevolent Ent Treebeard, who informs them that he is a forest herdsman whose task is to protect the sward from destruction. Mixing traits of trees and humans, the Ents provide moments of comic relief as they stomp through the forest, protecting Merry and Pippin from danger, while enunciating solemn ecological pronouncements. The Ents kick in, like Birnam Wood in *Macbeth*, as they step forth to fight the army of Sauron whose minions they see as a threat to their dominion. Trees too are living, talking, and mobile beings, providing a vision of Nature as a living, breathing force, worthy of preservation. Yet a tree can also be dangerous and catch the Hobbits in its tentacles.

The vision of nature is on the whole complex and quite engaging in Tolkien's novels and Jackson's films. The ecological theme that endeared audiences in the 1960s to Tolkien now infuses Jackson's cinematic trilogy with a warm ecological glow. Yet the vision of ecology in the films is limited, showing the dangers to forests and the earth from industrialism and war, but celebrating the warfare that is a highly dangerous threat to the very survival of human beings and the earth.

Large sections of the narrative in *The Two Towers* follow the adventures of Aragorn, the Elf Legolas and the irascible and comic dwarf Gimli. This plot line revolves about awakening Théoden, the King of Rohan, whose kingdom is threatened by Sauron's Orc army, so that he will fight and protect his kingdom. Théoden has fallen under the sway of his evil counselor Wormtongue, who is himself under the spell of Saruman. Here what is obviously allegorized is the need for politicians to avoid false counsel, recognize evil, and mobilize their forces to fight – as did certain European countries and leaders who fought Hitler while others were appeasers. Yet in the contemporary epoch, it is Bush and Blair who are claiming to lead the fight against evil in the so-called "War on Terror," although here the issues are more complex as evidenced by the many Internet discussions and articles equating Bush with Sauron.[3] My

---

[3] A picture circulated through the Internet in 2004 of Bush-as-Sauron exhibiting the One Ring (see Hart; Yerovi).

argument is that *The Lord of the Rings* indeed best resonates in the present moment with Bush's crusading militarism and is, at this moment, a profoundly conservative text.

Gandalf the White joins forces with the crusaders and prepares to confront the evil Saruman who is Sauron's minion. Gandalf and his crew go to Théoden's castle to try to rally him into action, but he resists, giving time for his daughter to become attracted to Aragorn.

Théoden eventually comes to his senses and decides to evacuate his peoples to the fortress of Helm's Deep where the decisive battle will take place. His moment of awakening is highlighted by assuming his sword, a figure of phallic power throughout the film. Much of *The Lord of the Rings* is about becoming a True Man and the seizing of the sword is a privileged talisman to masculinity in the trilogy. Théoden takes his sword with intense light shining on it and religious music sacralizing the deed. He buries his dead son Boromir, with women looking on and accepting to bury the body, one of the few essential tasks for women in this patriarchal epic. Swords indeed emerge as a key symbol of patriarchal power throughout the epic and patriarchal succession also emerges as a key theme.

While the action unfolds, Merry and Pippin find themselves in the forest with the Ents, who warn them of dangers ahead and advise them to return to the Shire, expressing conservative traditionalism that affirms minding your own business and staying out of trouble. Pippin is taken by the advice and suggests they indeed return home, but Merry proclaims that they should join their comrades in battle and of course they choose the path of peril, danger, and eventual ascension to manhood through military valor.

In the DVD commentary and documentaries, Peter Jackson, his partner Fran Walsh, and scriptwriter Phillipa Boyens go out of their way to proclaim that this passage has been misinterpreted as an embrace of militarism in Tolkien's novel and the film. Jackson and his colleagues insist in their commentary that Pippin and Merry's choice to soldier on to battle is not a pro-war message, but rather an injunction that there are some things worth fighting for, like that Good War, World War II, where the enemy was indeed a threat to life, liberty, and the pursuit of happiness and did threaten Europe, the United States, and much of the world with totalitarian domination. But the two Hobbit's choice of war, and that of other more obviously militarist characters in the film, is not for a clear cause against a determinate enemy. They go to make war against the abstract Forces of Evil themselves. Indeterminate crusaders against Evil now reflect Bush's war against terrorism, where you're either with us or against us fighting the Evil Ones and Evil itself. Evil, here configured, is a vast panorama of enemies in which Saddam Hussein soon morphed into Osama bin Laden (see Kellner *Media Spectacle*).

But each of the two coalitions fighting the key battle at Helms Deep and the final battle in *The Return of the King* is itself both multicultural and disparate. While Saruman's army is presented as Evil, there is a key scene where he recruits masses of ordinary townspeople and soldiers, in which that army is shown to consist of diverse groups of people coming together to join in the fight. The iconography of the scene, that Jackson and company highlight in their DVD commentary and interviews, is clearly that of Hitler at Nuremburg, with Saruman casting a spell over the masses and leading a massified totalitarian horde to battle. And perhaps Tolkien had German fascism and Russian Communism in mind when he imagined the destruction of countries and peoples by evil political forces and evoked an alliance to fight and defeat them (although he vigorously proclaimed that he was not producing a political or religious allegory).

But in *The Lord of the Rings* there are no clear political referents in the battles, no specific political goals, and no politics except fighting for land, achieving heroism, and, ultimately, restoring monarchy. Democracy is not being fought for, and indeed the iconography is profoundly anti-democratic with wizards like Gandalf and heroes like Aragorn proclaiming higher truths and carrying out great deeds that lesser beings follow. The political structure throughout is that of feudal and premodern hierarchy with celebration of military valor as one of the highest forms of human achievement. The film trilogy is highly militarist, spending tremendous amounts of time, energy, and money on creating the great battle scenes that were highly acclaimed by fans and uncritical critics. As I will argue in the next section, the trilogy on the whole is a celebration of military valor and heroism linked with valorizations of patriarchy, whiteness, and hierarchy, highly conservative themes that link the films with contemporary conservativism.

Indeed, there are few films that have shown more bodies stabbed, shot with arrows, crushed by monsters, and killed off in a myriad ways than *The Lord of the Rings*. The trilogy is one of the bloodiest epics in contemporary cinema and celebrates military valor as the highest form of human virtue, a necessity for survival in a world full of violence and evil. Yet to the film's credit, the cost of warfare is clearly shown and *The Two Towers* has an extremely melancholy feeling to it. Faramir of Gondor sees after killing an enemy that his enemy's sense of duty was no less than his own, and notes: "War has made corpses of us all."

Jackson's trilogy does not flinch from showing bloody killings, corpses strewn about on the battlefield, and the melancholy horrors of war. Few cinematic blockbusters have such a sense of the frailty of human life, where one stray arrow can mean death. Conflicts between courage and fear, and goodness and greed, lay at the heart of the narrative that has a strong sense of the mortality of human beings and the need for good character to survive in a violent and uncertain world to preserve fragile order and social stability.

Yet the evocation of finitude, contingency, and the frailty of human life is undercut somewhat in *The Return of the King* as Gandalf solemnly invokes belief in an afterlife, "another path" to higher states of being. Gandalf evokes the "White Shores" and beyond of the afterlife, bathed in a glow of white light, obvious invocations of a (white) Christian heaven and the possibilities of salvation. Indeed, the trilogy is teeming with Christian references to sin, redemption, and salvation, giving rise to a cottage industry of Tolkien Christian readings. But, as I will attempt to show in the next section, on the whole the trilogy has more to do with conservativism and militarism than faith and Christian redemption.

The Return of the King and Triumph of Conservatism

The Fellowship of the Ring appeared in the months following the September 11 terror attacks on the U.S., when battles against the forces of "evil" were being fought in Afghanistan and elsewhere in what the Bush administration proclaimed as a world war against the Evil Ones and terrorism. The marshalling of the Fellowship corresponded with the attempts at organization of a coalition to fight global terrorism by the Bush administration, and so the film resonated uncannily with key historical events of the era. This gave it extra relevance and force (although one could argue that the largely unilateralist and militarist Terror War waged by the Bush administration failed to learn the lessons of alliances and multilateralism from *The Lord of the Rings*, leading to eventual identifications of Bush with Sauron).

The Two Towers appeared in the tense period between a seeming victory over bin Laden and the terrorism in Afghanistan. Yet it was a period in which bin Laden and Taliban leaders remained at large, while the Bush administration marshaled its energies for a big fight against Saddam Hussein and Iraq. The melancholy, unnamed apprehension, and anxious mourning of the second film thus also uncannily responded to its historical epoch. *The Return of the King*, however, opened at the end of the year after Bush and Blair's largely unilateral militarist invasion and occupation of Iraq, about the time Saddam Hussein was captured, giving rise to a momentary euphoria that quickly died as the Iraqi insurgency greatly intensified its fight against the occupation. At this moment, *The Return of the King* arguably provides ideological ballast to the militarism of the Bush and Blair administrations, while ultimately legitimating military intervention in terms of its assault on dangerous and absolute Evil.

While *The Two Towers* takes place in a mountainous terrain and in the dark night of the soul, where superior beings can rise above the masses to become warrior heroes – or, in the case of Frodo and Sam, fight temptation and lust for power to exemplify goodness – *The Return of the King* takes place on a vast canvas in which the epic quest of destroying the Ring of power is achieved, Sauron's minions are defeated, order and harmony are restored, the heroes mature and establish themselves, and the narrative threads are pulled together.

Cinematically, *The Return of the King* is an epic paean to Whiteness. Never before has Whiteness had such extravagant visual apotheosis, nor has it triumphed so completely in cinematic spectacle. The film unfolds a panorama of white clouds, snowcaps, towers, and fortresses, tents, long flowing gowns worn by both men and women, and of course white faces bathed in a reverential halo of white light. Rarely has a film had so many blonde-haired and/or blue-eyed characters, and even the darker-complexioned Caucasian characters often have their faces suffused with a white glow to signify their goodness. There are even some white-faced/masked Orcs in the film, although there are still many very black evil forces, including the darkest villain of all, Sauron, described as a Dark Lord who lives in a Black Land and unleashes Black Riders, including a faceless Witch King dressed in black, possessor of a black flying dragon that looks like a pterodactyl.[4]

In the film and the trilogy as a whole, Whiteness is affirmed as the sign of good and virtue while black is the color of evil and villainy in a passion play between the forces of Light and Darkness. There also seems to be an aesthetic in play in which the more virtuous characters are portrayed as beautiful, or at least attractive, or cute and homey like the Hobbits, while the monsters are largely ugly, even hideous and repulsive. The idealized heroes and few women characters are portrayed in classical Western terms of beauty, while the evil ones are so extremely ugly that one can almost read the moral value of characters by where they fit on a scale of beautiful to ugly.

The action opens in *The Return of the King* with a flashback showing Sméagol in an idyllic fishing scene in the Shire in the sunny days before he found the Ring and became the corrupted Gollum. Sméagol obtained the Ring by killing a friend who found it at the bottom

---

[4] *The Lord of the Rings* films are not as racist, however, as the *Star Wars* films. Yet they present offensive stereotypes of human groups, with their robed, conniving, and deceptive Asians; their greedy hook-nosed Semitic merchants; their fawning, heavily-accented black figures; and other caricatures of current racial groups.

of a pond. After this murder he was ostracized from the community, condemned to a life of loneliness and wandering. Exile in the harsh mountains evidently ate away his flesh and human features, reducing him to a miserable skeleton of a human. Sméagol's corruption by the Ring provides a cautionary warning about how the tempting quest for ultimate power can destroy a person; throughout the final episode both Frodo and Sam undergo such temptations and conflicts before finally achieving their quest and destroying the Ring.

During a confrontation between the White Wizards Gandalf and Saruman, Saruman appeals to his "old friend" Gandalf, suggesting that they form an alliance and work together again, this an implication that Saruman is a White wizard because he was once good. But Gandalf sees into his soul, knows he is evil, and quickly dispatches him before proceeding to the castle of Théoden to try to prepare him for battle.

Meanwhile, Gandalf and Pippin attempt to rally the King of Gondor, Denethor, to defend his kingdom by mobilizing his forces against the invading minions of Sauron, but driven mad by the death of his son Boromir, this King is unable to effectively mount resistance. After first refusing to mobilize, King Théoden is persuaded to raise armies to defend Gondor, providing an allegory about how the threats to the freedom of a neighboring people require alliances and intervention, an obviously positive message when it came to marshalling nations and peoples against fascism in World War II, but less attractive as George W. Bush tries to assume leadership in the war against terrorism in what many see as a misguided invasion of Iraq and threats in 2005 against Iran, Syria, and other "outposts of tyranny."

Théoden's Roharian forces include his niece Eowyn, who secretly becomes a woman warrior when she is unable to woo Aragorn. Aragorn joins the crusade against the evil forces of Sauron along with Gandalf, the Elf Legalos, the dwarf Gimli, and the Hobbits Pippin and Merry. In the fighting, both Pippin and Merry take up the sword, are initiated into battle, and emerge into Manhood. Eowyn achieves heroine status when she stabs Sauron's dark and menacing Witch King, who tells her that he cannot be killed by man; she whips off her helmut, declaring "I am no man," and stabs the monster, achieving phallic power. Likewise Aragorn, like King Arthur, takes up the mythic sword of Elendia and is revealed as the true King of Gondor as he leads the disparate Coalition of the Willing to victory.

At first, it appears that the powerful army of Sauron will take the Gondorian stronghold of the very white fortress city Minas Tirith which is assaulted by armies of Orcs, bestial Trolls pulling back the springs for catapults to hurl boulders against its walls and towers, and a fire-breathing assault machine that pounds against its gates. Even Gandalf is pessimistic, believing that Frodo has been taken and that defeat is on its way. But in a fleet of ships Aragorn appears with an Army of the Dead. In the Battle of Pelennor Fields, these join the Fellowship and their allies, who together carry out an epic struggle against Sauron's Legion of Evil with its mechanized Orc army, assorted Trolls and mutants, giant elephants, winged dragons, and other beasties.

Audaciously drawing on the imagery of Abel Gance's *J'Accuse* (1919) which in a March of the Dead sequence showed legions of wraithlike spirits bemoaning their senseless deaths on the battlefields of World War I, Peter Jackson's army of souls comes from a painful Purgatory. They are mobilized by Aragorn, who promises to release them from their limbo after the defeat of Sauron's legions. Transforming Gance's anti-war symbology into figures of military heroism gives away the militarist proclivities of the film trilogy which invests its greatest energy and cinematic elan in the spectacular war scenes. The battle is also graced by eagles which are allies of the Coalition of the Willing. Eventually Gandalf will fly away with these creatures, perhaps joining with a will-be-upon-a-time American hegemony for future battles.

As noted, the trilogy is an epic of militarist Patriarchy as each hero solemnly takes up the sword in scenes bathed in white light and accompanied by operatic or soulful music. Militarism is the privileged route to manhood and virtue in *The Lord of the Rings;* the manly character takes up the sword, displays valor, and achieves honor, thus sending out the message that the sword and the military constitute the best route for manhood and social validation.

In a parallel story, Sam and Frodo trek to Mount Doom to destroy the Ring. In one horrifying sequence in a cave, Frodo battles a horrible giant spider that evokes fear and loathing of female sexuality. The spider monster Shelob has what appears to be a threatening vagina detenta, classically signaling fear of castration. Curiously, the Eye of Sauron also appears as a flaming vagina, putting on display male fear of women and presenting images of the feminine as menacing and castrating, thus infusing the film cycle with infantile and harmful notions of female sexuality. Indeed, Jackson's *The Lord of the Rings* cycle bifurcates its female characters into idealized female fantasy figures or symbolic images of castration, with the exception of Eowyn who becomes a Woman Warrior after she is spurned.

As the spider entangles Frodo in its web, it looks as though it might be curtains for the little Hobbit, now alienated from Sam by Gollum who has convinced him that Sam wants the Ring for himself. But Sam turns out to be a loyal servant, stealthily taking the Ring away when Frodo is captured by Sauron's minions and then accompanying him through Sauron's territory and up Mount Doom. Just as Frodo fights greed and temptation in order to throw the Ring into the fiery depths that will consume it, Gollum creeps up to snatch the Ring. After he fights with Frodo, both figures appear to fall off the top of the mountain into the fiery pit below. But Frodo emerges seconds later, intact and now a full-fledged hero and True Man, as he has carried out his task and defeated Evil.

Sam embraces him with joy and Frodo returns Sam's affection, saying, "I'm glad to be with you Sam Gamgee, at the end of all this." After a period of manly embracing and homoerotic bonding, Sam fantasizes returning to the Shire and marrying Rosie Cotton, perhaps to demonstrate that he and Frodo were not gay. The same cannot be so easily affirmed of Merry and Pippin who, after the victory over Sauron's forces, discover themselves still alive on the battlefield. Both have attained manhood, and fulsomely embrace and demonstrate their manly love.

Yet on the narrative surface *The Lord of the Rings* is a heterosexual text and so Aragorn and Arwen must marry in a triumph of Whiteness and Matrimony. When the couple reunite the spectacle is bathed, as usual, with intense white light and their very white faces are brightly lit and gleaming. Aragorn declares that "Now comes the day of the King," establishing that all of the fighting was for the restoration of monarchy. The Royal Couple bow to the Hobbits, Merry and Pippin, affirming their ascension to manhood, and the audience is told that "the Fourth Age of Middle Earth, the Fellowship of the Ring, founded by friendship and love, has ended."

Before the audience can return to Real Life, in a series of premature endings, Frodo and Sam return to the Shire, bathed in a warm glow of white light. Sam marries and has a family, and Frodo writes *The Lord of the Rings,* following Baggins's "Hobbit Tale," and thus achieves his own patriarchal succession as the Hobbit chronicler. The life of the writer is not so cheery, however, for Frodo appears despondent in the closing scenes and is shown at the end taking leave of Sam and his family and joining Gandalf on a ship for unknown adventures.

And so it is that the writer and the critic of *The Lord of the Rings* do not live happily ever after, but have further tales of the Battle between Good and Evil to recount and ideological extravaganzas to follow and critique. Novels and films are quite dissimilar, enable various readings, and have disparate effects in diverse social contexts. In an era of Terror War, *The Lord of the Rings* film cycle enjoins patriarchal and crusading militarism that reflects Bush's crusade against terrorism and a post-2005 as-yet-not-articulated-crusade-against-tyranny.

In a previous historical era, Tolkien's novels articulated politically with anti-German fascism and pro-countercultural rebellions against the "system." The story is rich and complex enough that it could also motivate alliances between forces of Good against evils of the present, such as an alliance against the Bush administration and its militarist agenda. The Ring could stand for capital and the ways that greed for money corrupts individuals. Yet the cinematic militarist and patriarchal spectacle of *The Lord of the Rings* is so great that more progressive readings are undercut by the mise-en-scene and its presentation by Jackson and his crew. Moreover, the fetishistic attention to details, well-documented in the multi-volumed DVD set, is so loving, and the creation of an alternative universe is so involving, that many viewers may miss the critical ideological subtexts and political unconscious of the film cycle altogether. That the world of *The Lord of the Rings* is so very appealing and the ideological subtext hidden makes it an even more powerful political force, thus requiring critical readers and a critical response.

Note

For discussions of *The Lord of the Rings* film that were extremely helpful in developing this paper, I'd like to thank Rhonda Hammer. For indispensable help in navigating the Tolkien universe, I am grateful to Lola Calderon and Clayton Pierce.

The Lord of the Rings and Family: A View on Text and Reception

Ernest Mathijs

> *"Become what you were born to be"*
> Elrond to Aragorn when handing him the sword of Elendil

Family in *The Lord of the Rings*[1]

Middle Earth is everywhere, in different versions. It would prove difficult to find anyone in the Western world, and perhaps even beyond, who hasn't heard of *The Lord of the Rings*. But is there consensus on its final meaning as a coherent text? Without recounting the wide variety of cultural meanings the books had taken on before the first film's release (see Chin and Gray "One Ring"; Speake "Power"), there are numerous versions of the filmic story in existence, with the 124 minutes of difference between the combined length of the theatrical release and the extended DVD version the most obvious example.[2] This essay argues that because the various versions of *The Lord of the Rings* films can take on

---

[1] I want to thank my wife Emily, for giving this essay a heart, and my brother Hedwig, for giving it a cause.
[2] To be exact: *The Fellowship of the Ring* (theatrical: 178 m; extended DVD: 208 m); *The Two Towers* (theatrical: 179m; extended DVD: 223m); *The Return of the King* (theatrical: 201m; extended DVD: 251m).

different meanings, they challenge the idea that the story has acquired a single meaning that is calibrated, consensually agreed upon, and culturally sedimented.

Using the well-known problem of film historiography and reception studies to determine a "correct" version of a film and/or its public presence, I will investigate alternate readings of *The Lord of the Rings* with regard to the differences between the theatrical versions and the extended DVD versions, and offer one of my own. But instead of insisting on the importance of textual properties, I wanted to suggest that by favoring one or the other version, theatrical release or extended DVD, audiences, critics, and academics indicate a preference for a particular understanding—indeed, a particular text. In theoretical terms, this beckons a rapprochement between textual analysis and reception analysis, because my claim is that each analysis of a film text needs to state very clearly its allegiance to a particular version. This in turn requires stepping back and being relentlessly reflexive, judging the personal reception of the film within the context of its wider cultural status. [3]

Specifically, I argue that representations of family are at the centre of disparities between the theatrical and the extended DVD editions. But my argument is more complex. Two kinds of family ties are portrayed in *The Lord of the Rings*: troubled ones, which stand as exceptions to pedigrees, heritages, and traditions; and accomplished ones, which are forged through the story's developments, opportunities seized, or obstacles overcome by characters, especially in relation to patriarchy. The roads leading toward these accomplished family ties are conspicuously

---

[3] Some of these questions are at the heart of a research project analyzing the launch and reception of the third installment of *The Lord of the Rings*. It was developed as part of the International Lord of the Rings research Project, supported by a grant from the UK Economic and Social Research Council (ESRC Grant No. 000-22-0323) to whom we record our gratitude. The project had three stages: a study of the prefigurative materials in each country (marketing and publicity, press, magazine, radio and television coverage); a databased questionnaire combining multiple-choice with free-text responses, available on-line but also completed on paper in a number of countries; and follow-up interviews with individuals chosen to typify response-positions from the questionnaire responses. The volume and density of materials produced by the project is enormous – with 24,739 questionnaires across the world. Because of this, over time it should permit systematic investigation of many questions which have, to date, been mainly the subject of speculative claims. A book of core findings from across the world is currently being developed: Barker, M. and E. Mathijs (2007). *Watching the Lord of the Rings*. New York: Peter Lang.

absent from the theatrical versions of the films. Their inclusion in the extended DVD edition forces a new understanding of the kind of story *The Lord of the Rings* is: less epic, and more personal. This issue of family and its representation has implications for the film's presentation as epic (its main marketing tag), for critics' attitudes towards it, and for general considerations on the distinctions between viewing environments.

Theories of a Film's Final Moment

The key to my approach lies in the consideration of the so-called "final moment." A film's "final moment" is the moment when most opinions on its meaning seem to converge into a larger consensus. This process is one that can be slow and continuous (as with the debates on the meanings of *Citizen Kane* (1941), or that is almost instant and immediate (as with *Titanic* [1997]) (Kael *Raising Kane*; Rosenbaum *Orson Welles*; Sandler & Studlar,*Titanic*). From a historiographic point of view, the problem of the "final moment" concerns only the text, and one's ability to determine its precise features. As Robert Kolker has pointed out, film historians are often confronted with the fact that the film versions they study and teach are significantly different from the film originally intended, released, or archived. Kolker cites *Greed* (1925) and *The Magnificent Ambersons* (1942) as examples, asking which edition should be granted the status of the definitive text: the released one, which audiences viewed, or the intended one, perhaps never released (Kolker "Film Text," 13-15).

Apart from being a problem of authenticity, it is also a problem of reception. Controversies, rediscoveries, revivals, retrospectives, and even casual cultural references can challenge a film's "final moment." For example, much to the annoyance of the director, David Cronenberg's *The Fly* (1986) became seen as a metaphor for AIDS (Mathijs "References"). As far back as the late 1980s, Barbara Klinger has rightfully called attention to the ways in which accompanying actions in the reading of a film allow for moments (she calls them "digressions") in which contextual information will provide more clues for enjoyment and communication with the text than the text itself seems to offer (Klinger

"Digressions"). What Klinger implies is that at least in part these actions are informed by an ability to connect the (experience of the) text to an active knowledge of (and willingness to use) contextual or ancillary information. As Thomas Austin has pointed out in coining the term "dispersible text" (a text fanning out in different directions in time and space), many high-concept Hollywood films of the 1990s no longer allow a straightforward "final moment" for a film text (Austin *Hype*). And for cult films, whose reputation is so dependent upon continual celebration, a "final moment" may well mean the end of their appeal (Mathijs & Mendik *Reader*).

The "final moment" is, of course, also an issue when adaptations are involved. Forced comparisons between different source materials invoke discussions of authenticity as well as reception, with battles between readings taking on hierarchical characteristics that go well beyond legal matters or issues of comprehension (who owns the right to a story's "justness"?), and often involve fan discussions. Recent debates over the faithfulness of the numerous editions of *The Exorcist* (1973) testify to this ambiguity (Hoxter "Possession").

Now, being a Hollywood-hyped adaptation with a preexisting cult reputation, *The Lord of the Rings* is a perfect example of a text without a "final moment." Even that ritual point of exposition of the text that a theatrical encounter is supposed to furnish has been undermined. Prior to its release, *The Lord of the Rings* had been spoon-fed to us, through leaks, trailers, clips, photos, and additional stories (gossip, facts, exegesis), to the point where even those who had not read the books came to know who the main characters were, what they looked like, what they wore, how they talked and functioned in the narrative. So much of the film text had already been shared with us that it was possible to form a pretty accurate idea of the text without actually going through the ritual encounter of a screening. Obviously this is connected to the ways in which producers "prepare" audiences for the reception of the film, something of particular importance to *The Lord of the Rings* because of the fact that it is an adaptation of a book with a huge, well-organized fan base. Its activeness is reflected in some of the debates surrounding the anticipation of the film text. There were concerns about the role of

Arwen, about the exclusion of Tom Bombadil and Glorfindel, and debates on "color coding" (discussing how good and evil seemed to be ethnically determined, with white associated with good, black with bad). With particular regard to the third episode, there was a short but fierce debate over the cutting of Christopher Lee's Saruman from the theatrical version.

The fact that *The Lord of the Rings* was a trilogy, a franchise with releases spread over two calendar years (December 2001 to December 2003) complicates things even further. The periods in between the releases become, in the mind of viewer and market, bridgeable by the insertion, at calculated intervals, of reminders of the past and upcoming episodes. Bennett & Woollacott's analysis of the James Bond franchise, and research into the Hannibal films (*Silence of the Lambs* (1991) and *Hannibal* (2001) (Bennet & Woollacott *Bond and Beyond*; Mathijs "Monster") demonstrate how the meanings and interpretations of such tent-pole productions become based on more than just the individual film texts, and how their narratives "spill over" the textual boundaries, at least for the viewer. If we look beyond the viewer's concerns and think of the text only, the striking thing is that these are all debates about the composure of a coherent text. They are not just elements of fan concerns but also worries over the status of the text and its meaning.

In the case of *The Lord of the Rings*, and increasingly so in general, such worries also have a pressing relevance for post-premiere releases, such as VHS, DVD, and various sorts of "cuts." *The Lord of The Rings* trilogy pioneered the idea that such materials would not just be identical or contain chapters which would include "deleted scenes" or materials cut by theatrical censors, but that each scene could be altered intrinsically, by adding and prolonging shots, music, dialogue, and effects internally. Peter Jackson has always refused to see the extended versions of the films as "director's cuts," insisting that the theatrical releases are as much his own vision as the DVDs. But there is no denying the dissimilarities between them. This goes beyond the mere length disparity. Jonathan Gray discusses the differences between the theatrical and extended DVD editions of *The Lord of the Rings* extensively, arguing that with the abundance of bonus textuality in existence ... it becomes incumbent upon analysts to study this textuality to see exactly what it adds to 'the text itself,' and, by extension, what DVDs are doing to textuality in this new age of bonus materials (Gray "Bonus").

Why is there so much worry over this textuality? Gray makes a helpful comparison with Walter Benjamin's concept of the "aura" of the work of art. In film much of that aura is preserved in the "screening encounter" with the film, with fans and experts distinguishing themselves from others by rushing to the earliest screenings (be they press screenings or avant-premieres), or by performing their expert knowledge of the text, sometimes in celebratory fashion. With *The Lord of the Rings* some of that aura may shift to the celebration of (or complaints over) prefigurative and post-release materials, and of discussions of extended editions. Gray's essay concentrates only on *The Two Towers* episode of the trilogy, but, as he concludes: "Other close readings of the same DVD could well reveal further and equally rich meanings. In studying texts, it becomes an open trap for us to examine 'the text itself,' its political economy, and its audiences alone" ("Bonus"). Such isolationist analyses should indeed be shunned. I want to take Gray's suggestion to task. That is why in focusing on the different layers of family representations (an "equally rich meaning" indeed) suggested in theatrical and extended DVD editions of *The Lord of the Rings*, I will take first the text, then its public presence into account.

Family in *The Lord of the Rings*

Family plays a crucial role in *The Lord of the Rings* story. Much of the narrative centers on kinship relations, and they have a profound impact on the development of the plot. The very beginning of the film, which recounts the battle of the Last Alliance, not only provides a historical framework for the story to follow, but also introduces the concept of family as an important complicating factor by inserting into the prologue the story of Isildur and his father Elendil. Such intimate connections between family troubles and big history are not unusual, in fact they are one of the trademarks of epic cinema, from *The Birth of a Nation* (1915), through *Gone with the Wind* (1939), to *Ben-Hur* (1959). But in the case of *The Lord of the Rings*, it is remarkable how fractured family lineages run parallel with failures to cast off evil. Jackson's prologue narration implies there is an Arthurian imperfection in the relationship between Elendil and Isildur. It means that the mere fact that it is the son Isildur, and not Elendil himself (the archfather of the story, the founder of Minas Tirith), who needs to take on the responsibility to destroy the Ring already indicates that he will fail to carry out this heavy task, or even the one of wielding the Ring; as if any son is the lesser of such a father. In doing so, the narrative immediately suggests that only certain types of (perfect) family bonds are capable of resisting corruption and evil.

Image 2: Fractured family lines and failure to destroy the ring. (Courtesy of Dr. Kristine Larsen, Central Connecticut State University).

This is not new, and there are several interpretations of *The Lord of the Rings* that refer to these views on family, mostly through discussions of love and friendship (Bassham & Bronson *Philosophy*, 68-71; Rosebury *Phenomenon*, 42-44). My particular interest in family representations is related to the "final moment" of the film. In the filmic versions there is a substantial discrepancy in the way diverse family situations are portrayed, and this has implications for their meaning and status. The theatrical version insists on painting a much bleaker portrait of fractured, troubled, and non-existing or non-consumed family ties than the extended DVDs, as if all instances of family happiness, or at least approaches towards that happiness, have been deleted. One reason for this may be that allowing more references to happy family life in the theatrical films would have more forcefully suggested that everything would eventually turn out all right, which would diminish the tension and suspense in the narrative as well as shift attention away from the action of battles and chases. As so many screenwriting textbooks remind us, there should be no harmony or peace for the characters until the end of the film, or else the audience will stop craving for that end, and hence stop paying attention to the narrative that takes us there. The story would lose its drive. For the extended DVDs, the drive of the story is of less significance. Most people watching these DVDs will already know the story quite well and there is no longer a strong need to provide theatrically graded impulsion. More space is available for reflective, embellishing moments, especially the ones in which family ties can be further explored. The DVDs function in this sense as exegeses of the theatrical text.

This cinematic/DVD dichotomy in representation is visible in virtually every family present in the films. In contrast to allusions on love in *The Lord of the Rings* by Rosebury and Bassham & Bronson, the love situation of the two lead protagonists, Aragorn and Frodo, is not a traditional one, at least not until the end of the story. This has to do with their status as single men. Neither is married, though they are at an age when they are receptive to such commitment. Both Frodo and Aragorn always smile serenely when marriage, or love leading to it, are mentioned, giving way to suggestions that a "normal life" is what they desire. But, curiously, such moments are much more present in the extended DVD editions. In the case of Frodo it is most notable when he observes his friend Sam's love for Rosie Cotton. In the theatrical version, that blooming love is only hinted at through one glance of Sam towards Rosie when, unnoticed by Frodo, they are leaving the Green Dragon, and then brushed aside for more serious matters, namely Gandalf's return with news of the real nature of the Ring. In the extended DVD scene of the Green Dragon, however, the film lingers on the subject a bit longer. Frodo boasts a little in the pub, and when he exits with Sam, his comforting of Sam's doubts is shown more elaborately, making the tension between Frodo's public pride and his personal wishes tangible.

In the case of Aragorn, the desire appears when, fleeing to Helm's Deep with the Rohan, he is being made aware of the feelings of Eowyn. When asked, he tells her about his true love Arwen and about their difficulties in realizing union (symbolized by the Evenstar). Again, the scene is much more elaborate in the extended DVD version, even including a more prominent presence of Arwen and more personal details about Aragorn (including the revelation that he is 87 years old). This gives their relationship a history and cements it deep within the core of the narrative – in effect it is a narrative root, rather than a branch.

The other family bonds of Frodo and Aragorn are ambiguous. Frodo's closest relative is his uncle, Bilbo, a well-respected member of the Hobbiton community.[4] Bilbo entrusts Frodo with the care of his estate, a clear sign of their closeness. But neither Frodo nor Bilbo seems a typical Hobbit, and this is poignantly encapsulated by villagers describing them as "cracked." In a few funny scenes, the Hobbits' custom to enjoy, or in the case of Bilbo endure, extensive family relations, are mocked. In his birthday speech, Bilbo's derisory comments on the Sackville-Bagginses, and his obvious though polite discomfort when he addresses his "dear Bagginses and Boffins, Tooks and Brandybucks, Grubbs, Chubbs, Hornblowers, Bolgers, Bracegirdles and Proudfoots" show how alienated he is from the "normal" Hobbit way – something evidenced by his (and Frodo's) status as outsiders. The scene in which Frodo welcomes Gandalf to town, both of them conspicuously watched by a Hobbit not coincidentally standing in front of his family home, is a clear indication of how Frodo's and Bilbo's family status is associated with a place outside the nucleus of Hobbiton. A relatively large amount of screen time is devoted to the exposition of this mutual discomfort, and nothing

---

[4] Like many Hobbits, Frodo has a wide circle of relatives. Both Peregrin Took and Meriadoc Brandybuck are among his cousins. My thanks to Taija Queen for bringing this to my attention.

appears in the extended DVD to ease it. The fact that the scenes are, by themselves, quite funny relieves some of the discomfort. But it does not do away with their significance as representations of the fractured sense of family belonging Frodo and Bilbo experience.

For Aragorn, the only clear kinship is with his deceased mother and father, both of whom are remembered regularly throughout the films. Especially with regard to his mother many scenes are fleshed out in the extended DVD (I will come back to this in detail later). Aragorn also maintains a family-like relationship with Elrond, the King of the Elves, who acts, *mutatis mutandis*, as his adoptive guardian, most explicitly in two sequences in which he takes a fatherly role towards Aragorn. In the first of these, Elrond shares his concerns with Aragorn regarding Arwen's feelings for him and the consequential implications for her status in the Elven community. This is actually a series of scenes spread out across the three installments of the films, neatly tied together through recurrent style (cold blue colors, windy autumn settings, slow motion, switches between on- and offscreen dialogues). Arwen, Elrond's daughter, will lose her immortality if she stays behind with Aragorn. Elrond counsels both Arwen and Aragorn and tries to make Arwen see that she belongs with the Elves. At the same time, he is reluctantly approving of the bond between them, as he knows it will be a factor in the battle against Sauron. It is a perfect example of the troubled, fractured family representations typical of the theatrical release (in this case even structurally so, as it permeates all three episodes). In the extended DVD edition much of this is still present, but subtle details point towards a shift: while it may seem in the theatrical release as if Arwen is really the one instigating the break with her father, choosing Aragorn out of true love, the impression is created in the extended DVD that the situation is more complex than that. Through the exposition of Aragorn's background – initiated by Elrond's remark to Gandalf when Aragorn arrives in Rivendell that "he turned from that path a long time ago, he has chosen exile" – the viewer gets a sense of how intrinsically intertwined the histories of Aragorn and Arwen are. Although the exact nature of their mutual history is never made explicit, it is nevertheless strongly implied in the extended DVDs that concerns greater than just Arwen's love for Aragorn govern a fair part of

The Lord of the Rings *and Family* 51

their relationship. When Elrond gives Arwen away as a bride at the end of the story, then, it is not just a final acknowledgement of his consent that they marry. The act is also a public recognition of the ties they have been sharing for so long.

The second sequence in which Elrond's paternal role towards Aragorn becomes apparent involves Elrond's traveling to the camp site of the Rohan riders, where they are gathering to ride out to help Gondor. He hands Aragorn the sword Andúril, forged from the chars of the sword Elendil wielded in his battle with Sauron. It is a strongly symbolic act of initiation and the handing over of responsibilities, of which the family overtones are reinforced by Elrond's command that Aragorn should become what he was "born to be."

Image 3: Elrond's father figure hands Aragorn the sword Andúril, re-establishing an allegiance. Digital frame enlargement (Copyright © New Line Cinema).

The scene is a turning point in the third film: from here on, Aragorn sheds his despair and sets out to win allies on the authority conferred by possession of the King's sword. It is a point of no return in the narrative; war (and the consequential responsibility of Aragorn as leader of the people of Middle Earth) is inevitable. Again, in the extended DVD edition, much more emphasis is placed on the familial-type bond between Elrond and Aragorn as the impetus for Aragorn's noble behavior.

Frodo and Aragorn are not the only ones with fractured family backgrounds shown to contain different implications through the additional materials included in the extended DVDs. One of the most extended family lineages, and also one of the most doomed, is that of the Stewards of Gondor, exemplified by the relationship between Denethor and his sons, Boromir and Faramir. In the theatrical narrative Boromir and Faramir are presented as two quite separate individuals, with their own paths towards destiny. In fact, through the personal madness of their father Denethor they are almost positioned as adversaries, tragic brothers battling each other over the approval of their father. It is only in the extended DVDs that they seem closer. In the extended editions of *The Two Towers* and *The Return of the King,* Boromir re-appears briefly, alongside Faramir, showing a clear fondness towards his brother and even a hint of disapproval of his father's dismissiveness towards Faramir.

Image 4: Family in the Extended DVD edition: Faramir and Boromir. (Courtesy: www.theonering.net)

The two appear far more congenial than in the theatrical release, begging an understanding of the narrative that is more harmonious, and less fractured. As a result, Faramir becomes a less isolated figure in the extended editions. As illustrated by the scene in which he gives Pippin the Gondor guard uniform he used to wear as a child (in itself already a token of a less troubled family past), Faramir's position shifts to inclusion among the main protagonists, aligning with their actions and perspectives. Through this material and thematic identification with the core group of characters, Faramir also becomes more acceptable as a match for Eowyn.

The only exception to these dissimilarities between fractured family representations in the theatrical releases and more harmonious (at least hopeful) representations in the extended DVDs, is the ending of the narrative. There is no difference here between the substance of the theatrical release and the extended DVDs. However, the dissimilarities still shine through because the meaning of final events is constructed by all that has or has not preceded them. There has been some criticism of Jackson for making the ending too long and melodramatic, out of tune with the rest of the film. This, in my view, is true only for the theatrical release. Indeed, when compared to the action-packed drive of the theatrical narrative, the ending does seem long-winded. It seems to focus too much on the farewells of the individual characters, melodramatically over-emphasizing their mutual bonds. This personalization fits the extended DVDs much better. For me, Jackson has made the "error" of putting extended DVD scenes into the theatrical version, thus creating an imbalance and leading to comments about sentimentalism. Fittingly, and in line with the more hopeful view on family relations expressed through the extended DVDs, the ending of the story places emphasis Sam's future life. He woos and wins over Rosie's love, and after the goodbyes of those characters unable to step into or return to family life (Frodo and Gandalf in particular), the film's final shots are of him, in his family environment, filled with happiness. Married, with two children, he embodies what Hollywood has long held up as the "ideal" nuclear family. It is no surprise, therefore that this is the end of the story: there is no longer a need for a further drive toward any goal. The building or restoration of family ties has conquered evil.

It should be noted here that on a less literal level, "family" also serves as a signifier of many friendship bonds between characters. The one between Sam and Frodo is the most obvious one, but those between Pippin and Merry, Legolas and Gimli, and Gandalf and Frodo also carry family undertones (in that sense, it is natural that Frodo and Gandalf leave Middle Earth together). The scene in which Frodo wakes up and is reunited with the other members of the Fellowship evokes a very homelike feeling, associated with childhood weekend mornings. Through its soft-focus, sepia colors, clever use of sound (much of the dialogue and vocal sounds are muted, as if soft-spoken, and the music is elegantly prominent), and slow-motion movement, it references happy family memories. Given this, it can surely be convincingly argued that depictions of close friendship in *The Lord of the Rings* use conventions of, and references to, family representations in order to increase their significance for the story.

The Faith of Women:
Aragorn's Maternal Strength, and Eowyn and Faramir

With so many disparities between the two versions, the extended DVDs become, in fact, a different trilogy altogether, with an alternative meaning. The essence of that difference lies in how the extended DVDs represent less fractured family bonds, and in how, through emphasizing ways in which those fractures are mended through women's activities and presence, it invites a gendered reading of the impact women have on the resolution of the conflict, and, hence, on the narrative itself. I want to explore this through two examples, the maternal influence on Aragorn, and the relationship between Faramir and Eowyn. Both relationships have great narrative significance. The first helps Aragorn take his responsibility: claim victory over Sauron, become King and rule Middle Earth, and marry Arwen, representing the everlasting alliance between Men and Elves. The second solidifies the renewed alliance between Rohan and Gondor, representing their mutual responsibilities in looking after each other in times of need.

Aragorn's lineage is of crucial value to the narrative. Although he is linked to both his mother and his father, there is a difference in the type of linking. Aragorn's connection to his mother is remembered by himself; his connection to his father by others. "This is Aragorn son of Arathorn," retorts Gandalf when Boromir, at the council of Elrond, refers to Aragorn as a mere "Ranger." Likewise, Elrond, when pushing Aragorn towards his faith ("Become what you were born to be"), uses Argorn's father as an argument to bestow royal responsibilities upon him. All of Aragorn's links to his father are present in the theatrical release and nothing is added to them in the extended DVDs.

This is not so in the case of Aragorn's mother, references to whom are scattered throughout the films. In the most significant, we see Aragorn visit the grave of his mother, Gilraen. It is a scene exclusive to the extended DVDs, and it is placed, significantly, right after the council has decided to form the fellowship and bring the ring to Mordor, one of the most decisive moments in the story. The scene strongly suggests Aragorn receives his strength and determination to carry out the task ahead of him through his mother. But maternal influences come to Aragorn from more than his mother. It is also invoked in two other scenes associated with decisive moments in the story. After Elrond hands Aragorn Andúril, the extended DVD includes a brief encounter between Aragorn and Eowyn. She is the first to notice he will leave the Rohirrim and take the Paths of the Dead. Such a presence, straight after a turning point, invites speculation as to her influence on Aragorn. Eowyn urges him to stay, and Aragorn first seems a little confused, then recomposes and tells her that although he cannot give her what she wants, he recognizes her importance for him ("I wished you joy since first I saw you" indicates maternal respect). In another, earlier, scene, we see Aragorn sing a song dedicated to Luthien, a legendary Elf woman, when watching over the Hobbits at the Midgewater Marshes, near Weathertop, the place where Aragorn's courage will be tested firmly for the first time. Much more than simply adding weight to his background, these matriarchic influences in the extended DVD edition give the story a gendered meaning. With the picturesque exception of Rosie's role for Sam, Aragorn is the only significant character with any matriarchic bond in the entire trilogy.

Among these influences, that of Aragorn's mother stands out as particularly important. Where Elendil, Denethor, Elrond, Theoden, and Sam are all patriarchic family heads, there is a conspicuous absence of any mothers. This is even atypical for epic stories. From Homer's *Odyssey* to *Ben-Hur*, and even Talia Shire (no pun intended) in *The Godfather* (1972; 1974; 1990) mothers are at the core of family representations. Yet there are no such mothers in *The Lord of the Rings*, with the exception of Aragorn's remembrance of his mother in the extended DVD edition. Her presence is crucial to a new understanding. Aragorn's courage and power, which he only gradually develops through the narrative as he changes from a lonely doubtful Ranger to a King who leads armies and alliances, is drawn from his mother. With Gandalf mysteriously losing his wit and presence near the climax and with Frodo's faith unknown, Aragorn becomes what the people of Middle Earth rely upon in their hour of need. To have this clear maternal influence, then, at that point, makes a determined difference in not only the hero's deeds but also the meaning of the power associated with that hero. Unlike the theatrical releases, the extended DVDs seem to suggest that the dark forces of Sauron can be overcome only by someone who pays rightful tribute to the role of the mother. When contrasted with the prologue, in which feeble Isildur was unable to live up to the tasks his father carved out for him, the success of Aragorn's personal journey seems to suggest that true strength is transmitted by the mother.

With Eowyn and Faramir, the case is slightly different, but it leads in fact to the same conclusion. Faramir is the second son of Denethor, seen as less able in spite of, or maybe because of, his greater thoughtfulness. Yet Faramir shows his courage and abilities in battle and conflict at every available opportunity. He leads guerilla attacks against Sauron's mercenaries, he is wise enough to see the importance of Frodo's and Sam's quest to destroy the rings thus releasing them from custody, and he twice attempts to courageously resist the Orcs' attack on Osgiliath. Yet he receives only scorn from his father. After being rescued, more dead than alive, from a funeral pyre set by his father, he recovers from his wounds (one would imagine them to be not only physical ones) in the Houses of the Healing in Minas Tirith, where he meets Eowyn. Eowyn finds herself in a similar position as Faramir. She is the "shield maiden of Rohan," niece (and adoptive daughter) to their king Theoden but kept outside the inner circle of decision making through a strong hierarchical patriarchy in which Theoden's deceased son Theodred and her brother Eomer occupy a position of power and command that she is barred from reaching. Like Faramir, her courage and determination are not gratified by the exclusively patriarchical family situations. In spite of this, she sneakily rides into battle with the Rohan and distinguishes herself by killing the Witch King, an act through which she attempts to rescue the fallen Theoden. The Witch King is invincible, unable to be killed by any man. Eowyn proclaims, "I am not a man," and kills him. Theoden dies nevertheless, but not before he recognizes the one who saved him from an even more grueling death as none other than his niece, the very person he refused to let join him in battle. Wounded herself, Eowyn, too, recovers in the Houses of the Healing (she is in fact healed by Aragorn who uses Elvish healing, presumably learned from his mother). In the theatrical release of the films, this healing scene and the subsequent meeting of Faramir and Eowyn are absent. Yet the healing scene provides a logical prelude to the eventual marriage between them. In the theatrical edition this marriage comes out of nowhere, and though a lot of the filmic story relies upon prior knowledge of the books and thus need not be apologetic about ellisions it is still a sudden introduction so near the end of the narrative. In the extended DVD edition, however, the Houses of the Healing scene provides a perfect framework for the marriage. Through it, the scene also demonstrates how these two victims of strict patriarchy in the kingdoms of men will, together, lead the way to new views on the alliance between Gondor and Rohan. Tellingly, neither Faramir nor Eowyn is eventually rewarded a leader's role. Descendant of a steward, Faramir stands aside for the rightful King (Aragorn); and it is Eomer who succeeds Theoden as King of Rohan. But it is safe to assume both will enjoy considerable influence at their respective courts.

Image 5: The new alliance between Rohan and Gondor: Eowyn and Faramir. (Copyright © New Line Cinema, available from Yahoo Movies.com)

The Missing Family in the Reception of *The Lord of the Rings*

If these family ties are so important and lead to such disparate interpretations of the text, then why are discussions of family ties absent from most writings on *The Lord of the Rings* film texts? There are several explanations. First, critics still see the theatrical text as basis for the "final moment" of a film. For them it is the Ur-text. Many magazines and newspapers publish only short DVD reviews and commentaries, ones limited to a reiteration of the main arguments put forward in the theatrical release reviews. Often they are simply edited editions of those reviews, with a paragraph or two on the additional materials (almost never linking these extras to the rest of the film). The changes in the readings of *The Lord of the Rings* indicate a growing need for extended DVD reviews to be separated from theatrical release reviews.

There is also another, more complex reason why critics have ignored the family ties reading of the films: they reveal films more focused on personal journeys and center the story on people rather than large-scale actions. A survey of the public configuration and critical reception of *The Lord of the Rings* shows how the vast majority of reviewers saw the film, and by extension the entire trilogy, as epic.[5] This was the case for reviewers who both praised and criticized the films. Comparing reviews from three British newspapers (*The Daily Mail*, *The Times*, *The Independent*), we find an overwhelming emphasis on the epic scale of the story. All three publications use the word "epic" to describe the films. *The Daily Mail* calls it "the greatest cinematic trilogy ever – surpassing by far its nearest competitors, *The Godfather* and the first three *Star Wars*. *The Lord of the Rings* is a major cultural landmark, a masterpiece that will inspire future generations of filmmakers, and it will be watched with admiration for as long as cinema exists" (Tookey "Long Live"). *The Times* concurs, calling the film "the greatest trilogy in cinematic history," adding a range of references from Shakespeare to The Bible, and ending by saying that Peter Jackson "started off filming a legend; now he is one" (Baillie, "One Film"). *The Independent* also writes that the film has "little time for anything much smaller than a rhinoceros" and "builds up to the most flamboyantly apocalyptic spectacle ever filmed" asking what the purpose is of this "gargantuan scale" (Romney "OK"). It is interesting to see that this stress on size tends to ignore individuality in favor of bigger events. It forges the idea of an epic film, with epic politics for epic times, with massive scenes, big budgets, and great new technology to create special effects.

    A brief look at the issue of ideology shows how attention to family representation becomes impossible within this paradigm. For Tookey, *The Lord of the Rings* is symptomatic, even emblematic, for the times we live in; he does not hesitate to lift the story out of its context and superimpose it onto contemporary politics. Such a take invites ideology into the discussion. Likewise, *The Times*' references to the Bible, British history, Henry V, King Lear, and "blood ties" with "dark Shakespearian overtones" indicate a desire to see it in ideological terms and in relation to large-scale events. Even Jonathan Romney's negative critique essentially

---

[5] The survey included a study of press clippings held in the Royal Film Archive library in Belgium, and a three-month tracking study of how the British, American, Belgian, and New-Zealand press reported on *The Lord of the Rings* in the run-up to, and immediate reception of, its theatrical release.

concurs with that view, summarized neatly in his description of the film as "totalitarian cinema" ("OK").

Such an ideological reading prevents attention to personal stories like Farmir or Eowyn's, or Aragorn's mother's, or even to the subtleties of the friendship between Merry and Pippin (reserved for the extended DVDs). Instead it invites discussions of the imperialism of Saruman and Sauron, the self-contained isolationism of the Hobbits, the arrogant neutrality and non-interventionism of the Elves, the honor-driven Rohan, the nationalism of Gondor, even the mercenary beliefs of the Army of the Paths of the Dead. They invite links to "grand narratives" but disregard the personal – the pockets of smaller communities and less stentorian unions, forgoing an engagement with family representations in pursuit of an ideological reading.

The focus on "epic" also has a root in the presentation of the product. The run-up to the premiere of the last installment of the trilogy (released 17 December 2003), put a lot of emphasis on its "epicness." This related to the scale of the enterprise: the production of the film trilogy shot back-to-back, its premieres spread over three years with intermittent DVD-releases, leaks, press releases, marathon-screenings, and other tie-ins, was itself turned into a media event. Even its local distribution was occasionally turned into a media event: note the shopping frenzy surrounding the film at the 2001 Cannes Festival (Biltereyst & Meers "Distribution") and that many distributors had to sign up without receiving much guarantee. Recent work on the branding of contemporary Hollywood and the negotiation of filmmakers' integrities in relation to that machinery, suggests that such practices are, if not new, then at least trendsetting; they have altered the ways in which high-concept blockbusters are put into the world. It is easy to see how issues like the family ties I have discussed above do not fit this pattern of grandiosity. In that respect, *The Times* critic does well to mention *King Lear,* as it is one of the few "blood ties" stories making the connection between epicness and kinship.

The Times published as many critical discussions/reports prefiguring the film *before* its release as afterwards, and never before have so many opinions on a film been made publicly available before it was released. This has an important implication. It provides a political-economical logic for the domination of epicness over family ties in the critical reception of the film. Reviewers picked up on the stories about the vastness of the enterprise and cleverly linked these to actions depicted in the story (it also gave them an opportunity to gape at the special-effects), a rhetoric not uncommon to film criticism (Bordwell *Meaning*). To strengthen their argument they also developed connections with current affairs and politics. The discussions of the trilogy's ideological overtones demonstrate a willingness to lift the film story out of its fictional context and treat it as a symbolic representation of our times. Several reviewers and discussions lists noting that *The Lord of the Rings* is about the price of triumph cannot be seen as disconnected from the events in Iraq. National Geographic linked it to American frontier mythology and presidents like Franklin Delano Roosevelt. Even then-Tory leader Ian Duncan Smith's attempt to show how Gandalf is really Churchill falls under this category. For critics like Romney, who realize the epic interpretation is forced by prefigurative and publicity materials, and by the producers' desire to turn the product into a media event, the epicness of the story becomes a point of contention. His epithet, "OK, Peter, message received" needs, I think, to be seen as a complaint about the impossibility of seeing the theatrical release as anything other than epic.

In this light, the concept of the "final moment" needs to be extended to the prefiguration of films through publicity, marketing, and previewing. In an online email discussion list, Gray asserts that:

> before the first film was released, fans had already decided whether they were going to love or hate the film, and already engaging in what could only be called close reading and textual analysis (of an as-yet non-existent text). But it's not just fans who do this: many of us already had our responses and suppositions about, for instance, the films' racial coding and signification before watching it, I'd bet, and on hearing snippets or reading bits about the film here and there. (Gray "Those Rings").

Such an observation is not new. It has, in bits and pieces, surfaced in recent considerations of the relationship between film and its public presence (Barker "News, Reviews"). But in the case of *The Lord of the Rings* we are faced with a unique opportunity in that the sheer abundance of ancillary materials surrounding the trilogy accounts for the potential emergence of new, not just deviant, interpretations of its meaning. This cannot be reduced to disagreement between critics, as has often been the case. Nor can the oft-cited recuperation of critics as "auxiliary PR-troops" (Romney "Diary," 66) be seen as the sole cause. Romney's discomfort is evidence of a realization that a film's meaning fans out in different directions, and that its material conditions and appearances are at least as important for its significance as its inherent features.

Conclusion: My Brother and *The Lord of the Rings*

In conclusion, I want to point out a curious parallel between the viewing environments of the various editions of *The Lord of the Rings* and the film's various interpretations as either epic or intimate and familial. Ever since the recovery of theatrical film attendance in the late 1980s, induced by the emergence of the multiplex theatre and the high-concept blockbuster, theatrical releases have come to be seen as serving a certain demographic as generically based spectacle in which size, scale, and the creation of a night-out experience are of utmost significance. The theatrical release of *The Lord of the Rings* is the epitome of this type of film. Since the late 1990s, DVD viewing has become an addition (some say a competition) to that. It generally takes place in a home environment, involving quite another demographic, and in substantially different commercial surroundings (no opportunity to sell popcorn maybe, but other possibilities arise, pizza for one). It seems only logical that producers and media corporations will want to cater to that new viewing environment by suiting their core product to the perceived needs of customers. Is it really only a coincidence, then, that the edition which facilitates an understanding of the trilogy as being about family representations happens to be the extended DVDs which are typically watched inside the domestic bubble? Can there not be a connection between seeing *The Lord of the Rings* as a film about *family*, and having the experience of watching it at *home*? An arrangement such as this warrants further research into how a film text's various public presences relate to its viewers' attitudes.

As to myself, until recently I was never really in any way attracted to Tolkien's *The Lord of the Rings*. In fact, I resisted the story as long as possible. It was only with the release of the films that I became interested, inevitably perhaps. There is a very personal reason for my decade-long avoidance. When he was twelve years old or so, my brother, younger by two years, read the books and became fascinated by them. It was endearing to see him plow his way through *The Hobbit*, the three Rings books, and then *The Silmarillion,* and perhaps every other affiliated story. It should have made me curious enough to want to investigate the books myself, but I was at an age when one doesn't want to be seen as even remotely associated with the interests of a younger brother. So great was my need to disavow the objects of his fascination that I even managed to resist when those very objects attempted to associate with me, infiltrating my universe in the form of cover-art on many a revered heavy metal album (these were the early eighties). Looking back, I realized it was a silly attitude, and as soon as the first film was released I tried to atone by plowing my own way through the books, observing the differences between book and film, and, later, between theatrical and DVD versions. By then it was too late. I found that years of neglect had created an insurmountable gap between my brother and myself. He had achieved an understanding I would never have, essentially different because of the conditions under which the story was encountered: his reading is a book-reading, mine a film-reading; his the reading of a seasoned fan, mine that of a novice.

I have yet to watch *The Lord of the Rings* with my brother, as I have yet to watch it with others I deeply care about. But I am certain those viewing experiences will offer new insights, some only marginally different, some radically new. Far more than I read into these films, these films read into me.

The Fading of the Elves: Eco-Catastrophe, Technopoly, and Bio-Security

Sean Cubitt

Aotearoa

This chapter is an attempt to trace some of the emergent properties of an ecological aesthetic in *The Lord of the Rings*. This new aesthetic is especially important for all of us who live in Aotearoa/New Zealand, site of all the locations and most of the miniature and computer generated image (CGI) material in the film. Not only was Jackson's trilogy (with an estimated turnover well over one per cent of the nation's GDP) an extraordinary achievement for an industry with basically a single product. It has also become totemic of the country's self-understanding as an environmental paradise kept free by sundering seas of the industrial and genetic pollution of Asia and the North Atlantic nations. The double naming of the country juxtaposes the geographical specificity of the ancient Maori name, "Land of the Long White Cloud," and the colonist's passion for combining the old country (the rich agricultural lands of the Dutch maritime provinces of Abel Tasman's birth) with the indefinite expansionism of the New. There could be no more fitting home for a film which addresses with passion and intelligence the dialectics of home and exile, harmony and expropriation, the clean and the destructive than these islands born of the guerrilla victory of the Maori over the greatest army the world had ever known, and the treachery that stole their victory from them in the dishonoured Treaty of Waitangi. As the Treaty regains its status as the founding constitutional document of the nation, the dialectics of secular and sacred understandings of identity and land have become the cores of politics, economics and biculturalism, from the economics of organic farming to the ethics of eco-tourism.

Like many small nations, Aotearoa New Zealand has diminishing power over its internal policies. The limitations on sovereignty imposed by GATT and GATS alone circumscribe the policy options open to governments. In many ways, what remains in the hands of the nation state, restricted if not determined by transnational agreements in policy and economics, is culture. In a bicultural nation, the question will often be about the delimitation of culture: does the prohibition against pollution of shellfish colonies count as economics or religion? And what is to be the status of the new New Zealanders arriving not only from other ex-colonies of the British Empire but increasingly from South, East, and Southeast Asia? At its most general, the political culture of the nation can be summed in a single question: how far can an exporting economy retain its complex identities in a globalising world? *The Lord of the Rings* has a remarkable place in the imagining of this uniquely local yet in many ways typically global discourse. It is not just that government invested heavily in the film, or that Air New Zealand has decorated its planes with *Lord of the Rings* logos, playing, in early 2003, a documentary guide to locations on all inbound flights. It is also that, *pace* the postmodern truism that "nobody" believes in grand narratives anymore (Lyotard *Condition*), eco-politics has become the single largest unifying political discourse of the early 21st century. Toby Miller and his collaborators (Miller et al, *Hollywood*) claim that film, and by extension all creative practice, needs to be understood in terms of the global arts and media industry. Likewise, they need to be understood in terms of an emergent global political culture, that of anti-globalization and ecology movements. What makes *The Lord of the Rings* significant in this context is that it balances the common fear of environmental Armageddon (Cubitt, *Partition*; *Aliens*) with the potentiality of a country in which it is still possible to imagine the green triumphant.

Ecological Aesthetics

All Middle Earth's peoples are defined by their designs and their technologies, which stand in the film as the languages do in the novel. These technologies, traits, and techniques – horsemanship among the Rohirrim for instance – are proper to each race and thereby both authenticated but also bounded, their mystery guarded like those of the mediaeval guilds and anchored in the spirit of place. At the same time these crafts are all communicative within and between communities, as garment, weapon or gift. Respect for boundaries is critical to the stability of Middle Earth, a respect mirroring the bio-security measures of the Department of Conservation, the environmental agency charged with protecting the island environments of Aotearoa New Zealand. The contradictions between communication and border patrolling, between the flow of trade, gifts, and meanings on the one hand and the policing of biological integrity on the other (Clark, *Demon-Seed*), structure the desecrations of Saruman in *The Lord of the Rings*, for example in the hybrid figures of the Uruk-Hai, all too easily legible as allegories of genetic modification and genetic engineering. In its imagining of Aotearoa New Zealand as Middle Earth, the film is in some senses closer to Hundertwasser, the Austrian environmentalist and artist who took Aotearoa to his heart, than to the influential but controversial phenomenologist of technology and Nazi sympathizer Martin Heidegger.

One clear example of this comes in the elimination of some backstory for the Balrog sequence. Tolkien is unambiguous: the Balrog has been awakened by the dwarves, because they have transgressed the unwritten law against delving too deep. In the film, however, the Balrog is just a force in the mines of Moria, linked by color thematic to Sauron's eye, otherwise unexplained. New Zealand's mining heritage, its ghost town relics of a typically brutal gold rush, and its volcanos sacred in Maori tradition, may have helped Jackson make this cut, which absolves the dwarves of being the instruments responsible for the arrival of teleological technology – mining for its own sake. (And mining has stood as symbolic of the end of the Golden Age throughout the European tradition. For a modern revisitation and reaffirmation, note Lewis Mumford's statement: "One must admit the devastation of mining, even if one is prepared to justify the end" [Mumford *Technics*, 72 and passim.])

Nonetheless there are spatial boundaries in *The Lord of the Rings*. There are also distinctions operating between the different temporalities of the authentic and inauthentic technologies of Middle Earth. The pleasures of Hobbiton are repeatable – pipeweed, ale – and the great artefacts, the Ring itself, but also Sting, the mithryl shirt, Isildur's sword, are long-lasting. Saruman's instrumental inventions on the other hand are ephemeral because self-consuming (again a minor change from the book reverberates here: Saruman's tower is simply his tower in the films; in the book it is the historic construction of the Men of Gondor). The contradiction that makes the film so interesting is that it is a technological triumph in the service of a green mythology. In Jackson's account the aim of the production design was verisimilitude, particularly to provide the various sets and locations with a history. Entirely in keeping with the novels, this history is ingrained in the overgrown, used, broken, and deserted. Likewise the actors wield their hand tools and weapons with as much familiarity as possible, to give the viewer the sense of skills learned not in the mind but in the sinews. The designs of tools, architectures, and weaponry speak of the "long intersubjectivity" of Paul Ricoeur and Georg Gadamer, not least because production design has to stand in for the wealth of linguistic inventions that characterize the book. Yet insofar as it is marked as intersubjectivity, the temporality of each design family operates very precisely within geographically bounded regimes, so much so that their discovery beyond their own territories makes them evidence, and so objects distinguished from their environments rather than elements of them. Their placedness is integral; travelling objects are evidence not only of alien intruders but of the breakdown of a "natural" order of rooted location, a quasi-feudal anchorage in the turf of home.

Saruman's sin, for example, for which he is punished by Fangorn, is that he does not respect the *genius loci*. Aotearoa New Zealand shares with Australia a popular concern for the replacement of "invasive" or introduced species with "native," paralleled in the European movements to rescue and restore lost species of fruit and livestock largely eradicated in agribusiness's drive to standardization. Separated from Gondwanaland before the evolution of mammals, Aotearoa has only one native bat, a scanty population of reptiles, a rich and unique bird-life, and a range of trees, ferns, and mushrooms that have evolved in their own style largely because of the absence of mammals. This unique ecology was first treated as wilderness by the European settler culture, with the introduction of pastoral and dairy farming in particular, but is now the object of extensive efforts to conserve, exactly, the genius loci, the unique spirit of the place. Assaults on the ecosystem of Aotearoa are popularly seen as two-fold: introduced species and genetically modified species. Conservation, however, at times veers close to conservatism. While on the one hand the film arises from a specifically New Zealand belief in the necessity to conserve a unique ecology, to a global (and indeed to an urban New Zealand) audience, it may also speak of a more sinisterly Heideggerian conservative cult of the Land.

This is why boundaries are so significant to the film. Clearly boundary crossing can happen: in the Fellowship itself, in the picaresque structure of the journey, and, most significantly, in the added weight given by the films to the love between Arwen and Aragorn (with its comic parallel in the mateship between Legolas and Gimli). Otherwise matters of high seriousness, these interracial relationships are marked by duties, obligations, responsibilities, and sacrifices, including the loss of community and of race-specific qualities (immortality), which must be deliberately chosen by an act of will in full knowledge of their consequences. It is at such junctures that the fear of contamination that belongs to the conservation movement meets the racism of the conservative protection of local culture. In our case, the strange symbolic absence of Maori from the re-imagined New Zealand of the films suggests that the culture to be protected is not that of the first inhabitants, but the civilization of the Pakeha settlers.

The races of Middle Earth are constituted as themselves in both endogenous and exogenous communicative networks that include trees and rocks, networks that exceed the human. In the production of the film, machine-machine communication is axiomatic. *The Lord of the Rings* is distinguishable from the French eco-apocalyptic cycle (in cinema the films of Luc Besson – *Subway* [1985] and *The Fifth Element* [1998] – and Jean-Pierre Jeunet and Marc Caro – *Delicatessen* [1991] and *The City of Lost Children* [1995]; in *bande dessinée* comic strips and graphic novels since the *Pilote* and *Métal Hurlant* of the 1970s); and also from Hollywood's eco-armageddons since *Soylent Green* (1973). What makes Jackson's films different is that they posit a possible resolution based on the very apparatus of illusion.

What is false, inauthentic, vile, amoral, anethical, and anaesthetic in *The Lord of the Rings* is manufacture – the smokestack industries. The good and true is craft – the craft of the armorer and the smith, the weaver, the sculptor, and the brewer; and likewise of the smiths, armorers, weavers, and sculptors who worked on the film alongside the more contemporary guilds of cinematographers, editors , production designers, and CGI crews. These guilds are organic: what they make is morphologically connected to its origins in the world. By contrast Saruman/Sauron are denaturing, as when greed for the Ring morphs Bilbo into a mask of snarling avarice at Rivendell. The crafts are physis, *natura naturans*, organic in Kant's sense that every part is an end in itself as well as an element of totality; the dark magic is closer to genetic modification/genetic engineering, determined externally, a hierarchy of parts subordinated to a purpose that overrides its elements.

There is, in this binarism, a certain ambivalence about white magic and about Gandalf, who falls to the monster unleashed by the Faustian delvings of Moria. That provenance is muted in the film to preserve the pride in craft of the miners' guild. Gandalf's guild is harder to analyze (or too easy to allegorize – the filmmaker's avatar as storyteller, master of destinies, weaver of spells – an allegory then transfigured by the return of Gandalf the White as Christ allegory parallel to C.S. Lewis's Aslan, again a theme muted in the second film). Saruman and Sauron work against nature and/or to control it. Their quest is to uproot the autonomy of the green world in order to reduce it to the status of Heideggerian standing-reserve, a mere pile of resources for purposes of which nature knows nothing. The white wizard, at the opposite end of the scale, is concerned to nurture a potential into existence, as he does most clearly in the scene of Frodo's moral education, when first we catch a glimpse of Gollum near the end of *The Fellowship of the Ring*.

Two features of this sequence are noteworthy in this context, the shots of Gollum's fingerpads and eyes, the latter of which will feature so strongly in *The Two Towers*. Both are canonic indices of discrete individuality – fingerprints and retinal identification. Both are sensory and at the same time sensed, thresholds between inward and outward realities, telling as much as they learn. The full figure has more to do with constituting Gollum as object. Eyes and fingertips bring him into the networks of intersubjectivity. What has removed him from those networks – and has damaged Bilbo and will damage Frodo – is the artefact of inwardness, the construction of self over and against the genus and the world. Gandalf's craft lies in sympathetic magic, fellow-feeling with Shadowfax or with the moth that brings the eagle to his rescue at Isengard. Contrast here the gradual construction of Frodo as object of the Nazgûl, an objectivity that both forces heroism upon him and deprives him of both joy and freedom, other than the freedom to accept the quest. Wisdom then, as it occurs to Frodo, is an outside event that happens to him, a matter of loss. It is a loss he will bear on behalf of Middle Earth when the Elves depart and the age of magic will be over. The price of the defeat of manufacture is the loss of that natural magic too. In their place there will remain only a human world. In this sense the trilogy moves towards the ending of illusion as narrative goal although its appeal lies strongly in the artifice of illusion. This sense of heroic destiny and heroic loss is characteristic of recent U.S. hits, not least in the theme of undying love in James Cameron's *The Abyss* (1989), and *Titanic* (1997) and the Wachowski brothers' *Matrix* cycle (1999-2003).

In certain respects, the communicative universe of *The Lord of the Rings* is peculiarly premodern. In the 19th century, ladies could still view battles from adjacent hilltops, so tightly were the codes of battle limited to the professionals. At this stage war was "narrowcast" in the sense that it was composed of a dialogue between defined sets of interlocutors and governed by codes that forbade the involvement of civilians. (Of course civilians suffered and were killed, but they were considered illegitimate victims, not collateral damage or intended targets, as they were at Dresden, Hiroshima, and in Vietnam). The age of narrowcast war ended somewhere between Sherman's March to the sea and the bombing of Guernica during the Spanish Civil War. War is now a broadcast medium: as Hobsbawm notes (*Extremes*), twentieth-century wars were indifferent to the neutrality of civilians, who are statistically more likely to be victims than warriors in the conflicts of the early twenty-first century.

The same historical drift has happened in the case of pollution. Industrial and population waste were at one time demarcators of class, intensely local to factories and the workers living in walking distance of them. But waste export, atmospheric pollution, and global warming are broadcast. Skin cancer is no respecter of class or politics. Susan George points out that the transfer of industries to the *maquiladoras* sweatshops along the Mexican border has resulted in waste from factories and sewage travelling north back into the United States (George, *Boomerang*: 26). Waste, in other words, is a mode of communication. It may be as natural as a gift – a child's gift of poo to its parent – or as counter-natural as the trade in nuclear waste. It may be as conscious as the export of dirty industries or as unconscious as the use of deodorant sprays. One upshot of ecological understandings of network communication is that consciousness is not a requirement – we communicate by virtue of our place in the network, by having a bank account or driving a car. Humans do not need to intend communication by the medium of petroleum by-products or savings accounts, yet all unconscious as we are, those actions communicate through the medium of greenhouse gases and stock market fluctuations on the widest planetary scale. If there is a consciousness in such communications, it is global and transhuman, an ecological effect, not a quality of individual agents. Similarly, the Elvish sixth sense that allows Galadriel to know in advance of the Fellowship's arrival is evidence of an ecological radiation of meaning and presence through the world. Nonetheless, even these unconscious communications can become tradable items, as in the U.S. proposal for a world market in pollution credits allowing for the commodification of pollution. This is the meaning of Jackson's *palantír*, the Seeing Stone in Saruman's tower.

The Fading of the Elves

Image 6: Point-to-point technology: Saruman using the Palantír. (Copyright © Quintessential Lord of the Rings Movie Shots – www.logicalcreativity.com)

Unlike Galadriel's ecologically networked vision, the *palantír* is a channel opened point-to-point, a narrowcast communication which has become, as we learn, a means for the delivery of moral pollution from Mordor to Isengard. Tolkien's backstory has not only more detail but a very different notion of the Stones. Of old, Gandalf tells Pippin, they were used "To see far off, and to converse in thought ... each *palantír* replied to each" (*The Two Towers*, 248). Like early cinematic accounts of television (*High Treason* [1927], *International House* [1932]), the Stones could see anywhere the viewer desired, and were to that extent an expression of a global environment that gave itself to vision. Jackson's Stone has lost that capacity (which is reserved, differently, for Galadriel's mirror) and become a medium of command, of a spectacle hiding a one-way commerce.

This triad of natural, instrumental, and lost magic might be restated as a movement between *physis*, *techné* and *polis*. Physis, in Dylan Thomas's beautiful definition "The force that through the green fuse drives the flower," is dialectically opposed to techné, the black arts of manufacture. For Aotearoa New Zealand, still in the early 21st century largely a commodity-exporting, agrarian economy, the smokestack industries have made little dent. The extraordinary local economic impact of the films can be seen as indicating a unique path to development for the national economy, bypassing the manufacturing era to move straight to an information economy. In this sense the human magic of information technologies, the technologies deployed in the construction of the film, announce themselves as resolving the disputation between green and iron. Their resolution, in which both will be transformed, lies in the human world of the polis, the restoration of the King in the fable of *The Lord of the Rings*, a new socio-cultural order derived from the marriage of technology and ecology celebrated in Jackson's Weta Workshops as a model not just for the creative industries but for the renewal of the whole national economy. Yet what makes this resolution so implausible is that it ignores the position of the films' making – and much more so their marketing – in an integrated global economy of exploitation and environmental degradation.

Creative Technology

If we are to understand *The Lord of the Rings'* eco-politics, and especially how it has changed from Tolkien to Jackson, we must also grasp something of the historical ecology of the global political economy in which the books and now the films were produced.

In the New International Division of Labor, the production of exchange value is divorced geographically from the consumption of use-value, and use-value, so divorced, is the more readily transformed through branding into sign-value. More traditional use-values (shipbuilding, tools manufacture, components and subassembly for finished goods) are made by a Third World proletariat who are nowhere *near* the use-values of their products. The production of exchange value is restricted to the developed world and among national and regional élites, and is rewarded in the consumption of sign-value. The production of sign-value resides in a creativity reserved for the metropolitan élites and is most highly prized among transnational corporations where the production and ownership of intellectual property, sign-value, has superseded ownership of the means of production as the core engine of wealth. Scott Lash (*Critique*, 84) argues that what is produced at this level is no longer goods but ideology.

Neither Tolkien nor Jackson and his team can be accused of attempting an allegory of contemporary globalization and its effects. Nonetheless, the films cannot but articulate with their own time, especially through the kind of second-guessing of audience tastes which must inform aesthetic decision-making in industrial filmmaking. While some emotional configurations can be relied on to keep their forms (fear of the dark, fear of spiders), others shift in time, such as the modes of schizophrenia attendant on 21st century immigration politics, and the movement of anxieties, till recently attached to computers, onto the feared futures of biotechnology. Considerations of North and South thus re-emerge in the film, echoing a more distant imperial paternalism from Tolkien's youth, but now devoted to new forms of anxiety.

As is the case with the paradox of magic in the service of the disappearance of magic, the narrative arc of the film trilogy takes us through wonders and marvels to return us at last to the natural cycle emblematized in Sam and Rosie's babies. In this sense, its task is to assimilate the miraculous, both narrative and technical, into the settled world of the Shire. The appearance of both Jackson and Weta effects supervisor Richard Taylor among the Haradrim corsairs in *The Return of the King* suggests a perverse sense in which both these magicians of the film world are in effect the enemies of a normality to which the film will ineluctably return. These wild Southerners, ragged and bloodsoaked, are the antithesis of the ethereal and Aryan Elves, whose ancestors the Eldar seem to revive the ancient Edda mythological cycle of the far north of Scandinavia.

    The Hobbits, on the other hand, are charged with maintaining the deep-rooted use-value of things. Their love of food and drink anchors them in the homely virtues, even when these veer to excess, as in the scene when Merry and Pippin are discovered guarding Orthanc and filling themselves with beer, salt pork and pipeweed. Men, Dwarves and, most of all, Saruman, have exchaged these uses for power and honor, though Gimli is tempted by the pork, and in the director's cut gets to drink deep in competition with Legolas. But for the two great magicians, Sauron and Gandalf, material things have vanished, even the exchange-value that turns wealth into might. Of the two, it is the one for whom the world has most completely turned into sign, Gandalf, who will triumph. Sauron's downfall is his confusion of sign-value with exchange-value, a confusion Gandalf refuses when he refuses to carry the ring. Like the Elves, Gandalf seems to subsist on air and magic, and to experience the world not as food and drink, nor as power and wealth, but as an accumulation of symbols that point away from the material world. This raft of attitudes seems almost to map the characters of Kipling's imperial romances, *Chalky and Co* for example. Kipling's rambunctious sergeants and their officers, whose patriotism lies furled silently in their hearts, are entirely at home together, like Gandalf and the Hobbits. Alien to both are the parsimonious and the greedy, the authoritarian and the despotic. This articulation of use with sign to the exclusion of exchange is utopian to the extent that it removes from the scene the site of contradiction (who feeds the city of Gondor?). In Tolkien's book, the stash of pipeweed would be explained by Saruman's occupation of the Shire. In the films a hoard of luck, it serves simply to anchor the Hobbits in their bodies, and their bodies in the earth. Technologies like Saruman's great pit lie in the hinterland between use and sign, between the old world of peasant farming and the new of information technologies. In Tolkien, the distinction was simply between ancient, which was both magical and wholesome, and modern, marked by the advance of industry across the rural Midlands. For Jackson's team, Aotearoa New Zealand leaps across the developmental model's middle passage, linking agrarian economy to information economy without having to pass through the smokestacks of industrialization. Yet the old belongs to the colony, and the informational to a global future.

In this way the South is condemned to the old ideologies in which the relations between people appeared to them in the fantastic guise of a relation between objects, the commodity relation under manufacture. Meanwhile in the North those relations appear as signs: identities and relationships forged as brand loyalties and fandom. As entrepreneurialism was once the royal road out from the old working class, so now creativity is the most prestigious and lucrative route for escape from the humdrum proletariat of consumerism.

Creative production takes this on board not only by selling interactive media like games but by the creative production of software, media for making other media. Office and design software can only work with an active audience. One step down the same is true of operating systems and communications protocols like TCP/IP, SMTP and FTP. Equally significant are encoding and engineering standards for laser optic and magnetic media, broadcasting transmission standards, the infrastructural intellectual property on top of which the skilled craft operators produce the custom plug-ins, cameras, mikes, etc., on top of which another tier of designers, writers and office workers produce consumable symbolic discourses. This is the new international political economy in which *The Lord of the Rings* films are being made. It explains, among other things, why not only *The Lord of the Rings* but any film or TV program is never purely a New Zealand product, unless it is made with tools – cameras, computers, filmstock – derived from New Zealand. New Zealandness is only another lens through which the filmstrip passes, another focal plane, another composited layer.

In the global economy, creativity (and increasingly a socialized creativity) based on team spirit rather than studio discipline, recruits from radical politics models for the reproduction of capital under a new guise. Failure to be a team player or to have creative engagement with the work in hand is seen as a moral failing. Contractual obligations to customers, students, patients, and clients order creative production and the delivery of services. But those goods and services proper to the circulation of sign-value demand also an emotional and creative commitment, almost regardless of the quality or nature of the commodity, from cinema to plumbing, requiring a commodification of the "duty of care" promulgated by Heidegger as an essential attribute of humanity.

Even the quality of being unknowable (the sublime) becomes a tradable entity. At one end of the scale, Sauron's eye indicates (but cannot demonstrate) the ineffable Evil. At the other, the unnameable loveliness of the South (see note on N/S distinction above) Island mountainscapes stands at once for the healing beauty of the natural world and as marketing for tourist destinations. In this sense at least we can agree with Derrida: there is no *hors-texte*; no transcendental subject or object. There is mediation, mediation that can be taxed and hoarded in the same way that finance capital flows are taxed and hoarded in the global market. The production processes of the movie are entirely of this order, the more so for the fact that much of the craft element was produced offshore. Most absurdly, the franchise end of the movie as event links it to practices in fast-food, toy, and garment manufacture, games development, and printing industries whose business practices tie them to the global business of sweatshops, pollution, and environmental degradation.

Philosophy and *The Lord of the Rings*

Was Tolkien a Heideggerian – not by influence perhaps but because both the Oxford don and the German philosopher derived their systems from a shared fascination with the etymologies of the Germanic (and in Tolkien's case the Celtic) languages? It may well be that both share, in Heidegger's phrase, a belief that "Whatever stands by in the sense of standing-reserve no longer stands over against us as object" (Heidegger *Question*, 17). At opposite ends of a spectrum, both Fangorn and the Balrog are autonomous of the human, and they stand over against the human as things that have their own presence. But their autonomy will end when the Elves leave Middle Earth, and the old things fade, as Heidegger writes of the fading of presence since the time of the pre-Socratics at the dawn of history. The autonomous presence of objects disappears, in Heidegger's later philosophy, as they cease to be apart from the human, and instead become a collection of tools and raw materials waiting to be fulfilled – and utterly changed – when they are used in human technologies. But in many ways, Tolkien's vision is less modern than Heidegger's, grounded in the collapse of Nazism and the post-war Germany of NATO and suburbanization. It seems fair to say that Tolkien was more of a Kantian, sharing with the 18th Century Sage of Königsberg a founding distinction between technology and the organic. For Kant the internal logic of life combines parts into a unity such that "an organised natural product is one in which every part is reciprocally both ends and means" (Kant *Judgment*, 24) where technological logic subordinates parts hierarchically to the function of the whole.

When Hegel revised Kant's distinction decades into the 19th century, he emphasized the distinguishing factor as the internal logic of organic beings. In contrast to the organic, technological mechanisms are characterized by their "external purposiveness" (Hegel *Science*, 736): the *telos*, the first and final destiny of a knife, a saddle, or a wagon is determined not by their parts, still less by any internal logic, but by the purpose they have for a user who is not a knife, a saddle, or a wagon. Yet finally, that distinction arrives quite logically at Heidegger's principle, that "the essence of technology is nothing technological" (*Question*, 35). Tolkien's trilogy shows a distinct distrust of the motives behind specific technologies, and of failure to observe the Natural Law against excess, while accepting the morphological principle that sees Hobbit technologies like watermills or Elvish technologies like weaving as wholly appropriate because their forms are so deeply determined by the nature and purposes of their makers.

Is the Jackson movie Heideggerian? The answer is clearly no. Not just because of the relation with "The Question Concerning Technology" but because this is, very explicitly, a world picture, again in Heidegger's phrase "the making secure of the precedence of methodology over whatever is (nature or history)" (*Question*, 125). Its concern is with the authenticity of artifice, the finality (*Zweckmäßigkeit*) of play. Against this authenticity is ranged the inauthenticity of Saruman, and the counter-authenticity of Sauron. Between them lies the guild mystery of mining and metal craft, the craft of the dwarves. Heidegger feared the arrival of a teleological technology, a technology whose own rationale would lead it towards a conquest of the world. Tolkien perhaps shared this fear, but in the films the fear is shifted, made more subtle, in order to accommodate the intrinsically technological dimension of the films' making, and in deference to the changing nature of our technologies.

The link between nature and imagination as it functions in *The Lord of the Rings* should by now be clear: it is the work of natural magic. The fading of the Elves is the sacrifice that allows for the emergence of Men, the polis of laws. The cost of this transition is the hyperindividuation which Frodo suffers, the delivery of attention to the commodity media as the construction of an obsessively determined subjectivity – subjectivity as teleological technology. In that movement, the world becomes Other, and the option of immersion in it is removed from the magical to the informatic. There can be no healing bath of nature, but there is the balm of the loss of subjectivity in the embrace of this cycle of films, and beyond them in the vast ocean of human communication. The special effects technologies so skillfully deployed stand not only for Middle Earth but for themselves, as crafts of mundane, rule-governed magic. That they are also marked as fallen, as imbricated without possibility of redemption in the global nets of the commodity, marks them out as the internally conflicting harbingers of the new dialectical of the new commodity: between the manufacture of sign value and the discipline of consumer attention. The utopian dimensions of the film are less about a green world untouched by technologies than about the possibility of a post-commodity communication in which techne and physis are embraced in the polis. The mood of regret masks an etymologically precise glamour of futurity.

On Being a 1960s Tolkien Reader

Martin Barker

The desire to interpret texts – the structured examination of their formal organization, patterned associations, intertextual constructions and, thence, organized cultural meanings – is a pretty ineluctable one. It is at its strongest when people sense that something is at stake, when the emergent meanings matter in some wider sense. And it was inevitable, with the astonishing resonance that *The Lord of the Rings* has created and sustained across its various embodiments, that a squadron of interpreters should home in on it. The risk is that we will come to love a resulting conflictual scene. A combination of the strong tendency among academics to compete for intellectual "novelty" of interpretation, well described by David Bordwell, with our own version of the Third Party Effect (divining a meaning/effect that will be true only of others, not of ourselves [see for instance Peloff "Third-Person Effect"]), will produce a rush of judgments on story, book, and film. Judging quickly will not only be unhelpful, it will be, I want to argue, untrue to a spirit which invested the early responses to Tolkien's world. For the caricature of the "1960s reader" who rang Tolkien late at night to ask about the Ents, wore a "Frodo Lives" badge, and was "into weed" misses some vital aspects of the story's early reception. I know, because I was there. This essay has to start with an account of a difficult personal experience engendered by the Jackson/New Line Cinema films.

On Discovering One's Ideal Interpretation

I had to see each part of the film adaptation of *The Lord of the Rings* twice: once, to find out just what the makers had done with it; a second time, I hoped, to enjoy it for whatever it had turned out to be. This was not from some kind of literary purism, an a priori preference for books over films. There are many cases where I have been only too grateful for a film adaptation of a book that I just can't get through, or where a book has stayed cold and impenetrable to me until a film has made it come to life. Differently than that, I have had a longstanding affair with *The Lord of the Rings* and went to see the films in a state of some nervousness. It would be only by first coming to terms with the nature of the adaptation that I would be able, as I very much wanted, to let myself go with it. And it is as well that I did this. Along with the many moments of sheer happiness at seeing the story-world enacted in ways that just made me smile with pleasure, there are others – very important others – where I was seriously aghast. What surprises me, even now, is that I didn't know what they would be. Knowing now, I understand things about my involvement in Tolkien's world that I had not understood up to this point.

I first read the books in 1959, when I was thirteen. I can't remember any detail of what they meant to me then, but I know that I was seriously engrossed – sufficiently that when I was asked to write a story for a class by my genial elderly English teacher Mr Francombe, I wrote a full sequel. It took me all of about five pages to recount the history of the discovery, quest, and destruction of a second Ring. Moved by my efforts, Mr Francombe asked me what I thought of the books. I admitted my fascination. Then he asked me: did I think the story was an allegory? I don't remember my answer, but what I do remember is that I knew that I didn't know the meaning of the word. It prompted my first ever visit to a dictionary.

The books of *The Lord of the Rings* remained important to me thereafter. I re-read them regularly through the 1960s. I introduced them to Judith, whom I would marry (it is her copies that I have revisited regularly ever since). In the 1970s we discovered the extraordinary radio adaptation of the BBC, and for years lived off our illicit recordings of them. We even rather liked Ralph Bakshi's half-adaptation. It was only in the moment of rejecting some very particular aspects of the first two parts of the film – more in fact than feeling strangely distanced from the third part – that I came to see *how* the books had mattered to me and even, in retrospect, made sense of an unease I had had about the radio adaptation but had never put into words. Since then, discussing the films with many friends and colleagues, I have realized that I seem to be almost alone in my "reading." And that interests me, almost as much as the understanding of what *The Lord of the Rings* has meant in my own life.

My refusals centre around three most symptomatic moments, one from each part of the film. Other disappointing aspects I tended to note, but was willing to let pass: for example, the casting. Pippin and Merry were just too leprechaunish for my taste, but I marginalized them in my mind, and that made them a topic of simple dislike, not part of my refusal. I forgave that the Shire was to me too clean and sentimentalized. Dropping Tom Bombadil was no problem. And so on. My first real unease came with the Council of Elrond. In the film, the emergent Company sits on a balcony with the Ring exposed in front of them, and under its baleful influence they begin to squabble, argue, even fight. That was to me utterly wrong. I cannot yield to the filmmakers' explanations of the need to trim the wordiness of the entire chapter that Tolkien devoted to the retold histories, slow assembling of understandings, detailed workings out. To me, the ratiocination of the Council was the nub of the story. Here, in space carved out of difficult times, the characters *reasoned*: what is the nature of Evil? It is not self-evident, it has needed research, discussion, a coming together of minds. How big is the threat? How could it possibly be combated, defeated? Do we have the strength ... the will ... the courage? Without that reasoning, the story was to me no more than an adventure story, a "fantasy."

The second problem was worse than the first, and this time lacked even the thin justification of saving screen time. In *The Two Towers*, Pippin and Merry meet up with the Ents after their escape from Saruman's Orcs. The Ents to me were well visualised, with excellent voices. But in Fangorn a debate arises – will the Ents go to war? In the books we do not hear their debates – the two hobbits, whom we accompany, are left to await the outcome. But I always "imagined in" these discussions – building up to the decisive "Hoom" as the Ents broke their Entmoot and began their march on Isengard. As Treebeard says, they are almost certainly going to their doom. This will be the last march of the Ents. But this is right, and inevitable. The film disposes of this, without compunction. Jackson's Ents *refuse* to go to war, and have to be *tricked* into it. Led the wrong way by Pippin, Treebeard is shown the devastation of the forest wreaked by Saruman (as if he would not already know: he, the shepherd of the trees) and is enraged. The Ents, from being embodiments of long wisdom, became foolish, grumpy, diminished creatures. Instead of reasoning their way to a decision, and accepting the fate this imposed on them, they became servants to others' wills.

In the third film, the battle scenes were fantastical and fantastic. I regretted the manically chuckling King of the Dead, but could pass on. But I was deeply discomforted by what to others has seemed the tiniest thing – indeed, some to whom I have pointed it out have had to go back to check that I was right. After the Battle of Pelennor Fields, the Lords of the West gather in Council. What must be done next? This was just a pause, not a victory. In the books, Aragorn calls on Gandalf to guide them, as he has ever done. And Gandalf counsels them to draw Sauron's eyes away from his own land – they must take an army south and attack the Gates of Mordor, even though they cannot possibly win. In the film, these words are *transferred to Aragorn*. Gandalf has for a moment despaired – he does not know what to do – and Aragorn has to step in with the solution. This was to my ears impossibly wrong. Gandalf, who may have looked and sounded so right in the films, was here made weak. He would never, but never, be at such a loss. He might listen, research archives, travel to hear news and gather information. And then he would know. His wizardry lay not in his sword, but in his intellect. He was the philosophical opposition to evil embodied. In a sense that I could not have articulated at the time of my reading of the books, it was important to me that Gandalf was a source of reliable, generalized wisdom. Somehow he stood outside time, and embodied a principle of understanding and best course of action.

In conversations with friends afterwards, I realised that I had had a fourth refusal, but only in retrospect could I place it: the prologue. The films begin, as in fact did the BBC's radio adaptation, by retelling the history of the Ring. In one sense, everyone who has read the books knows that history. And of course having such a prologue tidily establishes the good/evil opposition; and saves much time from later retelling. But, the harm it does! The Prologue is simply incompatible with any notion that we, like the characters, *might not know* the nature of the threats and dangers. I had never until this point been able to name the unease I had felt at the opening to the radio adaptation, until I identified this much wider set of shifts in the films.

To me, there is a clear pattern linking these four refusals of mine. The chain that combines them is the certainty that for me *The Lord of the Rings* is a very particular fictional treatise on the nature of evil. Only a deeply reasoning assembly of peoples committed to its defeat could unmask its deceits, see past their own ignorance and uncertainties, and assemble the sheer will and courage to keep fighting, no matter what the cost. The story did not need to be as simple as an allegory (now that I know what that word means!). It was a sensibility. There was a structuring principle to the evils of the world – the Vietnam war, the Bomb, apartheid, and so on – but it hid itself. The principle behind evil in the world was huge, and dangerous, and could only be defeated by acts of unlikely will. But if there is no space for reason to operate, no Kantian moment when humans can rise above the first impulses and work out the principles of operation of Evil, there can be no Hope.

The Concept of Interpretive Community

Mine was, I am sure, a 1960s reading, in the sense that it was definitely forged in that period, and in that it played a role in the emergence of my political views and engagements. Yet it is hard to find any sign of this in the quite copious writings which have told the story of that first phase of Tolkien fandom. As *facts*, the standard story may be right, but I believe it gets the situation wrong in several important ways. Yet it raises a problem: implicit in the various writings about 1960s readers is an account of their interpretive strategies – how they made the books meaningful to themselves. These readers – among whom I count myself – are presented, in effect, as a troublesome interpretive community, with whom Tolkien himself felt uncomfortable. Not only do I sense that this account misses much that is important about 1960s readers, I sense that it hangs upon a use of the concept of "interpretive community" that I want to question.

Consider this excerpt from an interview with a young woman, part of our International *Lord of the Rings* Reception project; she had been selected because she exemplified one tendency we had identified. Her hesitations indicate that the conclusion she arrives at was almost a *discovery* she made about her own reactions in the course of being interviewed:

> I just liked his character, and also afterwards, after they see him and they go out and get lost on those mountains those, they're like kind of weird ghost things come in and kind of *get* them and he comes and saves them, and I just quite liked that bit of the story ... and I thought that was quite a big, well not a big *part*, but like for me I really liked that character and I liked his wife, she was like magical and mystical and she sounded really nice but it kind of made it seem like the journey in the film, it made me feel like the journey from the Shire to the *Prancing Pony*, it's made it seem quite a lot shorter distance than I think it was in the actual *book* ... quite a lot easier to get to and I kind of think they could've maybe put something in there. I know two of the hobbits get stuck in a tree or something ... and it kind of tells how *little* they *know* about the Middle Earth." (viewer interview)

The concept of "interpretive community" has become the most widely used expression to indicate a range of features attending how audiences read, listen, and watch. Its obvious first intent is to stress the group nature of such activities. When we read a book, the way we read is a function not just of our private self but of how we have learned to look at a book of this kind. Why we read it, what we seek in it, how we interpret characters, follow narratives, forge analogies with the world beyond the book are all in part shared with others. But what kind of thing is the "community" that results? Easiest to understand are local groups who meet, discuss, share ideas, and reinforce tendencies in each other – even through disagreement. Jenny Hartley's *Reading Groups* draws attention to one such widespread phenomenon. Janice Radway's well-known study of one more informal group delved deeply into the shared practices of a group of women romance readers.

But not all uses of "interpretive community" presume such intimate connections among members. As Kim Schrøder ["Audience Semiotics"] has pointed out, many writers are content to use the expression to describe people who have never met or communicated, but who somehow are thought to share the same mentality. In what sense are they a "community," then? More importantly, to me, there is a striking contrast between the frequency of use of the expression in works of theory and textual interpretation and a scarcity of close empirical studies of actual communities. We find ourselves in the cleft of a problem, therefore. The concept is very valuable, but uses of it are preventing that value being realized.

The great potential strength of the "interpretive community" concept lies in its necessary Janus nature: it points simultaneously in two directions, towards the ways people understand themselves and the ways people understand texts: how they invest their sense of self in being kinds of people and in belonging; and how they thread together elements within circulating cultural texts to form meaningful wholes, centering on some components, marginalizing – or disputing – others, and thus attaching significance to them. It is surely this double potential that has made so many scholars turn to the concept. The quotation above brings such a process strikingly into view. "Sasha" discovers in her own responses an organizing principle that provides her with criteria for judging the rightness and effectiveness of the film's presentation of the story, which is also the ground of her pleasure and participation. It is important to her that the hobbits do not know the extent of their danger, or the Enemy's power, when they set out. They have to learn as they go, and thus in supporting each other discover the strength to continue. She does not watch the film, she evaluates it from the requirements of this standpoint – even though it is very unlikely that, until the circumstances of the interview, she had ever expressed the commitment even to herself in so many words. What she thus finds is a *principle of the importance of true friendship*. In that sense, of course, she is very like me.

But Sasha's resonant account at the same time reveals a key problem. She is doing this alone. Although the bones of a reading strategy are emerging, it is not clear in what ways this will count as connecting her to any identifiable interpretive community. We could label it as such, but that would be essentially gestural. And that points towards a more general problem. In their overview of the field of reception research, within which the concept of "interpretive community" has found its happiest home, Machor and Goldstein note that by 2000 the MLA database had recorded more 3,900 pieces of published work [*Reception Study*, xv]. The volume is impressive, but the greatest proportion of these has consisted of essentially theoretical enquiries. There has been very little address to the question: how to investigate empirically the formation, operation, and functions of real interpretive communities.

Let me briefly consider just some of the questions that ought to be asked about interpretive communities if the concept is really to become an active tool for research, instead of a convenient labelling device, offering rhetorical closure:

What are the conditions for the formation of different kinds of interpretive community? It might seem obvious that a reading group coming together and agreeing to read *Lord of The Rings* would thereby constitute an interpretive community. But that is to presume that its members give themselves over to its shared practices, rather than reserving other reading styles for other situations. Could we say when and under what circumstances people may tend to give themselves over wholeheartedly to a new way of using texts?

What happens when the practices of different interpretive communities come into conflict? A simple illustrative example: suppose someone watches the *Lord of The Rings* films first with friends (who share an emphasis on its action elements), then with family (where an older member of the family is "passing on" the story to her children), then in the context of having visited Internet sites and discussed the films online (this is based on real examples). When will their responses and assessments of the film be simply an *assemblage* of these circumstances and potential interpretive communities, or how might conflicts express themselves? When will conflict result in refusal, rejection, withdrawal, loss of pleasure?

How long do interpretive communities have to operate to become effective? An evening out with casual friends will often result in pub conversations afterwards, and a very temporary community will be formed – but it is arguable that the very institution of visiting the pub after the cinema, and wider conventions for using cinema in this way, constitute the grounds of the kinds of conversation that will ensue, and constitute this as an interpretive community.

For the more fugitive kinds – the categorial memberships (for example, being a woman reader) or imputed memberships (for example, feeling myself to be a "1960s reader" although I have hardly ever discussed the book with my co-members!) – what kinds of knowledge and involvement are necessary for these to become operative? For instance, a woman watching the films may well find herself uneasy at the marginal position of women in the story. But this could crystallize in more than one direction. Involvement with certain kinds of feminist formation may take it in the direction of a naming of *Lord of The Rings* as a "male" story, and thus make pleasure in the film much harder to achieve. But another kind of sense of female community could celebrate a "modernizing" tendency in the film – as contrasted with the book – and thus take pleasure in the struggle to introduce what would be seen from the first perspective to be marginal components.

How do people leave interpretive communities? For instance, someone who has had contact with the Tolkien Society and experienced its ways of "reading" the books (for their literary and ethical value), but subsequently withdraws (as some have, calling it puritanical): does s/he automatically shed that reading style as part of the act of withdrawing? What happens to their capacity to enjoy and find meaning in the books/films as a result?

What conditions might we be able to determine for the real strength and longevity in reading styles and strategies? It may be obvious that such elements as a formal organization, regular communication with other members, perhaps publications that consolidate responses would all serve to bolster a common reading strategy. Equally, they could generate factionalism, and fissiparousness. I would pose the possibility that reading styles may operate and survive most strongly when they are part of wider common projects, be they cultural, intellectual, spiritual, or political in all the senses of these words. This proposition runs counter to many tenets of postmodern thinking which tends to seek and celebrate diversity in people's identities and involvements. I wish it to be an empirical question

Finally, how may we as researchers best gather and analyze the information, symptoms, and evidence necessary to identify and fully account for the way interpretive communities operate?

Preparing and writing this account of 1960s readings has been the impulse to clarifying these questions to myself. And in one crucial respect I want to extend the range of kinds of interpretive community about which we may talk. Schrøder distinguishes *actual* communities (ranging from living communities of family and friends to the more momentary ones of an interview group) from *categorial* ones (genders, ethnicities, classes). Others distinguish live from virtual communities, and so on. All these are ways of discovering and labelling actual, already-achieved communities. I want to propose the notion of a *projected* community – that people may conceive of a set of shared values, even of sorts of people with whom they would want to form a kind of community, but so far only in their heads, or partially, or fragmentarily. That conception might become the stimulus to action, to finding others who share it. And of course, because that finding would inevitably be accompanied by talk, and by sharing of ideas, the project would develop and unfold and take clearer shape.[1] I want to argue that 1960s Tolkien fandom can best be understood as a very particular kind of projecting towards an interpretive community.

---

[1] This is, in my view, exactly what E. P. Thompson was describing in his *Making of the English Working Class*, a point which Marc Steinberg has reminded us of in a wonderful revisiting and extension of Thompson's ideas, in his *Fighting Words*.

The Story of 1960s Tolkien Fandom

Writing in 1969, one of the early academics to pick up the Tolkien flag introduced a book of "readings" with this caution:

> Usually, when initial critical reception has been so warm that it has contributed to great popular success ... the resultant popular success has apparently occasioned critical second-thoughts, with revaluations downwards. But this recurrent phenomenon has not really had any effect on Tolkien's reputation. One difference is that Tolkien's mass popularity was not fostered by the mass media; it grew from the excellences and appeals of the work itself and was simply reported in the media. There was never any promotional bandwagon for Tolkien. But the major difference is that there never was a critical bandwagon either. (Isaacs and Zimbardo *Essays*, 1)

This is salutary, given the common tendency to over-represent the few critical voices (such as Edmund Wilson and Philip Toynbee) who assaulted *The Lord of the Rings* when it first came out. This problem displays itself in the generally useful essay by Bruce Beatie ("Tolkien Phenomenon"), who uses as his source material almost entirely the resources of "official" publications: reviews, academic sources, and the Tolkien Society. From this he constructs a tripartite periodization of the books' reception – but one which has almost nothing to say about its spread through vernacular cultures. Actually, Tolkien fandom grew out of widespread acceptance and celebration of the books (especially in America) among some very particular groups. There, it took its place among the formative manifestos of science fiction fandom. But this was to be an interest in science fiction which could fuse it with alternative religiosities, with a celebration of "play" that would sow the seeds for the rise of role-play gaming (Gary Gygax, creator of *Dungeons and Dragons*, was inspired by the Rings to give up an insurance job to develop his idea), the Apple Mac, and the Free Internet movements (and in a way that could readily be linked with the playground attitudes to culture and wealth evinced by George Lucas, Steven Spielberg, and others). And this pot pourri could bring in other weird elements:

> Tolkien fandom exploded in the 1960s, when badges like FRODO LIVES and GANDALF FOR PRESIDENT popped up on college campuses and the nascent Tolkien Society started serving *mushrooms* and cider at costumed "hobbit picnics" up and down the West Coast. Hippies in particular *grokked* the woodland mysticism of Tolkien's elves, not to mention their fashion sense. But *Lord of the Rings* influenced technologists as well. By the mid-'70s, the printer at SAIL, Stanford's *AI* lab, was outfitted with fonts for Tolkien's Tengwar alphabet. (fusionanomaly.net)

Speake ("Power") retells this story well. Riding in large part on the back of Ace Books' unauthorized paperback edition, Tolkien took American campuses by storm at just the time when Marvel Comics were taking off again, the seeds of political activism were spreading beyond the Civil Rights movement, and a generalized critique of American economy and culture was emerging. Through early fanzines, through local happenings that grew into area conventions, through the distribution, exchange, and networking possibilities opened by the rise of shops and dealers in and around comic books, gradually there emerged a particularly self-aware and indeed self-celebrating fandom, with some academics willingly joining in that celebration (see for instance Jenkins *Textual Poachers*).

Other writers have placed the stress elsewhere. Andrew Blake's excellent introduction to Tolkien's work puts the emphasis on an emergent ecological consciousness:

> The generation that came to regard *The Lord of the Rings* as great literature was the first to become aware of the environmental problems associated with industrial development and human population growth. The peaceful Shire seemed a perfect antidote to these threats. Ironically, Tolkien's work then became part of the modern popular culture which he held in suspicion. Poster designers, rock bands and night clubs began to use Tolkien's iconography. Pink Floyd, whose first album *The Piper at the Gates of Dawn* was named after an episode in Kenneth Grahame's children's fantasy *The Wind in the Willows*, played at a club in West London called "Middle Earth." Heavy metal band Marillion was named after *The Silmarillion*. Clothing company Rohan – named after the Riders of Rohan in *The Lord of the Rings* – made outdoor wear for people who wanted to escape from the cares of urban life to the freedom of the "will." (*Guide*, 14).

It is not surprising therefore that this "movement" has had its history well recorded, and in particularly collaborative fashion. See for instance the emerging web history of such fandoms at *www.jophan.org*, which documents, event by event, and convention by fanzine, the assemblage of Tolkien among other fandoms in that period. Arguably, the current round of pop philosophical "takes" on Tolkien, such as *The Lord of the Rings and Philosophy* (2003) should be seen as attempts to reabsorb all this into the American intellectual landscape without critical digestion. And so, the image of Tolkien's radical 1960s readership has been almost entirely colonized by an image of American hippies wearing "Frodo Lives" badges, eating (magic?) mushrooms, and pretending to be hobbits.

What is singularly missing from these accounts is any sense of how people read the books. Speake recycles some of the easy explanations of Tolkien fandom, from hostile versions (ranging from "escapist entertainment" to drug-fuelled fantasies) to more welcoming ones (from early ecological tendencies to simple morality versus the cynical Watergate age [on this see also Birzer "Myth"]). But at best these only imply how people read the books. What were the important elements in them? I made an attempt to reach some members of that early generation of fans, to ask them about their memories of talking about the books. What was discussed, argued over, valued, invested in, in those early readings of Tolkien? None of those whom I managed to contact could really answer my questions – whether because memories have faded or because the questions were not particularly meaningful to them.[2] What is evident from these communications is the sense of fans going on collaborative journeys to find precedents, to share pleasures. Recruiting new fans was a significant part of the pleasure. In short, it was a very particular kind of interpretive community. Let me explain the significance of this by pointing to a puzzling situation. In preparation for writing this essay, I have read many accounts and communicated with many people about the ways in which Tolkien's popularity grew in the 1960s. All agree that Tolkien appealed then, and still appeals now, to a very wide range of people. To take a couple of examples:

> First and foremost, the *Lord of the Rings* is a myth for the modern world, and like all genuine myths it has a sort of elasticity that allows readers to find in it

---

[2] Thanks in particular to Ed Meskys, Joyce Worley Katz, Earl Kemp, and Cuyler Brooks for their friendly and interesting communications.

whatever messages they are looking for. It resonates with Tories and Greens, software designers and Luddites, monarchists and anarchists, devout Christians and tree-worshippers. (angelfire.com)

Part of the trouble for some of Tolkien's more jaundiced critics is the political culture that surrounds him. Certain detractors, like Grer, cannot forget the 1960s, when "Frodo Lives!" graffiti and T-shirts abounded. Despite Tolkien's conservative – some would say reactionary – Catholic politics, *The Lord of the Rings* became required reading for counter-culturists during the Vietnam era. In the wizard Gandalf's counsel that the powerful but corrupting Ring be destroyed, rather than used as a weapon against Sauron, antiwar activists saw a clear allusion to the scourge of nuclear weapons. Environmentalists, meanwhile, pointed to Tolkien's beloved Ents, the ruminative tree-creatures who are "roused" to protect their forest of Fangorn from the axe-loving wizard Saruman – who, with his "mind of metal and wheels ... does not care for growing things, except as far as they serve him for the moment." And then there are the hobbits' frequent time-outs to enjoy mushrooms and "pipe weed." Pot smokers felt they knew exactly what Tolkien was driving at. (Mooney, "Kicking").

I don't doubt at all that this is right, but it raises two puzzles: (1) apparently "everyone knows" how these different groups found their meanings in the text, yet (2) this can't be on the basis of position-taking because *there is no record of any arguments over the meanings of the books.*

A "Reading" of 1960s Readers

This is my proposition: many 1960s readers, and especially those who would in different degrees and manners constitute the emergent fandom around the books in that period, read as part of a seeking for a *new mode of imagining*. This meant that the differences in interpretation mattered far less, if at all, than exploring the new possibilities for conceiving that the books offered. It also meant that the books could be arrayed alongside others that, in parallel fashion, opened new imaginative doors. Thus, the field of operation of reading Tolkien was an opposition to enclosure, a challenge to perceived fuddy-duddiness, a refusal not to imagine. This required what I would term a "generosity of imaginative inclusiveness." Books and other materials that within ten years would be reclassified, in another context, into acceptable or unacceptable fantasies, would be reread for their failures to represent, for example, women, or black people, or political systems in politically allowable ways.[3] We can see this in the relations, noted earlier, between responses to Tolkien and responses to the writings of a man now considered to have been in important senses fascistic: Robert Heinlein. Heinlein's *Stranger in a Strange Land* was another book I recall reading in that period, and celebrating for its exploration of something which it knew, and I knew, was hitherto highly censored: forms of sexual desire. The fact that its proposed alternative is now one which many would challenge was nowhere near as important as the fact that it *proposed an alternative*. The same can be said of the SF writer John Norman. Nowadays condemned as a virtual pornographer for his fantastical S&M Slave-Girl novels, he was then appreciated for the thrill of considering the illicit.[4] This inclusiveness makes sense of the way in which, in this period, Tolkien's work could sit within the gateways to science fiction, fantasy, utopian writing, gaming, and a number of other emergent fan communities – without significant tensions.

What this proposition does, is to suggest a new, and perhaps central and transformative strand in the concept of an interpretive community: the idea of a *project-based* community, one which is finding, drawing together, and inventing uses for cultural materials as the means to conceive a project for itself. People in general did not argue over the books, rather, they talked together about possible expansions of their meanings. The pleasure was in the unlimited new possibilities, rather than specific achieved meanings. The story could not just be private property, for important reasons. In America, this sense of it being especially a public domain was assisted by its circulation in that near-illegal Ace Books version – this was something defying privatization. The slogan that arrived from the French May Events captured this expansiveness: "Be realistic, demand the impossible." It is easy to sneer at this as simplistic utopianism. The sensibility which underpinned it was without doubt a

---

[3] I consciously avoid the expression "politically correct' since it now comes so freighted with unhelpful meanings.
[4] See his *Chronicles of Gor* series of novels.

significant energizer of the political and cultural movements which came to dominate the latter half of the decade.

Yet at the exact time this generosity of imaginative inclusiveness was taking shape, a converse pattern was emerging. Within politics, in the student movements, in the anti-Vietnam war movements, in the various associated or independent movements such as Civil Rights, in industrial campaigns and so on, a greater and greater tendency to position-taking was occurring. The movements of the 1960s are simultaneously famous for their slogans about imagination, and for their factionalism and sectarianism. To understand what may have been at work in this, we need a wider context. Some years ago Adrian Mellor published an essay on a sea change that took place in science fiction in the late 1960s which can helpfully be seen to be one of the points when these opposite tendencies struck against each other ("Crisis"). Mellor explored the motive forces which led to a series of interrelated shifts: from technologically-optimistic to pessimistic narratives; and from a readership primarily based in the technically-trained middle class to one more inclusive of humanities and social science-based readers. Mellor ascribes this to a fundamental shift in the character of the (especially American) middle class, from being and seeing itself as upwardly mobile, managerial, and hopeful of participating in the "goods" provided by capitalism to a more proletarianized, alienated social position.

Mellor calls upon the work of Lucien Goldmann to establish the connections. Goldmann was the author, most famously, of *The Hidden God* (1964), a study of political Jansenism and its parallel expressions in the works of Pascal and Racine, exploring how the divided loyalties and possibilities of the *noblesse de robe* generated a "tragic world vision." This vision was centred on the impossibility of a rational choice or hope, because of which all that a person could do was to make a "wager" on the future. Mellor adopts this approach not only for its method, but also for its substantive content: the same pessimism, he argues, the same "loss of social hope, abandonment of science and rationality, its historical passivity" ("Crisis," 39) all characterized the situation of 1960s science fiction.

Mellor may have been right about science fiction, pure and simple. But in this period, of course, the boundaries of the genre were blurring and shifting with the rise of fantasy – energized by Tolkien's vision. And the tropes of fantasy were anything but pessimistic. One might say that the problem with science fiction was its too close inscription with capital, with labour technologies, and with structural conditions. To achieve optimism, it was necessary to move further off, in order to return with alert critical faculties and hopes for different conditions. This is what I believe Tolkien offered to me, at any rate: the exact opposite of Mellor's "loss of social hope." Even, I would argue, science and rationality could be maintained in my reading of Tolkien, because it was now about reasoning out the nature of evil.

In one other, final way, Mellor's turn to Goldmann is of importance. For Goldmann's is a theory of the possibilities for social consciousness of definite social groups. Although Goldmann arguably blinkered himself by looking only for fully developed, coherent, and highly articulated "world-views," in principle his conception of cultural formations can be used more widely. It lends itself to the study of communities in formation, emergent projects for judging and changing the world. What is distinctive about it is its focus on the notion of the wager, the project, the possibilities for action inherent in conceptions of the world. That sense of a project is just what I found in Tolkien. It is the cornerstone of my investment in his fantasy. It is what was so nearly lost in Jackson's films, whatever their other qualities.

The Return of the Four Refusals

At the beginning of this essay, I explained my "four refusals" in response to Peter Jackson's films of *The Lord of the Rings*. What more can be said about them, once they are set within the contexts I have proposed here? It is important to reiterate that until I saw the films I simply had not realized the depth of my attachment to a way of participating in the story. I can however be sure that this was formed in most ways during the 1960s. This was the period when I re-read them many times; during the 1970s I was too busy with my first job, with family and children, and with political work, to do much reading; and it was in 1981, when the BBC radio adaptation was first broadcast, that I first felt that inarticulate discomfort at the inclusion of a prologue. So what intersection of forces and practices might help explain my refusals?

During the 1960s I became intensely involved in radical politics, learning fast during the process about the causes and impacts of exploitation and oppression, but also – being on the Far Left – being engaged in debates, arguments, and faction fights. But this was coupled with an intense interest in ways of thinking how society might be reconstituted: discussions of the overcoming of alienation, and encounters with Karl Marx's early writings on human species-being combined with a fascination with Immanuel Kant's notion of reason as a necessary human task. Kant, as I learned about him, was the philosopher of human possibilities *par excellence*; he was interested to ask about the directions of human history, and what a fully rational society might be like. At the same time, I was caught up in the radical poetry movement in Liverpool, where I studied. This produced in me a driving interest in the notion that through the arousal of emotion by formal mechanisms, new conceptions and understandings of the world might emerge. It was worth the wager, anyway.

I do not doubt that there could be many others who would recognize chunks of my response to the films, or close parallels to those, without being either 1960s readers, or without the attached political investments. Sasha, almost two generations younger than me, catches some elements – albeit with a different emphasis. My aim is not to argue some hermetic separation of responses by decades. I am also conscious that, because of its particular self-awareness, American fandom's history has been told to an extent far outstripping any other country's. Even so, I believe it is unarguable that in these senses mine was a "1960s reading" of *The Lord of the Rings*. There was and is a will in me to find a secular exploration of the motive forces of evil, coupled with a wish to find imaginative resources to keep me committed to acting against its manifestations. There was always a sense that there were "others out there," whom I would mostly never meet, but with whom I felt that I would be sharing a common project; we would recognize each other, at need, through shared references and a common imaginative utopia. I also somehow felt that, despite himself, Tolkien had somehow done this for our benefit. Now, on the basis of a stronger understanding of the sociology of culture and of authorship processes, I would not bother with the last. For me, the other two still constitute an odd but decisive combination of beliefs and hopes.

Epic Fantasy and Global Terrorism

Ken Gelder

> *"If fantasy is the means by which we in some sense place ourselves
> 'out of this world' at the 'end of the world,'
> it is also a means for securing our adaptation to it"*
> Eric Santner *Psychotheology*, 40.

Introduction

This chapter will look at J.R.R. Tolkien's *The Lord of the Rings* trilogy alongside recent commentaries on, and anxieties about, the rise of global terrorism and the "war on terrorism."[1] This may seem like an odd thing to do, not least because a fantasy about Middle Earth no doubt seems very far removed indeed from contemporary political realities. But the point of this chapter is to examine how popular fiction can not only survive (in contradiction to the usual view of it, as ephemeral and disposable) but become relevant as if for the first time to world events at a much later date. This is an especially strange outcome for fantasy, which is supposed to be an escape from reality rather than the basis for a commentary on it. Nevertheless, Tolkien's trilogy – transformed into a massive cinema/entertainment experience fifty years after its publication – found itself put to use in the context of a twenty-first century debate over global

---

[1] A shorter version of this chapter appeared originally in Ken Gelder, *Popular Fiction: The Logics and Practices of a Literary Field*, London and New York: Routledge, 2004, 142-157.

terrorism, much of which itself relied on what we might call "fantasy discourse."

A few connections have already been drawn between Western reactions to global terrorism and literature; for example, Jason Epstein has compared the United States, in its pursuit of terrorists, to Herman Melville's Captain Ahab in *Moby Dick* as he frantically searches for the white whale (Epstein *"Leviathan,"* 13-14). But it may be that some genres of popular fiction, such as fantasy, are able to speak more directly and insistently to this predicament. An article by Mike Davis in the *New Left Review* in fact situates the terrible aeroplane bombings of the World Trade Center in the context of fantastic images of the fire-storming of Lower Manhattan in a bestselling work by H.G. Wells, *War in the Air*, first published in 1907. Under zeppelin attack by Imperial Germany, "ragtime New York" in Wells's apocalyptic novel, Davis suggests, "becomes the first modern city destroyed from the air" (Davis "Flames," 34). Davis has been one of a number of commentators on 9/11 who has read the reality of the event through the logic of fantasy, as if it was a moment of terror, or terrorism, that made it impossible to distinguish between the two:

> The attacks on New York and Washington DC were organized as epic horror cinema with meticulous attention to *mise en scene*. Indeed, the hijacked planes were aimed to impact precisely at the vulnerable border between fantasy and reality" ("Flames," 37).

That phrase – *the vulnerable border between fantasy and reality* – already alerts us to the possibility that fantasy can find itself inhabiting (rather than escaping from) the world we know. It also resonates with anxieties about terrorist activity itself, planned and executed in the case of 9/11 from within the borders of the U.S., and thus speaking to America's own sense of border vulnerability: of the possibility that what is outside the world it knows best can actually come inside. It may well be that counter-terrorism policy itself has something "fantastic" about it, the more so since terrorism (like Islamism, to which it is now so often aligned) became the demonized Other of the U.S. and its allies.

But fantasy already flourishes inside the world we know best. Davis has also written about Los Angeles as a city upon which fantasies of self-destruction seem endlessly to be projected: "No other city seems to excite such dark rapture," he comments at the beginning of a long chapter on the many literary and cinematic representations of the obliteration of Los Angeles (Davis *Ecology*, 277). It is, he says, "the disaster capital of the universe," destroyed in fiction and film at least 138 times since 1909. Davis sees all this as an expression of fantasy wish-fulfillment, the destruction of Otherness *inside* the United States: "The obliteration of Los Angeles is often depicted as, or at least secretly experienced as, a victory for civilization" (Campbell "24 Reasons," 2). So how real are these fantasy accounts of obliteration at home? A sense that Davis relished the telling of the sequential story of Los Angeles's destruction – and self-destruction – led to accusations that this social commentator was too enmeshed in the generic features of epic fantasy and SF, turning into a kind of latter-day Wellsian. Davis himself noted in an interview with Mark Dery, "I've profited greatly from peddling apocalyptic visions to people" (Dery, "Downsizing").

The connection between the twenty-first century "war on terrorism" and the genre of epic fantasy – especially Tolkien's *The Lord of the Rings* – was helped along by a cheeky visual image circulating around the Internet, titled "Frodo has failed: Sauron prepares to invade Iraq" (Fig.1). It shows U.S. President George W. Bush wearing the Ring of Sauron. "Frodo has failed" is taken from just one of many sites showcasing the image: *www.myirony.com*, posted 2 February 2003. *Myirony.com* is an open website and people offer their own commentaries on what it posts. Here is one of them, posted underneath the image of Bush wearing the Ring of Sauron:

> Sauron was trying to take away the freedom of the peoples of Middle Earth. Is Bush doing the same thing? Is taking away the freedom of a corrupt and dangerous government truly evil? OK – so I just set myself up for the comment that some people think the U.S. is corrupt and dangerous. But, are we as corrupt and dangerous as Iraq? Is the current administration making up the stories of Iraqi horrors? It seems to me that Saddam Hussein is a very bad man and his regime puts the U.S. at high risk. One thing is for sure. The current technology of weapons means that wars can't be fought on old terms. The idea of preventing Saddam from hurting us before it happens might sound

a bit like "Minority Report"... but, what if none of the war-talk had ever happened? Would we have been the victims of an attack from Saddam or terrorists he's funded? If so, wouldn't we all wish we'd gone to war? (*Myirony.com*)

Image 7: Frodo Has Failed. (www.myirony.com, 2/02/2003)

This posting captures an ambivalence found in much of the commentary on terrorism and the "war on terrorism" today, an ambivalence that wonders whether the "evil empire" of the U.S. is more, or less, evil than terrorism itself. The question of evil is central to these commentaries and, of course, central to the fantasy genre as it developed, through the nineteenth century and into the twentieth, into the kind of epic fantasy that Tolkien pioneered: a genre that I would suggest became more otherworldly and more worldly simultaneously. The posting in fact connects itself to another fantasy text, Steven Spielberg's film *Minority Report* (2002), based on a story by the SF writer Philip K. Dick. This is followed in turn by a sequence of fantasy projections that work again as wish-fulfillments ("wouldn't we all wish we'd gone to war?"), but only in some indeterminate past-future realm ("would we have been the victims..."). The account here imagines terrorism as a sort of phantasm: a terrorism that is yet to make itself manifest, a terrorism in which the principal villain, like Sauron himself in *The Lord of the Rings* or like Osama bin Laden, is both manifest and simply not there. As it is currently conceived, what is now called global terrorism does indeed seem to have both an immediately felt and an ethereal "body," a violently registered presence, and a disconcerting absence that seems, almost against the odds, to continue to keep itself that way. For Binoy Kampmark, bin Laden is nothing less than a kind of hyper-reality living as a perpetual "afterlife," his body and voice needing ceaselessly to be verified or authenticated (Kampmark, "Spectre"). Roland Jacquard's 2002 book, *In the Name of Osama bin Laden: Global Terrorism and the bin Laden Brotherhood*, makes a similar point about bin Laden's terrorist organization itself: that "al Qaeda, bin Laden's creation, no longer needs either his physical existence or his funds; alive or dead, he has become a talisman for a diffuse, self-sufficient terrorist network with every intention of fulfilling its mission to 'lead the world into the apocalypse'" (Baird "Review," 31). These various tropes, yoking terrorism to an absent source, to a phantasm, but also to networks of alliance and to a global apocalypse, should begin to further identify and clarify the connection between terrorism and the modern genre of epic fantasy exemplified in *The Lord of the Rings*.

The Lord of the Rings and "the War on Terrorism"

Even though he disavowed them, allegorical readings of Tolkien's work are commonplace, especially those that place the fantasy works in the context of Tolkien's own experiences during the First World War where he lost a number of close friends and was himself stricken with trench fever. The three parts of *The Lord of the Rings* were written during the 1930s and throughout the duration of the Second World War. The first installment of Peter Jackson's cinematic version appeared just a few weeks after 9/11, and the annual release of the other parts meant that they were necessarily caught up alongside the "war on terrorism," the invasion of Iraq, and the search for "weapons of mass destruction" (apparently another phantasm), as well as the search for Osama bin Laden and for global terrorist cells and networks. It is certainly possible to situate *The Lord of the Rings* cinematic project, as well as the trilogy's contemporary publishing fortunes, in this context, as if entertainment really does touch the sphere of contemporary political reality. By 2001, Tolkien's publishers – Houghton Mifflin (which publishes hardcovers and gift editions), Del Ray, Ballantine, and HarperCollins – had sold eleven million copies of *The Lord of the Rings* and "Tolkien-related" book items even before the film of *The Fellowship of the Rings* was released. The epic fantasy lodged itself atop the bestseller lists at the end of 2001, sitting alongside non-fiction books on Osama bin Laden and Islam. In 2002, sales reached nearly thirteen million. Clay Harper, Houghton Mifflin's director of Tolkien projects, is quoted in a *Publishers Weekly* article as saying that Tolkien's trilogy endures, especially in the United States, because "you can reflect on the history of your own time in the characters. The Hobbits realize the world is larger and more frightening than they wanted to know, but they have to engage with it." Harper's point, the article goes on to note, "might speak to an American audience still wrestling with a new sense of vulnerability" (Maas "Future"). By drawing vulnerable Hobbits and vulnerable Americans together, the point explicitly recalls Mike Davis's phrase, *the vulnerable border between fantasy and reality*: fiction and non-fiction, epic fantasy and global terrorism.

The Center for Libertarian Studies is a non-profit organization based in Burlingame, California, with a website that links to Antiwar.com for coverage of U.S. foreign policy. Carlo Stagnaro, an Italian who is co-editor on the Libertarian magazine *Enclave* and who has written a book on Waco, has posted an article on this site, titled "Tolkien's Lesson for September 11." "The conservative and liberal élites," he writes, "have been portraying Bush's war on terrorism as a sort of crusade of good against evil. They have even tried to enlist John Ronald Reuel Tolkien... author of the 'Book of the Century,' *The Lord of the Rings*, for this endeavor. In their view, the coalition led by the United States is like the 'league of the free' who fight against Sauron of Mordor – that is, bin Laden of Afghanistan" (Stagnaro "Lesson"). This is an informed article that answers back to the conservative appropriation of Tolkien's work, placing this writer instead in a tradition of civil dissent. "J.R.R. Tolkien," Stagnaro writes, "would hardly have taken a position in favor of the war on terrorism." The aim of Tolkien's work is the destruction of the Ring itself, the source of unlimited and always-corrupting power – a point which leads Stagnaro not to read the fantasy of *The Lord of the Rings* as an allegory for reality, but the inverse, that is, *to read reality as an allegory for fantasy:*

> Today's war on terrorism seems a war to own the Ring, rather than a war to destroy it. Neither Bush's nor bin Laden's supporters fight for liberty; they all fight to strengthen their own power. One can hardly choose to join one or the other – and should ask whether there is still a place for common, peaceful people in the lands of opposing war lords. Indeed, the only rational position is that of Treebeard [an Ent in *The Lord of the Rings*]: "I am not altogether on anybody's side, because nobody is altogether on my side, if you understand me... And there are some things, of course, whose side I'm altogether not on; I am against them altogether." (Stagnaro "Lesson")

Here, *The Lord of the Rings* provides the very means of articulating one's position on global terrorism. This epic fantasy text from the 1950s gains its power because it now accommodates, and speaks on behalf of, a contemporary war scenario. It "picks up" a terroristic allegory, just as Chris Mooney notes in an article first published in *The Washington Post* on 29 December 2002 (around the time of the release of the film of *The Two Towers*), titled, precisely, "Tolkien picks up a few more bits of cultural baggage." Mooney focuses on the Orcs in the epic fantasy as dissenters, complaining about the Ringwraiths and wanting only to be able to slip away and loot in a place where there are no "big bosses." "One can easily imagine," Mooney writes, "a similar conversation among lower-level al Qaeda henchmen or Iraqi troops." Mooney then goes on to register the ambivalence of evil, both in the novel and in the context of global terrorism: "The analogy between bin Laden and Sauron is not an empty one," he writes, but "for the bearer of the Ring of Power, he would need to look no further than George W. Bush" (Mooney "Baggage").

The second and final commentary to note here comes perhaps surprisingly from the Hong Kong-based *Asia Times Online*: a front-page piece titled "The 'Ring' and the remnants of the West," by a correspondent identified only as "Spengler," named, presumably, after Oswald Spengler, author of the apocalyptic socio-political tract, *The Decline of the West*. This commentary takes the release of the films of *The Lord of the Rings* as the "most important cultural event of the past decade," since in these texts "No better guide exists to the mood and morals of the United States" (Spengler "West"). It charts Tolkien's relation to Wagner and the Ring of the Nibelungen cycle, seeing them both – even though Tolkien thoroughly "recast" the earlier text – as elegies that track the departure of the immortals: in Tolkien's case, the Elves, who finally renounce the world and depart. The difference between Wagner and Tolkien's works is that whereas the former was neo-pagan and heroic, the latter is Christian (Tolkien was a devout Catholic) and anti-heroic. It is centered on the role of the Hobbit Frodo as Ring-bearer, who wishes that the Ring "had never come to me." Spengler thus sees the end of *The Lord of the Rings* as a return to ordinary life, and so casts the work not as epic fantasy at all, but as an anti-epic. This commentator accordingly reads the U.S. not as an empire but as an "anti-empire": "Boorish and gruff as the new American empire might seem, it is an anti-empire populated by reluctant heroes who want nothing more than to till their fields and mind their homes, much like Tolkien's hobbits. Under pressure, though, it will respond with a fierceness and cohesion that will surprise its adversaries" ("West").

In this article from the East about the West, Americans are indeed like Hobbits, content to remain *in* the West, insular and isolated from the outside world, the pressures of globalization and, in this case, the threat of global terrorism. This is a commonplace view of the U.S., as an empire-building nation that can also seem ignorant of the world beyond its own vulnerable borders, beyond the world it knows best. It is a view shared by, for example, Naomi Klein in a short article first published in *The Nation* in October 2001: "In the weeks since September 11, we have been reminded many times that Americans aren't particularly informed about the world outside their borders" ("Signs," 146). Susan Buck-Morss has also presented this view of the United States as a place which has refused to become global. For her, there are in fact *two* United States, the one shadowing the other much as Frodo is shadowed by Gollum in Tolkien's trilogy. The first is founded on what she calls "the deeply human, I will say it, universal political freedoms of belief, speech, assembly, due process, and equality before the law" (Buck-Morss *Thinking*, 29), a democratic republic, in other words. But the second is "another United States over which I have no control... a wild zone of power, barbaric and violent, operating without democratic oversight" (*Thinking*, 39). We might say that one of these United States is real and the other is fantastic. Or, like Frodo and Gollum, we might say that the one is the other's dark fantasy, its companion and its contradiction. I'm partly tinkering with the conceit here that Hobbits are Americans at their folksiest; but of course, if the Hobbits have any equivalent nationality in the real world at all they are probably English. Tolkien certainly claimed them as such, locating the Hobbits' Shire just outside of Oxford where he worked as a Professor of Anglo-Saxon. His biographer Michael White notes that Tolkien liked to identify *himself* as a Hobbit, equally sealed off from the outside world in "his ivory tower in Oxford" (White *Tolkien*, 159). Tolkien's Oxford, his Hobbits' Shire, is echoed by Michael Taussig when he describes an American university where a discussion of state terrorism is being held: a "middle class, largely white, fortress", as he puts it, "with fear-ridden blocks of lofty spires": "a perfect copy of an Oxford college" (Taussig *Nervous System*, 15). Fantasy and reality are entangled in Oxford and then simulated back in America in this account of places sealed off from the world outside. But through the production and release of Peter Jackson's films of *The Lord of the Rings*, a newer, twenty-first-century entanglement of fantasy and reality takes place: the perhaps rather unexpected identification of Middle Earth itself with New Zealand.

Epic Fantasy, "War on Terrorism," and New Zealand

The allegorical connection between epic/fantasy films and the "war on terrorism" is complicated by four major factors. The first one is the connection to a "real" location; the second is a shared resistance to "closure"; the third lies in the ways in which Evil is cast and put to use; and the fourth lies in the ways in which terrorist acts are mythologized.

In the wake of 9/11 and the "war against terrorism," this kind of fantasy identification – where a small, outlying nation claims a Middle Earth identity simply because that is where Jackson shot his films – has a particular resonance. New Zealand Tourism speaks of New Zealand as a "safe destination" in an otherwise unsafe world, an innocent place, untouched by terrorism, much like the Hobbit's Shire just prior to the events of *The Lord of the Rings*. New Zealand has de-militarized itself and no longer contributes to the Australian-U.S. alliance. It also refused to join the "coalition of the willing" in the war on Iraq, distinguishing itself carefully from Australia in this matter. At the same time, *The Lord of the Rings* films have given New Zealand global recognition: through scenery that is simultaneously natural and otherworldly; and through the development of sophisticated computer-generated effects, locally and cheaply produced, that have made New Zealand the preferred destination of other cinematic fantasy productions. New Zealand in this account becomes a place that "fits" Middle Earth perfectly even though the latter doesn't really belong there. It offers a safe, secure place in a globalized world, a remote and tiny nation identified both locally and globally as terrorist-free, innocent, and unworldly, which is precisely the fantasy at stake in its identification with Tolkien's trilogy.

Jacqueline Rose has been one of only a few recent commentators to talk about fantasy in relation to the nation, although she takes fantasy as a psychic condition, not a literary genre. In *States of Fantasy*, Rose nevertheless begins her commentary precisely by following the formula of modern epic fantasy as it is laid out in *The Lord of the Rings*. That is, she goes on a quest: "This book begins in 1980," she writes, "during a visit to Israel," a journey "to a country where you do not belong" (Rose *States*, 1). Exile becomes the means of experiencing a fantasy state, belonging yet no longer belonging, like Freud when he leaves Vienna and like Frodo when he leaves the Shire. The state itself exerts a magical, fantasmatic power over its subjects, as Max Weber had noted (*States*, 8); but fantasy also travels *beyond* the state (like the exiled Jew or the

Hobbit) and so both undoes it and provides a means of articulating its deepest yearnings. Modern epic fantasy also plays out this role, protecting the state's identity and yet troubling the state as it continually moves beyond its borders, or as it renders those borders vulnerable or porous, as the Shire becomes in *The Lord of the Rings*. It is still common to regard works of popular fantasy as, to quote the title of a recent study of the genre by Richard Mathews, a vehicle for "the liberation of the imagination" (Mathews *Fantasy*), since fantasy seems free enough to imagine other worlds that are "unknown" and not real. But modern epic fantasy in fact continually worries about reality, about the place it has left (usually, traumatically), its borders and its vulnerability, about whether that original or originating place can still be, like New Zealand, a "safe destination." The genre knows that "liberation" must also entail occupation (rather like the war in Iraq), border protection, regulation, surveillance, constraint. As fantasy proceeds into exile, its characters and places lose their identities, only to return to them in desperation (and nostalgia) over and over again.

The epic fantasy genre, or subgenre, grew out of the experiences of world wars to become literally the grandest and greatest of the literary genres: nostalgic for "safe destinations," but charting the vulnerability of borders and identities with an almost masochistic intensity. The genre can therefore often refuse to resolve itself: Robert Jordan's bestselling *The Wheel of Time* series is, as I write, up to its eleventh volume, each one around 600 pages, with no signs even at this stage of reaching (to use a word often associated with traumatic memory) "closure." Tolkien's sagas also grew, escalating into a series of volumes published posthumously by his son, Christopher, as if the battles and struggles could never stop or be stopped. Indeed, the genre charts what Dilip Hiro, in a book on the global response to Islamist terrorism, has called a "war without end" (Hiro *War*); or what Taussig in his chapter on terrorism (and under the influence of Walter Benjamin) refers to as a permanent state of emergency, or what Fredric Jameson has called, "a new sort of war without . . . a foreseeable end" (Jameson "Dialectics," 310). Characters in modern epic fantasy are mobilized on a quest and a war that may similarly be endless, sent to realms beyond their borders, as the Hobbits are in *The Lord of the Rings* or as Lyra is in Philip Pullman's contemporary series, *His Dark Materials* (1993-1999), which actually begins in the ivory towers of Oxford but soon travels far away. Exile is necessary in epic fantasy. Indeed, its characters travel incessantly, almost obsessively, into other lands and other people's territories. It is evil that drives them outwards: it comes into their home (that is, it is proximate) and yet it remains utterly remote, distant, absent, unable to be seen even as its effects are continually registered: much like the perpetual absence of Osama bin Laden. In *The Lord of the Rings*, Sauron is an eye that sees the Hobbits only when they become invisible. Paradoxically, when they can see themselves they remain out of Sauron's sight. Jane Chance, in her book on Tolkien, thus reads these epic fantasy novels in the context of Michel Foucault's account of the Benthamite panopticon with its universal "gaze," its sense of total surveillance, which is as good a reading as any (Chance *Mythology*, 21). A similar reading might turn back to Taussig, who describes the atmosphere of terror as one "whipping back and forth between clarity and opacity," generated centrally through some organizational force and yet which is radically de-centred, everywhere: "an eye watching," he says, "an eye knowing," like Sauron (Taussig *Nervous System*, 21).

The best academic study of Tolkien's work is Tom Shippey's book, *J.R.R. Tolkien: Author of the Century*. Shippey's discussion of evil in *The Lord of the Rings* emphasizes both its power and its intangibility, signified through the Ringwraiths: shadowy figures who were once men but who were utterly changed through their "addiction" to the Ring, and who seem able to go anywhere in Middle Earth, creating "panic." These are certainly terroristic creatures. "The spectacle of a person 'eaten up inside' by devotion to some abstraction," Shippey says, "has been so familiar throughout the twentieth century as to make the idea of the wraith, and the wraithing-process, horribly recognizable, in a non-fantastic way" (Shippey *Author*, 125). Links between fascism and terrorism, drawing the mid-twentieth century into the end of the millennium, have been made by commentators such as Christopher Hitchens; but it seems to me that Tolkien's shadowy, panic-causing Ringwaiths are more terrorist than fascist both in their devotion to abstractions and through their sheer otherness. Shippey has a slightly different argument to run, however. For Shippey, the Ringwraiths and the Ring itself form the two sides of evil in the fantasy work. The first is "Boethian," generated internally: absent as a thing-in-itself, and causing self-alienation and corruption. The second is Manichean, generated externally: an outside force, remote but powerful, and never inactive. The Boethian conception of evil is cast by Shippey as a literary trope, deployed especially by Tolkien's modernist counterparts: "the cosseted upper-class writers of the 'modernist' movement," as Shippey had called them (*Author*, 142). Epic fantasy, however, is able to deploy the Manichean conception of evil as well, which for Shippey thus makes fantasy (unlike literary Modernism) more directly relevant "to the real world of war and politics": communal or affiliated, not individualized or alienated; universal, not contingent; militant, rather than dialogic and introspective. The category of evil has certainly been reconfigured in recent years away from ethics and the question of individual choice and into something more worldly and universal. A key figure here is the French philosopher, Alain Badiou, who thinks ethics itself out of the realm of self-interest and back into the realm of the universal and the community, with its "militant conception of truths," its "combative" approach to situations and its commitment to "what is going on" (Badiou *Ethics*, xxxi, 2, 75). Badiou has also mobilized the concept of Evil as a universal category.

This philosopher has argued with Levinas, whose own ethics is underwritten by the requirement that one come face to face with the Other, the "Altogether-Other," or God. For Badiou, there is no God. His own project is irreligious, and that Levinasian respect for differences is dismissed as a project of Sameness. Sameness is embraced here, rather than refuted: truth is, he writes, indifferent to differences, "*the same for all*" (*Ethics*, 27). Badiou's conception of Evil is important to note here since it is terroristic, and close to the logic of epic fantasy – although few philosophical readers of his work may agree. Evil, he writes, has three names: terror, betrayal and disaster (71). An "ethic of truths" attempts to ward these off even as it is entangled in them, needing them dialectically. Badiou's concept of Evil is a delirious one, fantastic in its nature (a "simulacrum of truth") and terroristic in essence: "a terror directed at everyone" (77). Terroristic evil is itself a simulacrum, a betrayal of the truth, in response to which (in order to "ward off Evil") one can only "Keep going!" Indeed, Badiou advises – much in the way of epic fantasy – the following resources: "discernment (do not fall for simulacra) . . . courage (do not give up), and . . . moderation . . . (do not get carried away to the extremes of Totality)" (91). This account may be religious in spite of itself. But certainly, it is difficult not to think of Frodo and Sam in *The Lord of the Rings* here as they make their way to Mount Doom, trying almost beyond endurance not to fall for the simulacrum of the Ring itself – trying not to get carried away by the "extremes of Totality" offered to them by Sauron, an image of Evil so deep and resonant as to appear unmotivated: simply and always there, somewhere.

Epic Fantasy and *The Lord of the Rings* as Terroristic

I have suggested that terror in modern epic fantasy is both proximate and remote, here and always at the same time elsewhere – so that is bears both an allegorical and an arbitrary relation to contemporary realities. It was, of course, difficult not to note the synchronicity between New York's destroyed twin towers and the second book of Tolkien's epic fantasy, *The Two Towers*, signposted as an already completed film-yet-to-come shortly after the 9/11 attacks. Tolkien's dark towers (and so many works of epic fantasy have dark towers, as Stephen King readers would know very well) are evil and remote; New York's towers became proximate; but both have functioned as "marvellous" symbols, installed at the centre of an epic struggle. The fantastic aspect of the twin towers and of the 9/11 attacks themselves was not lost on some of the better-known cultural commentaries that followed. Slavoj Zizek's essay "Welcome to the Desert of the Real" takes its title from Jean Baudrillard via *The Matrix* (1999), drawing on that overwrought SF/fantasy film's evocation of fantasy as false comfort – with the rubble of 9/11 as the real and banal supplement to the fantasized abstraction of the towers themselves. Everything in this reading is infected by fantasy: the dream of the United

States as a safe haven, for example; or the identification of Osama bin Laden as "the real-life counterpart of Ernst Stavro Blofeld, the master-criminal in most of the James Bond films, who was involved in the acts of mass-destruction" (Zizek "Desert," 387). The United States, creating "catastrophes" everywhere else, also ceaselessly imagined its own self-destruction, so that "in a way," Zizek notoriously suggests, on 9/11 "America got what it fantasized about" ("Desert," 387). This is just as Mike Davis had said of Los Angeles – except that Davis was indeed talking about fantasy. Baudrillard himself, in "L'Esprit du Terrorisme," takes this point a little further, reading fantasy as wish-fulfillment: "We could even go so far as to say it is *they* who perpetrated the attack, but it was we who wished it"; "The West," he adds apocalyptically, "has... declared war upon itself" (Baudrillard "Esprit," 404-405). Baudrillard puts into effect precisely the fantasy of *The Lord of the Rings*, that "power itself is accomplice with its own destruction." The nearer it gets to "perfection," the faster it propels itself towards self-destruction: this is one of the available logics of modern epic fantasy. Baudrillard has no time for this popular genre, of course. Even so, 9/11 seemed to show through its very spectacle that reality and fiction, as he writes, "have become a tangled mess," impossible to separate ("Esprit," 413), the kind of entanglement Tolkien himself ascribed to children, the most "natural" readers of epic fantasy (see Turner "Reasons," 17).

These claims and perspectives return us to the question about the "war on terrorism" posed by our anonymous *myirony* commentator at the beginning of this chapter, namely, where is the greater evil: here, or over there? Inside or outside? In the West, or elsewhere? Epic fantasy's ambivalent conception of evil, as I have noted, locates it inside and outside simultaneously, although, since Hobbits survive the corrupting power of the Ring, it may finally and inevitably lean towards the latter. Evil performs at its most terroristic as a remote Other, like Sauron and his network of alliances. It has in fact been commonplace to talk these days of terrorist "networks," dispersed groups which affiliate across and beyond state borders to conduct what has been called a "netwar," where the "protagonists... use networked forms of organization, doctrine, strategy and technology attuned to the information age" (Voll "New

Age," 4). Networked alliances have been crucial to modern epic fantasy. Think of Sauron and the Orcs, Trolls, Warcs and various birds and so on in *The Lord of the Rings*, or the witches, the gypsies and the armoured bears in Philip Pullman's trilogy. *The Lord of the Rings* even deploys its own "coalition of the willing" to deal with these networks, the "fellowship" between men, Elves and Dwarves. It could well be worth thinking of George W. Bush, Britain's Tony Blair and Australia's John Howard as real-life counterparts to Aragorn, Legolas and Gimli (and more or less in that order). These leaders' counter-terrorist rhetoric has absolutely relied upon a Manichean conception of evil from which liberal democracy in the West is then earnestly distinguished. But there have been plenty of recent academic and journalistic commentaries operating in exactly the same way. Roger Scruton provides a spectacular recent example: an hysterical commentary which sees the West under threat from a network of "death-intoxicated" Islamist "brotherhoods" whose effect has been intensified and extensified, paradoxically perhaps, by Western-driven globalization. The work of Bernard Lewis (*What Went Wrong?*) or Simon Reeve (*The New Jackals*) or any number of media commentators following in the wake of Samuel Huntington's "clash of civilizations" prognosis reproduce exactly the apocalyptic scenarios of modern epic fantasy: Manichean divisions between the West and Islam, "awakening" antagonisms, ignoring "evil" until it rises up, etc. The opposing position is held by commentators such as Gilles Kepel and Edward Said. Kepel, in his book *Jihad: The Trail of Political Islam* (2002), takes globalization as a force that necessarily dilutes the identity of Islamism, which leads him to read 9/11 as "a desperate symbol of the isolation, fragmentation, and decline of the Islamist movement, not a sign of its irrepressible might" (Kepel *Jihad*, 375). This is an anti-apocalyptic response, standing *against* the prevailing logic of modern epic fantasy. Said had advocated "secularism" over "fundamentalism" in his work, which is equally anti-apocalyptic. Islamists, he writes (pouring cold water on the apocalypse, even before it has begun) "have by and large lost the battle" (Said *Islam*, xxvii). Said has been critical of Bernard Lewis, amongst others, for demonizing Muslims "as one terrifyingly collective person enraged at an outside world that has disturbed his almost primeval

Epic Fantasy and Global Terrorism   *117*

calm and unchallenged rule" (*Islam*, xxxii). For Said, this is indeed a fantastic perspective, the kind of thing one would find, precisely, in modern epic fantasy.

    The genre of modern epic fantasy, as it battles an evil without end, offers a form of literary fundamentalism that troubles secular ideals.[2] But it can also trouble the kind of political fundamentalism that relies on Manichean binaries of good and evil. For Said, Bernard Lewis and others satisfy a "market" in the West of representations "of a monolithic, enraged, threatening, and conspiratorially spreading Islam" which is "much greater, more useful, and capable of generating more excitement, whether for purposes of entertainment or of mobilizing passions against a new foreign devil" (*Islam*, xxxviii). Modern epic fantasy can indeed generate an "excitement" for the purposes of entertainment (as all genres of popular fiction do) that may well rely upon a "monolithic" representation of evil, terroristic in its incarnation. But in a work like *The Lord of the Rings*, the question of where evil actually resides is never fully resolved. It remains, as I have noted, outside and inside, elsewhere and here, simultaneously. As it charts *the vulnerable border between fantasy and reality*, Tolkien's trilogy knows that evil is both remote and already inside the world one inhabits and knows best. Modern epic fantasy thus conveys a loss of innocence. Its characters, like Frodo, are in fact paradoxically called upon to lose their otherworldliness, to become *worldly*. Readers have remarked on the despair of *The Lord of the Rings*, as a work that turns upon itself, "quietly running down," as Jenny Turner has noted. "It's a struggle with despair," she writes, "a panoramic portrait of the depressive state" (Turner "Reasons," 23-24), as if worldliness brings depression with it. The despair of the novels lies not so much in an externalized sense of evil, but in what is lost as the occulted otherworld changes – the Elves in particular, who "diminish" after Sauron has been

---

[2] Not all contemporary epic fantasy can be co-opted into a tradition of civil dissent, and of course, the reactionary aspects of much in this genre should also be noted. The work of bestselling contemporary usus fantasy novelist Terry Goodkind, who is influenced by Ayn Rand, is a good example. His novel, *The Pillars of Creation* (2001) – part of his "Sword of Truth" series - is earnestly dedicated "to the people in the United States Intelligence Community, who, for decades, have valiantly fought to preserve life and liberty, while being ridiculed, condemned, demonised, and shackled by the jackals of evil" (Goodkind, *Pillars*: n.p.).

destroyed. The video release of *The Fellowship of the Ring* was accompanied by a disc produced by National Geographic, which uses Tolkien's work to chart a commentary both on the impact of the world wars on Britain, and on a romantic mode of anthropology, concerned with the loss of ancient northern European oral traditions. The latter focuses on the Finnish epic song tradition of the Kalevala, linking it to Tolkien's research behind the language of the Elves and mourning its actual passing from the modern world. The elegiac mode of the National Geographic disc shows another "clash of civilizations," important to Tolkien as an anti-modern who loathed everything about the industrial West even as he ceaselessly registered its ever-encroaching presence. Michael White writes that Tolkien hated "technologists, modernizers, polluters and inveterate consumers" (*Tolkien*, 209). His vehement anti-modern position can situate him, these days, perilously close to the prevailing caricatures of Osama bin Laden and Islamism. For Colin Wilson, in fact, *The Lord of the Rings* was nothing less than an "attack," as he saw it, "on the modern world" (White *Tolkien*, 209). Epic fantasy, soaked through with nostalgia for lost traditions and dying cultures which it then systematically reinvents and reanimates, has been venting its spleen on the modern world for over half a century now. This is another reason why it is possible to see epic fantasy today not as escapist, but as terroristic on a global scale.

A Land of Make Believe: Merchandising and Consumption of *The Lord of the Rings*

Ian Conrich

The phenomenal global reception of *The Lord of the Rings* cycle is partly the result of the new film market's determination to maximize lucrative concepts. As with the *Harry Potter* (2001-) and *Star Wars* (1977-2005) series of family film fantasies, there is a dependency on an existing popular appeal, character familiarization, and the opportunities offered by heavily financed, digital effects driven, extended narratives for the creation of a film franchise.

But there are other issues that have been central to Jackson's screen epic succeeding where Ralph Bakshi's 1978 quasi-animated film adaptation of *The Lord of the Rings* failed. Through a consideration of the post-production of Jackson's *The Lord of the Rings* it can be seen that the spectacularity and sublimeness of the New Zealand landscape, this Edenic garden, is being exploited; the local myth of the resourceful pioneer and enterprising craftsman harnessed to manufacture a fantasy of a folk culture; a distant country which is on the edge of the world cleverly manoeuvred and adjusted into a perceived Middle Earth which can be reached through mass culture and corporate packaging; and fans' insatiability for all things Tolkien neatly controlled through a heightened protection of production images and the steady release of executive and toy related products.

In this land of make believe, Peter Jackson, New Zealand's foremost film magician, has demonstrated that New Zealand is not just a pastoral paradise but a producer's paradise offering a diversity of effective screen locations. A 1999 Production Guide, published by Film New Zealand to attract and assist locally based filmmaking projects from overseas, carried the title "The World in One Country"; following the beginning of the production of *The Lord of the Rings* a new campaign was launched which widened the location possibilities and equated New Zealand with Middle Earth. Here, the response to Jackson's adaptation will be considered as significantly local as it is global. Undoubtedly, the international fan base for *The Lord of the Rings* is huge, and this will be addressed through the audience's consumption of the trilogy in relation to promotions and available merchandise. Local issues will be addressed through the ways in which New Zealand industry and the national population have embraced the film as distinctly Kiwi.

Mass Merchandising

The impression made by the merchandising of *The Lord of the Rings* is not entirely unprecedented. In the age of the blockbuster, patterns of synergy between media industries and the inventiveness of licensed manufacturers in continuing the screen myth into a myriad of promotional possibilities have demonstrated the cultural power of the event movie. For instance, as I have written elsewhere, the *A Nightmare on Elm Street* films (1984-1991) triggered a vast series of merchandise that ranged from yo-yos and pyjamas to plastic replicas of the infamous Freddy Krueger's razors-for-fingers glove, and a talking Freddy doll (Conrich "Seducing"). With this merchandise phenomenon it was surprising that a group of films that was generally released for a mature audience was generating products with an advisory age as young as three. Significantly, despite the diversity of products, children were the dominant consumer fixation of manufacturers.

Whilst the merchandising of *A Nightmare on Elm Street* was impressive, it pales alongside recent blockbuster films, such as *Star Wars: Episode II - Attack of the Clones* (2002), *Star Wars: Episode III - Revenge of the Sith* (2005), *Spider-Man* (2002), *Spider-Man 2* (2004), and the Pixar productions *Finding Nemo* (2003), and *The Incredibles* (2004), which have been increasingly active in securing movie merchandising and tie-in opportunities.[1] New Line Cinema, the producer of both *A Nightmare on Elm Street* and *The Lord of the Rings*, is also the studio behind the *Teenage Mutant Ninja Turtles* (1990-1993) and *Austin Powers* (1997-2002) groups of films, both of which have been phenomenally successful franchises not least in terms of their generation of related merchandise. Justin Wyatt wrote on New Line in 1998, which he termed even then, prior to *The Lord of the Rings*, a "major independent," and he noted the value of the franchise to the studio, which astutely used revenue gained for supporting "less viable projects" (Wyatt, "Formation," 78). For Wyatt, this creation of "tent pole" movies – known or hoped-for major productions around which a studio builds its portfolio of films for the year – recalled Paramount's release schedule of the mid-1980s and its highly commercial *Indiana Jones* (1981-1989), *Star Trek* (1979-2002) and *Beverly Hills Cop* (1984-1994) franchises (78). But, whereas New Line appeared to learn from others in regard to the power of the movie franchise, in terms of merchandise and *The Lord of the Rings* the studio was also able to draw upon and advance the knowledge it had gained from the success of marketing its own productions. Here, New Line's earlier franchises had attracted not just young consumers; and often merchandise revealed fan appreciation and suggested cult film status.[2]

The extent of the merchandise for *The Lord of the Rings* went beyond earlier New Line productions such as *A Nightmare on Elm Street*,

---

[1] For a discussion of the highly successful movie merchandising of *Spider-Man* (2002) see Wasko, *How Hollywood Works*, 163-64. Fantasy films are often the best type of productions for generating merchandise or tie-ins, "movie magic" that can be taken home. For a discussion of the marketing of *Willow* (1988) see Wasko, *Information Age*, 197-199; and for *The Dark Crystal* (1982) and *Labyrinth* (1986), see Wright, "Selling," forthcoming.

[2] For a discussion of New Line's marketing of their films, and the creation or sustaining of fan bases through the use of the Internet, see Landro "Power of Synergy." For a focus on New Line's Internet approach to fans and the marketing of *The Lord of the Rings*, see Landro "Hobbits in Cyberspace."

Teenage Mutant Ninja Turtles, and *Austin Powers: International Man of Mystery* (1997), in being aimed at different consumer groups, each of which will be assessed below. An examination of the range of products and the placement of promotions reveals the expected mass markets of the mainstream consumer and the family as consumer, with associated childhood products in addition to consumer cult collectibles, the last of which, for *The Lord of the Rings*, has extended into a recent obsession for specially crafted full-size replicas of screen props. This superior movie merchandising is just one aspect of the fascinating series of high-class products marketed for an executive consumer; materials of this sort have never before been so well exploited in the selling of a film. Moreover, the celebration of *The Lord of the Rings* generated a range of products that addressed the central nation, New Zealand. Within this local economy is a consumer market absorbed in a *Lord of the Rings* culture involving both an insatiable desire for, and a patriotic defense of, anything from the trilogy that maintains and enhances the myth that the country is a living Middle Earth.

Mass-produced merchandise for *The Lord of the Rings* ranges from the expected posters, mousepads, books, bookmarks, calendars, mugs, postcards, trading cards, board games, computer games, puzzles, apparel, magnets, and key chains to the less familiar latex masks, snow-globes, paperweights, maps, 12-inch poseable talking plush Gollum, and Barbie and Ken dolls dressed as Arwen and Aragorn.[3] Among the many film-related books produced for the trilogy, *The Rough Guide to The Lord of the Rings* makes some attempt to organize the associated merchandise. One division made by the author is based on price, with products listed either under "The Ten Most Expensive *Lord of the Rings* Items on eBay," or "Ten Cheaper Items on eBay" (Simpson, Rodiss, and Bushell *Rough Guide*, 246; 249). Of the expensive items offered on eBay there is a "Seven-foot tall carved *Lord of the Rings* wizard, $2500," crafted by an Oregon carver, and of a much smaller dimension an almost complete set of figurines from Toy Biz, with a starting bid of $999 (246). Figurines have been popular toy tie-ins for films for much of the period in which

---

[3] www.donnagrayson.com/movies/lordoftheringsgifts, www.starstore.com/acatalog/Starstore, www.lotrfanshop.com, www.xs4all.nl/~rossnbrg/movies, and (accessed 21 April 2005).

the modern blockbuster has existed. The important texts here are the *Star Wars* films which marketed not just a vast series of figurines for capturing and representing the many notable characters in the epic tale but also representations of some of the many briefly seen cast figures, as well as multiple figurines to cover certain key characters in alternative situations or dress. With its different lands, distinctive cultures, and quest narratives that introduce many friends and foes in the course of the trilogy, *The Lord of the Rings* lends itself well to such merchandise (see Gillam *Treasures*, 182-194).[4]

Figurine Collectibles

A ten-figure set of *The Fellowship of the Ring* characters was available in 2001 as a Kinder Egg collection, but these miniature surprizes within chocolates were found only in Germany. A mightier tie-in campaign was orchestrated by Burger King who, in the tradition of previous fast food/film promotions, marketed a set of eighteen "must have" *Lord of the Rings* figurines between 23 November and 16 December 2001, in the period leading up to the release of the first part of the trilogy.[5] Less extensive than the Toy Biz series, and seemingly cheaper to collect as a set, this promotion was available only inside Kids Meals and Big Kids Meals but would have had a wide appeal within the mass market, attracting adults and children alike, fans and collectors. The figurines were stand-alone toys, with either light or sound functions (the figurines for Frodo and Gandalf had both), but could also be combined and added to a nineteenth toy giveaway, a centre-piece "Ring of Power," which held heat-activated messages on its sides. The eighteen figurines were designed for placing around the Precious object, forming a ring enclosure.[6]

The figurines included Arwen, Bilbo, Boromir, Celeborn, Elrond, Gimli, Saruman, Lurtz, and a cave troll. But as collectors noted, locating

---

[4] See the Toy Biz range of figurines at <http://www.toybiz.com> (accessed 10 January 2004).
[5] See <http://www.media-file.net/various/lr/lordoftheringsrelease.htm> (accessed 5 September 2003). Burger King's previous significant movie tie-in was for *Shrek* (2001).
[6] See <http://www.toymania.com/features/bklotr/index.shtml> (accessed 5 September 2003).

124 *Ian Conrich*

all nineteen pieces was in itself a quest.[7] Despite the online auction site eBay offering a quick alternative to furthering the figurine collection, certain pieces were elusive depending on where in the U.S. consumers were located. Moreover, variants existed for some models, and various countries sold different versions of the set. Burger King in Singapore, for instance, marketed nine figures, each with a film cell, with three different possible film cells per character.[8]

Image 8: The Burger King "Ring of Power" of figurines (www.fastfoodtoys.net).

Offering such pieces of celluloid free with convenience or fast food would have given the consumer the impression of an exclusive gift, not to say a piece of the film itself. For a production that controlled the images for each part of the trilogy before and during release, the acquisition of pieces of filmstrip in a fast food lunch box for children does seem paradoxical. Burger King would not have been alone, among those who were licensed to produce merchandise for the trilogy, in having special

---
[7] http://www.toymania.com/features/bklotr/index.shtml
[8] http://www.toymania.com/features/bklotr/index.shtml

secrecy clauses written into contracts. As Michael Perry, a miniature-model maker for the fantasy gaming industry, said,

> Working on anything to do with *Lord of the Rings* was a bit like working for MI5. It was all such a closely guarded secret. Even something as simple as a couple of stills from the film – if any of those had ended up on the Internet, we'd have been right in the sh**. (Scott "Relative Values," 13)

The Lord of the Rings was created and promoted as a prestige production, with the most advanced technology used to create the effects and illusions; specialist craft folk employed to manufacture admirable props; and magnificent locations incorporated as dramatic backdrops. Even though much of the merchandise for the films was mass-produced, New Line guarded its product while also maintaining its concern that anything associated with it presented a sense of distinction, quality, or precision.

Burger King did market "King of the Ring" enhanced onion rings available in three sizes, which commentators labeled "Lord of the Onion Rings."[9] But it was the collectibles Burger King emphasized, and made clear in press releases were superior movie tie-ins. New Line announced at the time that the deal with Burger King was its biggest ever for a movie tie-in, "eclipsing the one for *Austin Powers: The Spy Who Shagged Me* in 1999."[10] Richard Taylor, Burger King's Vice President for U.S. marketing, was quoted as saying "The literary significance of …[*The Lord of the Rings*] coupled with its superior entertainment value and tremendous built-in fan base, make it a smart fit for our global brand."[11] Alongside the figurines, Burger King also promoted four thirteen-ounce light-up goblets, each free only with the purchase of a Whopper sandwich Value Meal. Of these, Chris Clouser, Executive Vice President and Chief Global Marketing Officer for Burger King, said they represent "our commitment to bringing the magic and adventure of quality entertainment to our customers in authentic, creative ways," and that the Corporation

---

[9] See <http://www.media-file.net/various/lr/lordoftheringsrelease.htm> (accessed 5 September 2003).
[10] See <http://www.tolkien-movies.com/words/2001/06-19-01.shtml> (accessed 5 September 2003).
[11] See <http://www.tolkien-movies.com/words/2001/06-19-01.shtml> (accessed 5 September 2003).

understands "the importance of staying true to the film and giving our customers high-quality premiums they would be proud to give as gifts."[12] The union between fast food and products presented as sophisticated and not mass-produced plastic giveaways, is fascinating. Despite initial appearances, even the figurines were no mere toys and were refined collectibles featuring "high-quality laser scanned images of the movie characters."[13]

The Burger King figurines were surpassed by those released by Toy Biz, a company which is a division of Marvel Enterprises. The Toy Biz figurines were marketed in waves and in specific series during the trilogy's release. They were sold alone, and in combination, as electronic "specials," Deluxe sets, gift sets, twin packs, playsets, or as dioramas: Frodo in a Gothic forest, or Samwise defending a door from attack. All figurines come with attachments, such as weapons and clothing add-ons, but some have much grander accessories with mechanisms that can introduce controlled action. Saruman, as with other figurines, has a magnetic palm, in which he can hold the palantir, or magic ball, an attachment which can also be placed "floating" magnetically on its plinth. The Orc Overseer comes with a whip, and a figure of an Uruk-hai, which with a push-button mechanism rises from its birthing sac. In an early review of the figures, James H. Gillam wrote "Fine detailing to hands and brows only add to their authenticity... [accessories] look truly authentic. Made of soft and pliable vinyl, they [cloaks and robes] 'hang' properly and appear to be 'in motion'" (*Treasures*, 182). Toy Biz had been acquiring a growing reputation for such toy collectibles and *The Lord of the Rings*, while demanding quality merchandise, presented an opportunity to advance their expertise in creating what can be a lucrative side of the movie product business. As one reviewer explains,

> Toy Biz has utilized the talents of toy sculptors as well as laser scanning technology to create authentic figures. Many of the actors had their faces scanned by Gentle Giant Studios to create miniature editions of the actors'

---

[12] See <http://www.media-file.net/various/lr/lordoftheringsrelease.htm> (accessed 5 September 2003).
[13] See <http://www.media-file.net/various/lr/lordoftheringsrelease.htm> (accessed 5 September 2003).

> likenesses to smooth the approval process and create faithful renditions. The armour, weapons, articulation and action features were then designed to complete the process. The figures are designed around a six-inch scale, meaning that a character six feet tall would be six inches in toy form. All the figures in the first assortment are over six inches tall (the Easterling is a full seven inches), so they should fit in with both six and seven inch toys...
>
> Toy Biz has been setting high standards for articulation in their figures, and this line is no exception. All the figures are highly articulated, with many points designed to be hidden from casual view. They have also incorporated some of the joints that have been used in other lines, such as the ankle joints that have a side-to-side swivel on them.[14]

Gillam, like the fans, praised the detail and craftsmanship: "The likeness of the action figure faces is truly remarkable and unlike anything that has been seen in the toy industry before... In many ways, these figures are as much a work of art as they are a toy" (Gillam *Treasures*, 182).

Prestige Merchandise

Lord of the Rings merchandise has existed before, primarily for the Bakshi film of 1978, with, among others, action figures produced by Knickerbocker Toys, vinyl finger-puppets by Mystry, and porcelain figures by Royal Doulton (see Gillam). Merchandise for Jackson's *The Lord of the Rings* has, however, completely over-shadowed all previous related products, and equally significant is the way in which much of the merchandise has crossed over or moved away from being recognized as a possible toy or plaything to being valued as an exquisitely manufactured, sculpted, or crafted object. Other films have produced quality movie products aimed at adult consumers and connoisseurs, or those perhaps with stronger obsessions (and healthier disposable income), within fan or collectors' markets. Delicate and fragile ornaments, minted plates, and chess sets have been seen before and a recent trend for full-scale replica props and crafted (often lifesize) copies of movie weapons has taken off with films such as *Blade* (1998) and *Troy* (2004). But, never before has a

---

[14] <http://www.toymania.com/columns/spotlight/twotowersasst1.shtml> (accessed 3 March 2005).

movie production led to such an industry of what I will term prestige merchandise.

The Lord of the Rings is different from the aforementioned films in that it comes with a formidable heritage that includes not just the respectable literary foundation of the novels but also the fantasy gaming industry, where, according to Perry, "Tolkien is the godfather of the whole genre" (quoted in Scott "Relative Values," 13). Perry continues by observing that

> Merchandising is an important part of a film like this. Most Tolkien fans are either gamers, modelers, collectors or all three. There are plenty of people out there who buy two of every figure that Games Workshop produce. There'll be one for gaming, and one that they never take out of the packet. (Perry, in Scott)

As part of the gaming culture, Games Workshop produced a tabletop strategy game tie-in, which promised battle re-enactments from the films. Offering similar cerebral contests, *Lord of the Rings* collector's chess sets could be bought, but at a price: $495 for a chess board, with a relief map of Middle Earth under the playing surface, and thirty-two pewter pieces, plus $109 for twelve additional three dimensional characters from *The Two Towers*, to decorate the edges. And there were others, with The Royal Selangor chess set with pieces made of pewter and bronze costing £450, and the shot glass chess set, with pieces sculpted and designed to carry alcoholic doses presumably to be drunk on capturing a player's piece – cost: £750. Gaming, however, can also move beyond a board with representative pieces, with devotees role playing by acquiring the appearance of a chosen character.

A wealth of visual fantasy is presented in *The Lord of the Rings* films, with one aim being to establish a "believable" and enchanting realm in which the viewer can be immersed. The merchandising of clothing and props copied from the screen models, recreates the fantasy beyond the screen and extends the imaginative designs into a space of appreciation where they can be collected, most likely worn, and presumably treasured. Such merchandise is imbued with a manufactured magic that comes through association with the screen character from which the clothes and props have been "borrowed." As with the Harry Potter craze, which has led to merchandising packages of assembled props and clothes that enable children to "become" Harry, for *The Lord of the Rings*, Frodo, Gandalf, Legolas, and Ringwraith accessory and costume kits, for children aged seven and up, were available, interestingly through some sellers who promoted the gear as intended for Halloween.[15] Costumes have been marketed to cater to the fantasies of adults, too, and range from knitting patterns by Simplicity (designs 9891 and 4940, similar to the dresses worn by Arwen, Galadriel, and Eowyn) to basic copies of Arwen's white dress at $69.99 ($27.99 for children) – an Arwen wig is an extra $11.99[16] – and high-quality replicas of Arwen's blood-red gown at $450, described as "exquisite enough for weddings" (Simpson, Rodiss, and Bushell *Rough Guide*, 252). *The Lord of the Rings* is not just a blockbuster fantasy epic; it is also a romance with a sub-plot of undying love amidst medieval-styled costumes. Clearly, the extension of the films into wearable merchandise promoted not just screen magic but also fantasy-romance and a sense of elegance and refinement. The associated clothing that was marketed is notable for its appeal to different consumers for different reasons, functioning as playwear, role-play costumes, fancy dress, evening wear, and even bridal wear.

The vision and craft of the costumers working on the films was just one of the celebrated factors of the production, and part three of the trilogy was awarded an Oscar for Best Costume Design in 2004, after two years earlier being nominated in the same category for part one. Such is the high regard for the costumes that a web community has emerged to understand and appreciate their manufacture. The site is heavily documented with discussion and advice on specific items of screen clothing: Pippin's scarf, "How to build a Hobbit skirt," and "Galadriel's Prolog dress in obsessive detail." As the site advises "We're here to study everything about the costumes from fabric to patterns to metalworking... *The Lord of the Rings* costumes are just too fantastic not to research!"[17]

---

[15] See <http://www.costumeshopper.com/lord-of-the-rings-costumes.html> (accessed 3 March 2005).
[16] <http://www.costumecraze.com/index-lotr-arwen.html> (accessed 3 March 2005).
[17] <http://www.alleycatscratch.com/lotr/> (accessed 3 March 2005).

The screen costumes, which were constructed with attention to detail and quality, are not alone in being copied for prestige merchandise, with jewelry and weaponry available in seemingly endless options. Jewelry includes necklaces, earrings, rings, and brooches and ranges from Galadriel's ring (solid sterling silver and European crystal) at $129, Arwen's Evenstar Pendant at $95, the Ring of Aragorn at $129, and the Elven Brooch at $65, to Eowyn earrings and necklace (14-carat gold) at £400. Many of the items were sold by The Noble Collection and were described variously as "a precise reproduction," as "reproduced in stunning detail," and as "reproduced with extraordinary workmanship," the advertisements emphasizing craftsmanship, "authenticity," and the power of the simulacrum. The Evenstar Pendant of Arwen, given by Arwen to Aragorn in *The Lord of the Rings* as a sign of love, exists as a symbolic piece of merchandise. It supposedly transfers the romantic legend of the epic fantasy and allows a distinctive item of jewelry, worn by a mythical Elven princess, to be captured in duplicate and worn seemingly undiluted by ordinary consumers. A popular product, its desirability as a jewelry copy was second only to that of The One Ring.

It was perhaps inevitable that the most copied item of jewelry merchandise for the trilogy would be The One Ring. The very idea that it was unique inspired the copies, while the power it held and the fact of its desirability within the story added to its significance, despite the point that it corrupts each owner. Bizarrely, this is reinforced in the advertising for the Compton and Woodhouse official replica: "It has seduced the most powerful rulers of Middle Earth (sic), all consumed with lust for its power, and now 'The One Ring' has been recreated and cast in 9-carat gold for you to own and wear." Clearly, the ring is more "precious" when bought in the UK, with British based consumers charged £350 for the 9-carat version; the 10-carat version, $295, and the 18-carat version $495, in the U.S. Individually engraved in Elvish with a post-Tolkien laser, each ring comes with a certificate of authenticity and in a "rich wooden treasure box," which suggests the item is to be prized.

Among consumers, The One Ring as an item of merchandise would probably be worn, as much as treasured and kept within its wooden box. Other items of prestige merchandise associated with *The Lord of the*

Rings include replicas of the staffs, swords, and arms used in the films. Some of these, such as "The Arms of the Fellowship" collection, sold for £48, are for display purposes and are scaled miniatures of the original, mounted with a "handsome oval plaque." These 12-inch copies are "the ultimate collector's treasure" with the consumer advised that they were created by "the swordsmiths who crafted the actual weapons used in the [first] film." More impressive, is the 76-inch full-size replica of the Staff of Saruman, cost $223.99. Similar full-size replicas were sold in The Noble Collection: of Gandalf's sword (47 inches; $295) and The Sword of the King – Anduril ($395), the former "forged to the highest standards by the master swordmakers of Toledo, Spain," the latter also crafted in Toledo and made in a limited and numbered edition of 3500. But this is just the tip of a weapons and armory iceberg for the films, with the website for Blades by Brown Cutlery selling a vast selection of full-size swords (eighteen different items, covering all the main characters), helmets (8 different), scabbards (6 different), shields, axes, spears/pikes, and crowns/tiaras, as well as leather belts and bracers.[18] The limited edition helmet of Lord Sauron retails at $300, and can be purchased as a set with other Sauron crafted replicas of the gauntlet and ring and the mace. The manufacturers appear to be supplying an army and, clearly, from the scale of their operations and the list of forthcoming additions, there is a strong demand for such prestige merchandise. Many of the items are intended for display: swords are sold with a wooden wall plaque, while the helmets each come with a plinth. However, the manufacturer also produces what it describes as "heirloom" swords as part of its "Museum Collection." These are "fully functional" reproductions.

Made in New Zealand

Many of these items in their original screen form were created, crafted, forged, and manufactured in New Zealand, with *The Lord of the Rings*

---

[18] <http://www.bladesbybrown.com/lotr.html> (accessed 3 March 2005).

employing local crafts people to assist in producing a vision of Middle Earth. In 2001, Film New Zealand produced a poster-size map of New Zealand to promote *The Lord of the Rings* to trade, industry, and media figures just prior to the release of *The Fellowship of the Ring*. On one side of the poster is a Tolkienesque map of New Zealand in old manuscript style and calligraphy writing, which is headed "New Zealand home of Middle Earth." The map not only establishes in detail the set locations employed in making the first part of the trilogy but also places on the map, through a series of icons, the locations of artisans in New Zealand who were employed in creating film props and aspects of *The Lord of the Ring*'s mise en scène. The list of artisans is quite extensive with local crafts folk and specialist makers of rustic ware – such as glassblower, basketmaker, cooper, cabinetmaker, slipcase potter, rugmaker, boat builder, saddler, bootmaker, milliner, thatched roofer, and stone wall builder – indicated across the two main islands of New Zealand.

The map functions as a promotional aid for *The Lord of the Rings*, but it also promotes the local independent businesses and small industries (though without naming them) in what has been widely recognized as an enterprise culture; it suggests the detail and professionalism brought to the film production by artisans working to create the desired fantasy; and it suggests through an "ancient" map of New Zealand, complete with legends and icons, that this is an exotic country of "treasures" that demands exploration. Moreover, it equates Middle Earth with New Zealand, with the latter depicted cartographically in a style associated with the period and nature of the former. Following the success of *The Lord of the Rings*, New Zealand, with its myth of a pastoral paradise, has been compared repeatedly with the idyllic rural culture of the hobbits in Middle Earth, despite the fact that Tolkien's story is based on the English shire. The production's celebration of resourceful New Zealand industry, with defined local craft and efficient service industries, has even drawn comparisons between New Zealanders and hobbits. Certainly, the myths of New Zealand identity are foregrounded and enhanced in the marketing and publicity surrounding *The Lord of the Rings*, to the point where there is almost an obsessive "belief" in New Zealand being Middle Earth.

A 2004 Television New Zealand programme, "The Real Middle Earth (sic)," did nothing to dampen such a belief. The programme advises that it is a "unique look at Kiwis" who have worked in support of *The Lord of the Rings*, both in and post-production, as well as generally at the role of the country itself in manufacturing a screen vision. As the programme's host, Jim Hickey, concludes, whilst standing atop a high mountain point, "the little guys of New Zealand, ordinary Kiwis, helped to produce the success of the *Ring*'s trilogy from within the scenic magnificence of their own backyard." Including interviews with specialist crew, artisans, and extras – helicopter pilots, caterers, breeders of rare sheep for weaving the required fabric for the cloaks, and soldiers from the New Zealand army who played Orcs and Uruk-hai and took part in battle scenes – the makers of the programme both explore and celebrate the ingenuity, enterprise, and graft of a local population. Jackson is interviewed, too, and talks of the "get-stuck-in Kiwi spirit," "the broad skill base of New Zealanders," and "New Zealanders hav[ing] a great do-it-yourself abililty." The cultural myths of New Zealand identity are fuelled by Jackson and the programme makers, with an impressive and epic screen trilogy harnessed, even exploited, to validate the existence of a competitive national economy.

Many areas of local industry have benefited from association with *The Lord of the Rings*. Harrington's Brewery, in Richmond, at the top of the South Island, was approached to produce a special 1% low alcohol and dark-coloured hobbit beer for certain scenes in the trilogy. The official hobbit brewer, whose premises display a large sign reading "Proud to be 100% Kiwi," now welcomes visiting tourists and tours are provided by staff wearing specially designed T-shirts and caps, with ale-tasting supported by special mugs. The owner, Craig Harrington, advises that the tourism trade has been "massive," and that they are planning to market the hobbit beer under the name "Sobering Thought." Nearby, in Nelson, which could be viewed as almost geographically at the centre of New Zealand (or the middle of Middle Earth), is Jens Hansen Jewellers, which forged the One Ring used in making the trilogy. With both visits from tourists and emails flooding in from overseas aficionados, the jeweler's business has expanded to presumably meet demand for rings cast from the same forge as The One Ring. Of the licensed manufacturers of the *Lord of the Rings* merchandise and products, certain major New Zealand corporations were given unique rights to market the movies, and New Zealand Post sold first special commemorative or collectors stamps for each part of the trilogy as the films were released.[19] Later, in 2003, New Zealand Post also issued, with approval from the Reserve Bank of New Zealand, a series of official *Lord of the Rings* coins, with the most exclusive item being The Premier Gold Crown Collection of three $10 22-carat gold proof coins—cost: NZ$4295.[20] The coins were made by the British Royal Mint and New Zealand's Prime minister struck the first on a visit to Wales in July 2003.[21]

An additional set of stamps were issued by New Zealand Post in 2004, under the title "New Zealand - Home of Middle Earth," which commemorated the relationship between landscapes, specific movie scenes in *The Lord of the Rings*, and what the publicity defined as "their 'real life' counterparts." As four pairs of two stamps, each pair depicts a notable movie scene such as The Ford of Bruinen and the Rohirrim city of Edoras, and on the companion stamp the actual location, such as Skippers Canyon on the Shotover River or Erewhon, with movie sets and props removed. The publicity asks the consumer, "Who can forget the scene..." and employs descriptions such as "spectacular," "magnificent," "dramatic," "remote," "towering," and "mystically magical" to emphasize the cinematic nature of New Zealand views, which have now acquired a dual recognition as New Zealand and Middle Earth. The "100% Pure New Zealand" Tourism New Zealand campaign also exploited the power of the landscape for assisting a phenomenally successful movie franchise, by distributing posters, leaflets, and postcards featuring a spectacular scenic view and, to the side of the image, a clapperboard for *The Return of the King*. Underneath is the line, "Two years to film the trilogy. Millions of years to build the set." And these are sets that will not be destroyed. Many of the locations were already protected, as they exist in

---

[19] See <https://secure.nzpost.co.nz/cgi-bin/nzstamps/web_store/web_store.cgi> (accessed 3 march 2005).
[20] See < https://secure.nzpost.co.nz/cgi-bin/nzstamps/web_store/web_store.cgi> (accessed 3 March 2005).
[21] See <http://www.scoop.co.nz/stories/BU0307/S00174.htm> (accessed 3 March 2005).

New Zealand's national parks. But to assist in their discovery, various fantasy adventure and 4 x 4 tour operators – Safari of the Rings, from New Zealand Nomad Safaris; Red Carpet Tours; and the Rings Scenic Tours, which guides visitors around the Hobbiton set at Matamata – have emerged to transport tourists to the sites so that they may experience and be awestruck by the landscape of movies. A most detailed record of the locations employed can be found in the best-selling *The Lord of the Rings Location Guidebook* (Brodie).

Such profiting from the films has been encouraged by New Zealand Prime Minister Helen Clark, who established a government budget to promote the country as the "Home of Middle Earth" globally, and resituate it within the international cultural economy. New Zealand is a country that has geographically been viewed as down under and on the edge of the world. Maps predominantly depict the Pacific in two, with the West coast of the U.S. on the far left and New Zealand in the far right corner.[22] New Zealanders have challenged this view with maps that not only unite the Pacific but invert the globe, declaring on general merchandise, "New Zealand is not down under!" Such cartographic arguments place New Zealand on top and central but, with *The Lord of the Rings* the country seems to have been repositioned not just as Middle Earth but also as a nation that is being globally recognized as being at the heart of a production with tremendous international cultural attraction.

And Middle Earth can be reached, journeyed to with its own official airline, Air New Zealand. In a promotional campaign that saw the airline unite with the trilogy, Air New Zealand became "Airline to Middle Earth," a claim proudly announced on its products and assets from flight ticket wallets to the fuselages of three planes – a Boeing 747, a Boeing 767, and an A320 Airbus.

---

[22] Many maps have depicted the world this way, due most likely to two historical factors. Greenwich Mean Time, the British system of timekeeping, places Britain in a central position, at zero degrees longitude, with the world to the left and right. Also, many of the world's great explorers came from a group of countries – the U.K., Spain, Portugal, Holland, France – that sought new trade routes and lands, and journeyed to the East and West. Geographically, these countries can almost be joined with a vertical line when viewed on a map, on which they are positioned centrally.

Image 9: Air New Zealand's flying billboard for *The Lord of the Rings*. (Copyright © Brinkley Wings Collection, www.brinkley.cc)

Each plane was repainted with an individual collage of images specific to a film in the trilogy and acted as flying billboard, while transporting more visitors to a perceived Middle Earth.

New Zealand has been experiencing an increase in visitor numbers, especially from the key markets such as the U.S., following *The Lord of the Rings*. As Sean Murray, Chairman of the Tourism Research Council, stated, the films have been proving "a tremendously powerful catalyst in prompting travelers who've thought about visiting New Zealand to make that final decision. It's tapping into the latent desire to travel here."[23] Painting the fuselages of enormous planes is a bold statement for a national carrier to make about the impact of a film. While traveling on the Airline to Middle Earth, passengers have been shown the documentary "The Real Middle Earth," unable to avoid a cultural phenomenon, which has seen a movie trilogy consumed on different levels. From the Kinder Egg figurine or a fast food plastic giveaway to a gold replica One Ring, or the adventure tours, *The Lord of the Rings* has created a marketing craze that will continue long after the trilogy's release.

---

[23] <www.scoop.co.nz/stories/CU0301/S00068.htm> and <http://www.bandt.com.au/news/> (accessed 3 March 2005)

Fic Frodo Slash Frodo: Fandoms and *The Lord of the Rings*

Jennifer Brayton

Summer 1980: An Introduction to Fandom

At the age of eleven, I discovered my life's ambition... to become a Rider of Rohan. It didn't matter that I was just learning to horseback ride, or that the Riders only existed in a fictional book. It was the start of my summer break from school in 1980, and my parents, desperate to keep me occupied, gave me *The Lord of the Rings* trilogy to read. Three weeks later, I was done and all I could talk about were the Riders of Rohan and their amazing horses. When I grew up, I was determined to own a mearas, one of the treasured horses of the Rohirrim. Like Gandalf with Shadowfax, I wanted a horse that would let me ride him free of tack, so that we could communicate via our bodies and he would accept me as a trustworthy friend. As a young girl, I fell in love with Eowyn, the Lady of Rohan who masqueraded as a boy on her horse Wildfola to join battle against the Dark Lord. It was my first time reading the famed books by J.R.R. Tolkien, and that introduction, so long ago, started me on the path of *The Lord of the Rings* fandom.

Fans are commonly understood as people with a shared common love or admiration for a specific interest (McQuail *Theory*). Whether it be for sports, celebrities, artists, or various products of popular culture, there exist numerous fandoms that are aimed at a single true love and passion. While fans are, in one sense, simply audiences to a cultural activity or product, they are distinguishable from the general audience in their emotional connection to their specialized interest. They emotionally relate to their interest, and take pleasure from engaging with it. If the audience consists of general consumers of mass media and popular culture, fans are emotionally focused towards one specific topic or interest. The global audiences for the *Lord of the Rings* books and films include fans, but not all audience members are fans. Fans may share the experience of *The Lord of the Rings* with the mass audience by reading the books or watching the films and DVDs, but it is their specialized interests that distinguish them from the larger audience (Attallah *Audience*).

The *Lord of the Rings* trilogy, since its first publication in 1954/55, has appealed to readers from all over the world, from its inception sparking the formation of a new fandom based on Tolkien and the rich complex world of Middle Earth. Similarly, Peter Jackson's cinematic adaptation of the trilogy has also spawned a new generation of fans, creating new fandoms above and beyond the original fan base for the book series. In fact, the popularity of *The Lord of the Rings* in both formats has spawned its own documentary, *Ringers: Lord of the Fans* (2005), about the very nature of fans and fandom over the last fifty years.

While fans and fandoms of *The Lord of the Rings* date back to the first release of the book, the movement of the Internet to the public realm in the mid-1990s has changed the very nature of fandom. As this article will illustrate, Jackson's trilogy has spawned a new generation of fans whose love has been specifically influenced by the film series. The advent of the Internet has positively contributed to the global popularity of Jackson's cinematic vision of Middle Earth, and has had significant impact upon the fans. First, the specific interests of the fans have changed from the books to the films, and as a result fan consumerism has been extended and expanded. Secondly, fans are even more actively involved in the production and creation of content based on Middle Earth. There is no one and only way of being a fan of *The Lord of the Rings*, but an inherent feature common to all fans is a shared passion and devotion to the overlapping worlds created by Tolkien and Jackson.

Fanning the Early Flames of Obsession

The original book trilogy by Tolkien appealed to many readers from its first publication. While Tolkien expected a limited readership of family and friends, his trilogy was instead a gradual but solid success. At the 15th World Science Fiction Convention in 1957, it won the International Fantasy Award, indicating its popularity and recognition (tolkiensociety.org, FAQ). In 1966, Tolkien was recognized by the Royal Society of Literature when they awarded him the acclaimed Benson Medal for the trilogy. That same year, *Time* ran a story, "The Hobbit Habit," on the popularity of Tolkien and his Middle Earth books on American college campuses, as a result of the paperback release of the trilogy in the United States ("Hobbit Habit").

Following the popular success of the trilogy, many readers became fans and started to form clubs and organizations for other like-minded individuals. Formed in 1960, The Fellowship of the Ring was the first known organized North American fan group, a sub-group of the famed Los Angeles Science Fantasy Society (Meskys *Fandom*). Ted Johnstone, founder of the Fellowship, was the editor and publisher of four issues of their journal, *I-PALANTIR* (the first *Lord of the Rings* fan-driven magazine) before it folded. One of the Fellowship members, Ken Chelsin, brought Tolkien fandom to the United Kingdom with the 1961 publication of *Nazgul's Bane*, the first British fanzine based on Tolkien's books (Hanson *THEN*). In 1965, Richard Poltz formed the first formal Tolkien fan association, The Tolkien Society of America. They organized what is recognized as the first conference on Middle Earth and Tolkien, though the conference was academic in focus and featured papers by many notable academics and science fiction writers. The Mythopoeic Society was formed in 1967 for the discussion of fantasy literature, including Tolkien's work (mythosc.org). In 1969, the Tolkien Society first opened its doors for fans to share their love and knowledge of the books, and gave birth to the first recognized non-profit charity organization dedicated to Tolkien and his writings (tolkiensociety.org). By that time, the book trilogy had already been favorably reviewed by the *New York Times*, had been published in America with and without Tolkien's authorization, had been adapted for airing on BBC radio, and been subject to the first negotiations for a film adaptation. Many of these originating fan communities, groups, and organizations still exist today, demonstrating the ongoing love affair fans have with Tolkien and his trilogy.

In the 1960s, fans of the book trilogy had only two real focal points for their specialized interests: J.R.R. Tolkien, and the world of Middle Earth. Tolkienists were interested in Tolkien as an author, and studied all of his literary texts including the trilogy. Some early fan interest focused on the development of the Elven languages invented by Tolkien for the trilogy (Meskys *Fandom*). Other fans were interested in the complex mythic history Tolkien developed in the creation of Middle Earth. However, other fan/readers were interested only in the book trilogy itself and the magical world of Hobbits, wizards, Elves, and Dwarves contained inside. They were less interested in Tolkien and his career, and few of these fans had interest in his other texts outside the trilogy. "Ringer" was the term later introduced to distinguish the fans of *Lord of the Rings* books and films from Tolkienists.

This is not to suggest early fans of the trilogy and the works of Tolkien were in any way passive readers. Early fans of Tolkien were actively creating their fan communities as far back as the early 1960s. They began self-producing their own journals and fan publications, sharing their ideas and thoughts further afield. They created pins and t-shirts, sprayed "Frodo lives!" in subways, and designed their own clothes and costumes. Conferences and conventions were planned and formed, and more fans created more fan communities, including some early Internet fan communities. Musicians, inspired by the books, created bands and songs paying tribute to Tolkien's world.

Tolkien himself recognized his active and engaged audience of readers, making changes to the books based on letters that had been written to him (Tolkien "Forward"). Fans of his work picked up on typographic errors and mistakes, but also pushed Tolkien to further expand upon his mythology and to provide more detail and context for his Middle Earth world. Later revised editions of the book trilogy included a prologue detailing the Hobbit culture, an index, appendices, maps, and corrections to inconsistencies in the plot narratives. While the fandom surrounding *The Lord of the Rings* and Tolkien was small in scale compared to the fandoms surrounding the film franchise, members were still actively engaged in interacting with the trilogy narratives.

The Internet and *The Lord of the Rings* Films

By the time the Internet reached the North American public landscape in the mid-1990s, fans had been sharing a common love and fascination with a book trilogy that was about forty years old, with little new material to drive the fandom forward. While fans could debate the finer nuances of canon with the trilogy – what is considered to be genuine or authentic to Tolkien's mythology – they were accustomed to material that had only been successful in book form. In fact, many fans were angered by the few animated interpretations that had been attempted commercially, such as the children's TV movie *The Hobbit* (1977), or the cinematic flop *The Lord of the Rings* (1978) and the televised special "The Return of the King" (1980). The animation was of poor quality, significant plot points from the books were changed or left out, and fans felt that the films were being wrongly oriented towards a children's audience. With Ralph Bakshi's animated version of *The Lord of the Rings*, fans had major complaints over the exclusion of Tom Bombadil and the changing of Saruman's name to Aruman. More significantly, with "The Return of the King" major characters such as Legolas and Gimli were simply removed from the finale. These early visual texts were largely ignored by the fans of Tolkien and the book trilogy, who felt that Tolkien's voice and vision had been mutilated and changed too much from their original source.

    With the advent of e-mail, usenet groups, and web sites, fans had a new medium in which to share their fandoms and connect with other fans, facilitating a higher degree of activity and communication (Newman

Videogames). *The Lord of the Rings* and Tolkien fans were able to share and communicate across greater distances, no longer limited to their local geographic communities. Early fan sites dedicated to Tolkien, his literary works, and especially the trilogy made their appearance on the Internet. People shared information, bibliographies, and interests, and the original fandom surrounding the books and Tolkien's life became part of the early Internet culture.

The presence of online fans also worked to Peter Jackson's favor as he began to work towards bringing the book trilogy to cinematic life in the late 1990s. Early fan interest in the film trilogy quickly appeared on the Internet, and as far back as 1998, TheOneRing.net and Tolkien-Movies.com were covering all news stories pertaining to Jackson and his film deal with New Line Cinema. Before *The Fellowship of the Ring* was globally released in December, 2001, trilogy book fans and Tolkien enthusiasts were already discussing their concerns over the cinematic adaptation. Book fans wondered to what degree Jackson would stay faithful to the canonical text. Some had concerns over the casting choices made by Jackson, and had their own suggestions for actors: Bo Derek for Galadriel, for example, Sophie Marceau for Arwen, and Sean Connery for Gandalf (tolkien-movies.com: 2000 forums). Others were worried that the trilogy would again be too youth-oriented, or special-effects oriented. While some fans felt that the film version would help spark a renewed interest in Tolkien and his books, others feared it would detract from the authenticity of Tolkien's detailed creation. Fans were actively using the Internet to share their concerns about the adaptation, and to exchange knowledge about the making of the film trilogy.

One of the earliest major debates in the online fandoms was over the expansion of Arwen's role from the book to the film adaptation. Some fans felt that by expanding Arwen's role to a more predominant position, and developing the romantic plot line between her and Aragorn, Jackson was catering to the mass audience and not remaining faithful to Tolkien. Others felt that Jackson as the director had the authority to make changes based on his vision of the books. For example, Mark posted to the Tolkien-Movies.com forum:

> I respect the concerns of those who wish to see the movies as close to Professor Tolkien's original conception as possible. Yet, I have always felt that female characters were neglected in the Hobbit and the Lord of the Rings. With the notable exception of Galadrial [sic] and Eowyn, women, when present at all, tend not to be integral to the story and their characters are not developed (November 12, 1999).

By contrast, as Chris argued in the same forums:

> To make Arwen a rebellious, barely post-teen warrior princess goes far beyond stretching credibility. It argues that Peter Jackson doesn't understand or care about the central mythos of the LOR. Again, as many posters have said, this fact alone doesn't mean the movies will be bad. They'll simply have NOTHING to do with Tolkien. In which case, why bother? (February 22, 2000).

Jackson, recognizing that the previously existing book fandom would need to be interested and attracted to the film series in order for the films to be fully successful, worked hard to access these fans online. On April 7, 2000, New Line released an Internet-only teaser trailer for the film trilogy, which wound up breaking all previous records for film promotional Internet downloads (New Line Press Release, April 2000). The revised official web site was launched on January 12, 2001, the same day as the teaser trailer for *The Fellowship of the Ring* was officially released in film theatres (New Line Press Release, December 2000.) And instead of attacking existing fan sites for *The Lord of the Rings* over copyright and ownership control, Jackson made the decision to invite fan web sites to become part of the official web site through affiliations.

The Fellowship of the Ring sparked a firestorm of global interest. The first of the three films opened globally to popular acclaim and packed theatres. It succeeded in bringing old fans of the book trilogy and of Tolkien to the theatres, but also appealed to a different type of fan existing outside the Tolkien fandom. Fans of Peter Jackson as an oddball New Zealand filmmaker were interested in seeing how he could work with someone else's narrative. Fans of various well-known American and British actors, such as Viggo Mortensen, Elijah Wood, Ian McKellen, and Sean Bean, wanted to see their favorite stars in a new film. And those with a passion for science fiction and fantasy were interested in seeing whether a film of this genre could be commercially appealing and successful. Outside of the realm of the original *Lord of the Rings* fandom, these other types of fans were also engaged by the cinematic possibilities offered by Jackson.

The New Fan: *The Lord of the Rings* Consumer/Producer

Amidst the chaos of a three-year period where all three films were released commercially, a new breed of fan was born – the fan of all things *Lord of the Rings*. Some of these fans had never read the book trilogy and were inspired to go back to the original source after watching the films. Others fell in love with the film adaptation as envisioned by Jackson, and had no interest in the Tolkien material, fearing it would change their love of the films. Regardless, these fans of the films had an interest in *The Lord of the Rings* world that far surpassed book fandom, and became consumers on a scale never previously seen. All three of the Lord of the Ring soundtracks by Howard Shore have been certified Platinum in the United States, indicating that their individual sales each broke the one million unit mark. Each soundtrack attained Platinum status within the first year of its release, and they continue to be popular, as evidenced by the release of the original soundtracks, the enhanced CD versions of the soundtracks, and the 3-CD boxed set of the trilogy soundtracks. Each of the individual soundtracks, in addition to the boxed set, were also released in both regular and limited edition formats. Similarly, the video game for *The Two Towers* released by Electronic Arts for the Play Station 2 has also gone Platinum with 1.48 million units sold in the United States. And with the continuous global release of more and more *Lord of the Rings* merchandise, consumer desire remains stimulated to a high degree. Much of this had to do with the expansion of *The Lord of the Rings* into a marketing franchise. Outside of the release of the films, a mass-marketing campaign introduced related products for purchase, such as toys, board games, trading cards, video and computer games, membership to the official fan club, the fan club official magazines, action figures, DVD releases, and soundtrack scores for each film.

Fic Frodo Slash Frodo 145

Images 10, 11: A new breed of fan being identified through their consumer practices. (Photographs by Katherine Zion)

Fans of the film trilogy had a far more extension range of consumer products available for them, compared to the book fans up until the 1990s; the development of a fan base with more extended and sometimes divergent interests was thus facilitated.

This new generation of fans of the franchise became heavy consumers of cultural products related to their love of the film trilogy. They went to see the films in the theatres, often over and over again. They joined the official online fan communities through the trilogy's web site, and joined community discussion boards. They bought the DVDs as they were released, in theatrical and extended editions, individually and boxed. They read the books, and then went on to read the books that were being published in relationship to the films. They bought official merchandise, from replicas of weapons and chain mail, to collectible action figures. They bought unofficial merchandise, from knock-off collectibles and bootleg import DVDs, to pop culture magazines with features about the films or the cast and crew. They bought the licensed computer and video games to play at home, alone and with their friends. They learned all they could about Peter Jackson, the cast, and the crew, down to anyone who had even a vague connection to the process. They bought the soundtracks, and learned about Howard Shore, Enya, and Annie Lennox. In record numbers, fans attended the Museum of New Zealand Te Papa Tongarewa's traveling exhibition featuring the clothing, jewelry, and armor from the film trilogy. They attended galleries showcasing actor Viggo Mortensen's photography taken during the extended film shoot. And in Montreal, the sold-out live performance of the *Lord of the Rings* music conducted by composer Howard Shore was recorded for television broadcast and sold on DVD. It was no longer a fandom focused on Tolkien and his books, but rather a fandom attracted to and obsessed with any aspect of the *Lord of the Rings* franchise.

The relationship of fans to their interests in *The Lord of the Rings* is detailed and complex. While sharing a love and passion for Middle Earth, the fans themselves have divergent and extended areas in which they ground their interests. They consume different forms of content, and may not be interested in all aspects of Tolkien, Jackson, and the books and films. The fans may be insiders to one fandom, but outsiders to another, given the diversity of their interests. Within the overarching fandom, there are many internal debates, conflicts, and disputes (Hills, 2001). Some fans have been upset that the trilogy adaptation left out the significance of the relationship of Eowyn and Faramir, feeling that it was an important component to the books. Other fans were more upset with the presentation of Faramir in the films, arguing that Jackson made him seem more angry or nasty compared to the way the books treated him. With the announcement of the new *Lord of the Rings* stage musical premiering in Toronto in early 2006, some fans have already been debating the casting choices and arguing over the inclusion and exclusion of major plot scenes. Thus, fans have numerous different forms of relationships with the books, the movies, and the overarching *Lord of the Rings* franchise.

For example, one significant ongoing debate regards the very nature of what it is to be a *real* fan of *The Lord of the Rings*. Some people question whether fans of the film trilogy are truly fans if they have not read the original book trilogy. Fans of the book trilogy are often critical of those fans who became interested in Middle Earth after seeing the film, dismissing them as actor fans who have come to *The Lord of the Rings* fandom only as a result of interest in celebrity actors such as Orlando Bloom, Elijah Wood, and Viggo Mortensen. But those who have joined the Middle Earth fandom as a result of seeing the films argue their love of the films is equally valid to that of the book lovers, since it is the emotional investment that defines their fan status. Even within the book fandom, there are divisions between those who have read all of Tolkien's many published texts and those who have focused their interests solely upon the book trilogy. Some firmly believe that only those who have read all of Tolkien's works about Middle Earth are truly fans. And then there are the hardcore book fans who refuse to see the films under any circumstances, believing that any adaptation must by its very nature change the original expression. As Sophie L sums up in her posting to the tolkien-movies forum, "The fact of the matter is that I have absolutely no desire to see PJ's version of a story that is already completely, beautifully, perfectly drawn and brought to life – on the page" (August 15, 2001).

Yet, all fans are still inherently consumers of the mainstream popular culture that constitutes *The Lord of the Rings*: *The Lord of the Rings* is by no means alternative to, or outside of, the realm of the popular. The cinematic trilogy has all three films in the ten top-grossing films internationally, with their combined total gross standing at around US$ three billion (IMDB.com: All-Time Worldwide Boxoffice). If the revenue generated from official merchandise, DVD sales, collectibles, computer and video games, and other related sources is added, the figures go significantly higher. The success of the film trilogy, in turn, has driven even more book sales for the original Tolkien trilogy. *The Lord of the Rings* is a highly lucrative franchise with intense commercial success.

For fans, the commodification of *The Lord of the Rings* allows identification through consumer practice. Not only do fans connect to other fans through shared interests, they connect to one another through shared consumerism. It's not uncommon for fans to enumerate what they own that relates to their *Lord of the Rings* fandom as a way of making connections to other fans and establishing their status. Similarly, it also helps fans to distinguish themselves from fans in different fandoms, or from a general audience. Fans who collect different editions of the books are distinct from those who collect *Lord of the Rings* collectible action figures, though some fans may overlap in their interests. Someone who attends the film for casual entertainment has a different identity from a fan who engages in heavy consumer practices. For many fans, those who have only attended the films are not true fans unless they also engage in other forms of consumption of the Middle Earth world. Simply watching the films does not make one a fan; it is the expanded interest in all things Middle Earth that defines fandom. While the specific interests of fans surrounding *The Lord of the Rings* may vary, what unites them is their acceptance and enthusiasm for the franchise products and other related commodities. In this sense, the conceptualization of a fan has changed from having an intense emotional relationship with the object of interest to the commodification of that relationship.

While one unique feature of this film-influenced fandom is the broad range of fans' extended interests as consumers, another distinct feature is the intensity of fan activity. While the film trilogy allowed for fans to extend their interests as consumers of all things Middle Earth, the films also assisted in the development of even more active and interactive fans and fandoms.

For example, using the opportunities provided in cyberspace, new fans intentionally became their own producers of *Lord of the Rings* content. Creating fan web sites based on *The Lord of the Rings* film trilogy has become very popular. A simple keyword search for the phrase "Lord of the Rings" on any web search engine today will result in millions of hits for predominantly fan-based web sites. Fans use their *Lord of the Rings* web sites to host knowledge and information, discuss related news, create fan communities based on interests, and generally share their passion and love. Some fans create quizzes to test fan knowledge, while others create tests to help fans figure out which character best matches their personality. Fans have created their own original artwork, using traditional art tools as well as digital media, which can be shared through e-mail or by being posted on web sites. Some fans even sell their own artistic creations to other fans by vehicles such as eBay.com or fan sites. Creating new fictional content (fan fic) based on the film trilogy has also become quite popular, with fans creating their own narratives that build upon the canon of the films, and the books. For example, Nethien wrote a short fiction from the viewpoint of Faramir, as he contemplates his relationship to his father:

> I used to think you hung the stars in the sky, and now when I think of you, I just feel empty and cold. When I see you, I still feel the feelings I always felt. I still think you could move the Earth for something you wanted, if you truly wanted it, and that you can do anything. Thing is, there's something else there now. For the longest time, I could only say that it was a coldness. That's true, I felt extremely cold around you. Cold, empty, confused" (lotrfanfiction.com).

One popular satire series that circulated the Internet for several years was The Very Secret Diaries series authored by Cassandra Claire. Each character had his or her own diary, sharing private thoughts through journeys. For example, Day 1 of Aragon's journal reads: "Ringwraiths killed: 4. V. good. Met up with Hobbits. Walked forty miles. Skinned a squirrel and ate it. Still not King." While writing stories is one popular forum for actively producing content, creating visual tributes (fan vids) is another way in which the fans can engage with the films and construct their own multimedia products to share and exchange with other fans.

However, within the Lord of the Rings fan community, some fans are actually rejecting and distorting the mainstream popular cultural form of *The Lord of the Rings*. While some would possibly consider LOTR fans as being part of a distinct subculture, given the fantasy basis to the books and films, being interested in something as commercially successful as the cinematic trilogy is inherently part of broader popular culture (O'Brien & Szeman *Popular Culture*). The franchise-based products being purchased and consumed by fans maintain the norms existent in the books and the films. But within mainstream fandom are those who actively reinterpret the meanings of the books and films to give radically new and alternative meanings (Jenkins *Poachers*).

Specifically, slash authors of *The Lords of the Rings* content, regardless of their medium of expression, are deliberately reinterpreting the sexuality of characters to challenge heterosexual norms embedded in the dominant narratives. Slash fiction, in general, is understood as the erotic writing of popular culture characters into same-sex relationships. Within the slash genre, fan-written stories and fan-produced songs and videos recast friendships as sexual or romantic relationships. Sam's chaste love for Frodo in the books and films is re-established in terms of his sexual desire for Frodo. Similarly, some re-interpret the friendship between Legolas and Gimli in sexualized terms. For example, the web site Least Expected (femgeeks.net/tolkien) is credited with being the first *Lord of the Rings* slash archive, going live in 1999. It hosted hundreds of stories based on numerous different types of fan-created character pairings, from Aragorn-Boromir to Frodo-Gollum. The Library of Moria (libraryofmoria.com) is a large-scale *Lord of the Rings* Internet fan site strictly devoted to archiving slash for all character combinations produced by fans. One particularly fascinating combo is Shadowfax and Bill, the pony; another is the brothers Boromir and Faramir. Other fan slash archives are focused only upon the specific pairings of certain characters, such as a certain fan slash site called 'Feed You with a Kiss' (crickhollow.net/kiss/welcome), which features only stories based on the relationship of Merry and Pippin.

In this way, slash writers are producing original content based on the world of Middle Earth, and simultaneously giving new meaning to the relationships between characters. Megan Baggins, for example, writes with an NC-17 rating of Frodo and Legolas at a lake in the moonlight, with Legolas swimming and Frodo in the bushes, "gazing at his silken nakedness":

> Legolas, (being an Elf with extraordinary senses and especially keen hearing) shot up, alert. "I demand you reveal yourself in my presence" commanded the Prince of Mirkwood. Frodo took in a breath and revealed himself from behind the brush; not completely, but peeked his head out anyway. "Legolas, ah, only me, Frodo. I'm sorry, I was, um, I was just..." Frodo did not want the Prince to know he had been watching him with great admiration for fear of the Elf's reaction. "Ah, Frodo" chuckled Legolas "it's only you. Please, come down, I wish to speak with you". Frodo, a little afraid, stepped out from behind the purple clover bush and clambered down the dirt trodden rocky slope to the jagged rock edge of the lake. Legolas lie back again, treading softly in the dark water, watching the Hobbit intently. "You were watching me" he said, a smirk on his face and suspicion in his eyes. Frodo stared ahead, his mouth lay unlocked; he knew not what to say. Should he deny it? Dare he admit it? (libraryofmoria.com/frodolegolas/ahobbitinthehand.txt)

Fans are active producers of content, in addition to being consumers of *Lord of the Rings*. But while the franchise-driven products are marketed towards the mass audience and the fan base together, fan-authored products are explicitly for consumption by other fans, and are typically free. Most slash fiction and fan vids are freely available all over the web, and the only limit to access is the actual cost to access the Internet. In fact, one fan fic author was lambasted online in the fandom_wank blogging community after asking for financial donations by readers so that she could focus full-time on her fan fic writing (journalfen.net). Fan writing is assumed to be made by fans, for fans, with no financial costs to the reader. In this manner, slash producers are more closely identified as being part of a subculture to the larger popular cultural phenomenon of *The Lord of the Rings*.

It is incredible to think that a book trilogy about furry Hobbits, a golden Ring, and a war between good and evil, written over fifty years ago by an academic, could have become such a recognized and accepted part of contemporary popular culture. The original fans of Tolkien and

The Lord of the Rings have been fundamental in driving the success of the books for many decades, and for first establishing a fandom surrounding the trilogy and its author. Tolkien, having died in 1973, could not have foreseen the impact that the Internet would have in facilitating the further spread of knowledge about his complex world of Middle Earth. But Jackson, in his acceptance of the existing book fan base, and his use of the Internet to create additional audience and fan interest in the film trilogy, has been crucial in the development of a new generation of fans. This new breed, attracted to all aspects of *The Lord of the Rings*, has been the driving force behind the success of the film trilogy and related merchandise. The extended interests of these fans are broader in range, and linked to the commodification of Middle Earth, where their identities as fans are wrapped up in consumer practices. Middle Earth has thus become a kind of fan mall. These fans are also more actively engaged with the cultural products surrounding the *Lord of the Rings* franchise, including the development of fan products, commodities, and original content. The commercial success of the films has ensured the longevity of *The Lord of the Rings*, and its fans and fandoms will continue to grow and expand over the years.

Summer, and Back Again

It's been twenty-five years since I was first introduced to *The Lord of the Rings*. I re-read the trilogy faithfully ever year, and have kept the original books given to me by my parents so long ago. I've seen all versions of the books in film and television, and participate in *Lord of the Ring* communities and attend conventions. I am still an avid fan, and I still ride horses.

It's sunset and the sky is darkening above me as I near the end of my riding lesson. I'm tired, hot and worn out, and my horse, feeling the same way, is no longer listening to me. I'm frustrated and sore, but I keep an active hand and gently communicate with my horse, asking him through hand, leg, and body to relax and bend. The sky keeps getting darker and I can barely see his neck when I finally get him properly in hand. We click, and suddenly we're together and listening to each other. The motion is smooth and fluid and graceful, and for long minutes I am simply in the groove, being one with my horse. In those precious moments where we connect, I *am* a Rider of Rohan, I have pursued my fandom all they way *into* the territory of Middle Earth, which is now all around me, and *The Lord of the Rings* has become real.

The Lord of the Rings as Melodrama

Sarah Kozloff

Derek Brewer, a distinguished Cambridge don specializing in medieval literature, starts his study of Tolkien's literary work with this assertion: "My argument will be circular: both that to understand *The Lord of the Rings* we have to understand the true nature of romance; and that romance can be understood as the kind of thing that *The Lord of the Rings* is" ("Romance," 249). I wish to restate Brewer's sentence, with a key substitution. My argument will be circular: both that to understand the cinematic version of *The Lord of the Rings* we have to understand the true nature of *melodrama*; and that *melodrama* can be understood as the kind of thing that the cinematic version of *The Lord of the Rings* is.

  Strictly speaking, medieval romances are narratives about chivalry, written in the vernacular (not Latin), set in some pseudo-historical past, and often including separated lovers and sensational and supernatural events. Romances first appeared in verse form in France in the mid-1200s, and then spread to England, Germany, and Spain, quickly evolving into prose (Taylor *Introduction*). However, Brewer uses "romance" as a term of opposition to the novel, especially regarding the novel's aspiration towards realism. "Novel and romance," he writes, "are often taken nowadays to be much the same kind of thing, except that romance is inferior; it is taken to be debilitating, unrealistic wish-fulfillment, or abstract fantasy, whereas the novel shows life as it truly is, in all its concrete tragic elements" ("Romance," 249). Brewer argues, au contraire, that romance and novel are fundamentally opposed forms because the novel has as its mission to represent historical and social reality, while romance is much more closely tied to dream, folktale, myth, and religion, and to eternal psychic processes such as the passage from youth to adulthood. Therefore the archetypal plot of the medieval romance is the quest.

Melodrama, like romance, has had to cope with disdain, and in melodrama, as with romance, this opprobrium is often motivated by its departure from conventions of realism. However, whereas chivalric romance was embedded in the worldview of the Middle Ages and aimed towards the small fraction of society that inhabited feudal castles, stage melodrama evolved shortly after the French Revolution as a theatrical genre addressed to the urban working classes in France, England, and Germany. This genre did not produce individual masterpieces – the only playwrights whose names are frequently cited are Pixérécourt in France, and Holcroft and Boucicault in England – but flooded the cultural landscape with immensely popular commercial entertainments.[1] According to Peter Brooks, author of an influential analysis, *The Melodramatic Imagination: Balzac, Henry James, Melodrama, and the Mode of Excess*, melodrama came into being at this specific time period for an explicit purpose: to find moral and psychic truths in a "post-sacred" landscape, a landscape torn from traditional certainties by the bloody chaos of the Revolution and Reign of Terror (15).

In film studies, the term "melodrama" has been used in a variety of contradictory ways: sometimes to refer to the silent films that distributors themselves labeled as melodramas (nearly everything other than comedies was so labeled); sometimes to define a genre of classic Hollywood films featuring female characters and addressed to women spectators, e.g. *Stella Dallas* (1937) and *Now, Voyager* (1942); sometimes to refer to a cycle of films produced in the 1950s presenting hyperbolically troubled family dynamics, such as *Rebel Without a Cause* (1955) and *Imitation of Life* (1959). Further confusion has ensued over

---

[1] The plays collected by Michael Kilgariff provide a handy sampling.

whether melodrama should be studied historically or in terms of broader thematic and rhetorical patterns. In "Melodrama Revised," Linda Williams offers the most sweeping definition, arguing, "Melodrama is the fundamental mode of popular American moving pictures." She continues:

> It is not a specific genre like the western or horror film; it is not a 'deviation' of the classical realist narrative... Rather, melodrama is a peculiarly democratic and American form that seeks dramatic revelation of moral and emotional truths through a dialectic of pathos and action (42).

Williams sees the melodramatic mode everywhere, in films addressing familial problems and in more male-oriented action genres:

> If emotional and moral registers are sounded, if a work invites us to feel sympathy for the virtues of beset victims, if the narrative trajectory is ultimately more concerned with a retrieval and staging of innocence than with the psychological causes of motives and action, then the operative mode is melodrama ("Melodrama," 42).

Given J.R.R. Tolkien's profession as an Oxford professor of Anglo-Saxon literature, a small cottage industry has arisen tracing the connections between *The Lord of the Rings* and the canonical literature Professor Tolkien would have had ingrained in him: Norse sagas, Beowulf, *Sir Gawain and the Green Knight*, Milton, etc. (Clark and Timmons *Resonances*). I searched Humphrey Carpenter's biography for evidence that Tolkien was fascinated by the plethora of stage melodramas of his youth in Edwardian England (or that he was a movie fan) to no avail. Nonetheless, I maintain that the melodramatic imagination is clearly apparent in the literary original. Suggesting indirect, even unavoidable, influence from the pervasive cultural saturation with melodrama – Elaine Hadley argues that "a version of the 'melodramatic' seems to have served as a behavioral and expressive model for several generations of English people" (*Tactics*, 3) – doesn't seem much of a leap of faith. Although we shouldn't get too hung up on surface iconography, *The Lord of the Rings* does happen to be set in exactly the same landscape as hundreds of French and English Gothic stage melodramas featuring "castles, forests, mountains, and rushing torrents," peopled by ghosts and monsters (Booth *Melodrama*, 44). Moreover, just like the military/imperialistic British stage melodramas of the mid- and late nineteenth century, *The Lord of the Rings* foregrounds nationalism, battles, swordplay, last stands, and faithful comrades (Booth "Soldiers").

However, I am on even firmer ground in arguing that the move from page to screen has resulted in a clear intensification of the melodramatic mode, and moreover, that the pleasure of the New Line adaptation arises from the emotionality and psychological satisfaction of melodrama. This intensification is not, in my mind, a commercial cheapening of the original – although undeniably these decisions have increased the films' international success – but an artistically coherent strategy, well suited to the subject matter.

The Characteristic Traits of Melodrama

The various definitions of melodrama offered by numerous scholars emphasize a cluster of traits recurring under diverse exterior trappings. As a way of moving into specifics, let us here use the framework of five features that Linda Williams offers in "Melodrama Revised" as characteristic of cinematic melodrama. According to her:

(1) Melodrama begins, and wants to end, in a space of innocence (Williams "Melodrama," 65).

In actual fact, *The Fellowship of the Ring* begins with a voiceover spoken by Galadriel, encapsulating the brutal history of Middle-earth, i.e., the story of the Rings of Power, and the finding of the One Ring by Bilbo Baggins. The images accompanying this prelude have been filtered in camera and color-timed in post-production so that scenes devoted to power struggles, greed, battles, death, and destruction are a cold blue hue. When the present action begins with Bilbo's voiceover in the Shire, a striking visual change takes place. A new color scheme of green, red, and gold prevails. The green of the Shire grass is conspicuous and lush, filling the screen with a vision of pastoral paradise, and the warmth of the community is represented in the citizens' rich red waistcoats, the golden sunshine and, at night, illumination by firelight.

The landscape's visual appeal is ratcheted up by the lyrical Irish dance tune that accompanies the Shire scenes. Moreover, Bilbo testifies that Hobbits are simple, unpretentious folk: "Where our hearts truly lie is in peace and quiet and good tilled earth. All Hobbits share a love of things that grow."

Such stress on the Shire as a bucolic, communal paradise holds up this land as the vision of innocence the fellowship will be fighting to preserve. Much is made, in both book and film versions, of the Hobbits' lack of experience with the outside world, their sense of being outsiders to grand events, and their homesickness for this idyllic representation of rural England. When Frodo and Sam are climbing Mount Doom, the sign that the Ring wholly conquers Frodo is that he can't remember the Shire; after the Ring is destroyed we know he is himself again because he can recall his home's comforts and beauty.

A key difference between the books and the films is that in the latter the screenwriters, Fran Walsh, Philippa Boyens, and Peter Jackson, have cut out most of Tolkien's shadings that point to the stifling, parochial nature of the Shire and the small-minded vindictiveness of some of the inhabitants (including Bilbo). Most importantly, they have deleted the besmirching of the Shire at the end of *The Return of the King*, when Saruman and Wormtongue take their revenge by sowing pollution, destruction, and tyranny in the Hobbits' homeland. As Christine Gledhill notes, melodrama wants a return to "the Edenic home... and the rural community," in short, "'a golden past': less how things ought to be than how they should have been" ("Field," 21). In the cinematic *The Lord of the Rings* instead of suffering the shock of the Shire's despoiling the audience is allowed the traditional pleasure of melodrama – a return to an unspoiled place of innocence.

An alternate way to interpret the "place of innocence" is to think of it as the bosom of the family. Historians of stage melodrama point out how often these plots revolve around families being torn asunder and then reunited at the end. Curious, is it not, how little a role blood relationships play in Tolkien's original; Bilbo and Théoden are uncles, not fathers, and all biological mothers seem to have vanished like the entwives. Instead of family per se, both Tolkien's books and Jackson's films highlight intense loving bonds among friends. The films create pathos through recurring scenes of wrenching parting and joyous reunion: Bilbo abandoning the Shire/Frodo finding him again in Rivendell; Aragorn leaving Arwen/their reunion at his coronation; Gandalf "dying"/the comrades meeting him again in Fangorn forest; Aragorn being separated from his companions by a fall off a cliff during the battle with the Wargs and Orcs (an episode wholly invented by the screenwriters)/an empathic horse rescuing him and bringing him to Helm's Deep; Merry being left alone in Rohan when Pippin rides off with Gandalf/Pippin finding his injured comrade on the battlefield. Most notably, at the end of all their trials the fellowship is reunited at Frodo's bedside after the destruction of the Ring. The filmmakers emphasize the unbounded joy of reunion scenes through lines such as Merry's plaintive, "I knew you would find me, Pippin," and through slow motion, soft focus photography and emotionally resonant music.

(2) Melodrama focuses on victim-heroes and the recognition of their virtue (Williams "Melodrama," 66).

"Recognition" is a central trope of stage melodrama. Characters are often in disguise, or hiding past sins, or wrongfully accused. Lines of kinship – finding out that so-and-so is someone's long lost son – must be uncovered (think of *Oliver Twist*.) How often in *The Lord of the Rings* does a character need to be unmasked or recognized for what he/she truly is? Wormtongue turns out to be a servant of Saruman; Saruman and Denethor are revealed as being in league with Sauron; the "white wizard" turns out to be Gandalf; the slightly built horse rider is Eowyn in disguise – Eowyn's dramatic revelation of her identity on the Pelennor Fields offers a shivering *coup de theatre*. Most importantly, the dour Ranger, dressed in drab raiment (as Bilbo says, "All that is gold does not glitter") turns out to be Aragorn, son of Arathorn, heir of Isildur, King of Gondor.

One overarching strand of *The Lord of the Rings* is the "return of the king," the revelation that Aragorn is the rightful ruler, and the reinstatement of order implied by the restoration of a benevolent monarchy. The books and films treat this plot motif in distinct ways. For instance, Peter Jackson underplays Aragorn's arrival at Minas Tirith and the way the populace accepts him, but stresses Boromir's vow of fealty as he dies.

The climactic coronation scene in Jackson's *The Return of the King* is extremely revealing because its emphasis shifts from the crowning of Aragorn and the reinstatement of the line of Númenor to a focus on the superior value of the Hobbits. The book's emphasis is all on Aragorn:

> But when Aragorn arose all that beheld him gazed in silence, for it seemed to them that he was revealed to them now for the first time. Tall as the sea-kings of old, he stood above all that were near; ancient of days he seemed and yet in the flower of manhood; and wisdom sat upon his brow, and strength and healing were in his hands, and a light was about him. (*Return*, 304)

The film, however, quickly slides away from the regal moment (too antidemocratic?) to Aragorn's romantic reunion with Arwen (in general, the movies increase the quotient of the love story.) Then the emphasis shifts to what Tolkien himself once stated as his central purpose in the trilogy – "the ennoblement (or sanctification) of the humble" (quoted by Chance *Mythology*, 79). As Aragorn and Arwen proceed through the assembled multitude they come upon the Hobbits, who bow before them. Aragorn, however, demurs: "My friends, you bow to no one." While the Hobbits stand embarrassed, the king and the entire throng make obeisance before the four halflings. Brooks notes that stage melodramas included a "remarkable, public, spectacular homage to virtue, a demonstration of its power and effect" (*Imagination*, 25). This homage to the Hobbits on the courtyard of Minas Tirith constitutes just such a moment. One might wonder, why honor the Hobbits rather than any others who similarly acquitted themselves bravely in the war? The Hobbits are both humble (that is, little, not rich or noble) and innocent, merely bystanders to the conflicts of Middle-earth when fate sweeps them into the fray. The trilogy puts them through trials in which they undergo more jeopardy and suffering – pursued by Black Riders, half-buried in snow storms, chased by Balrogs, captured by Orcs, suffering starvation, thirst, fear, and despair – than Pauline tied in front of train tracks or buzz saws. There's a great

Image 12: **Paying homage to virtue, the Hobbits at Minas Tirith. Digital frame enlargement (Copyright © New Line Cinema).**

virtue in perseverance; Hobbits are doughty folk, and they surprise the big people (and readers and viewers) by their ability to bear up under constant onslaughts without wavering or losing their purity of heart.

As Williams states, "The victim-hero of melodrama gains an empathy that is equated with moral virtue" through his suffering ("Melodrama," 66). The insistent claim of the innocent, powerless victim (such as Uncle Tom or Eliza in Stowe's influential novel) to our sympathy is the wellspring of melodramatic pathos. Incidentally, this is why, of course, the cinematic *The Two Towers* offers numerous shots of children (each young character revealingly referred to in the end credits as "Cute Rohan Refugee Child"), clutching their mothers in fear in the caverns of Helm's Deep, sure to be slaughtered by the Orcs if the citadel should fall.

All the Hobbits suffer, but Frodo suffers the most. He is the one who is most frequently and grievously injured: stabbed by the Black Riders, grabbed into the air by the watcher in the lake outside the door of Moria, crushed by the cave troll in the fight near Balin's tomb, threatened by Boromir, stung senseless by Shelob, stripped and mistreated by the

Orcs who capture him in Cirith Ungol, maimed by Gollum's bite, and tortured by the power of the Ring. Since melodrama as a mode grants status to those who suffer, Frodo, the ultimate victim, becomes the transcendent object of value, instinctively cherished and protected by the rest of the Fellowship as if he were the young virgin of French melodrama or Lillian Gish in a D.W. Griffith film.

  Jane Chance, a Tolkien scholar, objects to the casting of the actors who play the Hobbits because of their youthfulness; she argues that Tolkien created the Hobbits as fully adult, and that Jackson has infantilized them (*Mythology*, 80). I believe that Jackson did this both for the commercial appeal to teenage viewers and to emphasize the Hobbits' vulnerability, powerlessness, and innocence. Ultimately, however, his casting choices also serve to *feminize* the Hobbits, particularly Frodo. Elijah Wood was only eighteen when principle photography started, and he has the fine features, large eyes, and long lashes of a girl.

Images 13, 14: Fine features, large eyes. Elijah Wood before *The Lord of the Rings*

This softness helps motivate the protective, chivalric solicitude lavished on him by one and all. That the cinematic Aragorn would lead the assembled armies to their presumed deaths at the Black Gate with the cry, "For Frodo!" illustrates how Frodo figures as an ideal of innocence and martyrdom.

(3) Melodrama appears modern by borrowing from realism, but realism serves the melodramatic passion and action (Williams "Melodrama," 67).

The behind-the-scenes footage included on the expanded DVD versions provides abundant evidence of the scrupulous attention to detail guiding the adaptation. From set design to makeup to armor, everyone involved in the project was obsessed with making every element as credible as possible. Peter Jackson once told *American Cinematographer*, "We wanted to create a feeling that we'd gone to Middle-Earth and were able to shoot on authentic locations... The mantra of our design work became 'Make it real'" (Magid "Imagining," 61).

Yet all this effort towards "realism" is in the service of the film's patently impossible, manifestly imaginary spectacle. Visual spectacle is the characteristic of melodrama remarked upon by all commentators. Historians of the stage lament how hard it is to recapture the thrills this theater once evoked: anecdotes about onstage snowstorms, water tanks, shipwrecks, special lighting effects, sword fights, dogs, horses, and elephants, may sound silly now, yet these effects completely mesmerized contemporaneous theatregoers. Like the theatrical in *Moulin Rouge* (2001), these plays were unapologetically excessive; they didn't understand the meaning of restraint; they could all have been titled "Spectacular Spectacular."

Certainly the cinematic trilogy operates through what Brooks calls the "aesthetics of astonishment" (*Imagination*, 24). Its production design could hardly be more perfectly awesome: the caverns of Moria, the Argonath statues, the city of Minas Tirith are impressive even to the most jaded filmgoers. The Black Riders terrify (even their mounts' hooves are caked with blood) and Shelob is nigh unwatchable to those of us with a hint of arachnophobia.

Brooks points to the expressiveness of tableau and gesture in melodrama (*Imagination*, 56). Time and again, the films unabashedly play out the body language of romantic daydreams: Frodo *grabs* Sam's reaching hand to rescue him from drowning, Gandalf dramatically *casts*

The Lord of the Rings *as Melodrama* 165

aside his grey cloak in front of the bewitched Théoden and draws out Saruman; with a flourish Aragorn *grasps* the newly reforged Narsil and holds it aloft, Sam *cradles* Frodo on Mount Doom and *carries* him up the mountain. Legolas's feats of elvish agility, patently aimed to thrill teenage viewers, are dazzling.

The rhetoric of the denizens of Middle-earth is similarly situated on a high plane. The screenwriters are careful to keep the speeches short, but the sentiments expressed and the mode of expression exalted (Kozloff *Overhearing*, 235-66). All of the following quotes are original to the film:

> Arwen to Aragorn: "I would rather share one lifetime with you, than face all the ages of the world alone."
>
> Aragorn to Frodo: "If by my life or death I can protect you, I will. You have my sword."
>
> Boromir, dying, to Aragorn: "I would have followed you, my brother . . . my captain . . . my king."
>
> Aragorn to his soldiers outside the Black Gate: "A day may come when the courage of men fails, when we forsake our friends and break all bonds of fellowship, but it is not this day."

The cinematography capturing these sets, actions, and dialogue is of a piece with the films' heightened drama. Andrew Lesnie emphasizes moments of import through slow motion, which allows us to linger extra beats over the Black Riders' dreadfulness, Aragorn's courage, or Galadriel's unearthly wisdom. This mise-en-scène does not sit back, offering neutral wide shots of characters; this camera jumps straight into close-ups, filling the screen with portraits of the characters' handsome suffering or noble heartbreak. Have there ever been so many swooping aerial shots, created with such a sense of speed and grandeur? This camera flies over Arwen and Frodo's race to the ford and Aragorn, Legolas, and Gimli's pursuit of the Orcs; it swoops down aggressively into the pits of Saruman's war machine. The camera swirls exultantly around the beacon lights from Gondor to Rohan, reveling as each new mountaintop bonfire bursts into flame, exulting both in the steadfastness of the alliance between the two powers, and in its own omniscience.

The camera is matched by over-the-top sound effects such as the shrieking of the Nazgul or the beating of the wings of their steeds. The music track, composed by Howard Shore, emphasizes every emotional wave through pastoral flutes, Celtic fiddles, and orchestral thunder. The choral musical backgrounds, performed by Maori-Samoan and English boys choirs, rely upon lyrics composed in Tolkien's invented Elvish and Dwarfish languages. This may seem superfluous, over the top, but nothing is too extreme for melodrama, the mode of excess.

(4) Melodrama involves a dialectic of pathos and action – a give and take of "too late" and "in the nick of time" (Williams "Melodrama," 69).

From the moment that Gandalf first suspects that Bilbo's ring may be the One, a clock starts running in *The Lord of the Rings*, and every second becomes part of a breakneck race to destroy it before it falls into Sauron's hands. In addition, subsidiary cliffhangers punctuate the overall arc of tension. Recall: Aragorn appears on the top of Weathertop to save Frodo from the Black Riders in the nick of time; Arwen and Frodo make it across the Isengard in the nick of time; the fellowship jump off the bridge in Moria in the nick of time; Merry and Pippin escape from their Orc captors in the nick of time; Arwen turns back from her path to the Grey Havens in the nick of time; Gandalf brings Éomer's host to relieve the siege at Helm's Deep in the nick of time; the Rohirrim arrive at Minas Tirith in the nick of time; Gandalf saves Faramir from immolation in the nick of time; Merry stabs the Lord of the Nazgul in the nick of time; the sacrificial feint towards the Black Gate pulls Sauron's Orcs and the Eye's attention away from Frodo and Sam in the nick of time; Frodo and Sam are saved from the lava of Mount Doom by the eagles in the nick of time. Watching the trilogy is exhausting not only because the movies are so long, but because we experience so many nicks of time; the narrative brings us to the brink of catastrophe again and again.

And sometimes it leads us over the rim. Melodrama evokes tears because sometimes it is "too late." Gandalf is one step too late leaving the bridge at Khazad-dûm – the Balrog's lash curls around his ankle and pulls him into the abyss. Emerging from the darkness of Moria to the (purposely overexposed) barren hillside, the remaining eight companions embody and stimulate the viewers' grief. Seeing the funeral pyre of Orcs left by the Rohirrim, Gimli, Legolas, and Aragorn believe that their heroic, breakneck pursuit over the fields of Rohan has been in vain – they are too late to save Merry and Pippin. Finding Frodo pale and lifeless from the spider's venom, Sam assumes he is too late to save his master from Shelob. To the extent that the first-time viewer shares the characters' range of knowledge at these plot points, he or she shares the characters' sorrow. However, either because Tolkien couldn't bear to kill off the characters he loved so dearly, or because, as Ben Singer notes, melodrama always turns to "outrageous coincidence, implausibility, convoluted plotting, deus ex machina resolutions" (*Melodrama and Modernity*, 46), in each of these cases . . . Surprise! Gandalf lives!! Merry and Pippin escaped!! Frodo was just stunned, not morally wounded!!! Viewers can rejoice the more for the pain they felt and survived. Other than the heroic deaths in combat of Boromir and Théoden, whose parting moments are suitably touching and prolonged, the only irretrievable loss in *The Lord of the Rings* is the departure of Frodo, Gandalf, and the elves from the Grey Havens at the trilogy's end.

Indeed, the larger pathos of "too late," comes from the price that the war to save Middle-earth will exact. The time of the elves will be over; they will leave their realms and sail to the West, taking with them their grace and enchantment. "A melodrama does not have to contain multiple scenes of pathetic death to function melodramatically," argues Linda Williams. "What counts is the feeling of loss suffused throughout the form. Audiences may weep or not weep, but the sense of a loss that implicates readers or audiences is central" ("Melodrama," 70).

"A sense of loss" is central to *The Lord of the Rings* on another level. I submit that both novels and films work to engender a bittersweet sense of loss regarding the narrative form per se. To experience *The Lord of the Rings* in either form is to be implicated in nostalgia for royal and grand melodrama presented without irony, offered with no apologies. Our culture has lost this type of story.

(5) Melodrama presents characters who embody primary psychic roles organized in Manichaean conflicts between good and evil (Williams "Melodrama," 77).

One of the great satisfactions of *The Lord of the Rings* is that there is never any doubt Sauron and all his minions are wholly evil; were they to triumph in this struggle they would enslave, torture, or destroy all the free people of the land. Thus, we can rejoice in Sauron's overthrow and can yearn without compunction for the death of his servants. The numerous, highly wrought battle scenes thus fulfill our (not very admirable) bloodlust and satisfy our craving for exciting action without engendering the slightest doubt or guilt.

The question of the goodness of the fellowship and their allies is a touch more complicated. Chance believes the novels' characters have been flattened out in the process of adaptation (*Mythology*, 79-85), because film viewers have lost many of the novels' incidents. Moreover in the move to dramatization, we've lost access to the flow of the characters' thoughts, as in this moment on Weathertop:

> Frodo was hardly less terrified than his companions; he was quaking as if he was bitter cold, but his terror was swallowed up in a sudden temptation to put on the Ring. The desire to do this laid hold of him, and he could think of nothing else. He did not forget the Barrow, nor the message of Gandalf; but something seemed to be compelling him to disregard all warnings, and he longed to yield. Not with the hope of escape, or of doing anything, either good or bad: he simply felt that he must take the Ring and put it on his finger. (*Fellowship*, 264)

Though Chance's argument has validity, actually I agree with Graham Fuller, critic for *Film Comment*, that the movies attempt to deepen the literary characters' psychological realism ("Kingdom Come," 25). This rounding out is accomplished both through nuances of performance and through plot alterations.

The films' cast breathes life into Tolkien's original characters simply by concretely embodying them, by giving them face, form, and voice. Although, as mentioned earlier, Jackson is not above incorporating a broad dramatic gesture or tableau for effect – with the exception of

Gollum and other villains – most actors work in a realistic performance style. They rarely shout or proclaim; they do not faint, tear their hair, or hold the back of their hands to their foreheads. Viggo Mortensen, Miranda Otto, Sean Bean, David Wenham, and Elijah Wood give naturalistic performances, working with small nuances of voice and facial expression; this allows viewers to read into these characters plausible and quasi-normal psychological motivations and emotions.

Another way in which the screenwriters seek to complicate their heroes is to emphasize – much more than Tolkien did – the way each is tempted by the Ring. As Tom Shippey, another Tolkien scholar, argues, the Ring symbolizes the adage, "All power corrupts, and absolute power corrupts absolutely." (Shippey astutely points out that despite the general assumption of Tolkien's debt to medieval sources, this is not a sentiment that would have been recognized in the Middle Ages; this fear of power as a corrupting force is a distinctly modern element of the trilogy [112-9].) The cinematic Gandalf, Galadriel, Aragorn, and Faramir have to struggle against the Ring's magnetism more than they do in the original; the screenwriters put each through a test "to show their quality." In addition to being so young, Frodo is weaker in the movies than in the books; he falls even more under the Ring's spell and distrusts his faithful Sam longer and more hurtfully. By emphasizing the characters' weaknesses and temptations, the film version makes them more credible, but also, paradoxically, more heroic for winning out in their struggle against their flaws. Whatever Jackson and company have done to increase the characters' plausibility, they have done not for realism's sake, but to aid viewers' absorption in the melodrama.

As for melodrama's slotting its characters into universal psychic roles, viewers will find it hard not to see Gandalf as the perfect, wise, testy grandfather, Aragorn as the adult finding his vocation, Arwen as the faithfully loyal female love object, Frodo as the adolescent boy who journeys to adulthood. Faramir represents the dutiful son, Denethor, the unloving father. Galadriel might be a mother figure, giving gifts and advice, and Eowyn symbolizes the tomboy/feminist (if this wasn't recognized as a common psychic figure in Freud's time period, it certainly counts as one now).

However, aligning the characters with psychic role models doesn't really work for the comic figures: Gimli, Pippin, Merry, and Sam. Time and again Jackson turns to these four for lighter moments, grace notes of non-heroic, more common behavior, such as Gimli's fatigue on the chase through Rohan, Merry and Pippin's greedy feast at Isengard, or Sam's lugging along worthless pots and pans. Yet these characters serve the narrative in a deeper way than just by providing variety and a change in tone. The traditions of stage melodrama help us understand their function; Michael Booth informs us these plays included "comedians," who served an essential task:

> The comedian – servant, artisan, or tradesman, usually a member of the working class and thus closely identified with his audience – is a friend or manservant of the hero, and sometimes carries on the battle against villainy . . . in the absence or incapacity of his superior. In many plays he is much better at coping with the villain than the hero is, and is frequently entirely responsible for the triumph of virtue. (*Melodrama*, 34)

Just as Frodo is a more accessible, more middle-class ego ideal than Aragorn, so Sam, the deferential gardener, the working class fellow, is even more accessible than Frodo. In many ways Samwise Gamgee is entirely responsible for the triumph of virtue in *The Lord of the Rings*, which is fitting, since he is the most modest of the modest Hobbits. Once again the texts work their way around to "the ennoblement (or sanctification) of the humble," which – since we see ourselves most clearly in these regular fellows – is the ennoblement of the audience.

Melodramatic Appeal

Clearly, the cinematic *The Lord of the Rings* evinces all the typical characteristics of the melodramatic mode. But the crucial question remains: why does this matter? How does seeing *The Lord of the Rings* as a melodrama alter our understanding of the films?

If knowing the conventions of Elizabethan drama enhances the experience of Shakespeare, then recognizing its debt to the conventions of melodrama enriches the experience of *The Lord of the Rings*. Viewers should realize that the texts did not spring uninfluenced from either Tolkien or Jackson's heads, but interlace with a rich and varied artistic tradition, one with which readers and viewers are already familiar through exposure to countless renditions throughout our cultural lives.

The perceived need to enhance the melodramatic qualities also explains some of the changes made during the adaptation process. At the same time it provides the groundwork for critics to examine the filmmakers' achievement. For instance, enhancing the roles of female characters in the filmic *The Lord of the Rings* serves as a contemporary corrective to Tolkien's male-centeredness and aligns the films even more closely with melodrama, which frequently foregrounded women as victim-heroines. Those who might cavil at the movies for their implausible plotting or their Manichean vision of good and evil are importing standards from realistic narratives that are simply irrelevant to this type of story. More perspicacious is Derek Brewer's insight that Tolkien would have enhanced his story's pathos and power by killing off more of the central characters ("Romance," 260-1). As Linda Williams remarks, "We must study melodrama as melodrama, not as a form that wants to be something else" ("Melodrama," 56).

Brewer's aim in *"The Lord of the Rings* as Romance" is to defend Tolkien as high art by putting his trilogy in the context of canonical authors of medieval literature such as Chrétien de Troyes, and to praise Tolkien's achievement in capturing psychic truths. Since his life's work involves teaching medieval literature, he hopes, through reaching the audience of Tolkien, to contribute to a deeper appreciation of the medieval romance as a literary form.[2] Similarly, I would hope that the millions of readers and filmgoers (a good number of whom are male) who appreciate either version of *The Lord of the Rings* would learn to have

---

[2] The scholarly literature on medieval romance, such as W.R.J. Barron's English Medieval Romance, offers strikingly similar terminology and concepts to the scholarship on stage melodrama. The influence of romance on melodrama-perhaps via the Gothic novel of the turn of the 19th century, which deliberately revived medievalism just at the moment when melodrama was gathering steam-may account for these echoes. Although both the romance and the melodrama existed as concrete historical genres with obvious distinctions in terms of form, presentation, themes and audience, the broader terms, "romantic imagination" and the "melodramatic imagination," both refer to the artistic impulse that is baldly emotional, anti-realist, and anti-classical.

more of an open mind about melodrama. "Melodramatic" does not mean cheaply sentimental, and the term should not be used as a synonym for "cheesy," although melodramas – like comedies, tragedies, or realistic fiction – can vary in quality. At their best, works in the melodramatic mode are deeply serious and ambitious. Brooks argues that melodramas feature "the effort to articulate the moral universe" (*Imagination*, 52):

> Melodrama from its inception takes as its concern and raison d'etre the location, expression and imposition of basic ethical and psychic truths. It says them over and over in clear language, it rehearses their conflicts and combats, it reenacts the menace of evil and the eventual triumph of morality made operative and evident. (*Imagination*, 15)

In the cinematic *The Lord of the Rings*, certain "basic ethical and psychic truths" are offered to make sense of a chaotic and threatening postmodern, global environment: the transcendent importance of friendship, loyalty, perseverance, courage, humility, and self-sacrifice; a reverence for nature; and the abjuring of the will to power. These values may or may not match viewers' hierarchy of ethics, and unquestionably they are insufficient guidelines for the quandaries of our times, but their emphatic restatement (to me, at least) is neither offensive nor inappropriate.

Regarding the thousands of stage dramas that used to entertain generations of the fairly recent past, Michael Booth observes:

> Essentially, melodrama is a dream world inhabited by dream people and dream justice, offering audiences the fulfillment and satisfaction found only in dreams. An idealization and simplification of the world of reality, it is in fact the world its audiences want but cannot get. Melodrama is therefore a dramatization of this second world, an allegory of human experience dramatically ordered, as it should be rather than as it is. (*Melodrama*, 14)

The Lord of the Rings could be thought of as *escapist*, because in watching these movies one leaves behind quotidian cares, chores, and life "as it truly is, with all its concrete tragic elements." But perhaps *idealistic* would be the more appropriate description, and hasn't one of the roles of art always been to offer us a vision of the ideal?

Masculinity, Whiteness, and Social Class in *The Lord of the Rings*

Lianne McLarty

Introduction

Not having read *The Lord of the Rings*, I had little awareness of the story beyond the degree to which it has become part of the popular imagination through various cultural forms, especially Peter Jackson's films. In fact, I had not even read the book until after I saw the first film and was asked to contribute to this anthology. Considering the cultural currency Tolkien's story has obtained, I find myself wondering how I could have missed it! I avoided reading it because I assumed it to be all about dragons and magic, and knights rescuing damsels in distress, in short, a conservative romantic fantasy. Yuck. But, then I read *The Hobbit* and was hooked. What I had dismissed as a tale that abstracts social relations onto unreal landscapes, promoting a kind of escapist happily-ever-after consciousness, was quite the opposite. In *The Hobbit*, for example, considerable emphasis is placed on material exchange as a primary relationship among characters. They expect to be compensated for their efforts; Bilbo helps the Dwarves for a reward. Much is made of money and the labor done for it. The landscape through which the characters move is indeed magical, but it is also understood in terms of industry, mining, and the production of material goods. This anchoring of the action in the social relations of modernization and industry is also evident in *The Lord of the Rings*. Certainly there is romance and magic but the story is more an engagement with everyday life than a fantastic escape from it. And, it is more about the threats that are structured within social relations than about the tribulations of romantic love.

Certainly, the films make sense in relation to a variety of genres. They are a sort of war-road-melodrama fantasy. But, given that "the free peoples of Middle Earth" are in violent conflict with the monstrous armies of Saruman and Sauron, Jackson's films may also be understood in terms of the horror genre. Not only are there monsters but the very idea of difference (embodied in various races) structures the social relations among the characters. This focus on difference (both benign and monstrous) invites a comparison with the horror genre. More specifically, with landscapes marked by social and historical contingency these films recall the so-called postmodern (post-*Psycho*-post-*Exorcist*) horror film that imagines an internal rather than an external threat and a monstrous self more than a monstrous other. Like such horror films, *The Lord of the Rings* films invoke the practices and institutions of a familiar (if fantastic) world as a source of threat, and construct monsters that defy a clearcut separation between "them" and "us." The fantastic landscape of Middle Earth, far from being abstract, is very much characterized by cultural practices; it bears the marks of history.

Responding to fans who object to the films' departures from Tolkien's novel, Jackson observes that "there is no definitive *The Lord of the Rings*."[1] While there is never a single definitive adaptation or analysis of any novel or film (meaning is not fixed), Jackson's remark is particularly salient given the popularity of the story and the cult status it has obtained. For some, there is an expectation of authenticity, truthfulness, and faithfulness to an original over which a certain kind of ownership is exerted. Ironically, this is expressed toward a narrative that

---

[1] In this exchange between Philippa Boyens and Peter Jackson in the commentary that accompanies the DVDs, Jackson goes on to say that given access to technology, audiences could re-edit the trilogy in chronological order, thus creating another film. Given the appendices available in the various DVD versions, the possibilities for re-writing and interpretation seem endless.

is itself fantasy (by its very nature standing against an idea of an authentic "real") and one, further, that makes possession a problem. Tolkien himself, in asserting the dominance of the principle "applicability" over allegory, acknowledges that there is no definitive or fixed meaning of his work (*Fellowship*, xviii). In doing so, he releases it to the contingencies of history and the activities of interpretation. This contradicts the commonsensical attempt to account for the popularity of *The Lord of the Rings* by anchoring it to "universal" themes. Its popular impact is very often understood in the story's ability to access "eternal" human emotions and experiences and offer up a "timeless" tale of the value of friendship, loyalty, honor, faith, and hope in the battle between good and evil. These broad themes are indeed embedded in the text, but the narrative itself complicates a reading that brackets off history and social and political struggle. Tolkien's story situates its characters, and the relationships among them, not only within natural and at times animated landscapes but also within landscapes characterized by economic and social changes. Far from positing some universal notion of humanity and its nature, *The Lord of the Rings* locates a multiplicity of discrete subjectivities and proceeds to construct the relationships among them as a function of landscapes marked by history and culture, that is to say, by material conditions. Such a relationship between subjectivities and cultural and social practices reflects Tolkien's insistence on the interpretative possibilities implied by what he calls "applicability": rather than a direct and allegorical relation between his text and historical events, his meanings are not fixed but are open to different interpretations by different audiences in different historical moments. Against the fixed meaning of allegory or an abstraction that affords the story an apolitical timelessness, audiences are invited to read *The Lord of the Rings* in history as a means of social communication, as a site where particular meanings are negotiated. As popular commodity culture, *The Lord of the Rings* films escape the grip of both Tolkien and Jackson, mingle with other images and narratives within the cultural landscape, and enter into the arena of ideological struggle.

The politics of Jackson's films may be read not only in relation to the ways in which they imagine a familiar landscape as a source of horror but also, and more specifically, in terms of how they stage a struggle within patriarchy, casting masculinity in a dual role, at war with itself. What is monstrous in *The Lord of the Rings* is a particular masculinity that appears as a will to dominate nature as well as subjects. What further accounts for the critical stance of these films is the construction of variant masculinities that not only offer a progressive range of expression but undercut notions of fixed gender identity. Indeed, in the pluralistic world of Middle Earth, identities are multiple and difference is not necessarily monstrous. Yet, the expression of difference is restricted to a range of whiteness. It is not so much an inclusive undermining of a universalized white subject as a presentation of a hierarchy of whiteness dependent on conceptions of social and class status. To put it simply, the more a Middle Earth race is associated with the privileges accrued through learning and knowledge and with refined cultural production the whiter they are, almost whiter than white in the ethereal light of the Elves, for example. The lower levels of this hierarchy of whiteness are invoked through working class imagery (the Dwarves are miners) and through classist constructions of cultural crudeness and uncouth behaviors. It is the crude behavior of the "less white" that is exaggerated and used not only to locate the enemy as a site of disgust but also to code the monstrous as not white. The enemy is an undifferentiated mass, all darkness and fire cast against impossible light and illumination. Whiteness in *The Lord of the Rings* relies on a monstrous "non-white" other to differentiate it; it depends on constructions of class and race to give it meaning and lend it legitimacy. While fear is directed in these films toward a familiar social world, there is a way in which they contradict their own progressive stance about masculinity and the critique of patriarchy as a will to power, by relying on class and race differences to express it.

The Fires of Industry

The horror of the social world conceptualized by *The Lord of the Rings* is that of modernization and industrialization and a conception of progress as the domination of, and control over, nature. This adversarial stance towards nature is represented in part by Saruman, who exerts an oppressive and monstrous mastery over animals, crows, and wargs, for example, and by Isengard, shaped as it is out of sharp spikes and black volcanic rock. With its fiery pits and harsh sounds of forging metal, Isengard is evocative of a nineteenth-century factory carved into the earth itself. As Treebeard says of Saruman, "He has a mind of metal and wheels." His "factory" is a site intended solely for the manufacturing of armor, weapons, and Orcs, and nature is the raw material for their production. Saruman promises that the old world "will burn in the fires of industry," and Fangorn Forest indeed does. His is a war economy and Isengard his military-industrial complex. He is breeding – manufacturing – an army. Moria, too, as the place where the rings were forged, is a site of production. As with Isengard, the landscape around it is visualized as fiery, desolate, rocky sameness which supports no growing things.

Against this industrialized landscape (which suggests the production of cultural goods) "the ring of power" takes on qualities of the fetishized commodity in capitalist societies. In part, the problem of the ring is that human relations come to be understood through it; "the one ring" mediates relationships among diverse characters. Like the commodity described by Marx, the ring appears to have a life of its own. That the ring is a character or has subjectivity is suggested by the films' prologue, told from the ring's perspective. It is attributed with a gaze of its own that the audience shares (near the beginning of *The Fellowship of the Ring* the ring is given a point-of-view shot of Gandalf). It has its own subjectivity and agency, its own intentions and voice. In contrast to this, the mass of generally faceless Orcs has no subjectivity. Against the subjectivity of the ring, Orcs are things, reified labor. They are products of industry, manufactured and visualized as a burned, scarred, and mutilated mix of metal and flesh, their wounds repaired with metal slats and nails.

The horror of the ring is that it drains the bearer of his or her subjectivity. Sméagol endures the most radical transformation while he possesses it, forgetting his own name, mutating into something other, Gollum, as the ring consumes him. Gollum's refrain, "It's mine. My own. My precious," not only invokes extreme possessiveness but ties the ring to the subjectivity of the bearer. Sméagol is more interested in fish. Even Sméagol's voice (suggestive of personal identity) changes as the ring possesses him. Bilbo's sense of self is also threatened; the ring results in his feeling "stretched thin" and at one point mutating, his face taking on monstrous qualities as he attempts to grab it from Frodo. The hypothetical portrayal of Galadriel should she take the ring imagines a transformation into a terrible queen. That she comments in this state that she will "remain Galadriel" signals the ring's impact on identity. The monstrousness of the ring is possession: both the desire to possess it and its possession of the bearer. Through the ring, possession is fused with subjectivity. Through the ring, which takes on a life of its own, the subject is drained of human agency as the ring possesses him or her. Through the ring, people are subjected to surveillance by Sauron's lidless eye ("always watching"), suggestive of the power of the disembodied gaze in Foucault's analysis of the panopticon. It is this will to power and the consequences for those subjected to it that constitutes horror in *The Lord of the Rings*. What is monstrous is leveling the plurality of Middle Earth under the domination of the one ring.

The will to power and control is the only unambiguous threat in *The Lord of the Rings* and it is not located in an abstract notion of absolute "evil" but in oppressive material conditions and the characters' relationships to them. Indeed, apart from Sauron (who "embodies") this disembodied will to power) no one is "altogether evil." As in the progressive horror film described by Robin Wood, there is a refusal of a clear-cut opposition between good and evil (Wood "Introduction," 1979). This is most evident in the slippage between Sméagol and Gollum. He is figuratively beside himself, split. His internal conflict, his split subjectivity ("He loves and hates the ring as he loves and hates himself") is visualized in the shot/reverse shot presentation of Sméagol's arguments with Gollum. Reminiscent of David Cronenberg's heroes, whose humanity is invaded by monstrous forces, Sméagol (once one of the River Folk) graphically mutates into Gollum. A victim of the ring's terrible power, he is enslaved. Similarly, Orcs, once Elves "taken by the dark power," are slaves to the will of Saruman, "tortured and mutilated," living "a ruined and terrible form of life." The Uruk-hai, too, are servants,

Frankensteinian monsters bred "for a single purpose." Once "kings of men," the Wraiths have been manipulated (like the Wild Men) by the power of the ring. Sympathy is invoked for the Cave Trolls;[2] at the end of the final battle, once the ring is consumed in the Crack of Doom, the Cave Trolls stop in mid-swing of the sword and make for home. Even Wormtongue was not born evil ("You were a man once"). Both Galadriel and Frodo could become monstrous like Gollum if they succumbed to the ring. As with Bilbo's monstrous transformation when he reaches for the ring, Jackson filmed but did not include – even in the extended DVD version – a shot of what Frodo would become if the ring consumed him. His connection to Sméagol is clearly made as Frodo begins to resemble Gollum.

This breakdown in the binary between good and evil is progressive, because it refuses to project the monstrous outward as the exclusive property of "the other" but recognizes its possibility in "the self." It also signals a lack of fixity or unity in the subject. Rosemary Jackson argues that fantasy's subversive potential is tied in part to the "category of character" due to its focus on metamorphosis, on "the instability of natural forms" (Jackson *Fantasy*, 81). "It is precisely this subversion of unities of 'self' which constitutes the most radical transgressive function of the fantastic" (83). Fantasy rejects a unified character and with it the category of "the real." It "draws attention to difficulties of representation and to conventions of literary discourse" (84). This subversive function of fantasy is suggested not only by the indeterminacy of character in *The Lord of the Rings* but also through the emphasis on the diverse cultural practices engaged in by the characters. The act of storytelling frames the film and the characters within it. Bilbo begins transcribing the tale, Frodo continues it and passes it on to Sam to finish ("Each of us must come and go in the telling"). Culture shapes the characters and their understanding of the social world (Frodo is introduced reading, Gandalf singing). Sam makes direct reference to stories. He and Frodo wonder if tales will be told about their adventure

---

[2] In the DVD commentary, Peter Jackson indicates that he intended some sympathy for the Cave Trolls, imagining their mothers waiting for their return with a glass of milk. He means for them to be seen as creatures who got in with the wrong crowd and not "evil at heart."

and in *The Two Towers* he rallies Frodo with his monologue about "the great stories." In foregrounding the act of storytelling the trilogy constructs, not a naturalized landscape but one inscribed with culture and history.

If this landscape may be seen as a series of signs, the signs do not necessarily have fixed meaning. Nature is sentient; it has history and language. Legolas tells Gimli that the "forest is full of memory and anger." Treebeard writes and recites poetry and mourns the death of trees that "had voices of their own." The landscape speaks to, or is read by, the characters: Aragorn listens to the ground and reads the terrain to find Pippin and Merry; Gimli discerningly tastes Orc blood; Legolas reads the sky and senses that "blood has been spilled." The Landscape is a language. The films visually manifest Middle Earth as readable through the cultural artifacts and ruins it contains. The history of the Dwarves is carved into the walls of Moria; the paintings in Rivendell tell the story of Isildur's battle with Sauron. The landscape embodies layers of civilization, and is written with history. Architectural ruins and historical statuary punctuate the imagery (note Bilbo's frozen trolls that Frodo passes before the battle that ends Boromir's life). The circulation of signs marks Middle Earth. The emphasis on ruins suggests not only that subjectivity is produced through culture but also that cultural practices are only partial, ruined. The head of the statue that serves as the backdrop for Frodo's fight with Boromir does not tell a whole story, nor does the ruined Weathertop. Gandalf admits this instability of knowledge: "I don't know, Frodo. I don't have any answers."

In *The Lord of the Rings*, then, subjectivity is produced through culture, not essentialized. Thus it is in flux. With no unified, stable subject, the trilogy is about characters becoming more that being. It is through this refusal of the stability of identity that the films access the category of masculinity. The battle over masculinity in Middle Earth is a struggle between maleness (variant and shifting masculinities) and the patriarchal will to power that results in an industrial wasteland.

The Battle for Middle Earth Masculinity

It is oppressive power and control over subjects and the natural world that constitutes the monstrous in *The Lord of the Rings*. Set within an opposition between nature and industry, masculinity is alternately characterized as the will to shape the world according to a single vision or as a continuum of diverse and multiple positions. When Aragorn is crowned he says, "This day does not belong to one man, but to all." This sense of inclusiveness is in stark opposition to Sauron's one eye, "one ring to rule them all." Masculinity, then, is not fixed. Middle Earth is awash with male difference coded racially or ethnically. The "Elvish prince" mingles with the artisan Dwarf. Further, using the relative relation to nature of different male subjects, *The Lord of the Rings* disengages maleness from patriarchy and in doing so not only offers a spectrum of masculinities but holds the "Law of the Father" responsible for a potential apocalypse. Sauron, Saruman, and Denethor embody a dominating patriarchy that threatens to transform the natural world according to its own singular vision. Even Theoden, possessed by Saruman, is the image of the "bad father" and in some ways a failure. Of Eowyn he says, "I should have loved her as a father." These old "kings" have outlived their usefulness. Referring to his own inadequacies, and Aragorn's heroics, Theoden admits, "It was not Theoden who led his people to victory." In *The Return of the King*, he counsels Eowyn: "Do not grieve for those whose time has come, you shall live to see these days renewed." Renewal in the universe that the films depict means that patriarchy – to borrow from Sméagol's command to Gollum – must "go away, and never come back." It must be dismantled altogether, not just rehabilitated into a "kinder, gentler patriarchy": in flames, Denethor jumps from the walls of Minas Tirith; Saruman is washed away; and what is left of Sauron and his armies is consumed by the very earth he seeks to possess and exploit.

In battle, multiple male subjects are in the process of becoming. Gandalf the Gray becomes Gandalf the White, Aragorn becomes king, and Sam becomes a hero. Patriarchy is destroyed and replaced by male characters who do not seek power as a means of controlling others. Unlike the male heroes of many mainstream films (played by the likes of Sylvester Stallone and Arnold Schwarzenegger) those of *The Lord of the Rings* do not set out to be heroes. They are reluctant. This is perhaps most clearly exemplified by hobbits. Slight in relation to the "big folk," Frodo and company are anti-patriarchal heroes, demonstrative of a masculinity that depends on a "connection with" rather than a "disengagement from" other people. Hobbits are illustrative of male subjects who are neither fixed in their masculinity nor fixated on power. In fact, value is placed on nurturing relationships between them: Pippin assures the wounded Merry, "I'll look after you." Sam makes sure Frodo eats, cooking for him and sacrificing his own Elven bread. Sam's relationship to Frodo is as a nurturer, his masculinity expressed through signifiers usually reserved for female characters in mainstream films; he battles the Cave Troll with a frying pan and brings salt from the Shire in case he needs to roast a chicken. And at Sam's wedding, significantly, it is Pippin who catches the bride's bouquet.

The males endorsed in *The Lord of the Rings* do not exert a will to power over social or natural landscapes. Rather than occupying an adversarial position with respect to nature, the males of Middle Earth (exemplified by hobbits who literally live under hills) love "growing things and good tilled earth." The elves are the magical manifestation of this: they woke up the trees and taught them to speak. Positioned between magic and farming, both Aragorn and Gandalf have the ability to communicate with their horses (significantly Orcs do not ride horses). The culture of the Rohirrim is dependent on horses for its aesthetic: horsetails distinguish their helmets and horses figure as decorative motifs in Edoras. The architectural and art historical styles of the "good" peoples of Middle Earth who are referenced in *The Lord of the Rings* are not only "postmodernly" diverse (as though the films are a kind of Third Age *Learning from Las Vegas*) but are importantly set within, rather than against, the natural landscape. Helm's Deep, for example, is built into a rock face whose caves provide sanctuary for the people of Rohan. Lothlorien is integrated into trees and its structures shaped according to the fluidity of natural forms. The dissolution between inside and outside, and the consequent inability to tell the difference, defines Rivendell. Minas Tirith is built into a cliff, its tiered structure determined by the contours of the surrounding geography. Given the variety of ways in which patriarchal culture fuses nature with "the feminine" (de-politicizing them both), the fact that these films value masculinity in relation to – rather than against – nature is a progressive gesture.

Although the politics of feminism are not foregrounded in *The Lord of the Rings* (and it would be a stretch to argue that it constitutes a feminist critique of patriarchal ideology), it is important to note that the films do not renegotiate masculinity at the expense of female characters. They do not absorb and displace female subjectivities or feminism as a critical discourse in the interests of promoting the illusion of patriarchy without power. It is Galadriel's voice, after all, that provides the introduction to Middle Earth and tells the history of the ring, the history of male subjects. The trilogy presents at least a duality with respect to female subjectivities. This is suggested in the differences between the Eowyn (a "shield maiden of Rohan," a warrior who defiantly declares "I am no man!" when she slays the Lord of the Nazgûl), the more traditionally depicted Galadriel, and the "love interest" Arwen. Even Arwen is given an active role in the films (she rescues Frodo), more, indeed, than she is afforded in the novel. Yet it is also true that the social landscape is marked by the relative absence of female characters. As Gimli points out, "You don't see many Dwarf women." There are no Entlings because the Entwives have been lost. In fact, with the exception of Aragorn's visit to his mother's grave and the hobbit mother with her brood at Bilbo's party, there is a general absence of mothers in these films. Middle Earth (or at least the predominant heroic action there) is male.

However, the enemy is distinguished from the other races of Middle Earth by a *masculine exclusivity*. There are no female Orcs, here now, in the past, or in the imagination. Male Orcs are "born" wholly formed, notably without mothers. Thus, *The Lord of the Rings* does not associate the monstrous with female biology, as do some horror films (for example, in the depiction of a woman breeding multiple children on her own and on the outside of her body in *The Brood* [1979] [Creed

Monstrous Feminine; Bell-Metereau "Searching"]). Indeed, what is monstrous in the trilogy is reproduction set within the context of patriarchal masculinity without women. Breeding Orcs and Goblins in the "fires of industry," Saruman is responsible for monstrous creation. Such a system is able to reproduce monsters only in monstrous ways. This destructive pattern is contrasted with the earthy, agricultural style of reproduction exemplified by hobbits' "love of growing things." Of the hobbit mother with many children Bilbo comments, "My, you have been productive!" Although the trilogy privileges the homosocial non-sexual relations among men, the ending may be read as progressive: while the films' closure is characterized by all of the ingredients of recuperation according to the ideological imperatives of the nuclear, heterosexual family, it works to emphasize the "female" (as embodied in males). Sam, the gardener, makes things grow. He is associated with an agricultural style of reproduction. Given the films' emphasis on fathers and sons, it is also significant that in the final shot Sam holds his female child. But although *The Lord of the Rings* films do not resort to misogyny in their progressive stance toward masculinity, they do depend on problematic conceptions of class and race.

Armies of Darkness

Degrees of whiteness depend on culture and social class and it is through a class displacement that the "less than white" character of the enemy is secured. The enemies of Middle Earth are characterized by darkness, in contrast to the extreme luminosity of those who are most white ("fair" and "wise"), the Elves. When faced with Gandalf's blaze of light as he rides to the rescue at Helm's Deep, the Orcs and the enemy mass squint helplessly (more accustomed as they are to the cover of darkness). Behind his dark helmet, the Lord of the Nazgûl is only a pit of blackness. In fact the enemy is characterized as a black mass set against the earth tones, the gold, and the silver of the heroes' costumes. The legendary "Haradrim from the South and mercenaries from the coast" are costumed as being Middle Eastern, their bodies draped in robes and their heads covered under turbans. They have olive complexions, and of their faces only dark-rimmed eyes are visible (echoing the "great eye"). In opposition to the layers of "civilized" culture and art that characterize the landscape of the "free peoples," Orcs are tribal, their faces painted, their skin tattooed, their flesh pierced. They are defined by drums, not the orchestral strings that accompany the exploits of the "civilized" characters. Orcs are also manifested as cockroach-like, in the deep dark of Moria; it is not through culture (practices of the mind) that they have adapted to the darkness but through evolution (unconscious necessities of the body).

Orcs have no culture and therefore they are "classless." They have language (although certainly not the King's English) and can "speak," but their function as monstrous antagonists is communicated through grunts and growls, the beating of chests, and the stomping of spears. They snort through their face armor and one Orc has an iconic skull on his helmet. Monstrous forces are not defined by art, culture, learning, and knowledge but by the will to kill. Their armor appears mismatched, thrown together. Helmets are shoved haphazardly onto the heads of Uruk-hai and their weapons are crude and undecorated, not marked by the artisan. This is in contrast to the armor of the heroes, which is inscribed with the stylistic flourishes of their culture. For example, the Elves' armor mirrors the Art Nouveau style of their architectural spaces. Without culture and language, the enemy is an abject repository of dirt and disgust. The Orcs smell: Gimli sniffs and responds in revulsion when a fatally wounded Orc falls on him. Sam threatens Shelob, "Let him go, you filth!" During the Ents' revenge-of-nature destruction of Isengard, Treebeard says "the filth of Saruman is washing away." Orcs and their manufactured kin are also visual sites of disgust. Their features are misshapen, mangled and distorted; their teeth sharpened to spikes and decayed (this in opposition to the impossibly blonde and fine features of the Elves). Perhaps the most extreme representation of this visual horror is Gothmog, most notable for his command, "Release the prisoners." The monstrousness of his face is matched by his actions: he returns only the prisoners' heads.

It is arguable that the motif of organized meals and the social structuring they imply, helps to code characters as "civilized," as occupying an elevated social class. With their multiple meals, frequent cooking, and references to food, the eating habits of hobbits are central to the story. This is most clearly expressed in the distinction between the culinary habits of hobbits and those of the dwarves and other creatures. While it is Bilbo's hospitality to offer Gandalf tea, for example, Gimli looks forward to "red meat off the bone"; While Aragorn and Theoden discuss whether to fight or retreat, Gimli, apparently unengaged in the intellectual matters of state, eats and drinks, belching and slopping on his beard. Disgust is, in part, generated around these conventions of eating and their relative connection to social class and monstrosity. Orcs eat their own, raw; they are cannibals, going after the headless body of a fellow Orc like a pack of dogs, entrails flying. They eat men, too. Saruman promises them "man-flesh" as an enticement to fight. The Lord of the Nazgûl tells his fell beast to "feast on [Theoden's] flesh" in the battle at Minas Tirith. The films set up an opposition between the raw and the cooked. Sméagol insists "Give it to us raw and wriggling" in his debate with Sam about the relative merits of cooking rabbits. He bites into a rabbit and pulls out bloody entrails with his teeth. In *The Return of the King*, his mutation into Gollum includes an extreme close-up of him biting into a live fish with his deformed and rotten teeth, saliva dripping down his chin.

Even though *The Lord of the Rings* troubles an unambiguous distinction between categories of good and evil, self and other, the centrality of disgust is a reminder of the often contradictory positioning of the products of popular culture. Disgust reinforces the division between "normal" and "monstrous" bodies and is a central trope of the conservative culture of fear. It is organized around the idea of the organic, pure body, and depends on the physicality – the viscera, or in this case, the saliva – of the reviled object. Disgust is also a position offered to spectators, one that hinges on having or not having class, in terms of taste. It is doubly embodied, generated by the image of the monstrous body onscreen and experienced in the body of the viewer. Disgust depends on the physical reaction of the disgusted subject; it is manifested in a shudder or a gag of revulsion. The intense embodiment of disgust makes it a useful ideological strategy for managing social anxieties.

It is arguable that the category of disgust is rooted in the body and that it focuses attention on the visceral over the cerebral. To be disgusted is to have a physical, not an intellectual, response. Since disgust forces (or assumes) a disconnection between the mind and the body, privileging the latter, it also depoliticizes. Disgust is seen to be a natural bodily response and not an ideological position. The disgusted subject is not a subject of discourse, but one whose organic body reacts. Thus, reason is bypassed. It is arguable that disgust works to reinforce the idea of the essentially and universally human, by invoking the "universally disgusting," as though the labels "ugly," "disgusting," "revolting," and "unbearable" are not culturally determined. This logic suggests that if one is not properly disgusted when others are, one is either not human or less than human, because humanity everywhere is characterized by certain fixed aesthetic responses to the hideous. Disgust, then, has a dual ideological function: it works to enhance the biological identity of the disgusted subject at the same time that it singles out the non-disgusted as less than human. Disgust is a moral (as opposed to an ethical) category and implies that the disgusted subject holds a superior (more human) position. What is "disgusting" is essentially any opposition to the controlled body displayed by those with social status. The discourse of disgust defines and maintains distinct boundaries between normality and otherness. In *The Lord of the Rings* this is most clearly expressed in the difference between the cultured, proper, and ritualized eating habits of hobbits and the Orcs ravenously, barbarically, and habitually eating hobbits.

"…here, at the end of all things."

The Lord of the Rings is not ideologically fixed. It slips between reactionary and progressive stances, not unlike the Wraiths, neither living nor dead. It signals that popular image culture is a site for the struggle over meanings and interpretation and that the political is located as much within categories of gender, race, and class as in the undermining of "reality." It also suggests that historically positioning a narrative according to the time and place of its consumption influences the politics of cultural texts. As much as the circumstances of history, social definition influences how popular culture characterizes the monstrous, and the changing definition of "evil" over time influences the ideological positioning of cultural texts. The politics of the battle against Sauron shift as various interpreters understand them. Against the historical context of World War II the battle may be read as a struggle against fascism. But different meanings may emerge in the current culture of fear that shapes and motivates the so-called "War on Terror." In this ideologically charged narrative, the "civilized" world is at war with "barbarians" who whisper their plots in the dark corners of the world. Forces of "good" battle the "evil-doers" who originate in a "breeding ground" where they are "spawned" like "cockroaches" and "lethal mosquitoes." Discursive dehumanization of an enemy is achieved, in part, by provoking disgust by means of the images of rodents and insects, unclean domiciles (such as swamps and holes), and non-human breeding practices (spawning), all these being ostensibly outside the boundaries of "the good." *The Lord of the Rings* seems to occupy an unfortunate historical position as its depiction of "freedom-loving people" fighting a "great evil" slides into current terror culture that depends on a discourse of absolute "good" and "evil" to give it meaning. But the definition of "evil" may yet be redirected inward, the great eye collapsing in flames. In the words of Arwen, "There is still hope."

Urban Legend: Architecture in *The Lord of the Rings*

Steven Woodward and Kostis Kourelis

> *"Now and forever the architect will replace the set designer. Film will be the faithful translator of the architect's boldest dream"*
> Luis Buñuel

> *"The environments do become a character. That's the way of designing films really. You are looking for ways to tell the story in so many different ways, you know, not just the way that people are telling the story and acting out the story, but architecture becomes the story"*
> Grant Major, Production Designer, *The Lord of the Rings*
> (Jackson Audio Commentary)

Since J.R.R. Tolkien sold the movie rights to *The Lord of the Rings* in 1968, he must have suspected that his literary epic would one day be rendered in spectacular visual terms. It is ironic, of course, that while the trilogy dramatizes the conflict between a gentle tradition of land stewardship and the ruination of nature through machine culture (a conflict inherent to modernity that became Tolkien's obsession), it would be a technology epitomizing machine culture – the elaborate mechanisms and digital confabulations of the contemporary filmmaking enterprise – that three decades later would give the conflict a cinematic embodiment.

Through the same infernal technology that frightened Tolkien, Peter Jackson has created an alternate universe of intricately realized spaces and places, a materially bound Middle Earth visualized through the perverse amalgamation of stone with polystyrene and of flesh with latex, the secretive manipulation of propellers, cranes, cranks, rails, and smoke machines, and the uncanny operations of a labyrinthine computer network, the whole accomplished by a vast army of unseen laborers.

Steeped in a literary tradition of medieval epic, Tolkien had rendered his myth of the Ring of Power through an invented landscape. The fabric of Middle Earth was constructed as a fantastic version of Britain, one that Tolkien himself would have preferred to inhabit. Although taking cues from the Midlands landscape in which he grew up, the novels lack architectural specificity. In contrast, the movie is filled with spatial signification and architectural associations. Indeed, critics hailed Peter Jackson's *The Lord of the Rings* not only as a good narrative but as a masterpiece of set design, so much so that many actual props from the shooting were elevated to the status of self-sufficient art works, traveling as "*The Lord of the Rings* Motion Picture Trilogy: The Exhibition" through museums around the world (Schorow "Beloved").[1] Art direction for all three films produced nominations for Academy Awards, and *The Return of the King* in fact won. But given that this celebrated architectural vision did not take its cue from Tolkien's literary prototype, we may analyze it here as its own invented artifact.

In this essay, we will consider Peter Jackson's aggressive use of architectural form to tell a story. If the environments do become characters, we must evaluate those characters in relation to the traditions from which they arise. In the omission of architectural details, Tolkien makes a subtle argument about historical referents in the articulated space of fantasy. With an abundance of architectural details, Peter Jackson makes an entirely different argument appealing to the sensibilities of an audience schooled in the simulacra of visual narratives and too distracted

---

[1] March 13-June 4, 2004, Singapore Science Centre; August 1-October 24, 2004, Museum of Science, Boston Science Park; December 26, 2004-March 31, 2005, The Powerhouse Museum, Sydney Australia; June 5-August 28, 2005, Houston Museum of Natural Science; October 8, 2005-Jaunary 2005, Indiana State Museum, Indianapolis.

to fantasize. In these films, there is no room for subtlety but a call for immediate readability. Thus, although one might have expected the filmic challenge of Tolkien's fantastic epic to have warranted the creation of a new architectural language on a par with that of *The Cabinet of Dr. Caligari* (1920), *Metropolis* (1927), *Lost* Horizon (1937), *Blade Runner* (1982), or other movies of architectural inventiveness – and interestingly, Mark Stetson, who worked on the special effects of *The Lord of the Rings*, was chief model maker for *Blade Runner* – Peter Jackson's architecture is instead derivative of visual formulas developed by illustrators in the late 1960s and 1970s. A graphic (and hence flat) psychedelic universe is animated in space and time through special effects.

Beginnings in *Bad Taste*

As a filmmaker willfully restricting himself to the human and physical resources of the New Zealand film industry, Peter Jackson has always been pragmatically minded, and the massive *Lord of the Rings* project is no exception. The trajectory of his own filmmaking career demonstrates how he has harnessed his own strengths and interests, as well as labored to overcome his weaknesses.

A great fan of the James Bond films, and entranced by cinema's illusory potential from a young age, Jackson rapidly became a master of special effects. Indeed, his first feature, *Bad Taste* (1987), concentrates almost exclusively on over-the-top effects, primarily the evisceration by bullets, knives, and chainsaws of numerous humanoid aliens who have come to earth to harvest the inhabitants, beginning with those in a remote coastal village. Reminiscent of *Night of the Living Dead* (1968) in situation and with an opening nod to *Dr. Strangelove* (1964), the film draws more on Monty Python for its characterization and setting, with Jackson satirizing both his heroes and the community they have come to save. The humble domestic architecture and almost-vacant landscape add to this self-effacing ethos, but serve primarily as backdrop for the grotesquery in which Jackson clearly delights. Spaces and places are not part of the deeper experience of the film, as his explanation of his working method reveals: "There's a funny thing going on there where you're building the effects and thinking of a story to link them, and suddenly at the end of the day (actually four years later) you've got a movie and you're a filmmaker." Indeed, Jackson himself called his first three films, including *Bad Taste*, *Meet the Feebles* (1989) and *Dead Alive* (1992), "splatstick" or "splatoons" ("Peter Jackson Bio").

By the time Jackson worked with Grant Major and Richard Taylor on *Heavenly Creatures* (1994), the first of his films to achieve any kind of critical acclaim, he had developed a more complex understanding of the tactile possibilities of approaching space. The film begins with an early 1950s style documentary that literally maps out the city of Christchurch, charting its parks, city center, and schools, but ultimately representing it as a well-ordered, unthreatening "city of cyclists." Against this relatively static introduction, Jackson cuts to fast-tracking shots of two screaming, bloodied girls (Melanie Lynskey and Kate Winslet) running along a country path. From this point on, a highly mobile camera continuously tracks, booms, circles and tilts, often to the music of Mario Lanza, suggesting the giddy exhilaration of the two girls as they immerse themselves in their friendship, their shared medieval fantasy world of Borovnia, and the "fourth world," all of which represent an escape from the staid and parochial environment of their parents.

Despite the obvious association between Borovnia and Middle Earth, Jackson only considered making *The Lord of the Rings* after plans for a remake of *King Kong* fell through and he had to find another project that could utilize the increasing resources of his own effects company, Weta. In crucial ways, Tolkien's trilogy was a natural, if unwieldy, second choice, allowing Jackson to work with special effects to an unprecedented degree, to capitalize on New Zealand's sublime landscapes, and to explore the epic possibilities of cinema, something that had clearly impressed him in such films as Sergei Bondarchuk's *Waterloo* (1970) (Pryor *Peter Jackson*, 244). The great challenge, though, would be to create not merely a narratively delimited dreamworld like Borovnia but a fully realized fantasy world, a seamless alternate space in which the epic action could unfold.

Borrowed Fantasies

For all *The Lord of the Rings*' innovations in this regard – the digital manipulation of size and the fusion of the real and the virtual – the architectural environments were not designed afresh, but derived directly from a book. In 1991 the Houghton Mifflin Company celebrated the centennial of Tolkien's birth by hiring graphic designer Alan Lee to illustrate a new edition of the *The Lord of the Rings*. Lee had established himself as a leading illustrator of children's literature, especially of tales based on Celtic and Norse mythology. His illustrations for *Faeries* (1978) and *The Mabinogion* (1982) had earned him a great reputation in British children's books. As Houghton Mifflin had anticipated, the Centenary illustrations were extremely popular. Jackson wanted to replicate Lee's success in illustrating the books with the animated scenography of his movie and hired Lee as conceptual designer. Together with John Howe, whose cinematic illustrations typically emphasize moments of high tension in the narrative—Gandalf's confrontation with a fiendish and enraged Balrog on the precipitous Bridge of Khazad-Dum; Eowyn's defiant stand against the Nazgûl-mounted Witch King – Lee traveled through New Zealand to find shooting locations by sketching how the landscape before them might be made to appear in the film. In effect, Lee extracted his own drawings from the Centenary edition and implanted them into an actual landscape. By relinquishing creative control over the architectural settings, Jackson appropriated a visual system dated at least one decade prior to the movie's release. Lee's vocabulary (and Howe's to a lesser extent) became in effect Jackson's vocabulary. Compare, for example, Lee's illustrations of Rivendell, Meduseld, and the Black Gate, or Howe's illustration of Hobbiton, with Jackson's versions.

More problematically, Lee's designs belong to a style of drawing that dates back to the 1960s popular culture associated with psychedelia and the pastoral romanticism of the hippies. Taking its lead from surreal

Image 15: Pastoral view of the Shire of Alan Lee and John Howe. (www.tlotr.com)

art and specifically the dreamscapes of Salvador Dali, the figurative art of Lee's generation was rejected by the contemporary art world, which headed in alternative directions toward abstraction and the conceptual. At the same time, the visual exuberance of psychedelic illustration infiltrated popular culture, carving a market in genres of fantasy, science fiction, comics, posters, and rock albums. Particularly notable, for instance, was the work of Peter Max. The popular appeal of this style has thrived uninterrupted from the late 1960s to the present. Nor is it a coincidence that the infiltration of psychedelic art into British and American popular culture coincided with Tolkien's growing readership. As Nigel Walmsley has shown, Tolkien was canonized as a popular author by the hippie generation, and his book sales peaked in 1965-68; *The Lord of the Rings* provided literary fodder to the subculture of atavism and mythic pastoralism that emerged with them (Walmsley "The 60's"). Although psychedelia waned with the riots of 1968, its cultural influence persevered in the bedrooms of middle-class suburban adolescents through the rest of the twentieth century (and was surely not unknown to the seven-year-old Peter Jackson in Pukerua Bay, North Island, New Zealand).

Hollywood Down Under

Thus Peter Jackson chose to recycle a 35-year old marriage between psychedelia and Tolkien that had already proven a success in the ten-year old illustrations. As Grant Major observed about the source of the sets,

> It always began with Alan and John's pictures. Even before they both arrived in New Zealand, Peter Jackson would be talking about a setting or a scene and he'd reach for one of their paintings and say: "It's got to look like this!" When they joined the project, I simply wanted to harness their extraordinary talents and facilitate the creation of the worlds they envisaged. (Sibley *Making*, 47)

Jackson's reliance on this tested visual vocabulary, however, missed the opportunity of re-conceptualizing the scenographic space of the novel in terms of the "geopsychic space" particular to the cinema, as defined by Giuliana Bruno: "film is a modern cartography: its haptic way of site-seeing turns pictures into an architecture, transforming them into a geography of lived, and living, space" (Bruno *Atlas*, 8-9).

As early as 1920, the filmmakers of the German Expressionist cinema and their critics recognized the extraordinary potential of film to extend our sense of space, and began to develop a phenomenology of film's spatial and architectural language: "No longer an inert background, architecture now participated in the very emotions of film" (Vidler "Explosion," 15). However, the Expressionists depended primarily on set design for the creation of imaginary spaces that would, as Hugo Munsterberg observed, relate directly to the "inner movements of the mind" (qtd. in Vidler "Explosion," 17). Erwin Panofsky had noted, though, that film had a much greater potential for the "*dynamization of space*," not through the creation of sets but "through the controlled locomotion and focusing of the camera and through the cutting and editing of various shots" (Panofsky *Perspective*, 70). The Marxist critic and sociologist Siegfried Kracauer (who was trained as an architect) imagined that such potential could be applied, instead of to the fabrication of illusion, to a cinematic recasting and analysis of reality itself (Kracauer *Theory*). But Hollywood's cinematic code, as it developed after World War I, aimed not for such a critique but for the absorption of the spectator in the filmic experience, accomplished by maintaining the illusion of unity of space and time: "The cinema abandoned the architectural and theatrical model in favor of a literary one" (Ockman "Architecture," 173). It is the tension between these two uses of space – one primarily decorative and the other dynamically created; one based on literature's unity of space and time and the other drawing on architecture's fragmented vision – that creates the tension in Jackson's film architecture. On the one hand, Jackson is adapting an epic written by a literary scholar committed to the depiction of a fantasy world (which is nevertheless anchored to history). On the other, he is a filmmaker working (for the first time in his career) with unprecedented technical resources at a time when audiences are attuned to the discontinuity of virtual spaces as represented in such recent films as the Wachowski brothers' *Matrix* series (1999, 2003, 2003) and Hayao Miyazaki's *Spirited Away* (2002).

Undoubtedly, Jackson has gone some way towards realizing the potential of cinema's expanded architecture. To the extent that Tolkien's story is an epic, it organizes space horizontally and depicts arduous journeys through it. Not surprisingly, then, much of Jackson's film trilogy focuses on those journeys, set against sublime landscapes, and on the numerous clashes that result when two armies collide on a great plain.[2] Furthermore, Jackson's camera constantly works to place characters in uneasy relation to their environment. We often discover the protagonists only after the camera has scanned along the ridges of sheer-faced

---

[2] Jackson's psychological polarities belong to the aesthetics of the sublime where spatial extremes dramatize psychological states. Articulated by Edmund Burke as early as 1757, the sublime has been a constant source of reference in the film genres of horror and fantasy. The Piranesian spaces of the *Lord of the Rings* have formal characteristics – depth, light, color, point of view – that are tightly organized according to Gaston Bachelard's poetical system (Bachelard *Space*). Sublime extremes are, furthermore, enhanced by the extensive use of effects. What the viewer sees as small or large is frequently constructed by multifarious means. A helicopter flies over a mountain and films a bird's eye view of the natural topography, while a camera in the studio films a miniature set. The two views are digitally grafted into the movie's scene. Such conceptual and mechanical manipulations heighten spatial conflicts and dislocate the viewer. Inevitably, the movie's spatial effects are rooted in special effects.

mountains or surveyed bleak, frozen expanses. Dynamic boom, crane, and helicopter shots work to maintain the sense not only of diminutive heroes pitted against the landscape as much as against their enemies, but of a deeply unsettled reality on the verge of cataclysm.

At the same time, in the creation of the architectural sets Jackson has been entirely conservative, preferring to use his technical resources to reproduce, with an extraordinary degree of realism, Lee's two-dimensional book illustrations. As a result, the architecture remains superficial and engages the viewer in a flat iconicity. Of course, this is not to say that, in following the lead of the book illustrators, Jackson is not sensitive to Tolkien's themes, using the iconicity of the image to elaborate on the meaning of the epic conflict. For example, Tolkien's Middle Earth is a world in which the boundaries between the natural and the fabricated have dissolved, in which the synthesis of the two works either to idyllic or to monstrous effect. On one hand, the hobbit houses of the Shire are molded under the contours of gently rolling hills; the Elven habitation of Rivendell is enshrouded and interpenetrated by trees, cliffs, and rivers; and the human city of Minas Tirith takes the logic of its form and defences from the rocky pinnacle it encircles. On the other hand, Uruk-hai gestate in mines sunk into the bowels of the earth below Isengard and are torn from their fabricated wombs by hideous midwives; and both Saruman's and Sauron's towers soar abruptly out of desolate plains over which they exert panoptical control. Hence the contrast between nature and built form provides one of the chief means for Jackson to give visual point to the meaning of the great conflict in Middle Earth.

Furthermore, in orchestrating a struggle between the natural and the manmade, Jackson exploits spatial binaries: big/small, high/low, open/closed, and tight/expansive. Infinite exterior landscapes, for example, contrast with claustrophobic interiors such as Shelob's Lair, Farumir's base above the Forbidden Pool, the caverns behind Helm's Deep, the Mines of Moria, and the road under the mountain. Similarly, the characters are repeatedly forced across impossibly narrow bridges and paths: the bridge of Khazad-dûm; the ramp to the main gate of Helm's

Deep; the knife-edged ridge that hangs above the lava under Mount Doom.

However, when we look beyond these general qualities of space to the style and details of the architecture proper, we discover an architectural idiom drawn directly from European history. Rather than using the indigenous architecture of New Zealand, exploring its Polynesian culture or British colonial past, the production team, following Alan Lee's lead, erected new stage sets for the films' dramatic settings. New Zealand was used as a landscape of unconstrained filmic possibilities, a primordial land before history and without a cultural past. Imposed upon this "blank" space, all the realistically rendered sets communicate messages from European architecture. The movie asserts confidently that the practice of architecture exists within time, and specifically within western cultural history. Thus, the trilogy's selection of sets introduces a historical dialogue. Through specific stylistic quotations, Jackson constructs an air of historicity that is necessary to set the heroic ancestral tone. Timely architecture balances the timeless sublimity of the landscape.

A Battle of Styles

In a relentlessly formulaic fashion, Jackson uses four architectural types or categories drawn from European example: 1) the vernacular; 2) the naturalistic; 3) the grotesque; and 4) the archaeological. In general, this typology adds to the movies a sense of history, authority, and vintage. Like the movies' costumes, the architecture works as a signifier of periodicity situating the narrative in heroic time. Beyond that, the categories are coherent unto themselves and share aesthetic characteristics (scale, materiality, color) that are easily recognizable in popular culture. The readability of this typology provides visual coherence throughout the films.

Perhaps most importantly, the architectural categories relate psychological polarities to the unfolding conflicts of the story. All that is associated with the innocence of the Shire is depicted in the language of the British vernacular – rustic walls, wooden paneling – which evokes comfort and domesticity. The ethereal universe of the Elves is stylized with the naturalism of Art Nouveau – sinuous branches and intricate designs, for example. All that is evil takes on the dark, metallic forms of an ultra-Gothic grotesque, invoking caves, dark pools, vaulted arches lit by firelight. Finally, the heroic cities of kings are embossed with the archaeological signature of medieval monuments: vast reaches of white marble, ashlar courses, draftsman's elevations. This simplistic typology produces a unique filmic unity with the result that the heroic exploits are constantly surrounded by a grand filmic space befitting Hollywood's phantasmagoric tradition and familiar to the popular imagination.

The first architectural setting unfolds in the Shire, and inspires thoughts of the British vernacular. According to Lee, "the houses have the look of English vernacular architecture from different periods, suggesting the area had been inhabited for several hundred years" (Russell *Art*, 16). Tolkien had spent four idyllic years of his childhood in Sarehole, a country village uncomfortably close to the industrial center of Birmingham (Pryor *Peter Jackson*, 232), and the Shire clearly represents that specific environment , an environment whose disappearance at the onslaught of industry he lamented (Carpenter *Biography*, 132).

We are first introduced to the Shire as a place of pastoral bridges, water mills, and aboveground and underground houses, all nestled cozily in a lush and rolling landscape. The architecture reflects directly the unthreatening rural context. As Bilbo talks to Gandalf about leaving the Shire, he explains why he does not want to reveal his intentions to Frodo: "I think in his heart Frodo's still in love with the Shire... the woods, the fields, little rivers" (*Fellowship*, 43). Just as the scale of this landscape suits perfectly the hobbit physique and mentality, the interior of Bilbo's house is marked by its miniaturist comforts: warm whites and browns are accentuated by diffuse, warm lighting, and the (horizontal) ampleness of its space is conveyed through numerous tracking shots at Bilbo's eye-level (after Bilbo has left, however, we easily assume Gandalf's perspective and height). Furniture and decorations are simple and functional, but not rough. The kitchen table is spread with an ample supply of hearty foods (though Bilbo claims to have nothing worthy of serving to Gandalf). Even the disarray of possessions spread out over table and floor only adds to the sense of comfort in this bachelor's den. If Gandalf can barely stand upright in its entrance hall, that is a testament to its coziness and to the romantic association of Hobbits with children.[3]

Image 16: The miniature comforts and warm whites of Hobbit houses (http://img-fan.theonering.net)..

Indeed, although much of the architecture of the Shire is aboveground, its most distinctive form is this sunken architecture, the Hobbit houses that Tolkien explicitly prescribed as subterranean.

> All Hobbits had originally lived in holes in the ground, or so they believed, and in such dwellings they still felt most at home; but in the course of time they had been obliged to adopt other forms of abode... The poorest went on living in burrows of the most primitive kind, mere holes indeed, with only one window or none; while the well-to-do still constructed more luxurious versions of the simple diggings of old... and in the flats and the low-lying districts the Hobbits, as they multiplied, began to build above ground. (*Fellowship*, 8)

What Tolkien seems to have in mind is the Nordic domestic form of the medieval turf house. Remnants of this type are still found in remote Iceland; one such turf house at Keldur was bought by the Iceland

---

[3] In the party for Bilbo's 111th birthday, there is plenty of carousing, drinking, and dancing, but the essential innocence of the hobbits is reinforced by Sam's reluctance to dance with Rosie and by Merry and Pippin's mischief with the most spectacular of Gandalf's fireworks.

National Museum in 1947 and preserved for display. This domestic form had disappeared from England by the tenth century when it was replaced by wooden and stone architecture. In addition to the sunken forms, Tolkien is explicit about some additional features: the Hobbit houses have round openings, a form that defies the material principals of vernacular architecture: "A preference for round windows, and even round doors, was the chief remaining peculiarity of hobbit-architecture" (*Fellowship*, 8). Alan Lee remains faithful to the text; all openings, doors and windows, are circular, making reference to ocular brick windows of Roman architecture. The interior spaces contain folk artifacts (glazed ceramic plates, woven carpets, carved chests) and are roofed by shallow vaults articulated by structurally illogical wooden beams. At this point the space diverges from the vernacular prototype, seeking instead an aura of "organic" domesticity.

The notion of organic developed here is not strictly natural or even environmentally friendly (which the Shire is not); beyond its basis in Tolkien, it refers to a formal vocabulary of non-rectilinear design developed by Lee's contemporaries during the psychedelic 1970s. The direct model for the hobbit houses comes from the design of alternative communities, such as Willowater, designed by Roger Dean. Dean is best known for his psychedelic album illustrations for rock groups Uriah Heep, Yes, and Asia. Parallel to his career as an illustrator, Dean produced a model of curvilinear dwellings, an "alternative style of domestic architecture." Dean's designs were built for the first time as dwelling prototypes for the 1982 International Ideal Home Exhibition in Birmingham. That Dean's ideas are still current is evident from the fact that, in 1997, his Home for Life initiative found corporate sponsorship and an affluent New Age clientele (Roger Dean).

Like the Shire, Bree is directly modeled on the caricature of a rural village, an environment common to our popular images from Chaucer and Shakespeare or their American colonial-period manifestations. The Prancing Pony, a country pub with a creaky wooden interior where medieval foods and spirits are served up, completes our expectations. However, for the hobbits Bree is the first stop in their journey from the Shire, and as such it is clearly a liminal space between the familiar home comforts of the Shire and the strange and threatening places that they will cross as part of their epic undertaking. Its gate is thin, its narrow streets are dark and muddy, and its pub, despite the warm light of its interior, is ominous, especially in the absence of Gandalf. The simple elegance and order of Bag End is replaced by a coarseness of construction matched by its human inhabitants and emphasized through low-angle and tilted shots and through close-ups. Already, the hobbits are out of place here, terribly vulnerable to the Ring Wraiths who easily breach Bree's gate, and they are saved only by the intervention of Strider/Aragorn.

The second architectural type, the naturalistic, involves a dreamy stylized world set in the woods and vegetative in form, a vocabulary here limited to Elven cities, namely Rivendell and Lothlorien. When Frodo awakens in the house of Elrond he finds himself in an Art Nouveau city. Rivendell is not folksy or vernacular; its reference comes from cosmopolitan Europe at the end of the nineteenth century, from the exuberant designs of Art Nouveau. According to Jeremy Bennett, of the Weta team, "there are so many little influences—the whole kind of Prague architecture, there's a lot of Art Nouveau, some Italianate and other stuff, mingling with Celtic designs. Alan designed all that" (Russell *Art*, 48). The House of Elrond is made complete with statues and wall paintings of Pre-Raphaelite character, calling up the heroic figures of Edward Burne-Jones. Although inspired by natural forms, the vocabulary of Art Nouveau is far from natural. It is the product of infinitely repetitive stylized graphics executed in rich material. Lines twist and turn into dematerialized surfaces, working overtime to create an artificial illusion of the natural. The forms intend to elicit from the viewer an intense empathy for natural associations, a characteristic of both Art Nouveau and psychedelic naturalism. Here, Alan Lee's graphic talents are perfectly suited to helping fantasy overcome the limits of physical substance: the construction of Rivendell, for example, out of slender wooden forms that are intended to resemble trees, although no actual tree would look exactly this linear or this graphic. Art Nouveau went out of favor in the twentieth century because of its neurotic and decadent underpinnings. As with the psychedelic projects of Roger Dean, it is not surprising that Art Nouveau was rediscovered in the 1960s and, according to architectural critic

Herbert Muschamp is experiencing a further revival in the tastes of the 2000s (Muschamp "Arcadia").

The third architectural category is the grotesque. All evil cities are depicted in a consistent style: Isengard, Mordor, Barad Dûr, Minas Morgul, and the Black Gate (and even the entrance to Mount Doom itself) are modeled in an exaggerated Gothic fashion. The predominant color is black and the predominant material is metal. This overbearingly dark metallic environment resembles the torture fantasies of popular imagination.

Image 17: The gothic fashion of Isengard and Barad Dûr (from the poster of The Two Towers)

Everything is heavy and oppressive, like the Black Gate, which is moved by a torturous mechanism. Molten fire and machines underlie the environment of evil; even the Orcs have metal prosthetics which are all redundantly decorated with painful spiky elements. Here the molten process (industry) meets a perpendicular Gothic (a late development of the Gothic aiming at great height and lightness) that has metamorphosed into a machine.

This connection between metal and Gothic is far from new. In the nineteenth century, when iron became a prominent material, it was often manipulated into stylized Gothic forms. Viollet-le-Duc developed an entire vocabulary glamorizing the medieval mason and the modern engine. Closer to Tolkien's environment, we find a manifestation of this marriage between Gothic and cast iron in the Oxford Museum of Natural History designed in 1860 by Thomas Deane and Benjamin Woodward (Garnham *Museum*). In fact, Tolkien taught in just such a Gothic revival environment; although Exeter was not the most beautiful of colleges at Oxford, it featured a façade and chapel designed by George Gilbert Scott, a star of the Gothic revival movement.

Finally, the fourth architectural category belongs to the heroes. All the buildings of Gondor and Rohan, including Minas Tirith and Helm's Deep, are depicted in archaeologically correct fashions: they evoke specific medieval architectural monuments of Viking, Byzantine, Romanesque, and early Gothic age. The heroic cities are in turn divided into two categories, cities of wood and cities of stone. The villages of Rohan and the city of Edoras contain wooden architecture with thatched roofs, modeled on Viking and Anglo-Saxon prototypes, as seen, for example, in the reconstructed version of the tenth-century Viking fortress of Trelleborg, Denmark. Thus, King Theoden and his people are associated with an earlier and more northerly place than the other humans of Middle Earth.

Edoras, a hilltop city crowned by the Golden Hall of Meduseld, seems like an island rising on a rocky outcrop from a broad, desolate valley between two spectacular mountain ranges. Its lavishly decorated stables befit horse-based culture. The King's Hall at the peak is a grand and faithful reproduction of a royal audience hall. Its grandeur comes from the Celtic gold ornamentation (reinforced by musical theme), with horse motifs on exterior and interior decorations. The Golden Hall of King Theoden is not very extensively described by Tolkien, so Alan Lee created a composite idea, drawing on Heorot, the hall in *Beowulf*, and on knowledge of other medieval wooden structures from Northumbria, Germany, and Denmark. Although wooden, it has to seem highly decorated and already quite ancient (Sibley *The Making*, 40-41).

Again, we must note that Jackson uses the set of Meduseld in a fairly dynamic way. Its interior is first seen in diffuse light (in *Two Towers*), when Gandalf and his party enter it, with horizontal shafts coming from small windows in the clerestory. The effect is to emphasize Theoden's isolation from the outside world. Even though as Theoden decays under Saruman's spell he is raised on his throne which stands in an illuminated alcove, he is seen in silhouette, his head dropped forward and in shadow. Later, in *The Return of the King*, after the victory at Helm's Deep, a warmly illuminated Meduseld will be the site of both Theoden's memorial ceremony and of the subsequent victory celebration, with Merry and Pippin singing irreverent drinking songs.

An additional form of archeologically correct architecture is made of stone. Its greatest manifestation is Minas Tirith, the seven-tiered city of kings, the layout of which is described quite precisely by Tolkien. While Alan Lee considers this city "an equivalent for Ancient Rome or Ancient Byzantium" ("ROTK Production Notes!"), it has, at first glance at least, more in common with Pieter Brueghel's painting of the *Tower of Babel* (1563), which represents a medieval city gone haywire. Minas Tirith is an architectural fantasy, a historicist wedding cake with an Italian luminosity. Every possible urban form from the Middle Ages to the Renaissance is squeezed into a city that rises to a pyramidal peak. Its Babel of styles, however, communicates a singular and direct message to the viewer, that we are dealing with a learned historical city steeped in institutions (such as a library) and civility. As with its wooden counterpart Edoras, Minas Tirith is crowned by a palace on the summit, a pinnacle of human civilization in Middle Earth. The interior of this cathedral-like palace is clean, rhythmical, and precise, with white stone and fine, black columns, making it reminiscent of both Brunelleschi's church of San Lorenzo and Siena's cathedral, true exemplars of the architecture of Northern Italy in the early Renaissance.

Since Minas Tirith represents the height of human civilization in Middle Earth, Jackson and Lee employ architecture here in its most inflated way in the trilogy. As a result, we sense a historical burden quite different from the austere but ephemeral Viking cities in wood. The overabundance of architectural form reminds us of the late-nineteenth century at the peak of architectural eclecticism. Artists of that time, particularly aware of their position at the tail end of a long history, often painted dreamscapes of architectural piles, like Thomas Cole's "The Architect's Dream" (1840), which represents a montage of white architectural form accumulated through history. Of course, such self-consciousness about cultural inheritance might also provoke anxiety over the burden of history. Sigmund Freud's essay on the anxiety associated with viewing the Acropolis is but one example ("Disturbance in Memory").

Indeed, there is such anxiety and a corresponding paralysis within Minas Tirith. Lord Denethor, steward of Gondor, sits enthroned in the silence of the palace, surrounded only by the statues of Gondor's former kings. Like Theoden, he has been corrupted, partly by the death of his son Boromir and partly by his desire, like Gollum's, to keep something that is not his, in this case the kingdom of Gondor. This contrast between the achievement of civilization represented by the architecture and the corruption of the rulers who dwell within it is crucial to the sense of impending calamity in Middle Earth, and the ubiquity of ruins also contributes to that sense. The watchtowers on Amon Hen and Amon Sûl are depicted as ruins with fallen heavy masonry blocks. Here we find heroic sculptures with austere authoritative figures and walls in deep relief. Guarding the waters, we find two freestanding military figures, the Argonaths. And of course, the city of Osgiliath is an abandoned archaeological site full of fragmentary forms, its semicircular arched ruins contrasting markedly with the pointed forms of Mordor.

As we can already see, without this deployment of an architectural typology, the exact nature of the conflict in Middle Earth would likely remain unclear. With it, we can clearly and immediately see that the organic integration of race and place represents a kind of humility that stands in direct contrast to Sauron's monstrous and destructive lust for control. Thus, one review of *The Two Towers* noted the fact that this middle film in the trilogy "lacks a sunny Shire and an elegant elf kingdom" and that the conflict in this case becomes "a simple case of peaceful underdogs defying bullying power mongers" (Westbrook "Ward of the Rings"). Tolkien, who was using *The Lord of the Rings* as, among other things, an anti-industrial polemic framing humility and ambition in an extended, mythic conflict, would surely have been dismayed to think that all of this critique was lost in *The Two Towers* simply because a relevant architecture was missing.[4]

We must acknowledge, too, that the architectural typology is part of a larger discourse and accumulates meaning in combination with camera position and movement, lighting, costume, and characterization. For example, the ambiguity of Saruman's allegiance, when we first meet him in *The Fellowship of the Rings*, is conveyed both by the tension between his tower and the landscape and by the presentation of the interior: his study appears as a kind of dishevelled and disordered monastic cell, half lit with cool light. While he and Gandalf are alike in appearance, both their staffs and robes convey their fundamentally different natures: Gandalf's twisted stick, plain rough robes, and simple leather belt, all emphasizing the organic, contrast strongly with Saruman's metallic staff (mirroring the design of the tower itself) and heavily stylized and ornamented robes. When Saruman's allegiance to Sauron becomes clear, the cinematography works to emphasize the connection between the Gothic and the industrial: a crane shot from the top of the tower of Isengard travels down its full length then continues to plunge into the mines that have been carved out of the earth at the foot of the tower, emphasizing the link between the urge to survey and control the world and the abuse of its resources. The dizzying loss of orientation that results for viewers comments effectively on Saruman's infernal nature.

---

[4] Of course, it is also often read as an allegory of mid-twentieth century politics.

But as spectacular as such effects may be, they also become one of the chief liabilities in these films that, to an unprecedented degree, depend upon elaborate mechanical and digital manipulations to impress us with a fully realized fantasy world. Indeed, the *Lord of the Rings* differs from Jackson's earlier projects in the sheer size of a production team specializing in digital effects (Weta Digital Ltd) and special effects (Weta Workshops Ltd). Grant Major, the production designer, worked with a department which expanded to four hundred people at one point in production. This army of specialists constructed sets that ranged from full-scale to miniature. The city of Edoras, for example, was built full-scale in a dramatic valley, a difficult feat given the fierce winds that attacked the light set. After eight months of construction, all the scenes were shot, and every piece of the elaborate set was dismantled, including the mile-and-a-half roadway that led to the valley (Edoras). However, in most other cases the architecture was constructed in miniature, the filmmaker and his team relying on digital manipulation to render the model as life-size. The production team constructed sixty-eight such miniatures. In fact, most were large enough that a new term had to be invented: not miniatures but "bigatures." The Dark Tower of Barad-Dûr, for instance, which supposedly rose to 3000 feet, was represented in the studio by an 18-foot model (Calhoun "Hobbit Forming", 24).

At times, the artificiality of this technical endeavor is strikingly obvious. The mastery of the bigature is most dramatic in the siege of Minas Tirith, which like that of Helm's Deep involves a series of breached gates and walls and close combat within the courtyards and streets. Added to this, however, is a different sense of scale, as Minas Tirith is assaulted by catapults loaded by giants with massive boulders that dissolve the stone walls of the city and bring the fragments down upon the inhabitants. The soldiers of Gondor respond with even more massive artillery. Indeed, this superhuman scale and sense of action do not match well. Although the intention is doubtless to suggest the fragility of human civilization in the face of "such reckless hate" (Theoden's words in *Two Towers*), the effect is to reduce the architecture to a mere model, an elaborate weightlessness, which, of course, is what it is. For all the digital manipulations and the sophisticated effects, for all its look of gravity and hardness, Minas Tirith finally collapses like a house of cards. During its siege, the fall of its limestone blocks lacks the slightest relation to gravity, mass, and velocity.

Furthermore, because so much money and effort is invested in the creation and rendering of the models, the exterior of these often become the center of attention, to the detriment of the story. For example, we first experience Minas Tirith as Gandalf and Pippin ride to it to warn of an impending attack, coming over a ridge to discover the city rising precipitously against the rock out of which it is hewn, its white stone citadel on a summit glowing in the sun. As they gallop through its streets meandering up the switchback road to the citadel and the cathedral-like palace that stands there, we get only a very brief glimpse of daily life within its walls, a life which is placid without being rich or joyous, even as the camera remains in constant motion to impress us with the scale and dimensions of the place (which is in fact a model). Such scenes point to a peculiar absence in Jackson's Middle Earth: with the exception of the Shire, domestic spaces are out of sight and public places are barely inhabited so that Middle Earth seems like a world hardly worth the saving.

Clamorous Images

Without a doubt, *The Lord of the Rings* is groundbreaking in its innovative application of digital manipulation. The special effects and sophisticated sets produce sublime spatial tensions. Overall, however, the visual unity never challenges the viewer's subjective balance. The adventure unfolds in front of our perhaps too-relaxed eyes. The viewer is an excited spectator who never loses the comfort of a stable subjectivity. Even as she is twisted through adventurous impossibilities the experience is visual and apprehended through distance. In this sense, Jackson is faithful to a grand theatrical tradition where the architecture remains a visual backdrop heightening psychological effect. *The Lord of the Rings* fails to be a great architectural movie because its buildings spring from the aesthetics of illustration (hence painting) rather than from an existential exploration between space and artifact such as we see, for example, in Alfred Hitchcock's *Rear Window* (1954), Michelangelo Antonioni's *The Red Desert* (1964), or Jacques Tati's *Playtime* (1967).

In analyzing the relationship between painting and architecture, Walter Benjamin posited a great conceptual difference between the two art forms that had implications for film (*Illuminations*, 232-37). In painting, he argued, there is a distance imposed by the viewer. In contrast, the experience of both architecture and film is tactile because the viewer moves through spaces and is mechanically dislocated in the process. Using Benjamin's terminology, Jackson is a magician rather than a surgeon; he maintains the comfortable distance of stage set and visual effect. Although spatially lush, *The Lord of the Rings* is not dialectical and fails Benjamin's criterion for contemplation. We watch people moving through its spaces and buildings, but we do not move ourselves. Jackson does not engage in the spatial intelligence of Orson Welles, in the voyeurism of Alfred Hitchcock, or in the fragmentation of Sergei Eisenstein. Although "realistic" in effect, the trilogy offers no innovation in filmic realism ("Aesthetic of Reality"). The spatial flatness of *The Lord of the Rings* becomes even more apparent once we realize that its conceptual prototype is not rooted in the history of cinema but in the genre of graphic design. If Jackson had created a more dynamic and engaging architecture instead of offering viewers comfortably distant points of view, rationally coherent perspectives, and a historically articulated and easily decipherable architectural vocabulary, the films might have spoken more urgently to our current circumstances and perhaps carried more of the critical weight of Tolkien's original project. Thus we can conclude that Jackson's use of space, original in its technical facility, is philosophically conservative.

If so many of the movies' sets are accumulated icons of living or ruined monuments, we cannot but wonder how they relate to the vision of Tolkien who, unlike Lee or Jackson, was a professional historian of the Middle Ages. Despite Tolkien's intentions to set Middle Earth in a medieval heroic past, his narratives are bereft of any architectural referents. This observation makes the movie's architectural sets that much more original, but at the same time begs the question of architectural history's marked absence from the original. Why is Tolkien so distinctly vague about the buildings of his Middle Earth?

Both as Oxford linguist and as popular writer, Tolkien was involved in a deeply nostalgic project of resuscitating the lost medieval world – and its values – for the sake of British modernity. Although a contemporary of T. S. Eliot (whose conservative agenda embraced modernist forms), Tolkien's work better resembles the generations of British medievalists A.W.N. Pugin and John Ruskin, and unlike Tolkien, both Pugin's Ecclesiological Movement and Ruskin's aestheticism exploited medieval architectural prototypes to make their arguments: Pugin, toward the reformation of industrial society through a return to the values of medieval England; Ruskin, toward the realization of a future for modernity through the labor of the medieval stone mason. Furthermore, Tolkien's fictional project also belongs to a Romantic literary tradition dating to the late eighteenth and nineteenth centuries (Brooks *Gothic Revival*). Horace Walpole's *Castle of Otranto* (1765), Sir Walter Scott's *Ivanhoe* (1819), and Victor Hugo's *Hunchback of Notre-Dame* (1831), three landmarks of the Gothic Revival, utilized explicit architectural settings to elicit imaginary time travel into an idealized medieval past. Michael Crichton, author of *Jurassic Park* (1990), understood the power of medieval architecture to transport the popular imagination. In his bestselling novel *Timeline* (2000), fourteenth-century architecture becomes both the vehicle and the destination of time travel. Similar themes were explored in his film *Westworld* (1973), where the Middle Ages become one of three futuristic amusement parks. The Romantic Movement instilled Gothic monuments with unprecedented expressive potential; modernity imagined the Middle Ages with an architectural cloak of spires and rib vaults, tall cathedrals and castles with dark subterranean passages. Medieval architecture has, then, always been an integral player in the century-long tradition of reenacting medieval drama. With this accumulation of precedents in mind, what are we to make of the willed absence of architectural reference in Tolkien?

In fact, the absence of architecture from Tolkien's work has a simple explanation. Unlike the medieval ideals of his Oxford predecessors, Tolkien's was located in the age of Beowulf and an early medieval past from which we have very little surviving architecture. For Tolkien, "Beowulf's battle with Grendel was more interesting [. . .] than the squabbles between the American Eagle and the Russian Bear, even if the latter might end the world with nuclear warfare instead of merely putting a stop to the cannibalization of a minor king's army" (Jones *Myth*, 19). Tolkien's direct experience of grand architecture occurred during WWI, when his military unit disembarked in Amiens, the site of Europe's most spectacular cathedral (Carpenter *Biography*, 81). Thus, his introduction to Gothic was traumatic and coupled with a general dislike for travel. For Tolkien, all interest in the Middle Ages ceased at the moment that Anglo-Saxon purity was diluted by the French. Everything following the Norman invasion in 1066, and the consequent introduction of Romanesque architectural forms into England, was corrupt for him. According to Tolkien's official biographer, "the Norman conquest pained him as if it had happened in his lifetime" (*Biography*, 129).

With Middle Earth, Tolkien attempted to fantasize a pure Nordic and Celtic environment free of any French presence. Medieval historian Norman Cantor characterizes Tolkien's project as a "genteel Nordic neoracism in the form of neomedievalism" (Cantor *Inventing*, 227). To the extent that British medieval architecture was dependent on Norman models, it had to be eradicated altogether from Middle Earth. It is no coincidence that French neomedievalism used architecture as its key piece of evidence, claiming the birth of the Gothic as a national feat. Victor Hugo, the greatest popularizer of the Middle Ages, used a building, Nôtre Dame Cathedral in Paris, to stage a medieval revival.[5] With the further assistance of Viollet-le-Duc, who began preserving medieval cathedrals, medieval architecture was claimed by the French. The Anglo-Saxon purist Tolkien, in order to avoid French contamination, had to abandon architecture. Post-Norman England had to be rejected, and Middle Earth was Tolkien's visualization of Britain's fantastic

---

[5] It is no surprise that the visual potential of the Gothic Revival was quickly and frequently realized in the movies. Hugo's *Hunchback of Notre Dame*, for example, was dramatized in twelve movies between 1905 and the Disney animation of 1996. *Ivanhoe* had its silent-film debut in 1913 and is better known today by the 1952 adaptation staring Robert and Elizabeth Taylor, if not the 1958 television version staring Roger Moore.

patrimony, which had no physical monuments to advertise itself (Webster "Archaeology").

Given the relative silence about particular architectural features in Tolkien, Jackson had to invent a new architecturally inflected story for his screenplay in order to complete the vision of Middle Earth, and as we have seen his strategy was straightforward: to appropriate the visual vocabulary already developed by Alan Lee to illustrate Houghton Mifflin's centenary edition of *The Lord of the Rings* and to simply add the dynamics of camera movement and montage. The resulting visual environment, thanks to the movies' Academy Award-winning special effects, is extraordinary. Without reservation, the unified spatial vision could be described as follows:

> The whole must have succeeded admirably in creating in the minds of the poet's contemporaries the illusion of surveying a past, pagan but noble and fraught with deep significance—a past that itself had depth and reached backward into a dark antiquity of sorrow. (Tolkien "Beowulf," 124)

These words, nevertheless, are not reviews of the movie, but Tolkien's characterization of the historical space in the literary epic of *Beowulf*.

If Tolkien's objective was to write a modern *Beowulf*, it seems that Peter Jackson has helped him achieve the vision. The means for creating this popular filmic universe, however, are far from subtle. Through the eyes of Alan Lee, architecture both encodes the conflict central to the narrative and illustrates the movie's epic spaces in terms that even contemporary North American audiences, generally unschooled in the subtleties of European architectural history, can apprehend. Although architecture does not achieve Grant Major's formulation that it "becomes the story" or that the environments "become a character," it helps the readability of the story by means of iconic imagery. As a result, the movie is stuffed with architecture whose characteristics are generic, broken down, as we have seen, into four simple categories. Tolkien's age, the early twentieth century, was a lot more literate about historical architecture than Jackson's age, the early twenty-first century. But paradoxically, it is Jackson's vision of Middle Earth that is inflated with architectural form – even if its particularities are superficial. The Middle

Earth of Tolkien is subtle. By remaining silent about stylistic details, Tolkien resists packaging his work with a decorative wrap of architectural form. The Middle Earth of Jackson is inflated with architectural messages that ultimately belittle the expressive possibilities of architectural space and its contested history.

The Lord of the Rings and the Fellowship of the Map

Tom Conley

The sequence that follows the opening credits of *Distant Drums* (1951), a feature that film historians call a workaday adventure that rehearses the traits of Raoul Walsh's signature, says much about what makes it especially memorable. The Technicolor camera closes in on a map of the peninsula of Florida. Framed by the aquamarine surround of the Atlantic Ocean to the right and the Caribbean Sea to the left, pocked with marshes and lakes, a bright green landscape of the Everglades is set adjacent to two red stars, one in the distance that will be the point of departure of an adventure, the other a large wind rose nearby in the Gulf of Mexico, just below the legend indicating that the map has been composed "by the order of Gen. Zachary Taylor, 1840" (the legendary figure who rid the peninsula of its nasty inhabitants). When details of the map are shown early in the narrative, a black line traces the itinerary the narrator takes by cutting its way inland from the western shore toward "Gen. Taylor's Headquarters" and beyond, in the direction of the eastern shore of Like Okeechobee. An emblem of motion and drive, this black line symbolizes the path of any of the "desperate journeys" for which Walsh had been known in his films for Warner Bros. since 1939. The arrow that brightens the surrounding brown and aquamarine tints at the point of departure of

Distant Drums tells us that this journey will be colorful. The aquamarine edges indicate that the location of the film is ideal for treatment in Technicolor. The bright contrast exceeds the narrative and becomes the *raison d'être*, so it appears, of the feature.

The map on which the itinerary of *Distant Drums* is plotted while the narrative is engaged belongs to a classical tradition. Many films situate the time and space of their stories through allusion to maps in the credits or opening sequences. At these moments the map and the movie reflect each other: the presence of the one within the frame of the other indicates that a projective fantasy is about to take place a good part of which has to do with a paradoxical suspension of the spectator's belief, that is, with the spectator's accession to a state of consciousness located in – but also at a distance from – the imaginary geographies indicated by the film (see Jourde *Géograpies imaginaries*). It is not a "suspension of disbelief," a condition in which the spectator willingly seduces himself or herself toward identification with the time and space made manifest by the map but, rather, a state of being that seems at once settling and unsettling: settling, insofar as the film produces geographical fantasies that lure us into wanting to be, as Baudelaire stated in English in his *Tableaux parisiens*, "anywhere out of this world." What Baudelaire called "this world" is for us the movie theater or what is exterior to the visual field of the screen. And our viewers' condition is unsettling in that we enjoy letting ourselves be tourists in the film, especially in a film that turns its milieu into a travel advertisement. As with the Everglades in *Distant Drums*, we "see and visit" a fantasy born of inherited and often inert images that reach back to the first manuscript maps of the New World or pictures in early cosmographies and geographies.

The map that inaugurates a film quickly organizes our memory-images of the spaces it invents. In this way it is indubitably of a strong religious valence. The map in a movie is often the hidden guarantee of what it tells its spectator to be its truth. Having no origin in the film itself, it is merely there, like a sacred tablet, attesting to the spatial laws of the narrative. The religious effect of the map in films is deeply rooted in the history of cartography. In the early modern age many of the first maps that a public of both alphabetic and analphabetic readers first gazed upon

The Fellowship of the map 217

were found in printed Bibles (see Delano-Smith *Maps*). Editors (often of Reformed conviction) discovered that the names and places of the Holy Land found in the text of Scripture could be ascertained and made sensuously present by way of woodcut illustrations. Bibles combining text and maps could inspire illiterate children to read and their literate counterparts to discern the beauty of a world given by God, whose borders were found extending well beyond those in which it was read about. Furthermore, if the same Bibles figured prominently in the everyday lives of early modern users, they promoted graphic fantasies of holy places that existed beyond the reach or hold of Christendom.

At the same time the map itself had been felt to be a sign of the presence of God. This began with the circulation of maps in manuscript and printed editions of Ptolemy's *Geographia* from the middle of the fifteenth century up to the end of the sixteenth century, the moment when Mercator and Ortelius supplanted the Alexandrian cosmographer's authority with their new atlases. Ptolemy's projection of the world extended from the coast of Hibernia on the west (left hand) border to the fabled island of Zipangu at the east (right hand) side. Who, indeed, could look at the world from such a transcending point of view? It was clear that the geographer of 145 A.D. had been either imagining the world as God was seeing it or himself rivaling Creation.[1] The perspective that the new world maps were offering to their viewers could only have been – at least for those who reflected on what it meant to look at a map – seriously unsettling. The earlier *mappaemundi* of the Middle Ages, that had been abstract designs closed upon themselves or else memory-images of a highly circumscribed terraqueous sphere, now suddenly opened onto spaces that inspired wonder and doubt.[2] New maps printed on undiscovered areas the text, "terrae incognitae" or, in the case of the austral continent that was partially known but still very much a figment of

---

[1] According to Christian Jacob, ancient Greek cartographers (Anaximander, in particular) showed the world as only Gods could have seen it (*L'Empire des cartes*).

[2] Edson (*Mapping*) suggests that that enclosing frame—the "ring" or surround, as it were—of the medieval map changes as of the fourteenth century. She notes that "the world of maps began to undergo a revolution. Already the first nautical charts based on compass readings had appeared. Their accurate delineation of familiar coastlines were [sic] a revelation, and within the next century these forms were incorporated into world maps" (165). With new maps the world opens, and so do their borders of its cartographic representation.

the imagination, "terra australis nuper inventa, sed non plene examinata" [Oronce Finé, in Shirley 1987, frontispiece). The unknown was clearly evidence of the presence of God, but when the threshold of the unknown was receding as oceanic travel moved in all cardinal directions there was cause enough if not for the disappearance of God at least for the presence of a hidden or absent creator, a hidden god or *deus absconditus*.

Not immediately discernible but felt either in the shadows or crannies of the physical world or in the blinding or invisible rays of light, the cause of creation was something that had to sought, perhaps, in the sweat and toil of pilgrimage or in the itinerary of adventure and displacement. The maps that led the way to shrines, recounted the process of discovery or that were records of topographical investigations remain signs of religious quest, whether they take the form of city-views, chains of mountains among sinuous bends of rivers, or bird's eye views of the reach of dioceses and lines of their surrounding boundaries. In more than one projection executed by adepts of the Reform the sign of God is the map itself: the map stands in for God, it is a sign assuring creation at the same time it reveals an absent cause. In the cartouche of the Ortelian world-map at the beginning of Lancelot de la Popelinière's *Les Trois Mondes* (1582) the space reserved for "Totius orbis descriptio" or "Typus orbis terrarum" is filled with the title of the book in which an argument is made for Protestant colonization of Australia.[3] A synonym of God, "Le tout-puissant," is the term that describes the map. In the text adjacent to its placement in the book it is hard to tell if "the all-powerful" is either God or the printed map (Conley *Self-Made Map*, 283-284).

The confusion of god and the map that is witnessed in the early modern age informs some of the cartographic strategies of classical and contemporary cinema. If cinema is a tool of power (insofar as power is a mode of the control of perception and an agency that forms subjectivity) it bears resemblance to maps that aim to promote and channel both perception and cognition. In its history the map (as J. Brian Harley has shown) has become a tool of power itself, by virtue of the control it exerts

---

[3] Shirley *Mapping*, entries 120 (of unknown provenance, ca 1570) and 122 (Ortelius, world-map of his *Theatrum orbis terrarum* [Antwerp, 1570]), respectively. Lancelot's epitome world-map is found in entry 148.

the space it simulates. The map is a strategic tool for the ends of administration of the world and its inhabitants. In cinema, and especially *The Lord of the Rings*, the map can be seen as a strategic agent aimed at inspiring and controlling the fantasies of its viewers. *The Lord of the Rings* offers a classic model of cartographic control not only in its relation to its narration but also in its relation to the fantasies it elicits. The viewer discerns how the film is an agent of power through the ways that the map figures in its composition.

It is not by chance that a map of "Middle Earth" that is found at the beginning of the film version of *The Fellowship of the Ring* also accompanies the "special extended edition" of the slip-cased box encrypting four DVDs. The movie is part and parcel of an octavo book-box conceived by New Line Entertainment in a very old and a very modern shape; out of it the user extracts a codex. It unfolds to reveal five panels, two of which contain the two DVDs constituting the feature, two others "The Appendices" and a fifth a brochure that plots the latter. Part one is titled "From Book to Vision" and Part two "From Vision to Reality." The brochure itself takes the form of a flow chart and a map. To a historian of maps the sites and their names belong to a tree of knowledge – replete with branches, apples, and leaves adjacent to names and toponyms – that resembles, among other analogues, Christofle de Savigny's geographic world-map and other Ramist diagrams that seek to organize all of the world's knowledge (Shirley *Mapping*, entry 159).

The very ordering of the electronic information track by track follows the line of schematic reasoning that had substituted visual form for oral knowledge at the moment when, in the words of Father Walter J. Ong, S. J., the Christian world was undergoing transformation from an oral to a visual culture.[4] The colophon of the brochure uses the language of both rare book rooms and websites to tell the buyer to handle the material delicately. The secrets of the world of this rare edition can be found, the instructions note, when the user goes "on-line to unlock exclusive content" in order to "check out the latest of the *Lord of the Rings* updates."

---

[4] (Ong *Ramism*). Ong's work anticipates many of Michel Foucault's conclusions in the shift from analogy to representation that is taken up in chapters one and two of *Les Mots et les choses*.

The map that appears in the credits of the film is the frontispiece on the left hand and outer panel of the codex containing the brochure and the four discs. It seems to be both a guide and a secret. A topographic map from a tradition reaching back to works of early modern "king's engineers" who drew local maps for the purpose of crafting defensive systems along the borders of the countries, the device also belongs to the line of projections that the late David Woodward calls a "route-enhancing map" (Woodward "System"). A close up of the topographic map in the credits becomes the bookish credits for the inside of the boxed edition of the DVDs. The difference is that the details, seen in the frame of what would seem to be a zoom-in on the projection seen in the film itself, display four chains of mountains and other chains of peaks. The style of the mountains in the area of the "Argonaths" resembles forms seen on copperplate maps of the sixteenth century.[5] The other peaks, especially those around "Gondor" and "Moria" belong to a style associated with the eighteenth century. They confirm what Père François de Dainville noted about fantasy in the ostensibly scientific representation of altitude in the age of the Enlightenment. The most handsome terrestrial maps of the second half of the eighteenth century, he notes, "although constructed on a rather exact geodesic background, give little measure of altitude and do not seek to represent the real forms of the land. The viewer need only glance to see how imaginary [*fantaisistes*] they are even in areas where passage poses no obstacle. The engineers who drew them did not know how to look at the land. Nor did they want to" (Dainville *Langage*, 165). Like the scientist Cassini who indulges in fantasy when adding ornament to make his topographic map "more agreeable" in order to have it seen as a "sketch" or "a draft," the author of this map – designers working for Peter Jackson actually made it, of course, although Tolkien did draw maps himself – seems to seek scientific illusion by having a quasi-medieval script spell the toponyms in the context of cartographic anachronism.

Contrary to the greater map seen in the sequence following the credits, the printed version on the box includes a dashed line in red ink

---

[5] Jean de Beins's views of the area are comparable. They have analogues in the projection of Savoy in Ortelius's *Theatrum orbis terrarum*.

that follows a serpentine course from the "Falls of Rauros" to a land called "Hobbiton" (in small upper case characters) at the upper left corner. No wind rose or indication of cardinality yet accompanies the legend to the red line that is indicated to be "the Fellowship's Journey" (in text printed over a scale of miles inscribed near the lower left corner). The map is thus the anticipation of a travelogue or a narrative of displacement that can proceed – since no arrow is indicated – in one direction or its opposite. The map is cut from a greater whole in the film in which, the viewer discovers, the drawing provides more shading and greater relief in a bird's eye perspective.

In the movie, as the camera pulls away from a V-formation of nine males, each holding a ring, standing in an eerie milieu in such a way that four are on either side of a wizened sage who sports a long white beard and faces the camera, the map follows a suave and almost vampishly castrating feminine voiceover that states, "... and nine ... nine rings were gifted to the race of men who above all else desire power." The shot fades into black as the voice ends with emphasis on "power." Suddenly now the map appears. Within the surround of a mannered cartouche in the style of a gothic revival is "Middle Earth." Set over a region of the "Sundering Seas" above, the cartouche draws attention to the composite quality of the map in general: it is indeed a topographic map whose coastline of "Eriador" and "Gondor" includes a mountainous peninsula above the "Bay of Belfalas." A snake-like creature, a sort of miniature Loch Ness monster, swims in the water adjacent to two lightly drawn boats equipped with lateen sails. The paper of the map is creased and even pocked enough to display anfractuosity along lines where it might have been folded. This map has evidently been handled a lot, and continues to invite us almost to caress it.

As significant as the map itself is the voice-off that has associated it – quite as much as the nine rings – with *power*. Before the narrative is further engaged, the inner or third voice of the film implies that the film is producing a webbing of fantasy in which the map and the movie are coextensive. The inner or third voice is located indeterminately between what is seen graphically in the film and what this vision inspires the viewer to imagine. The cartographic projection is a guide for the "route-

Image 18: The map of Middle Earth according to Jackson. Digital frame enlargement. (Copyright © New Line Cinema)

enhancing" narrative to follow, to be sure, but it is also a cinematic "special effect" given to hold its spectator in a state of suspended attraction. A classical relation of cartography and power is shown where the map, filling the entire frame, is implicitly the "ring" – or magical object – that constitutes the enigma referred to in the title of the movie. It is with and by means of the map, after all, that our understanding of the journey of the Fellowship is made lambent and coherent.

The camera moves over and about the map, twisting and closing in on the land of "Mordor," the name inscribed in what seems to be a three-sided cartouche at screen right, complementing that of the "Middle Earth" at left, and whose outline is formed by two parallel chains of mountains attached (at its possibly western end) by another chain running along a vertical axis. "For within these rings was inscribed the strength and will to govern each race... but they were all of them deceived." As in the previous fade-in that associated the map with power, here the fade-out leaves the word *deceived* and the idea of deception in isolation. What or who is deceiving whom, and through whom or by means of what agent? The power of dissimulation is ascribed as much to the projection as to anything in the narrative.

The Fellowship of the map

In the same black interstice the voiceover continues, "For another ring was made...," before the film cuts to a close-up of the land of Mordor, its lake, its lower chain of mountains ("of shadow") and their upper counterpart (the "Ash Mountains"). For the first time the voiceover repeats what is seen on the topographic projection. "In the land of Mordor, in the fires of Mount Doom," she states, drawing the spectator's attention to the salient peak in the center of the land, before the map cuts to a shot of a volcano spewing flames and smoke, "another ring was made...." The shot cuts to a close-up of a masked man who is then seen in a medium shot as if he were a pagan priest dressed in golden fabric and metal armature. "The dark Lord Sauron forged another ring, a master ring to control all others... And into this ring he poured his cruelty, his malice, and his will to dominate all life... One ring to rule them all...." After a series of special effects: a ring falling and turning, its inscription in cursive gothic burning bright, a shot intercedes of two wooden buildings set ablaze, that stand behind a throng of armed men pillaging the land around them. This image quickly dissolves into the greater map that is implied, like the landscape, to be on fire. "One by one... free lands in the Middle Earth fell to the power of the ring." The greater map remains in the background as the crowd, brandishing clubs and axes, continues to wreak havoc and rampage. The crowd dissolves away, the map remains, and the voice continues as we again fade to black. The words, "But there were some who resisted," give way to a shot of epic proportion as thousands of men in armor holding swords erect in their right hands advance forward from left to right. The "some who resisted" can hardly be the endless legions of soldiers: in the gap between the voiceover and the image it may be the matter of the map itself that resists consumption. And if it is the map that resists and survives pillage and destruction, it can once again be associated with the ring and the film itself. The map is the perduring – the real – object of the tale.

Soon later the map returns after the voiceover explains that a Hobbit had found the magic ring and that the journey of the tale leads back to the area that the viewer might have seen in the upper left corner of the sheet. "For the time will soon come when the Hobbits... will shape the fortunes of all." As the sanctimonious voice utters these words, an aerial shot of mountains shrouded with clouds appears. The receding landscape dissolves quickly into an extreme close-up of the peaks of "The Misty Mountains" on the map. As in the preceding shot, the camera pulls back but now turns to follow the place-names and decoration of the map (mostly schematic trees and molehills). A new voiceover of a man hemming and hawing before beginning, "The twenty-second day of September... in the year 1400... " replaces the Cassandra-like tone of the female who had just spoken. The camera plunges in to close detail of the region of "Hobbiton" (between "Westmarch" and "Bywater") and then pulls back to show where it is situated vis-a-vis "The Shire" and "Bree." The voice enumerates the place-names as the camera pulls back to include the entire map of the "Middle Earth" in the frame. A resonant and reassuring orchestration of violins accompanies the movement that now locates the map in an office whose floor is paved with elegant oak tiles upon which other maps and manuscripts are strewn in what seems to be a careful chaos. The voice ends, pronouncing "the third age of this world" before the camera swoops through a tunnel-like room and past a chest of drawers over which hangs a framed landscape map.

Image 19: From the map to the world inside it. Digital frame enlargement. (Copyright © New Line Cinema)

The title, "The Fellowship of the Ring" (in the composite style of a gothic/humanist script) appears in white. It dissolves as the camera tracks into an office where Bilbo Baggins is seen from behind, seated at a desk by the warmth of a fire (a variant perhaps on Dürer's "Saint Jerome in his Study"), adjacent to a mantelpiece on which is posed yet another map. An easel adjacent to the desk bears what seems to be still another projection, as well as stacks of books and strewn papers. "There... and back again," utters the voice that may or may not be that of the man at the desk. "The Hobbit's Tale," continues he, "by Bilbo Baggins." The film cuts to a hand deliberately scripting the very words we have just heard.

Clearly the two titles, the one imposed upon the image through the sound track and the other suspended in the field of the image, ensure that the promise of the narrative resembles something of a cartographic fantasy, in all likelihood a composite tale whose origins are found in an intermediate area between a map and discourse of a genre that one historian calls "cartographic fiction" whose quality could be almost quintessentially British. Including *Treasure Island*, a tale that Robert Louis Stevenson avowed to have created from a map, the genre inaugurates "a space of visibility in the process of reading" (Jacob *Empire*, 365). In its most successful manifestations, the map (and map-as-landscape) undoes the narrative thread because it inspires alternative itineraries in such a way that an interactive relation between text and reader is legitimized. Christian Jacob notes that for Tolkien the imaginary map shows alternative worlds and is subtended by "a truly parallel geography but is not only physical but also of human political, and linguistic character. The sum of the novelistic saga assumes the form of a voyage in this fictive world by dint of the narrative motif of quest and its attendant displacement (Jacob *Empire*, 371).

These observations hold true for the map in the novel, but the cinematic medium alters the magic effects that the historian of cartography finds in the text of the *Lord of the Rings*. In the sequence in which the map is duplicated in the film, and in which the wizened traveler Gandalf, having ridden into the land of the Hobbits, enters the diminutive world in which the writer of the "The Hobbit's Tale" is scripting his story, the map figures as an anamorphotic tour de force, twisting and bending in perspective (in a way that reaches back to experiment with classical pictorial models), displacing the spectator in such a way that he begins to wonder where he is. The bearded sage enters into a miniature space. A shot from his point of view reveals an interior whose minuscule size is broadened through the effects of a lens of very short focal length. Windows and doorways that are rounded, oval, or elliptical suggest a microscopic but expansive interior in which a corner of the map is first seen near the lower left edge of the frame. In fluid omniscience the camera penetrates the room, swoops left, and centers on the map that rests on a picture frame set on a table, partially covered by others. The camera cuts to the old man whose eyes have caught hold of the sacred object.

The point of view is one of a free subjectivity. Is this subjectivity Gandalf's, or does it belong to the camera itself and the effects it is producing.[6] He picks up the map on the frame, sets aside the sheets that had been on top, and gazes upon what is now made clear in extreme close-up: "Here of old was Thrain King under the Mountain," written below a drawing of the mountain seen earlier, that is adjacent to the words, to the lower right, "The Desolation of Smaug." In the center of the image a tattered fold reveals a hole in the paper that seems to be the aperture opening onto an inner area, perhaps that of the "Lonely Mountain" (whose peak is beneath a great dragon that spits fire in red ink when the camera pans upward in a motion that not at all reproduces the effect of the human eye scanning a map).

The map suddenly disappears when the film cuts to a close up of the writer who says to the absent hero, "I can make you some eggs, sir... ." The camera cuts to a long shot of the small man standing in the circular doorway. This writer, standing in the midst of the circle, seems to be reflected on the pupil of an eye. The map figures in a play of hide-and-seek and of what might be called a special spatial effect. The lands on which the old hero has just placed his eyes appear to be great glacial planes, to be sure, but the way the map swirls in the first shot and then twists and is viewed askew attests to an anamorphosis. The map turns and bends as do televisual presentations of letters and words of familiar logos

---

[6] "Free subjectivity" is taken from Gilles Deleuze's reading of Pasolini (*Cinéma 1*, 109-114). According to Deleuze's reading of the Italian theorist wherever "point of view" becomes difficult to discern in a film it usually underscores the presence of the camera itself and the spectator whose imagination is in and of the space being shown.

The Fellowship of the map

Image 20: Bilbo's map of The Lonely Mountain. Digital frame enlargement. (Copyright © New Line Cinema)

(that include any and every major network) and icons in advertisements (say, familiar names of automobile manufacturers). The swirl of the map is equated with the power of the camera to produce special effects. In *The Fellowship of the Rings* the symbolic money of the film is fantasy, and fantasy is shown to be the product less of Tolkien than of special effects.

When Gandalf, the wizened and wizardly father-figure, studies the map at the beginning of the film he seems to be gazing upon it as if it were a palimpsest while at the same time his eyes seem to find in its figures a flow chart, a series of stock options, or a diagram for the production and arrangement of special effects. Each site that is seen on the map will figure in the voyage narrative to come. The sight of the mountain forces recall of the sequence of the burning peak that had preceded the second intervention of the same map in the narrative only minutes earlier. But far later in the film, when the survivors of the voyage that had led them into the bowels of the earth finally emerge into daylight, out of a stony portal on a high plateau, one of the valiant soldiers, Aragorn, would-be King of Middle Earth, seeing the two hobbits overcome by tears, yells, "Legolas, get the map! We must reach the woods of Lothlorien!... By nightfall these hills will be swarming with Orcs! Legolas! Get me the map!"

The soldier is indeed asking Legolas to produce what we see only in memory. Legolas never produces a map. The only indication about the place can be found near the credits, in the first images of the topography of Middle Earth, which re more present on panels of the box containing the DVDs than in the film itself. Confirmation of the place where the travelers are found can be made through consultation of the fantasy map, the legend that belongs to the slip case edition. It happens to be part of a self-authenticating effect by which the reality of visual fantasy is legitimized by the presence of the place-names which locate the effects. The sense of voyage depends not on the film itself or a map in the movie but the relation of accompanying paraphernalia to the visual material.

At the end of this portion of the epic, brave souls push ahead and move more into fantasy than into geographic space. They find themselves pursued by a cohort of stunningly ugly monsters, but the pursuit bears traits familiar to adepts of the many maps that tie literature to cinema. The passage through the straits of the Argonaths is made, it seems, to tell us that the special effects produced by the colossal statues at the narrows of the river dwarf those that Ray Harryhausen engineered in Don Chaffey's *Jason and the Argonauts* (1963). When infidels make a final attack on the band of fellows, one of the heroes, seeing that the end is near, blows a horn to remind us that we are in a primeval Roncesval that floats between computer-generated battles and memory-images of *La Chanson de Roland*. The entry into the depths of the lower world prior to the sequence is a nod to the episode, among others of its author, of the "Château de Pire Aventure" in Chrétien de Troyes's *Yvain ou Le Chevalier au lion* (Dufournet *Chanson*, 200-209; Rousse *Yvain*, 281-292). A vague but evocative cartography of sources, drawn from cinema and medieval literature, charts both the narrative and the memorial relation the spectator holds with images belonging to the medieval canon.

By way of conclusion it can be said that the topography of Middle Earth that follows the credits and that Gandalf discovers early on in the film belongs to a cinematic "map quest" bathed in an aura of religiosity. A story that tells a tale of travel acquires a sense of a quest for "truth." The latter is gained through the binding – hence religious – force of "fellowship" indicated in the title and plotted on a map that in its historical background is taken to be a sign of the difficult beauty of creation. What might be called the monotonous aura of *The Lord of the*

Rings – a condition emphasized in the appendices to the extended DVD edition by the copious testimony about the brilliance of the film – is owed in part, in the film itself, to the hundreds of medium close-ups of the blue-eyed Frodo looking in astonishment at what he sees. The adolescent sees events that have been scripted on the map of the movie, and by force of his repeated stare he cues the spectator to look at the special effects as creations of a hidden god. The effects become ends in themselves and, within the fictive world of the film, by virtue of its authenticating effect, the map stresses that they are also incarnations of truth. Yet, paradoxically, where the map is seen, a history of the relation of power and cartography enters into the film. The projection becomes a critical element showing how the religion of the film owes its presence to special effects. As with the imaginary world of Seminole-infested Florida in *Distant Drums*, the map is one of these effects, but it is also what calls them into question.

Enchantments of *Lord of the Rings*: Soundtrack, Myth, Language, and Modernity

James Buhler

Myth of Origin

Time before time: gray mist drifts aimlessly across the screen. An amorphous sound, ethereal and vaguely musical, shimmers in the darkness. The mist, however, is but a vision, a reflection on a revolving, thin, receding square, giving the impression of depth to the otherwise dark screen. A bright light, bluish in color and round like a distant sun, shines forth brilliantly but briefly in the distance only to be eclipsed again by the square. Two other abstract figures – ladders – appear alongside the square, all of which tumble disjointedly through what now appears to be a void. Three other ladder shapes appear, following straight lines toward the sun, vanishing as they pass by the square. The other three figures, the square and the two ladders, come together revealing the New Line Cinema logo ringed by a halo of blue light.

When it precedes other films, this animation is, of course, completely unremarkable, the standard New Line Cinema logo sequence, a repetition by which the corporation ritualistically conjures itself as origin – and so also the condition of possibility – of this film. The moment that the abstract shapes coalesce into the logo, the sequence suddenly disappoints: the logo is merely graphic, two-dimensional, the mundane mark of corporate authorship, underwriting, and ownership. The meaning of what we see – the square a representation of a film frame, the ladders its sprocket holes, and the light the projector's beam – is achieved through a clarifying movement, which mimics the movement of Hollywood narrative in general. Here as elsewhere, clarity is gained only with the loss of depth. Consequently, the meaning revealed is enigmatic: the square is devoid of an image, the sprocket hole on the right is broken. These are the ruins of modernity.

Sound, however, wraps this corporate credit in a veil of enchantment, restores the depth, so that the sequence can become something else entirely. In these opening moments of *The Fellowship of the Ring* we witness, it seems, the birth of a world. This is why a close analysis of this apparently insignificant sequence in terms of sound and image reveals such a profoundly ideological figure. Sound serves to confound issues of authorship, underwriting, and ownership and to place us on the cusp of myth, which exceeds the framing authority of financial control. Appearing in advance of the filmic image and consequently seeming to draw the latter into being, sound raises the question of origin: where does the film begin? This enigma in turn presses an ontological question: where does the world – indeed being itself – begin?

In using sound to bridge from the studio sequence to the film proper, *The Fellowship of the Ring* is doing nothing exceptionally novel. Many films, especially recent ones, begin with sound under the studio credit. It is a question of origin, not novelty. *The Lord of the Rings* self-consciously draws its origin, the origin of its world, from sound. This origin in sound is completely consistent with Tolkien's mythology, where the world is literally born of enchantment, sung before it is made. "And he spoke to them, propounding to them themes of music; and they sang before him, and he was glad" (*Silmarillion*, 3). This music, what Tolkien calls the Music of the Ainur, knows the future and determines the fate of the world. But the fate of Men, *The Silmarillion* tells us, lies beyond the Music (35-36). *The Lord of the Rings*, which recounts the end of the Third Age, is therefore necessarily a tale of disenchantment: as the old world of the Music – the world of Elves – fades, it gives way to the disenchanted world of Men. The destruction of Sauron and the departure of the Elves at the end of *The Return of the King* mark not just the end of the Third Age but the end of the Music. All that remains is its fading memory, which, in Tolkien's text, takes form as snippets of song (incomplete tales), especially those in Elvish.

The Lord of the Rings can be understood as a parable of modernization, whose icon is the machine. Although Tolkien had a famous distaste for allegory, even he could not deny the deep allegorical content contained in his mythology:

> I dislike Allegory – the conscious and intentional allegory – yet any attempt to explain the purport of myth or fairytale must use allegorical language.... Anyway all this stuff is mainly concerned with the Fall, Mortality, and the Machine. With Fall inevitably, and that motive occurs in several modes. With Mortality, especially as it affects art and the creative (or as I should say, sub-creative) desire which seems to have no biological function, and to be apart from the satisfactions of plain ordinary biological life, with which, in our world, it is indeed usually at strife. This desire is at once wedded to a passionate love of the real primary world, and hence filled with the sense of mortality, and yet unsatisfied by it. It has various opportunities of "Fall." It may become possessive, clinging to the things made as its own, the sub-creator wishes to be the Lord and God of his private creation. He will rebel against the laws of the Creator – especially against mortality. Both of these (alone or together) will lead to the desire for Power, for making the will more quickly effective, – and so to the Machine (or Magic). By the last I intend all use of external plans or devices (or apparatus) instead of developments of the inherent inner powers or talents – or even the use of these talents with the corrupted motive of the dominating: bulldozing the real world, or coercing other wills. The Machine is our more obvious form though more closely related to Magic than is usually recognized. (*Fellowship*, xv-xvi)

Tolkien's invocation of the Fall here is especially pertinent, because it brings to mind that other great mythological Fall, that of Eden. The departure from Eden, the separation from God, is the price of knowledge, which links Enlightenment and the acquisition of knowledge to disenchantment and loss. Although it would seem to bring darkness, the Fall is in fact a condition of possibility of enlightenment. A disenchanted world is the price of human autonomy and free will.

This notion of disenchantment descends from Max Weber, who used the term *Entzauberung*, literally "demagification." On the one hand, magic might be understood as already disenchanting, that is, as an instrumentalization of song. On the other hand, disenchantment assumes material form as the Machine, which is nothing other than a reification of disenchanted magic. This passage from Magic to Machine, the story of disenchantment, is precisely the Fall into the modern world of instrumentalized knowledge (Weber *Essays*). Disenchantment grows from the seeds of enchantment.

While the films follow Tolkien in condemning what Weber calls the "disenchantment of the world," they at the same time use music and sound to disguise their inextricable debt to modernity, magically exempting the cinematic apparatus from the disenchantments of the Machine. Very much in keeping with Tolkien's mythology, the soundtrack renders the modern world as a fall to earth, as a lamentable descent from enchantment to disenchantment, from the sung but wholly disembodied heavenly Music of the Ainur to the unsung instrumental or earthly embodied music of Men (with the Elves and other creatures from the old enchanted world serving as a mediating link between the Ainur and Men). This antimodern vision, filled with a characteristically modern nostalgia for a past that never was, twines the corporate origin of myth with the mythologized origin of international corporate capital, obscuring the historicity of the market in order to weave a veil of enchantment about the actual locus of modern power, that is, global capital. A close reading of the prologue in particular shows how music and sound serve this end: the representation of the mythic world in the film becomes at the same time a displaced representation of capital. Analyzing the relations on the soundtrack between vocal and instrumental music on the one hand and between embodiment and disembodiment on the other reveals this displaced representation to be a characteristic movement of the film, indeed an allegory of society as a whole, which is bound to live under the spell of capital.

Division and Disenchantment

Born of the mist, the celestial shimmer of sound, ever more musical but still formless, grows in intensity. As the screen plunges into darkness, the sound becomes disquieting, even unruly, panning across the stereo field before settling into a low string drone supporting harmonics in the upper strings. We immediately recognize this sound as not belonging fully – or even at all – to that image. The sound is now divided from the image that appears to accompany it. This original division will multiply throughout the prologue, indeed through the trilogy of films. And a longing to heal this division will power the narrative to seek a return to a moment of plenitudinous unity that never was.

"New Line Cinema" reappears as the strings emerge from the shimmer. This repetition of "New Line Cinema" also divides. Where the first image had appeared outside the film proper so that it set up the original division between image and sound, the second credit, in a font inspired by Tolkien's calligraphy, appears at the very origin of the world to come. This title in turn summons a sustained angelic tone that enters over a string drone as the title dissolves back into the void. A second corporate title, "Wingnut Productions," appears (in the same font as the second New Line Cinema title), dividing control between the two companies. This division, the appearance of the second title, motivates the voices into melodic declamation. This is the business of myth: to extend the corporate claim to a time before time. In putting the voice into motion, it also sets the world in motion; and the sound of this voice conjures the chant of an ancient world. If this enchanted opening reveals an origin in corporate ownership, which would like to extend the rule of capital, the pursuit of profit, and principle of private property from the beginning to the very ends of the earth, the way sound seems to escape the determinations of capital also conceals the extent to which these divisions are a product of that origin.

Divisions continually multiply throughout the opening of the prologue. A female voice whispers in Elvish, the marker of another division, and one that is now literally disenchanted, that is, spoken not sung. This voice, too, is divided: Elvish and English; and the storytelling, the history of a world that is fading into forgetfulness, is already figured as a loss by the need for a translation that is indeed inadequate to the idea it represents. This notion of translation inheres in Tolkien's own texts. The very opening of *The Silmarillion*, for instance, bears the trace of linguistic division: "There was Eru, the One, who in Arda is called Ilúvatar" (*Silmarillion*, 3). Then, too, it is well-known that Tolkien constructed his mythology as a way to explain the deep historical connection of the two forms of Elvish, Eldarin and Sindarin, his invented languages, which were themselves presented as a product of division, the sundering of the Elves. Moreover, his texts were not written primarily in Elvish, but English. And the fragments of Elvish that actually appear consist primarily of chanted songs, tales of ages past. In other words, Elvish appears in *The Lord of the Rings*, both text and film, as the language of a primordial, enchanted world that is already fading.

The opening words of the prologue – "The world is changed" – speak to this division, marking a separation between old world and new. Indeed even the narrator's perception of this separation divides the world into three of the four cardinal elements: "I feel it in the *water*. I feel it in the *earth*. I smell it in the *air*." This division, the perception of a world on the cusp of change, leads to a profound melancholy over the fading of the old world: "Much that once was is lost. For none now live who remember it." Instrumental music becomes associated with this loss, as it displaces song just before the narrator – Galadriel, as it will turn out – gives the loss voice. It is a loss linked in turn inextricably to the Ring, as the title, "Lord of the Rings," begins to appear on Galadriel's enunciation of the word "it." The statement of the languid Ring theme, which seems to carry the burden of the world, itself lags behind the title, sounding only when the title becomes fully manifest; the process then reverses, the title fading just as the motive ends.

The theme and the title fill the space of another division: the film passes from the timeless time of myth to the deep historical time of legend. Galadriel narrates a new origin: "It began... ": the shift to the past tense marks the beginning of history, but it is a false origin, or at least a disingenuous beginning. Anyone who has read Tolkien's texts knows that the changing world, the entry into history, began, if anywhere, with Fëanor, the Silmarils, the Kinslaying and the return to Middle Earth of the Noldor. Galadriel's narrative therefore itself mythologizes, "beginning" with precisely the particular history we are hearing about, a history told from the perspective of the Elves, that is, already in division. "It began with the forging of the Great Rings," Galadriel intones, passing over a second Fall, the Elvish will to power that prompts this alliance with Sauron. "There cannot be any 'story' without a fall," Tolkien writes. "All stories are ultimately about the fall" (xi). But where the first fall served to initiate history, the second is at root an attempt to arrest this history. In this sense Galadriel's opening lament on change is a sublated recognition that change is a sign not just of the fading of the Elves but of the waning of the Elvish power of enchantment over the course of history. The presence of the Ring theme bespeaks a truth that Galadriel's words do not.

Refrain of the Ring

History in Galadriel's tale begins appropriately with sound *effects*, a mode of disenchantment even further removed from song than the spoken voice. This move toward disenchantment is linked immediately to power and magic, the forging of the Rings. The appearance of the Rings also completes the unity of the four cardinal elements: water, earth, air, and fire. Fire had indeed been anticipated with a shift in color from the blue-white of the corporate credits to the red-orange of the title, a color scheme brought over into the original image of the history, and so also the original moment of synchronized sound with the pouring of molten metal into the mold. From this point until the inscription appears on the One Ring, sound effects are restricted to fire; and the sound of the inscription that marks the presence of its power on the hand of Sauron recalls, albeit faintly, the ethereal music of the very opening as if to suggest that the fiery power this ring taps is indeed primordial.

As the prologue continues, music momentarily drops out and sound effects multiply in a sweeping crescendo that announces the entrance into the time of epic narrative: the terrified crowd, a heavy breath accompanying a map of Middle Earth, the marching of the Last Alliance, the hissing of Orcs, the firing of arrows, the locking of shields and so forth right up to Elendil's cry of victory and Elrond's final sword thrust. While this crescendo begins with an alternation between the dark forces and the alliance, the soundtrack is more and more dominated by sound effects associated with the alliance and its display of might even as the music, which returned at the appearance of the alliance, boils up into mythic rage. The crescendo reaches its apex as the violent chorus grows frantic and the camera tracks quickly toward Elrond frozen in place.

Here, the sound quickly collapses, music reduced to four deep, ominous heartbeats, effects rattling superfluously in the background. Metallic footsteps reverberate offscreen as musical heartbeats pound, ending in a roar and an electronically generated effect – again akin to the primordial music of the very opening – marking the presence of Sauron and the Ring. The power of the Ring is manifested aurally by the way Sauron now dominates the soundtrack, which returns immediately to the previous apex and indeed makes a further crescendo. The music, too, picks up where it had left off before the collapse. The Ring allows Sauron to appropriate the mythic rage, turning it demonic; and the sounds of his clearing the field saturate the soundtrack on each swipe of his scepter until he strikes Elendil. Then, the soundtrack suddenly collapses into four distinct effects: the strike, Elendil hitting the wall, the sword landing on stone, and Elendil dropping to the ground. These effects punctuate the cry of a new musical motive, whose pathos-filled strings shift markedly from the violent vocal music that preceded it. The last note of this four-note motive is stretched beyond measure as though the music had nowhere to go, analogous to the narration: "When all hope had faded." A low rumble – apparently footsteps – obliterates this held note, as Sauron appears again looming over Isildur.

And yet, though the situation appears hopeless, music perceives that not all is lost: a faint horn note emerges from the rumble and swells defiantly as Isildur reaches for the sword. Like the theme that marked Elendil's death, the music here, too, is punctuated by a series of effects; and the scene plays aurally almost as a varied repetition of Elendil's death: Isildur's cry, the breaking of Narsil, a second cry, the cutting of Sauron's finger, the cry of Sauron, the Ring hitting the ground, the explosion, the piece of mail hitting the ground and finally Sauron's helmet. Here the effects form a breathlessly quick crescendo that matches the music right up to Sauron's explosion, after which music and effects make a second, even briefer crescendo that cadences precisely as the mail hits the ground. A moment of echoing silence, then the helmet lands heavily with the sound of doom, a metallic shudder that resounds as if the very gates of hell had snapped shut. Lying on the ground, Sauron's finger, Ring unscathed, sizzles, a last ember of the fire that had initiated the recounting of this history. As Isildur stares, bewitched, the Ring motive, which had not sounded since the title, returns, offering a closure that, however, does not come. It becomes a refrain rather than a recapitulation.

"The Ring passed to Isildur," Galadriel continues, "who had this one chance to destroy evil forever." The burden of evil is laid on Isildur and therefore Men. Galadriel's narration is again somewhat disingenuous, deflecting responsibility for the existence of the Ring from the Elves to the weakness of Men for not destroying it. "But the hearts of Men are easily corrupted. And the Ring of Power has a will of its own." As it does throughout the prologue, the Ring motive indicates the passing of the Ring from bearer to bearer, and the lugubrious sound of the theme represents both its attraction (the melodic figure dancing slowly around and gracing the upper dominant) and the weight of its burden (the drawn out tempo; the brief initial pause on and general emphasis given to the sixth scale degree in the melody, which makes the theme seem reluctant to return to the dominant; and the abrupt collapse to the tonic).

The recurrence of the theme thus serves not so much to underscore the presence of the Ring as to mark the passage of history (Abbate *Voices*). Each caesura in the line of bearers is filled by a refrain of the motive, which marks the moment of loss linking one bearer to the next. The line of descent follows a path of disenchantment from the mythic, magical Sauron to the legendary Dúnadan Isildur to the historical creature Gollum, to the adventuresome Hobbit Bilbo, to the reluctant Hobbit Frodo, ultimately reaching its furthest point of disenchantment in the servant Hobbit Sam, before the process begins to reverse itself; and it is this retrogression that provides the energy, as it were, to literally sever the line and return the Ring to its origin, bending the line of history back on itself and enclosing its power in the enchanted circle of myth. Once the Ring is destroyed, evil has been vanquished, perhaps; but the power of the Elves quickly diminishes with the destruction of the Ring, and Men inherit a disenchanted world.

Repetition and Return

The theatrical release of *The Fellowship of the Ring* and the extended version on the DVD disagree as to where the film proper begins (the introduction of the Shire is the first significant departure of the extended version from the theatrical release) and the relation that each of these beginnings forms with the prologue is decidedly different, even if both present the enchanting image of untroubled peasant life. In the theatrical release, the Shire is introduced aurally by the sounds of nature accompanied by Gandalf's singing and punctuated by wagon noises. The introduction of the Shire here thus offers a mundane variation of the opening sequence in the prologue: the music of nature yields to song and effects before dialogue is eventually introduced. Nondiegetic instrumental music assumes the narrative function of Galadriel's voiceover, marking the scene as peaceful, pastoral, mundane, the farthest thing from the grand mythic tone set by the prologue.

Yet, as with the prologue, the narration here is also disingenuous and unreliable; the representation of an innocent pastoral, an illusion. If the scene enchants with a nostalgic picture of a timeless Neolithic as yet untouched by the ravaging forces of modernity, its changeless appearance is nevertheless sustained through the power of machines, however absent forged metal might be from the image. The initial sound effect, the clattering wagon, suggests a parallel with the fire that forged the Rings of Power, the jingling bells an aural cue to the hidden presence of forged metal. The wheels of the wagon resemble the Ring not just in shape; they are also a form, as it were, of disenchanted magic, a machine that, like the Ring, harnesses and amplifies power. While we might object that it is

Gandalf, the wizard, who intrudes on the Shire with this wagon, the fact that a windmill revolves unobtrusively in the background in one shot and a water wheel turns in another makes explicit the connection between circular form and power.

"Concerning Hobbits" in the extended DVD version likewise plays as a mundane variation of the opening of the prologue, though with somewhat different emphases than the theatrical release version. A single note sounds, carried over as a transition, reminiscent of the drone that emerged out of the ethereal opening music. But instead of the black screen of the prologue, this sequence begins by panning across a map of Middle Earth. The vocal music is replaced by the faint sound of birds chattering in the background, and the sound of Bilbo clearing his throat serves as a sort of analogue to the whispered Elvish. Bilbo starts to narrate, beginning with the fixing of time and place, where Galadriel spoke of change. Instrumental music enters as Bilbo recounts the year: "In the year 1400, by Shire reckoning." Where the instrumental music behind Galadriel's narration had been preparatory to the Ring motive that followed, the music here is a pastoral meandering air, which unlike that in the theatrical release signifies "Shire" abstractly, much like its representation on the map. The Shire soon appears in actuality (albeit under the control of Bilbo's narration), with its unchanging character preserved through the force of Bilbo's representation of it. As Bilbo will put it later in his narrative, "Things are made to endure in the Shire . . . There's always been a Baggins living here under the Hill in Bag End. And there always will be." Bilbo's relation to the Shire is structured by nostalgia, which is a manifestation of the fear that the world has indeed changed and the Shire along with it. Even the very title of his book, *There and Back Again: A Hobbit's Tale*, reflects his desire to arrest the changing forces of history and return the time of the Shire to a cycle bound by the traditional rhythms of agrarian life.

After Bilbo's preamble on time, the music shifts to the Fellowship theme as the title appears. As with the prologue, where the "Lord of the Rings" title and Ring motive divided Galadriel's preamble from her narrative proper, so too the title and Fellowship theme here divide Bilbo's voiceover, fill the time of a narrative pause. The theme accompanies a meandering tracking shot into Bilbo's study, which focuses on a fire burning in the circular fireplace before settling on Bilbo writing at his desk. Whether we take the ambiguous sound effect here to be the hearth fire gently crackling or the scratching of Bilbo's pen on parchment, the sound follows the opposite course of the opening prologue, toward the representation of a domesticated commonplace rather than the unleashing of preternatural forces. As fire, this effect is the furthest thing from the raging flames of the mythical forge. Yet, like the concealed metal and machines working discretely in the background of the Shire, the affinity with the fire in the opening prologue can hardly be denied. As the sound of a pen, the effect makes the silence of the fire into an analogue with the prologue by negation. The emphasis would fall instead on the power of writing, the attempt to narrate in order not to forget, to preserve history and keep its changing force at bay by enclosing it in the pages of a book.

Where Galadriel's voice continued to hover numinously disembodied above the world it recounted, Bilbo's voiceover is quickly embodied, brought down to earth, as he recites the title that attempts to contain his tale (Silverman *Mirror*, 48-49). And this difference is emphasized in the initiation into narrative proper: Galadriel's "It began..." is echoed by Bilbo's "Now, where to begin?" And where Galadriel first presented an accounting of the Rings of Power, Bilbo can only "begin" by documenting the essential characteristics of the Hobbits, as though these are fixed and eternal qualities. What both share despite the difference in tone and apparent historical magnitude is a resistance to letting the narrative, and so also history, proceed. Although Bilbo's tale is a story of personal growth, it masquerades as cyclical comings and goings, there and back again. It is entirely consistent that Bilbo never manages to recount any of his story, jumping straight from descriptive prologue to final line: "I've thought up an ending for my book: 'And he lived happily ever after to the end of his days.'" If his story therefore ends with the recognition of mortality, the weariness he expresses to Gandalf on leaving the Shire is a product of his fall into self-knowledge, a loss of innocence that the fixing of the Shire seeks to repair and reclaim. Bilbo's disenchantment here accords with Tolkien's conception of *The Hobbit* as taking "a virtually human point of view" – that is, one whose fall is structured by a descent into knowledge – so that *The Hobbit* becomes "the completion of the whole [mythology], its mode of descent, and merging into 'history.'"

Terms of Disenchantment

The descent to earth and "merging into 'history'" – perhaps we might better say the fall of myth into history – starts from the premise that the modern world has lost the power to enchant, that history is the disenchanted form of myth. This descent is figured musically in two ways: instrumental music as a fall from vocal music; and embodied music as a fall from disembodiment. If the prologue already associates disembodied vocal music with the Elves and other forces of enchantment and thereby sets up the operatic idea of instrumental music as a corresponding figure of loss and disenchantment (Chua *Music*, esp. 29-50), the soundtrack as a whole is organized around this principle as well, and relatively consistently.

Most of the major themes of Men and Hobbits are, as director Peter Jackson puts it, "hummable," yet they are seldom, if at all, given voice. Thus the Shire theme that accompanies the fixing of place and time at the opening of Bilbo's narration is an unsung song of pastoral bliss, the instrumental scoring here transforming the music into a figure of loss. Likewise, the themes of Rohan and Gondor, while similarly characteristic of place, are also only instrumental. The world of Men and Hobbits, though bathed in unheard music, is marked as disenchanted by virtue of deafness to this music and, consequently, by an inability to sing the music of the world.

The Elves and other creatures of the old mythological world are characterized more often than not by disembodied vocal music. In the case of the Nazgûl, this music resembles mortal music in seeming wholly nondiegetic. The presence of the choir, however, weaves these figures in a veil of dark enchantment, and the diegetic cries of the wraiths seem to place all of them except perhaps the Witch-king beyond language, beyond music, beyond the world. It is in effect the inverse of Men and Hobbits; a mortal world whose bodily decay is arrested by the power of enchantment. Sauron's voice, although more sound effect than music, is wholly disembodied, most spectacularly in the Mouth of Sauron.[1] And the Black Speech of Mordor is clearly an enchanted language, even more so than Elvish, as the effect of Gandalf's uttering it in Rivendell makes clear. The Elves, on the contrary, are typically characterized by a vocal music that hovers nebulously between the diegetic and the nondiegetic, disembodied but of the world.

Like the voiceover, vocal music is available to mortals only as something embodied and strictly diegetic. Often, especially with the Hobbits, it is raucous and earthy, at furthest remove from the airy music of the Elves. When Aragorn haltingly sings snatches of the Lay of Lúthien, what comes across, despite his chanting sadly in Elvish, is the distance from the tale, its lack of completeness, and its raspy wavering tone. The mortal voice only ever achieves the status of allegory, signifying through its representation what it fails to reach: the enchantment that lies beyond the bodily voice. Aragorn's song is a music that has fallen to earth. Likewise, Pippin's moving lament before Denethor literally sings his disenchantment. It receives its power by acknowledging the descent to earth, which is underscored by the dissonant accompaniment added as the horsemen begin their hopeless charge on Osgiliath. The song is wracked with Pippin's painful recognition that music has no power over the world.

Those moments that fall outside this typology are typically marked as liminal: death, as in the fall of Boromir; divine intervention, as when Gollum seizes the Ring from Frodo or when Frodo and Sam are rescued from Mordor by the eagles; or apparitions of the old mythical world, as in Khazad-dûm, which like Elvish music hovers ambiguously in the space between diegetic and nondiegetic. Most of these exceptions also make use of slow-motion camera work and a severe reduction in extraneous diegetic sound, further cinematic signs of liminality.

---

[1] Like Hal in *2001: A Space Odyssey* (1968), Sauron is what Michel Chion calls an "acousmêtre," an acoustical being. See Chion *Audio-Vision*, 129-131 and *Voice*, 140-151.

Myth and Power

I have suggested that the sound and music, but also the films themselves, adhere closely to the mythological underpinnings of Tolkien's world, even if they take liberties in presenting Tolkien's narrative. Whether the films were ultimately faithful to Tolkien is, however, neither here nor there for any but textual fundamentalists. The films succeed or fail not on the faithfulness of the adaptation, but on the eloquence, insight, significance, and coherence they bring to the representation. We might nevertheless ask: what are the films' investment in the myth? What profit do they seek to extract in this retelling? If the profit is not purely monetary, their success nevertheless redounds to the film industry, which reaps not only the monetary profits but also, and perhaps more importantly, a claim to the image of enchantment these films sell to their viewers. And this is perhaps an even more insidious aspect of film in general and of these films in particular: they bewitch their audience, appropriating the power of myth by giving a semblance of what the audience wants. Like Isildur, we claim this Ring as our own.

Such criticism is, of course, voiced often enough against the film industry. But seldom does a film take up a story, indeed a whole mythology, so pointed in its attacks on modernity while also using the whole modern apparatus of illusionary filmmaking, apparently oblivious to that critique. Tolkien, for instance, demonizes the magic of the machine, linking it directly to the Two Towers, Isengard and Barad-dûr. The films follow suit. Isengard, says composer Howard Shore, represents "the industrial age," and he wrote his music for it in a 5/4 meter to evoke the feeling of "things being a little off-kilter." Appropriately, the music is repetitive and impressively menacing, grinding continuously like a giant, infernal machine, engine of modern industry run amok. And it is hard not to extend the allegory to the Orcs and Uruk-hai, who become by analogy the unwashed proletariat reproduced only to feed the ravenous machine that would consume the world. Yet the films differ from Tolkien in this important respect: far more than Tolkien's books, they require the very modern technology that they condemn.[2] To represent this enchanted world on film demands extensive technology, indeed, all the wizardry that the film industry can muster. The necessity of this technology testifies to the instrumentalization at the heart of filmic enchantment, its heavy debt to the capitalist power that finances, builds, and maintains the machinery of the film industry. However mythic the subject may appear onscreen, the mode of its representation is necessarily and thoroughly modern, the best that capital can buy.

Music becomes an important instrument in the production of this characteristically modern illusion, this enchanting cinematic sleight of hand. "It's designed really to transport you into another world," director Peter Jackson says of the music. It brings "the world of Middle Earth to life." As noted above, this function of animating the world, of stirring it into being, is present from the very outset of the opening prologue, where music serves not just to inaugurate the world but also to underwrite the myth of corporate origin. Music permeates the films to mask this corporate presence, and that of the technology that made the representation possible; it distracts its audience from recognizing the corporate machinery whirring in the background. The unreal presence of music is the point of distraction: the musical saturation allows the audience to hear the musicality of a world that has receded into the mythical past. Where the screened world hums with music, the modern world of the audience is by contrast silent. The Elves may sing of a world that exists no longer and may long for its return, but, unsung, instrumental music becomes, by contrast, an allegory of the fall of Men and Hobbits into a disenchanted world, a world of human – that is, mortal – knowledge. Although the films ask us to mourn this loss along with the Elves, the silence of our world is not necessarily a loss, but the legacy of the Ring passing out of this world, receding from history into myth.

The films, however, do everything in their power to discourage this reading. Like Frodo in the Crack of Doom, they have difficulty letting go

---

[2] Yet Tolkien does not escape the forces of modernity he decries any more than do the films, which are themselves but the latest manifestation of the Tolkien industry. The dissemination of Tolkien's mythic world indeed requires the printing press. And if we think that printing is merely a contingent aspect in the production of his texts, we should recall the lengths to which he went to reclaim his U.S. copyright over *The Lord of the Rings*.

of enchantment. Sam, the quintessential Hobbit, recognizes what needs to be done, but he cannot act. The task is not his but Frodo's. Only one who knows its charm has the power to break its spell. Frodo in fact fails, refuses to let go the power of enchantment, and his severed finger is the price he pays to disenchant the earth. Characteristically, disenchantment is thus allied with absence and loss. And if Frodo cannot ultimately bear the burden of disenchantment, he can always sail to the Blessed Realm, where enchantment is eternal.

Yet the scenario is incoherent on this point: in the films, the Shire remains what it was: the image of blissful pastoral life. Enchantment is apparently already eternal, and it is as though nothing really happened. History, rather than the nostalgic image of the Shire, becomes the illusion. Consequently, once the story has been written down, preserved, and so safely contained, paradise has been won. Frodo in essence simply exchanges one paradise for another. Sailing into the sunset is simply a conventional close, that superfluous cinematic cliché whereby Hollywood promises a utopia it cannot deliver: "And he lived happily ever after..."

But one cannot simply go there and back again. History intervenes. Knowledge and experience are acquired along the journey or there would be no story to tell. Even Bilbo appended the sign of mortality – "to the end of his days" – as a recognition of his disenchantment, of the impossibility contained in his title. Tolkien acknowledges this impossibility in *The Lord of the Rings*, too, with the otherwise superfluous "Scouring of the Shire." The decision to excise this episode suggests that the filmmakers either did not understand its place within Tolkien's text or understood it all too well, since the episode runs contrary to Hollywood's own tendency to arrest history, to see action only as a countervailing force to evil. Tolkien's episode, on the contrary, places emphasis on restoration, suggesting that a disenchanted world might still make its own magic if it but resist the forces of modernity. Whether or not we accept this charming ideological fantasy, we can at least acknowledge that Tolkien has the courage not to stop there. Frodo, Bilbo, even Sam are the ones who ultimately fade, who fade rather than die. Mortality – the "strange gift" of Ilúvatar – and also the fruits of disenchantment lay beyond them. They must sail beyond the world, leaving the world unchanged so that it might change, for better or worse. For if this mythology belongs to the Elves rather than to us, they, not we, remain caught within the veil of its enchantment.

It does not pay, however, for the end of *The Return of the King* to leave its audience with the fleeting thought that enchantment may not be the best of all possible worlds. This is the business of "Into the West," the haunting song Annie Lennox sings over the credits: it returns to the terms of enchantment laid out in the final scene and colors them with nostalgia. Singing of departing Middle Earth on gray ships, it nevertheless mourns our loss, our fall into the luciferous disenchantment to come as we descend from the theater and find ourselves not in Middle Earth but in the harsh light of the modern world. Naturally, our loss is the industry's gain, the sales of the song entering into the calculations of the film's ancillary revenue and so also the films' ultimate commercial success. The presence of "Into the West" if not the text itself thus recalls the myth of origin: in the beginning was the corporation. It is left to our disenchantment to break this spell that modern corporate capital would weave about its profit.

"Wicked, Tricksy, False": Race, Myth, and Gollum

Cynthia Fuchs

> *"It cannot be seen, cannot be felt,*
> *Cannot be heard cannot be smelt.*
> *It lies behind stars and under hills,*
> *And empty holes it fills.*
> *It comes first and follows after,*
> *Ends life, kills laughter.*
> *Answer: Dark"*
> One of Gollum's riddles, from *The Hobbit*

The Return of the King begins with a recollection. Like the prologues in the previous films, this one sets an historical background, marks a violence that frames the current crisis. But here the connection between past and present is intensely personal, the story of one character's brutal death and worse rebirth. The beginning of Gollum, this scene suggests, is yet another beginning of *The Lord of the Rings*. As he falls into sudden dread and eternal longing, Gollum comes to embody two related mythologies. The first, more familiar, concerns lost innocence, as Gollum is cast out into darkness. The second, stranger and messier, has to do with lost self. It is an origin story of metaphorical, cultural, and political dimensions. It is a story of race.

While *The Lord of the Rings* films showcase the racing of various communities and armies in order to produce moral and political order, Gollum's racing is a unique and uniquely disordering experience. If race is typically constructed by processes of objectification, identification, and especially categorization, Gollum, being the only one of his kind, is uncategorizable except as himself. Even more traumatic and emblematic, this character lacks a sense of his own identity, caught between Sméagol and Gollum. He is thus defined by his difference – from others and from himself.

The initial setting is serene: two Hobbits, Sméagol and his cousin Déagol, are fishing. The sun is out, birds chirp. The peace, however, is fleeting. When Déagol is pulled into the water by an especially large, dark fish, he spots a shiny object on the river's floor. Grabbing it, he clambers to shore, opens his hand, peers at and pets the Ring he has pulled out. An ominous, churchy chorus comes up on the soundtrack, and Sméagol appears behind him. "Give us that, Déagol, my love," he whispers, his voice suddenly transformed into Gollum's rasp, adapting the plural pronoun that signals Gollum's perpetual self-split. "Why?" asks Déagol, himself rather taken by the muddy Ring. "Because," insists Sméagol, the camera close on his face as his cousin is lost to view, a mass of wet hair and forehead, "It's my birthday and I wants it."

Indeed, it is Sméagol's birthday. Or more precisely, it is the day of Sméagol's loss and Gollum's birth, occasioned by the discovery – hardly accidental, but fated in the Rings mythology – of the One Ring. The music goes low and orchestral, throbbing and whooshing as if to indicate the introduction of a cartoonish ghost, and Sméagol becomes monstrous. He grabs at his cousin, they struggle, each trying to throttle the other. The camera careens to show the trees above, still dappled in light, and then tumbles downward, focused on Sméagol putting Déagol down, his face strained and intent as he strangles his dearest relative and closest friend. He pulls the Ring from Déagol's dead fingers and holds it to his face, the camera framing them as lovers: "My Precious," he gasps, just as he's literally zapped from view.

Sméagol's immediate reappearance as he is first being consumed by Ringness demonstrates the simultaneity that will plague him, as

Gollum: he's launched into a dark and rocky terrain, climbing up a hillside but descending into his own mind. Gollum's voice intones as Sméagol shivers and clutches at his own filthy wet body, bent into himself as the camera circles, denying him space for movement or location. The forest is dark and oppressive. The frame is his alone. The voiceover growls, "They cursed us. Murderer they called us. They cursed us and drove us away." A close-up of the Ring in his hand cuts to Sméagol's face as he gags and turns pale, speaking his new name, the name of a solitary being: "Gollum." At this point, the voiceover becomes more clearly Gollum's as it is integrated into the film's broader narrative fabric: the camera pulls out and up to show Sméagol-becoming-Gollum crouching in the rain. "And we wept, Precious," he mourns, the biblical rhythm intimating "their" beginning. The environment becomes synchronous with his internal state, and "Precious" becomes both part of that state and its externalized opposite, grasped and desired but never attained. "We wept to be so alone."

Possession and Consumption

Being alone precisely defines Gollum's race, not so much as he possesses race or raced identification but as though he is consumed by it. The Ring represents such lack of (self-)possession ("He wants the Precious," says Gollum, as everyone, from himself to evil Lord Saruman to Frodo to Sauron might be enveloped by the pronoun. "Always he is looking for it. And the Precious is wanting to go back to him... But we mustn't let him have it"). Imagining the Precious to have a desire that mirrors his own, Gollum, like any addict, yet knows its dangers, that possession means his end. The addiction transforms him, makes him unknowable even to himself. To an extent, addiction circumscribes his new self, as he is shaped solely as raw need and want. The Ring afflicts Frodo, but because he has the "strength" to fight its pull, because he is not like Gollum, Frodo is the films' hero, while Gollum will be their scoundrel, a character so depleted of identity and audience identification that he might be considered un-human in comparison to the many humanized Fellows; this even as he is as crucial to the Ring's eventual obliteration as any of the heroes.

The Ring produces Gollum, the aftereffect of Sméagol's enchantment and obliteration, the wholly bereft being, without self-knowledge or comprehension of time and place. Gollum is Gollum. He eats fish and worms raw ("so juicy sweet"), he abides in shadows, he scuttles rather than walks upright. "And we forgot the taste of bread, the sound of trees, the softness of the wind, we even forgot our own name." All this loss of "civilization," memory, and self is in order to focus only on "my Precious," the Ring that ordains Gollum's existence and leads the other, many communities in the *Lord of the Rings* movies to war and devastation. Slithery, gaunt, and convulsive, Gollum's split self is also perversely and intelligently nuanced. So desperate to hold the Precious, so quick to despise Sam and deceive Frodo, this transformed Hobbit is a most remarkably imagined "other," a newly raced being. Because he is unique, he remains frighteningly untethered to community or history (despite and because of his personal backstory). Without a knowable identity or ambition, haunted by traumatic memories, Gollum has no place to be, except the fiery Cracks of Doom into which he throws himself at last.

This essay examines Gollum's lack of definition in particular relation to race, as he evolves during the three films. Though the trilogy is surely troubled by race throughout, Gollum's is the only one deemed wholly other, gruesome and victimized (by the intoxicating Ring) and, most strangely, unfixed. This has to do with his literal construction as hybrid human-CGI, and with his narrative and thematic uses, at once mythic and mundane, the repository for protagonists' and viewers' fears and judgments.

Gollum is Gollum, but he is also, always, not. This conflict, which the filmmakers refer to as Gollum's "schizophrenia," forms and unforms his race. It makes him special, and "Precious," as well as emblematic. Race here is understood as an individual experience as well as a collective one, a movement toward meaning and also away from stability. It is, as Frantz Fanon has argued, a "fact" determined by objectification, that is, a "seal[ing] into that crushing objecthood," as an individual's "fragments [are] put together again by another self" (Fanon *Black Skin*, 109). For Gollum, the objectifying gaze is his own, and this is what designates his simultaneous difference and sameness. He forgets "our own name" and is transformed into "it," so deemed by skeptical helpmeet Sam and compassionate master Frodo. Although he is plainly masculine (he has a penis, at least), Gollum's engendering is of a piece with his othering, his body visible evidence of his devastating dearth.

He is so completely unlike all, that his unique race becomes a kind of gender and class, too. Although Frodo might be related to Gollum in their shared experience of the Ring, Frodo also remains Frodo, not newly named or reborn as another, but fighting the curse-addiction of the Ring. Frodo retains his connection to his past, yearning for the Shire. Gollum only regrets his past, recalling that he is Sméagol when Frodo tells him his name, in *The Two Towers* as they arrive at the Dead Marshes. "Once it takes hold of us," Gollum says as he watches Frodo clutch the Ring beneath his blouse, "It never lets go." "Us" here means "Gollum," as this is his consistent self-description, but it also means Frodo, resisting the power of the Ring, yet in the process of falling.

This process – metaphorical for loss of innocence as a coming into self – is made visible in the next few moments, when Frodo plunges into the marshes, where he thrashes about and the ghosty-green corpses grab at him until Gollum hauls him out. Shocked to be rescued by his seeming enemy and reluctant guide, Frodo asks the film's crucial question: "Who are you?" Gollum, only concerned that he has saved "our Precious," rejects the question out of hand: "Mustn't ask. Not its business." Here we come to understand that Gollum's absent gender not only pertains to how he is perceived by others, but also to his perception of those around him. Without a social context, Gollum has only the Precious. All breathing beings are only conduits or obstacles to that end. And so Gollum slides into one of his preferred elusive modes, reciting cryptic but relevant poetry: "Cold be heart and hand and bone. Cold be travelers far from home."

This description of "cold" speaks again to Gollum's own experience, as he is forever far from home and cannot remember warmth or closeness. But it is also his version of empathy: looking at Frodo shiver, he sees his own feeling reflected. In this compulsion to possess, or just be near, the Ring, Gollum is not unlike Frodo. Their bond and similarity – as well as their difference – are demonstrated later that night, when Frodo strokes the Ring and Gollum, crouching by water's edge, apart from the Hobbits, mirrors his action. Frodo sees him at last, not as a creature only to be roped, used, and abused, but as a being "not so different from a Hobbit once." Self-conscious and disheartened, Gollum looks down and away, as Frodo speaks his former name: "Sméagol." Gollum looks up and directly into Frodo's eyes. "What did you call me?" Gollum repeats the concept: "My name, my name. Sméagol." And with that, the trio is beset by Ringwraiths, an action interlude interrupting Gollum's potential memory and punctuating it at the same time.

As this scene marks both Gollum's utter difference and his sameness with regard to the Hobbits, it raises complex questions concerning race, as well as its associations with morality and culture, its representations and invocations. And so, its abrupt ending is probably apt, for the films cannot work through these complexities, given their focus on the triumph of what amounts to whiteness (affiliated with "diversity" in the forms of Elves and Dwarves). Instead, Gollum is the films' most prominent cipher, the sign of process that is forever paused, the story that can't be told. This doesn't mean he has no story, however, or that he is unreadable. It means that his story drives everyone else's. As co-producer Rick Porras puts it in "The Taming of Sméagol," one of the appendices to the *Two Towers* DVD, "Gollum was definitely this pivotal character in all three movies even though he barely shows up in the first film. He's so significant in the second and the third because of what happens with that Ring. No matter how successful Peter would have been in the telling of that story, if Gollum hadn't worked it all would have fallen apart. It would have been like a house of cards." While this pronouncement is surely promotional speech, it also suggests the character's foundational role. Gollum's fall allows everything else to follow. And his fall into this seminal identity is also a function of its opposite, necessary for Frodo's ascent and only possible by Sméagol's transformation into not-Sméagol. The final image of Gollum's origin story, at the start of *The Return of the*

King, shows his transformation into a not-self: "My Precious," he sputters, as the screen goes swiftly and portentously black.

In "Beyond Black and White: Race and Postmodernism in the *Lord of the Rings* Films," Sue Kim argues that raced representations in *The Lord of the Rings* films are troubled by what she calls "the problem of selective applicability" ("Beyond," 881). Tallying the many explicit representations of raced differences in the films, from Orcs and Uruks to Easterlings and Southrons, she concedes that such grotesque characterizations and "infelicitous casting" (of Caucasian, M ori, or S moan actors, for examples) are at one level, as the filmmakers contend, only an effort to "invoke" representations in Tolkein's books without judging their contexts or motivations. And yet they are also indications of broader structures. Kim goes on, "One of the most curious things about the films' racial codings is that they appear to have no referent; they function at the level of pure discourse" (880). And yet, of course, they do *have* referents, historical, aesthetic, and sociopolitical. Similarly, as much as the "films' production and distribution epitomize the logic of global late capitalism," Kim notes (citing labor, financing, and distribution systems), their effects and the stories they tell are hardly models of equity and transition. Tales of triumph written by the victors, they are, above all, reflections of the moments that have produced them – both Tolkien's and our own. Kim observes that while the story of *The Lord of the Rings* "stresses the importance and power of history, continuity, identity, and ethics, the films rely on discontinuity, alienation, moral vacuity, and suppressed pasts and presents. The films' "racializations," drawing on popular racial discourses, mystify race into the abstract (it is there while not being there), ignoring and denying the actual political realities of racialization and late capitalism while relying on those very processes" (895).

Gollum serves as the most egregious, revelatory, and mystified of such racializations. In part, this has to do with his "personal" story, but it also has to do with the story of his technical and cinematic coming into existence, the product of whole squads of designers and artists, from the Weta Workshop and elsewhere (Richard Taylor, Weta Workshop's creative supervisor, says on the *Two Towers* DVD, that "Tasked with bringing Gollum to life on the screen as a living breathing creature was all-invading in our thoughts for a long time"). Here such invention is rendered with an eye toward the inclusiveness of "race" as a category, exemplified by the collaboration of communities and transitions across time and space in the *Lord of the Rings* films. Still, Gollum remains fundamentally foreign, not like any other character, rejected for his severe appearance, dreadful groveling, and wretched obsessiveness. His story, unlike others, is not one of redemption, but one of destruction. So much a part of the Ring that he cannot live or even imagine himself without it, he becomes the necessary vehicle for the Ring's return to Mordor, and the release of the "good" armies from the potent aggression of the "bad." Donna Haraway has famously stated, "Every story that begins with original innocence and privileges the return to wholeness imagines the drama of life to be individuation, separation, the birth of the self, the tragedy of autonomy, the fall into writing, alienation; that is, war, tempered by imaginary respite in the bosom of the Other" (Haraway "Manifesto," 178). As war rages around him, the wasted Gollum hardly has a bosom; he is the other offering no gleam of respite, only the gloom of death. And yet his fall is the saving fall. Where Frodo fails to fall (or let go the Ring), Gollum cannot help himself.

Race and Naming

As the other others exemplify some recognizable racing – "Asiatic," or "black" or "Caucasian" – Gollum is only barely human, his huge eyes and Iggy Pop-inspired emaciation suggesting only that he might have been something or someone else. In his embodiment of absence, he reflects those who judge him. Gollum is fundamentally conceived in lack – of past, character, and belonging. He first appears, some eight minutes into *The Two Towers*, first just an idea, a point of view over a cliff gazing down – like the accompanying rain – on Frodo and Sam, and then as a bony hand, his long fingers gripping at the cliff's edge. Within seconds, Gollum is visible, climbing down the rock face, the camera following close on the digital creature as it approaches the Hobbits. He grabs and fights with Sam, violently, until Frodo comes with "Sting," a sword guaranteed to slice through his translucent skin. Captured and roped like a pet, Gollum proceeds to lead them on their journey by scrambling over the rough terrain, faster and more agile than the Hobbits, unconstrained by human physicality.

It's soon apparent as Gollum attacks Sam and Frodo that he is not what he seems, that is, merely antic or monstrous. But his oddness, while vague, is also worrisome. Sam, Gollum's victim on this occasion, sees no reason to keep him; Gollum writhes and moans upon the ground, spastic in his agony over the rope twisted by "nasty Elves." But Frodo, the master, pronounces, "Maybe he does deserve to die, but now that I see him, I do pity him." Gollum senses a sympathetic being. This emphasis on seeing remains crucial throughout Frodo's relationship with Gollum, as this relationship grows more intricate and convoluted. "We be nice to them if they be nice to us," he half-mutters and half-yelps. "Take it off us. We swears to do what you wants. We swears. We swears to serve the master of the Precious." Sam is disgusted by Gollum's manner, both submissive and conniving. Frodo sees something else, however, and soon the three set off to find the Black Gate, entrance to Mordor, where Sam, at least, means to destroy the Ring.

Their journey, intercut with those of the other Fellows – Aragorn, Legolas, and Gimli forming one team, Merry, Pippin, and Gandalf another – becomes a tangle of what might be seen and what remains unseen. For Gollum, being seen is essentially a risk, a condition frequently transferred to the Hobbits with whom he travels. When the Ringwraiths roll thorough, soaring and swooping aboard huge winged beasts, Gollum's first concern is that "They will see us." And so he promises to lead Frodo and Sam another way, "a secret way, a dark way," where being seen will be less likely. The Hobbits, less familiar with the dark, succumb to fear and illness as they travel, that is, they tremble and cough, and grow sunken, so that they begin to resemble Gollum.

In this visual connection, the film proposes that in appearance Gollum is not so very different from everyone else in the diegesis (a recurrent description of the CGI-ed character's seeming integration into the actors' physical world, helped certainly by the fact that most scenes were acted first by Andy Serkis, then rotoscoped, animated, key-framed, or digitally reshaped). Indeed, as Frodo begins to recognize their likeness, he also imagines in Gollum the potential for redemption, even the road home that Sam describes. Pressed to explain his willingness to identify with or protect Gollum, Frodo can only come up with a story, self-serving and hopeful: "I want to help, Sam, because I have to believe he can come back." Sam knows better, observing, "You can't save him, Mr. Frodo." And with this, Frodo proclaims his likeness to Gollum, if only in their shared experience of the Ring. But he can do so only with language that rejects sameness, because to acknowledge affiliation radically undetermines his identity. "What do you know about it?" Frodo yells at Sam. "Nothing! The Ring was entrusted to me, it's my task. Mine, my own."

Naming himself singular, inimitable, and important in his own right, Frodo ironically makes himself more like Gollum than not. Both are addicted to the Ring, craving it and not comprehending it, and yet both also are aware of its pain. Frodo's difference, at least for now, is his possession of language. Where Gollum skitters about in his speech, his pronouns symbolic but not sensible, Frodo calls up the language of authority and dominance by means of ownership. He defines himself by his task, his possession, and he denies that same identity to dear, doting Sam. The risk of such monumental naming, however, is dire. Trinh T. Minh-ha observes that naming,

> like the cast of the die, is just one step toward unnaming. A tool to render visible what he [here used in opposition to 'she'] has carefully kept invisible in his manipulative blindness. I never really start or end the trial process; I persist" (Trinh *Woman*, 48).

To be fixed, to start or end the process by naming it, is to be defined. For the "other" of Trinh's formulation, persistent movement becomes resistance. Frodo's assertion of a distinct identity based on the Ring (as mission, as designation of Fellowship, leadership, or specificity) is here contrasted with Gollum's continuous sliding, his lack of name, place, or affiliation, much less task. For Gollum, the process Trinh envisions is hardly a form of resistance, but rather, a form of incessant breakdown, a means to no end but more of the same.

As Gollum is raced – named – by Frodo, his only continuity lies in acquiescence to the master's orders. But this obedience demands deception, self-denial, or self-delusion. For Fanon, such a relationship, between master and subject, leads to resentment and destruction. He writes, "And so it is not I who make a meaning for myself, but it is the meaning that was already there, pre-existing, waiting for me. It is not out of my bad nigger's misery, my bad nigger's teeth, my bad nigger's hunger that I will shape a torch with which to burn down the world, but it is the torch that was already there, waiting for that turn of history" (Fanon *Black Skin*, 134). Gollum cannot transgress because his horizon – his "torch" – is pre-existing. He cannot pass from one community to another, he cannot "come back." He cannot pass from one condition to another. He can only wander and crave. Gayle Wald writes, "[I]nasmuch as it depends on race to be stable, transparent, and visibly embodied, the very authority of the color line must also give rise to he possibilities of racial transgression, or 'crossing the line'" (Wald *Crossing*, 5). The line for Gollum is exceedingly and unnervingly unfixed; this is in contrast to identificatory troubles for other characters like Gandalf (who passes from one state of being to another, gray to white), or Arwen (who decides to live with the mortal Aragorn rather than accompany her father Elrond to live forever in an immortal Elven paradise). Although other races are visibly marked, and certainly Gollum's transformation is visible, he has passed into no known community, no point of comparison, no status except as himself.

"An Ill-Favored Look"

This point of Gollum's pathetic singularity is emphasized repeatedly in *The Two Towers* and *The Return of the King*, in moments the filmmakers (in DVD commentaries) call his "schizophrenic scenes." Gazing on his alternate embodiment in *The Two Towers*, he laments his unremitting sense of loss. "They're thieves! They're thieves! They're filthy little thieves! Where is it? Where is it? They stole it from us, our precious.

Curse them! We hates them! It's ours, it is, and we wants it! We wants it, we needs it. Must have the precious. They stole it from us. Sneaky little Hobbitses. Wicked, tricksy, false!" His other, trusting, good, Sméagol self smiles feebly and protests that "master" could not be so "false." Abandoning himself more or less to himself, Gollum here can't maintain even a pretense of his social self, instead lapsing into a sinister self-stimulation, baiting and arguing with himself. This leads to his own version of self-recognition and assessment. While good Sméagol wants to believe that master is his "friend," bad Gollum knows better. "You don't have any friends," Gollum tells Sméagol,

> "You're a liar and a thief." Whimpering, goodish Sméagol tells bad Gollum to go away. Gollum has an answer for that as well: "Where would you be without me?... Gollum – -Gollum saved us! It was me! We survived because of me!"

Seeing himself as separate entities, a me and you and we made visible here, such that you share in his subjective split, Gollum can't tolerate himself. He is here Fanon's "wretched of the earth," self-colonized and self-tormenting, or at best, an anguished subject of the Precious, unable to control or contain himself. "The evidence was there, unalterable," writes Fanon in "The Fact of Blackness." "My blackness was there, dark and unarguable. And it tormented me, pursued me, disturbed me, angered me" (Fanon *Black Skin*, 117).

Pursued and disturbed, Gollum imagines that he might be saved by Frodo, who, he says, "looks after us now." Consider this an ultimate postcolonial moment, as Sméagol chases off Gollum (or so he supposes) and begins dancing about in a not-quite-new new incarnation, the grey night and rocky shore framing his celebration as the parody it might be. "We told him to go away. And away he goes, Precious. Sméagol is free!" he rasps, flailing his arms in a perverse instant of gamboling. Cut to the morning, Sam and Frodo wondering about their next move as Sméagol, bizarrely chipper, arrives in a veritable fit of glee, dumping two dead rabbits in master's lap as an offering of fealty. "They are young," he announces, snapping one rabbit's back as Frodo starts in disgust. But if Gollum can gnaw away at the dead meat raw and bloody, Frodo turns pale. Sam steps in, pulling Gollum away roughly: "You'll make him sick, you will, behaving like that!" That Sam here attributes Frodo's potential response to Gollum's behavior only reinforces his status as "criminal" and deviant, isolated by definition. He can't come back.

But he can be captured and tortured, in a sequence in *The Two Towers* that only underlines Gollum's inhuman status in the eyes of the sad and noble warrior Faramir. Coming on Frodo and Sam, he wonders, "Where is your skulking friend? That gangrel creature. He has an ill favored look." Cut to Gollum, catching fish by hand and slamming them against rocks, merry at the mere thought of the raw, oily, cold flesh he's about to devour in big bloody bits. Frodo relents at last, understanding that he cannot keep his own affiliation with the creature unknown. "The creature is bound to me," he murmurs, "He is our guide." Even so, Faramir distrusts the creature as does Sam. Frodo tricks Gollum into giving himself over to Faramir's men, who drag him off screeching with a bag over his head. "Master!" he squeals, betrayed by the one who had set him "free." The indignity and abuse continue when Gollum is locked up in a dank, grey cell and "interrogated" ("softened up," muses Peter Jackson on the DVD commentary track). While other violence in the films is surely grim and sometimes explicit, this scene shows acute and awful cruelty by Faramir, much-moralizing brother of much-missed Boromir (killed in *Fellowship* while protecting Hobbits). Faramir's tragedy is that this sympathetic and wise character ("War will make corpses of us all") is so wounded and reshaped by war that he is able to perform such brutality, tossing Gollum against the cell walls, slamming his body to inflict pain because he can. But Gollum's utter helplessness before such vigorous battering does more than demonstrate his vulnerability. It also reveals his lack of affiliation, again. "May death find you quickly if you visit harm upon them," Faramir warns Gollum, by way of encouraging that he look after Frodo and Sam as they proceed to Mordor.

Incapable of making such a pledge, Gollum leads the "Hobbitses" on to the Black Gate, by traveling the Secret Stairway, in *The Return of the King*. "Sméagol hates nasty Hobbitses," he tells his reflection in a stream. Of course he does. "Sméagol wants to see them dead. And we will. Sméagol did it once, he can do it again." The flashback to Sméagol's strangling of Déagol is unnecessary in terms of plot (the image is unforgettable) and yet makes visual the point of Sméagol's self-understanding, as forsaken but now self-remembering murderer. With his name returned, Sméagol's split self structures his internal struggle: he sees Gollum in the stream but Sméagol in his mind (the flashback), ensuring that his transformation from Hobbit to Gollum is a matter of changed skin, body, and capacity. Sméagol only "did it before" when driven by the Precious. "Patience, patience, my love," he soothes himself. "First, we must bring them to her," that is, the spider Shelob, leaving the act of murder to her. Sméagol is perhaps not so far gone as he imagines himself.

As they make their way up the cliff face, Gollum plainly able to cling to rock in ways the lumbering, depleted Hobbits simply cannot, Frodo takes a tumble. Though Sam warns Gollum to stay away, the creature reaches for him anyway, in a shot approximating Frodo's point of view, suggesting that Gollum might actually push rather than pull. But Gollum's interest is the Ring overpowers all, as Sam observes more than once. "Why does he hates poor Sméagol?" complains Gollum. "What has Sméagol ever done to him? Master carries a heavy burden. Sméagol knows. Heavy, heavy burden. Fat one cannot know. Sméagol look after master." He also plants the seed for Frodo's suspicion of Sam, because only Gollum and Frodo understand that burden, "He wants it, he needs it, Sméagol sees it in his eye." As Frodo *gets* this, has felt exactly the desire that overwhelms friendship, he also forgets that Sam's difference makes him trustworthy. Paranoid Gollum schemes to separate Frodo from "the fat Hobbit" by framing Sam for thievery of their last bits of food, scattering crumbs on Sam's "jacketses" just before he dumps the remaining bread supply over the edge of the mountain they're climbing. When Sam awakes and accuses Gollum of mischief, the creature has a ready answer, claiming – for Frodo's benefit, as Sam and Gollum are competing for his approval – that it is Sam who has stolen the food. "That's a filthy lie!" cries Sam, almost beside himself with outrage and frustration. "You stinking, two-faced sneak." With this, Gollum launches into a grim, almost wounded birdses routine, using Sam's own language against him: "Sneaking? Sneaking? Fat Hobbit is always so polite.

Sméagol shows them secret ways that nobody else could find and they say, 'Sneak.' Sneak? Very nice friend."

Sam can stand it no more, assaulting Gollum with alarming ferocity – alarming, at least, to Frodo, who calls him off (and will repeat this sort of attack later in the film, when left on his own with Gollum). Frodo's consequent faint returns Sam to "himself" even as his distrust of Sam grows. When Sam offers to carry "that thing around your neck," in order to share the load, Frodo sees him through Gollum's "poisoned" perspective, and tells him to go home. Of course he won't, as Sam is stubborn as well as loyal and sensitive, but for this moment, Gollum believes he has "won" the trust of master, and so, access to the Ring.

The problems here, sustained throughout the two films, have to do first with Gollum's absolute fealty and abject addiction to the Ring (as he's aiming to get access to Frodo by turning out Sam), and second with Sam's (and to an extent, Frodo's) own capacity for vicious denial. As Sam's attack here recalls Sméagol's on Déagol – all handheld, too-close camerawork and fast cuts to create a subjective hecticness – the correspondence between the fat Hobbit and Gollum is more emotional than physical. Their fight is staged as a frantic sort of performance for Frodo, for whose attention and allegiance they are competing. The film has in fact provided evidence for Sam's claim – the crumbs-dribbling and the bread-dumping – but Frodo, shuddering in his sleep on the rock shelf, hasn't seen what you have. And so he believes what the hallucinogenic Ring offers, as translated by Gollum's twitchy gesticulations, genuflections to the Precious.

Gollum's next self-encounter underlines his embodiment of miserable, unfulfillable desire. Seeing himself again, Gollum crawls along rocks in the dark Secret Stair, unable to settle for himself what he's done. "Too risky, too risky," he mutters. "They stole it from us. They knows, they suspects us." Just where he ends and they begin, or vice versa, is here unclear. The Ring, for all its mystery and unobserved for so many years, yet orders Frodo and Gollum's experiences, even as Gollum attempts to arrange for Frodo's death in the cave that houses Shelob. Sending the Hobbit inside the cave alone, Gollum is horrified as he watches the spider's methodical webbing and attacking begin, whimpering as he runs from the scene, frightened and repulsed, an act contrasted within minutes by Sam's own decision to "come back," to kill the spider and save Frodo from certain death. Gollum's own return to this scene is far less sanguine: he comes back to retrieve the Ring from what he presumes will be an incapacitated or dead Frodo. When Frodo beats him down and Sméagol/Gollum seems to re-emerge, crying that he "could never hurt master," the circle of servitude closes in on him. Beholden to the Precious ("The Precious made me do it"), Gollum is simply unable to think his way through the complications of loyalty. Frodo gasps that he must "destroy it for both our sakes," but Gollum leaps upon him anyway, flipping over Frodo as they wrestle for the Ring, and over the edge of yet another cliff. This time, he falls back, skinny limbs wriggling as he recedes from view, an image of yet another fall that prefigures what will be his final fall, into the fiery Cracks of Doom.

This fall is set up with a series of triumphant moments for other characters, from Aragorn and his audacious warriors (all inspiring themselves with the cry of "Death!" before they plunge into battle), and Sam, who insists that Frodo not give up just as they reach the end of their journey. "Do you remember the Shire, Mr. Frodo?" he asks, cradling him. "Oh Sam," sighs Frodo, gazing up on his best self-reflection and gardener, "I can't recall the taste of food, nor the sound of water, nor the touch of grass naked in the dark. There's nothing. No veil between me and the wheel of fire. I can see him with my waking eyes." Sam has home, a memory of who he was and what he wants again. Frodo, however, here recalls for us Gollum's tragic death-and-origin story, the litany of loss uttered at the start of *The Return of the King*. The Precious kills hope and sense, destroys self and desire. But even as Frodo is unable to move, literally, Sam moves him, carrying him to the Cracks so that he might let fall the Ring and lose forever that object that has so long ordained his fate, his sense of himself, his understanding of Fellowship.

No surprise, Gollum's reappearance, even his resurrection, at film's end, slows this process of destruction, as he leaps on Sam, snarling and scratching. Their struggle allows Frodo's ascent to the hellish fire, but the Hobbit cannot "just let it go." A heartbeat-like drum sounds as he turns to Sam, his eyes fierce and Gollum-ish. "The Ring is mine," he hisses, as a chorus comes up and Gollum appears one more time. It is at last Gollum who must sacrifice himself, the one member of his race who must annihilate the One Ring. And it is Frodo who must give himself over to Sam to achieve his sense of collective self. Frodo's death is portrayed as a joyous (or at least loving) reunion with the Shire's inhabitants, not a fiery hellishness, like Gollum's. Frodo can leave behind his story, to be shared like Bilbo's, now over and so, available for telling, for use in the construction of community, a history to be circulated as means to shared identity, "to save the Shire."

And yet, if the *Lord of the Rings* films are about the reconciliation of community and individuality, the necessity of violence and faith, they are also about the efficacy of myth and the definition of race, the institution or order in and as storytelling. Gollum's story cannot create community, though his death also helped to save the Shire. In ongoing conflict and conversation with himself alone, Gollum sees something he cannot share. He is raced alone, with his "ill favored look" delimiting his absolute alienation and cheerless dissimilarity. Talking to himself, or to his un-self, and thus to us, he denotes the race and community that everyone else can share.

"What does the Eye Demand": Sexuality, Forbidden Vision and Embodiment in *The Lord of the Rings*

Ruth Goldberg and Krin Gabbard

Introduction

Imagine that you are a psychoanalyst. A young male patient with big eyes and curly hair comes in with a dream full of suggestive imagery. It goes something like this:

> I dreamed I was very small. I lived in perfect happiness surrounded by other small people. Somehow none of us had any parents. One day a ring imbued with terrible destructive powers was handed to me. With that sudden responsibility my whole world changed forever. Whenever I put on the ring I became invisible to others and lost my place in the world. Putting on the ring also made me understand that a giant flaming eye was gazing at me. The eye, however, did not really look like an eye even though I knew it was meant to be one. More like a huge slit in the sky surrounded by fire, the eye was always trained on me. I set out with my male friends to destroy the ring in the place where it was created, in a fiery pit called "the Crack of Doom" on top of a

great mountain. My journey was made much more dangerous by a formerly good and wise wizard who bred a race of monstrous beings to pursue me and destroy all goodness in the world.

Meanwhile, the ring had a bizarre and enchanting effect on me. It made me intensely jealous of anyone who might take it from me at the same time that it sapped my strength and my will. The way to the black gates around the pit was repeatedly barred to me, and it was necessary to tunnel through mines and climb mountains along the way. At one point we were joined by a creature named Gollum, whose alternately servile and hostile behavior as well as his terrifying aspect were all the result of his obsessive pursuit of the ring. It was only through the deep loyalty of my closest friend Sam that we made it through the trials. Seeing Sam's great love and loyalty for me grow ever stronger made the ordeal bearable.

Pursued by the all-seeing eye we nevertheless arrived at the black gates, but as a final test, we had to make our way past the lair of a huge spider in a deep dark cave. The spider paralyzed me with her venom, but I was saved by Sam who ran her through with my sword. Finally I was able to evade the all-seeing eye and penetrate the fiery pit and destroy the ring, but only after a final struggle with Gollum, during which he bit off my finger. The victory, however, was bittersweet because it meant the adventure had come to an end and my friends and I would have to return to the old world. We went back home and Sam married and had a family, but for some reason I never did.

Could you, the analyst, even begin to understand Frodo's story without acknowledging the undercurrent of sexual ambivalence that runs throughout? The imagery in the dream, with its deep mines, dark caves, black gates, avenging swords, and fiery pits, consistently evokes and conflates images of desire with a terrifying vision of female sexuality. Faced with the challenge of analysis, what's a Freudian to do?

Of course, a great deal hinges on the idea of the dream being "told this way," in what Sigmund Freud has called secondary elaboration. The act of telling the dream and the language used to tell it are of critical importance for the classical psychoanalytic method. One could argue that using the tools of dream analysis to understand *The Lord Of The Rings* distorts the story to fit the preoccupations of the analyst. ("Freudian analysts have Freudian dreams," as the saying goes.) But you the analyst can respond that it is *Peter Jackson's* rendition of the story that calls out for a psychoanalytic reading. For it is Jackson's choice of images and words that bring what was latent in the original narrative to the surface in his retelling of *The Lord of the Rings*.

"Keep It Secret. Keep It Safe"

Jackson's version of the story is driven by profound tensions between fear and desire. It is colored by the fear of discovery as well as a pervasive reference to the forbidden, almost always shrouded in sexual imagery. The atmosphere is one of mortal peril and some terrible revelation is at stake. The opening line of the first film informs us, tellingly, that "the world is changed" and that there are unknown transformations ahead. Our tiny hero, who appears to be presexual at the outset of the film, teeters on the verge of madness as he risks losing his innocence; for along with the departure from the security of the known and familiar world comes the terrible and consuming fear of losing *oneself*. In these many ways, *The Lord of the Rings* films sound for all the world like the anxiety dreams of children. No wonder our hero is permanently small.

The moment Frodo accepts the dangerous burden of carrying the Ring of Power, he is charged to "Keep it secret. Keep it safe." In the dreamwork, a warning to maintain secrecy and avoid revelation under fear of death evokes the secret, often taboo wishes that stay with children even throughout their adulthood. With these wishes, of course, comes the fear that they may come to light or take on a life of their own. As Ella Freeman Sharpe phrases it:

> Psycho-analytic experience has shown that the ideas that are symbolized concern the fundamental basic factors of our existence, namely our own bodies, life, death and procreation. These fundamentals in relation to ourselves and the family of which we were a member, retain for us through life their

original importance, and energy flows from them to all derivative ideas. (Sharpe *Dream Analysis*, 53)

Further evoking the quality of a child's dream, Frodo and Sam have no parents in the peaceful and perfect world of the Shire, where the eye of Sauron and the Ring of power suddenly arrive to turn their world upside down.

What else does that flaming eye remind you of, Frodo?

As Joseph Campbell, Bruno Bettelheim, and many others have pointed out, hero stories always deal with the loss of innocence as a direct metaphor for the transition into adulthood. In *The Lord of the Rings*, however, the hero does not really lose his innocence, and although his friend Sam takes the familiar route into adulthood, Frodo never samples adult sexuality and Sam's choices hold no appeal for him. After all, the adult world that Frodo has seen includes female monsters, grotesque birth scenarios, absent or castrating father figures, as well as a range of terrifying images representing women and sexuality. No wonder he wants only to rid himself of the terrible Ring, return to the Shire, and live among its mostly asexual inhabitants.

The key elements in the world that Frodo must endure are, of course, a corruptive, irresistible Ring and a single, all-seeing, eye of fire. Both images are completely consistent with the film's spectacularized terror of female sexuality. The Ring perfectly resembles a wedding ring, the commonplace symbol of a man's extended commitment to a life of adult sexuality. And by no small coincidence, the eye looks like a giant flaming vulva. Just as the child knows that not all adults behave the same way in every situation, those who wear the Ring take on different personalities. Bilbo and Gollum are completely emasculated by the Ring, even though it makes Bilbo passive and morose and turns Gollum into a scheming killer. When Frodo wears the Ring, he immediately sees the flaming vulva and quickly removes it from his finger.

Although the films introduce a number of women, some of them presented as sexually desirable, none of them are for Frodo. And even the handful of fully grown males who bond with these women do so only in brief and awkward set pieces not nearly as exciting and exhilarating as the many battle sequences. At the trilogy's conclusion, Arwen is brought out for a quick smooch with Aragorn and then hustled off the screen so that the film can dwell at length on its child-like characters. For most of its many hours *The Lord of the Rings* suggests that these pursuits are an end in themselves. If a young man can resist the feminine and the passage into adult sexuality, he can engage in endless adventures such as playing in the woods with his male friends, even bonding with them at an emotional level entirely unlike what women have to offer. At the end of the first film, the kiss that Aragorn bestows on the brow of the dying Boromir is decidedly more passionate than any of the trilogy's occasional heterosexual kisses.

Many critics have maintained that the original narrative of *The Lord of the Rings* is suffused with homoerotic longing and a deeply rooted fear of the feminine. In her essay "No Sex Please – We're Hobbits: The Construction of Female Sexuality in *The Lord of the Rings*", Brenda Partridge makes this case at length about the original novels and explores the more difficult matter of what this fictional construction of sexuality might tell us about J.R.R. Tolkien's own proclivities (Partridge, "No Sex," 179).

Although the book's homoerotic tensions and gynophobia should be fairly obvious even to people who are not pyschoanalysts, some critics of both the original trilogy and its adaptations to the screen have fiercely rejected this view, protesting in raised voices that not all bonding among male characters indicates underlying sexual tension. While this observation about heroic narrative in general may be true, citing it here ignores the specific case of *The Lord of the Rings* movies and the wealth of carefully constructed innuendo in the three films.

Jackson plays up the latent homoeroticism of the novels on several levels. For one thing, he has given the key role of the good wizard Gandalf to Ian McKellen, surely one of the most unapologetically gay actors in the cinema of the late twentieth century. Jackson must have known what he was suggesting when Gandalf, astride his beautiful phallic white horse, more than once places a child-like male directly against his lap. And near the finale, when the several small males are united with Frodo, they joyously embrace and bounce about on his bed while Gandalf and the other tall men look on, smiling benevolently. There are no women to chaperone the boys while they gambol about on the bed. These are the kinds of scenes that prompted J. Hoberman to declare, "The Ring trilogy may be fiercely chaste, but its hobbituary denouement is gayer than anything in *Angels in America*" (Hoberman, *Final Fantasy*).

Most of the film's homoeroticism lies in the relationship between Frodo and Sam, in the way that they speak to each other, look at each other, and touch one another. But let's first consider the context in which it develops. The worldview of Middle Earth, with its flaming eyes and deadly Rings, requires a closer look.

Flaming, Indeed

The all-seeing eye of Sauron and the Ring of Power are the two disembodied and displaced elements of ambivalence around which this particular version of the hero's journey revolves. The characters in the narrative define themselves in relation to the eye and the Ring according to the polemics of attraction/repulsion and surrender/domination. Significantly, we are told several times that the Ring has the power to "disembody" a man or to reduce him to a shadow of his former self:

> Disembodied when the One Ring was cut from his hand at the Battle of the Last Alliance in the Second Age, the Dark Lord Sauron became a shadowy echo of his former self. Formless and terrifying, he returned to his rebuilt tower of Barad-dûr, and from there began to muster his strength to begin the long search for the only thing that might restore his form and power, the lost One Ring. Now no more than a terrible will, Sauron appeared as a great Eye, lidless and slitted, wreathed in flame. Against his piercing gaze none could stand. (*The Lord of the Rings Website*).

The Dark Lord Sauron is the most terrifying father imago in a world full of terrifying fathers. This world is practically without women, certainly without mothers. The Dark Lord is an overtly male presence but is embodied in the form of a giant flaming vaginal eye ("lidless and slitted"), to the extent that he is embodied at all.

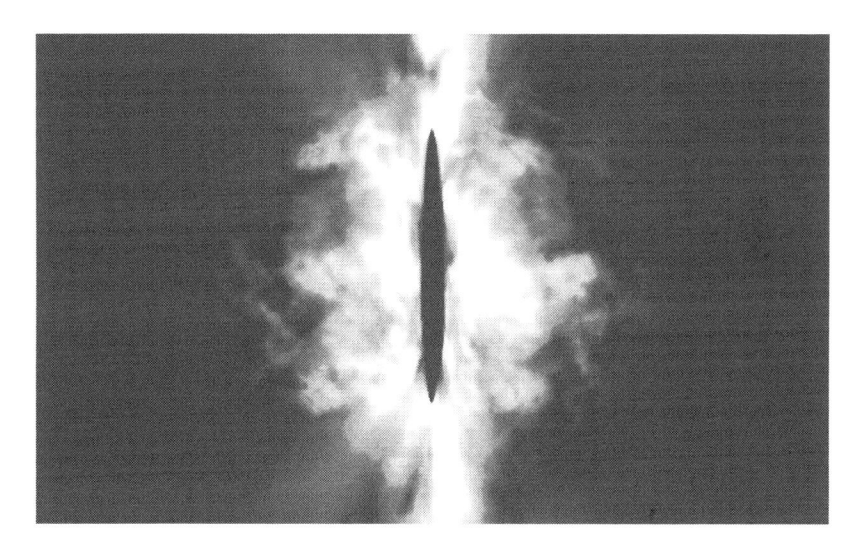

Image 21: Sauron's eye as a giant flaming vaginal slit. (directxscreensavers.com).

Moreover, Sauron takes on the most powerful aspects of the monstrous-feminine when he empowers Saruman to breed a race of monsters, the fighting Uruk-hai. The film shows the Uruk-hai being pulled up out of a mucilaginous pit in the ground in a vision of monstrous birth; procreation without women, conceived through the alliance of two men.

It is this eye/vulva that hunts Frodo, an especially perverse play on the idea of "vision." Not only does the eye see everything; Medusa-like, it also endangers those who look at it. Throughout the film, the association between forbidden vision (the trance-like state Frodo enters when he puts on the Ring and sees the flaming eye) and Jackson's undeniably sexual imagery evokes the classical ideas of the primal scene and the family romance. It is, after all, seeing the eye and being seen by it, as well as carrying the heavy burden of the Ring, that threatens Frodo's innocence. This is consistent with the way children experience the family romance and their own desires as both terrifying and burdensome, and, inevitably, bound to be detected.

In the dreamwork, forbidden visions may reveal taboo desires. Hunted by the eye and clinging to the Ring, Frodo has seen more than he should and desires more than he can have. *The Lord of the Rings* suggests that desire can in fact destroy the entire world, still another parallel between the film and a child's sense of terror about sexual taboos. Frodo both wants and does not want the Ring. Putting it on saves his life several times but also reveals him to the Dark Lord, putting him in harm's way and exposing his weakness. And when he finally has the opportunity to dispose of the terrible Ring, he cannot resist wearing it one last time. Of course, Gollum chooses this moment to bite off Frodo's finger, an upward displacement of the castration that is constantly threatened by the flaming vulva as well as the film's other nightmare symbols of female sexuality, including the vagina with teeth that is the gigantic spider Shelob.

The film's visual symbols are also ambivalent and confusing, betraying and reinforcing the idea of an underlying emotional conflict – is the eye that sees into Frodo's being male or female? The Dark Lord would seem to be a father reference, but the eye is clearly "embodied" as an aggressive and monstrous female image. The imagery of the dreamscape suggests that Frodo's only certainty is that the feminine is terrifying and that exposure of one's secrets may be fatal. In the indeterminate and displaced sexuality represented by the eye, Frodo's own ambivalence takes physical form.

In this way the eye/Ring dynamic evokes the secrets we must all hide, even from ourselves lest we face the terror of their revelation. A classical reading of this conflict might explore Frodo's panic about being seen; his fear that Sauron can see that he has taken what, by rights, belongs only to the Dark Lord; and his suspicion that Sauron might see just what he and the rest of these lads are up to, running around in the woods together with their "swords drawn." His vacillation between attraction and repulsion further illuminates Frodo's fear that his own desire will destroy him, that he will be split in two, polarized by the force of his own ambivalence. As long as he resists the Ring, he can continue on with his male friends, a bonded "fellowship" of loyal companions.

Choosing the path of fellowship rather than submitting to the Ring distinguishes Frodo from most of the human men in the narrative. Even though the Ring does tempt him, Frodo remains focused on its destruction. Seeing Gollum reduced to a monster by the Ring's seductive powers continually reminds Frodo that he must resist. The hobbits are referred to as "halflings" or half-men in this cosmology (particularly, indeed, by highly masculinized types like the Uruk-hai and the Rohan), and although ostensibly these epithets refer to their small size they also evoke the "half-heartedness" that Frodo feels towards conventional male sexuality, perfectly represented in the film as a common wedding ring transformed into a terrible destructive force. Traveling through a perilous landscape with Sam at his side, avoiding the eye, trying to destroy the Ring, Frodo is ultimately devoted only to returning to the Shire and to his small male friends.

A Topography of Desire

Having chosen an ordinary wedding band as the trilogy's dominant image, Jackson is very clear about how the Ring changes Gollum from a vibrant being into a craven repulsive thing intent upon repossessing his "precious." Suggesting that surrender to a woman reduces men to utter depravity, *The Lord of the Rings* clearly posits female sexuality as forbidden and dangerous. The Ring was powerful enough to disembody Sauron, to split Gollum in two, and to turn nine powerful kings into the phantom-like Ring Wraiths who hunt Frodo. This dark meditation on desire and manhood is further illustrated by the Ring's power to render its wearer invisible. When Frodo puts the Ring on his finger, he disappears and goes into a quasi-orgasmic trance state in which, suddenly, he sees things he is not ready to see, and, in turn, is exposed to the eye. As far as the mythology of the film is concerned, the history of the world revolves around a Ring that reduces men to animals or makes them disappear and is responsible for all evil and depravity. This is, of course, a matter among men, who are much better off avoiding contracts such as marriage that require a man to wear a ring throughout his adult life.

Jackson reinforces the sexual resonance of these ideas in both the language and the visuals in the films. He may even have taken a certain satisfaction in directing his actors to use phrases like "Crack of Doom" in a trilogy replete with sexual imagery. Around Mordor the landscape is dominated by structures and formations that either jut sharply upwards or emit some substance that shoots into the sky. Volcanic eruptions and exploding towers regularly appear. When the members of the fellowship finally reach the secret stairway that will lead them into Mordor beside the city of Minas Morgul, they watch as the ground shakes, a shaft of white light shoots up into the sky, and the monstrous brood of Uruk-hai comes tromping out of the black gates. The entire sequence is shot from above and unmistakably resembles a birth, with the gates swinging open and the Uruk-hai emerging. Like Ripley (Sigourney Weaver) in the lair of the alien queen in *Aliens* (1986), who watches fecal eggs drop out of a huge birth canal that resembles an elephant's trunk, the tiny heroes shudder in disgust.

Jackson's exploration of the monstrous-feminine and the visual representation of sexual metaphor is nowhere more explicit than in the encounter with Shelob in her cave. Jackson uses both script and camera to posit a vision of the feminine as a ravenous, devouring, and abject force. The sexual quality of the encounter with Shelob is first established by what the characters say about her. This particular monster is always referred to as female and is repeatedly described as a consuming, emasculating force. The description of going into a dark cave at the end of a narrow tunnel only to be devoured resembles nothing more than a young boy's nightmarish fantasies of sexual intercourse. Consider the internal dialogue between Gollum and Sméagol about leading the Hobbits to what both know will be certain death:

> Sméagol: We must get the precious. We must get it back.
> Gollum: Patience. Patience, my love. First we must lead them to *her*.
> Sméagol: We lead them to the winding stairs.
> Gollum: Yes. The stairs. And then?
> Sméagol: Up, up, up, up, up the stairs we go, until we come to . . . the tunnel.
> Gollum: And when they go in, there's no coming out. She's always hungry. She always needs . . . to feed. She must eat.

The dialogue between Gollum and Frodo in the tunnel itself is even more instructive. It plays out as a terrible fantasy of sexual initiation and the mythical vagina dentata that devours all who enter. This sequence also evokes the male child's conflict at the threshold of sexuality, facing adulthood or its rejection:

> Frodo: What is this place?
> Gollum: Master must go inside the tunnel...
> Frodo: Now that I'm here, I don't think I want to.
> Gollum: It's the only way. Go in or go back.
> Frodo: I can't go back... What's that smell? Aaah, its sticky! What is it?
> Gollum: You will seee... Oh yesssss... You will seee.

At that moment Frodo steps on a skeleton and realizes that he is surrounded by webs and dead animals. He hears a noise and panics, running in terror but quickly falling into a pit filled with cobwebs and bones. Then he remembers that he has a "most beloved star" in his pocket. In Galadriel's words it is "a light for you in dark places, when all other lights go out." Whipping out an object strongly resembling the secret weapon every boy ought to be able to count on in such a pinch, Frodo clutches the little glowing phial in front of him in a rather optimistic and suggestive way. But even this "most beloved" of gifts is simply too small, inadequate for the circumstances.

The light from the phial reveals Shelob, a giant spider, standing beside Frodo. Jackson's use of scale is masterful here. Not since *The Incredible Shrinking Man* (1957) has the fear of emasculation been so directly and effectively translated to the screen. Moments later, as Frodo is left struggling in a web after trying to flee, Gollum returns to taunt him: "Naughty little fly, why does it cry? Caught in her web, soon you'll be... eaten." Sam bursts in on the scene like a jealous lover, challenging Shelob to unhand Frodo: "Let him go, you filth. You'll never touch him again."

In spite of Sam's desperate intervention, Frodo *is* stung by Shelob, and time stands still as his eyes roll back in his head and white goo issues from the corner of his mouth. He collapses, spent. The metaphor of sexual climax is officially exhausted. Not even Peter Jackson can wring another drop from it. Sam grieves, thinking Frodo has died. But when a group of

Orcs arrive, Sam overhears them expounding on Shelob's method: "First she jabs him with her stinger and he goes as limp as a boned fish. Then she has her way with them. That's how she likes to feed."

The images of Shelob's cave as a dark, disorienting place where her helpless and doomed prey is about to be killed and eaten in a viscous medium is a nightmarish vision of a womb in reverse. It is guarded by an enormous, scuttling, stinking female monster, who is basically a hungry mouth on hairy legs – a larger-than-life vagina dentata. Everything in the narrative leads Frodo to this important encounter in Shelob's "cave." Only after his escape from the monstrous feminine does Frodo realize that safety lies in his connection with Sam.

There's No Place Like Home. There's No Place Like Home.

The third film in the trilogy is most instructive as it explores the mysteries of sex and death. *The Return of the King* relies on the most classic imagery of hero narratives. Like Gilgamesh, Odysseus, Orpheus, Aeneas, Dante, and many others, Frodo faces death in a horrifying underworld and then exits transformed. The last step in the journey should be the hero's return to his old world as an adult, emerging from the depths as a fully integrated being. Bruno Bettelheim elaborates:

> It does indicate that which alone can take the sting out of the narrow limits of our time on this earth: forming a truly satisfying bond to another. The tales teach that when one has done this, one has reached the ultimate in emotional security of existence and permanence of relation available to man; and this alone can dissipate the fear of death. If one has found true adult love, the fairy story also tells, one doesn't need to wish for eternal life. This is suggested by another ending found in fairy tales: "They lived happily for a long time afterward, happy and in pleasure." (Bettelheim *Enchantment*, 10)

Bettelheim surely had a heterosexual liaison in mind. On this topic, fans and critics of the trilogy are fiercely divided on the subject of Frodo and Sam and what their tenderness and devotion towards one another may mean. Even making allowances for an unusual amount of Sam cradling Frodo in his arms and teary impassioned entreaties, the films suggest a bond beyond a normal friendship which can only exist in the context of the "adventure," not in a world where men and women bear children and live and work together.

In fact, the story of Frodo, the Ring, and the eye of Sauron is not a conventional hero narrative. It has much more in common with narratives of what Freud called the "latency age," the stage between ages ten and fifteen before the child approaches adult sexuality. In latency age stories the protagonist does not leave home in order to defeat monsters and kings and to enjoy the sexual favors of women. Instead, the young protagonist leaves home – usually unwillingly – and struggles to return. What he (and often she) sees outside the home may be full of wonder, but it is no place for a pre-adolescent child.

The best example of a latency age narrative is *The Wizard of Oz* (1939). Dorothy (Judy Garland) has many encounters with extraordinary characters, some of whom have the potential to initiate her into a grown-up's world even if that world is not necessarily sexualized. (The Cowardly Lion [Bert Lahr] has possibilities, but we've always suspected that one of those witches might have been more willing to help Dorothy become a woman.) Dorothy knows that she belongs back home, and that is where she happily returns at the end. Much the same can be said of Spielberg's *E.T. the Extra-Terrestrial* (1982). Young Elliott (Henry Thomas) has his share of adventures, but ultimately he fondly returns to the bosom of his mother, who, as Ilsa J. Bick points out, becomes an increasingly prominent character as the film progresses (Bick, "Look Back").

All those bittersweet glances and passionate embraces shared by Frodo and Sam are best conceived as the pre-genital interactions of boys at an age when girls are still thought to be yucky. Jackson brings a certain pathos to the latency age narrative by allowing Sam but not Frodo to grow up and move on. The return to the Shire is fine for Sam, who becomes a sexualized man. But Frodo wants none of it. Seeing Sam take a wife and build a family, Frodo confesses that he feels "torn in two." He tells Sam, "How do you pick up the pieces of an old life? How do you go on? When in your heart you begin to understand, there is no going back.

There are some things that time cannot mend. Some hurts go too deep... that have taken hold."

Now that the Ring has been destroyed and the evil empire of Sauron has collapsed, all is right with the world. But Frodo is not at peace, and unlike Sam, who accepts the comforts of a traditional destiny, he must travel beyond the accepted male/female schema to an uncharted place where he is not "always torn in two." There is a final good-bye in which he makes this explicit.

> Sam: What does he mean?
> Frodo: We set out to save the Shire, Sam. And it has been saved, *but not for me*.
> Sam: You can't leave!
> Frodo: The last pages are for you, Sam (Gives Sam the Red Book).

Frodo hugs Merry, Pippin, then Sam. He kisses Sam's brow. He walks onto the ship with Gandalf, then turns and smiles back at the Hobbits. Merry and Pippin and finally Sam turn away. On the path to the house, Sam's daughter Elanor runs out to meet him. He picks her up and carries her. She grins and hugs him.

> Frodo (voiceover): My dear Sam. You cannot always be torn in two. You will have to be one and whole for many years. You have so much to enjoy, and to be and to do. Your part in this story will go on.
> Rosie carries their baby Frodo out to meet him.
> Sam: Well, I'm back.

Like Aragorn and very few others in the trilogy, Sam matures into an adult. The film hardly celebrates this passage, however. The gynophobia and sexual hysteria that drove the plot and provided so many monumental battle scenes can only provide wan and tepid visions of married life.

If *The Lord of the Rings* has little interest in tracing out the lives of sexualized adults, it does fill in some details about its asexual characters. Many critics complained that the final film in the trilogy was forty-five minutes too long, even without the credits sequence. Much of what happens in the film's long coda involves the fate of Frodo, who may be a little too old to fit perfectly into a latency age narrative. He may also have seen too much to return to pre-sexual innocence. Audiences must not be told too often that they're better off staying home and appreciating the simple life. If that lesson is stated too often and too aggressively, people might start staying away from movies. And the film industry wants us to feel that Frodo, like the rest of us, has been changed by his experience.

Frodo must therefore return to the Shire a very different Hobbit than he was before he left. Jackson uses Frodo's ambivalence toward his old home to create a sense of gravitas that the film must have for the ending to work. On a deeper level, Frodo's dilemma represents the film's unresolved ambivalence about female sexuality. Even if one goes to as much trouble as did Frodo to put it out of his life, one cannot be untouched in a world where sexuality is so terrifyingly empowered. Frodo's hard-earned purity is evident not just in the look of wide-eyed innocence on Elijah Wood's face. It is the residue of a child's fantasy that never really goes away – the dream that we can remain intact in spite of everything out there that threatens to unman us. Needless to say, this is the fantasy of a boy child.

So, you, the analyst, have heard the dream from the boy with big eyes and curly hair. You can read it as an especially vivid depiction of one stage in the universal developmental crisis that every child faces. You can also see it as the cumulative result of the heightened misogyny and sexual anxiety that seems more and more typical of the early twenty-first century. You could even read it as Peter Jackson's shrewd and playful exaggeration of the kinds of narratives that boys really want to explore when they go to the movies. You'd have to be very cynical indeed to see it as the stuff of not one but three hugely successful films.

Scale, Spectacle and Movement: Massive Software and Digital Special Effects in *The Lord of The Rings*

Kirsten Moana Thompson

> *– Grı́ma Wormtongue: It would take a number beyond reckoning, thousands to storm the keep.*
>
> *– Saruman: Tens of thousands.*

In *The Two Towers*, Saruman and Grı́ma Wormtongue discuss the logistical demands of the giant battle to conquer Helm's Deep. As they walk out on to the balcony of the Orthanc tower at Isengard, a flythrough camera movement rapidly pulls the spectator back over the spears of hundreds of thousands of Uruk-hai, who have been magically generated by Saruman and are assembled for a huge rally before the tower. This stunning shot was created by Steven Regelous's Massive software program, an advanced 3-D crowd simulation program specially developed for Peter Jackson's trilogy. A milestone in computer-generated filmmaking, Massive software and other digital effects enabled the visualization of vast battle scenes, with up to 200,000 Uruk-hai fighters in the Battle of Helm's Deep, Pelennor Fields and Minas Tirith. Combined with camera movement, bluescreen technology, and miniatures, the Isengard shot is typical of Peter Jackson's ostentatious style, in which the aesthetics of scale, spectacle, and vertiginous (simulated) camera movement produced by computer-generated imagery and special effects created some of the most striking visual set pieces in *The Lord of the Rings* trilogy.

Scale

Much of the extensive news, promotional, and fan-based commentary has described the extraordinary scale of the trilogy's production, budget, and shooting schedule in terms like "monumental," "colossal," or "epic." Over 1200 scripted pages, Tolkien's story took sixteen years to write, and Peter Jackson's production of the trilogy matched the epic scale of his source material by taking eight years to plan and shoot, with twenty-eight leads, 100 speaking parts, a cast and crew which totaled 2500, and thousands of additional extras. The monumental fifteen-month shooting schedule (from October 1999 to December 2000) included seven different units shooting simultaneously and was undergirded by an extensive budget and elaborate logistics. From the 48,000 separate props including 1000 suits of armor, swords and other items created by Weta Workshop, and the 1500 special-effects shots created by Weta Digital, much of the discourse around the trilogy has emphasized, if not fetishized, epic scale, monumentality, and numbers. The film's extensive shooting schedule and budget was matched by the scale of the marketing and ultimate commercial and critical success, with eleven Oscars and dozens of other awards, and about $3 billion in combined domestic and international grosses. The enormous commercial grosses paralleled the length of the theatrical prints with DVD releases of the film topping out at four hours per installment. In other words, not only was scale a central aspect of the material dimensions of both production and exhibition, it has also been a central component of the discourse around the film.t's been a balance of the epic and the personal. The Battle of Pelennor Fields taking place with millions of people on this massive plain and in the foreground there were two little figures climbing this mountain. (Andrew Leslie *The Return of the King*, Extended DVD).

Another major component of scale in *The Lord of the Rings* is the narrative's textualization of the juxtaposition and contrast between different sizes – from tiny Hobbits to huge Ents and from little Dwarves to giant Trolls, monumental buildings and the tall towers of Isengard and Mount Doom, the film foregrounds a narrative concern with contrasts in scale. These contrasts are epitomized by the culminating scene in *The Return of the King* when Aragorn and the city of Minas Tirith bow to the Hobbits for saving them ("My friends, you bow to no-one"). These contrasts in scale between tall Elves and humans, and short Dwarves and Hobbits, and the varying sizes of the props and sets of their respective environments necessitated special effects to preserve the illusion of this scale difference. From traditional tactics like forced perspective, oversized and undersized sets, and actors on scale rigs, to technical innovation, the film adopted a variety of strategies to construct the illusion of a fellowship whose members were widely varied in size. Two examples are *scale rigs* and *scale compositing*. Scale rigs involve actors on stilts in oversized costumes and hands (created by Richard Taylor and Weta Workshop). Scale compositing is created by shooting each actor separately in front of a blue screen, and then compositing his or her image into the scene. Connecting actors and props with motion-controlled cameras and synchronizing the movement of all three elements created forced perspective with moving camera.

The mise-en-scène's juxtaposition of contrasts in scale highlights a thematic opposition between the small number of the nine members of the fellowship and the vast forces of evil that are arrayed against them, from Saruman and Sauron and their innumerable armies of Uruk-hai and Orcs, which stretch from Mordor and the Mines of Moria to Mount Doom. In addition to the vast scale of the enemy's armies (a "number beyond reckoning" in Gríma Wormtongue's words), Jackson also added an array of oversized monsters in league with Sauron or Saruman – the giant squid The Watcher, the huge spider Shelob, Cave Trolls, the mammoth Mumakîl, and the Nazgûl-Ringwraiths atop their gargantuan winged Fell Beasts. Borrowing from the famous mythological creatures pioneered by Ray Harryhausen in films like *The Seventh Voyage of Sinbad* (1958) and *Jason and the Argonauts* (1963), the staging of fights and theatrical "reveals" emphasizes the disparity in scale of a Hobbit matched against a giant monster. Reminiscent of David and Goliath, Eówen battles the Witch King in *The Return of the King*, and Frodo fights a troll in *The Fellowship of the Ring*, for the trilogy repeatedly underscores what Galadriel reminds us, that "even the smallest person can change the course of history."

In addition to thematic and physical contrasts in scale, the mise-en-scène is dominated by colossal buildings whose monumentality recalls medieval cathedrals: from the walls of Mordor to the insides of Khazad-dûm, and from the giant trees of Lothlórien to the ruins of Osgiliath and the two towers themselves, the fellowship are repeatedly dwarfed by their environment. This physical monumentality suggests an Ozymandian theme of collapse and decay in which the remnants of earlier civilizations and monuments, like the weathered statues of the kings at Argonath, suggest the narrative themes of decay, loss, and decline.[1] One of *The Fellowship of the Ring*'s striking set pieces, the Pillars of the Kings are revealed in a nearly minute-long shot in which the camera begins with the fellowship canoeing on the azure River Anduin, cranes up and along the arm of one of the statues, and sweeps past its face to reveal a stunning lake background.

This scene was created through a combination of miniatures (statues designed by John Howell), tiled mid-level scenery (scenic unit) and background matte paintings projected onto a cyclorama and then composited with computer generated birds, river, and boats. Acentuated by Howard Shore's score, this stunning vista prompts Aragorn to muse, "Long have I desired to look upon the Kings of old, my kin," and also suggests the spectatorial desire which the narrative's own spectacle prompts and satisfies. As the canoeists paddle past the giant foot of Argonath, the image's juxtaposition of scale epitomizes the monumental task of the nine members of the fellowship. The epic dimensions of this task are manifold. The fellowship must journey from the Shire through

---

[1] This recalls Percy Bysshe Shelley's sonnet *Ozymandias* (1818) in which the narrator remarks "two vast and trunkless legs of stone /Stand in the desert…near them on the sand,/Half sunk a shattered visage …. My name is Ozymandias, King of Kings/Look on my works ye Mighty and despair!."

Image 22: The Pillars of the King. (Copyright © New Line Cinema)

forests and mines, across marshes and rivers, and up into mountains and volcanic realms.

In fact, the physical dimensions of this epic journey are repeatedly reiterated by the narrative's foregrounding of the landscape as map, in what Tom Conley (in this collection) discusses as the narrative's "cartographic impulse," typified by one of the concluding shots in *The Return of the King*, which zooms out from Minas Tirith and dissolves into a 2-D map. Throughout the many journeys across Middle Earth, repeated zooms-out, aerial and high angle photography, and extreme long shots punctuate the beginnings and endings of each narrative sequence as the fellowship move from one kingdom to the next. All through the trilogy, topography and maps are central in demonstrating the progress of the fellowship toward Mount Doom, but also in orienting the viewer to the fellowship's spatial placement in the furtherance of this narrative goal. The enormity of the task to return the Ring to Mount Doom is underscored by the placement of tiny characters in vast landscapes and suggests the second major stylistic hallmark of the trilogy; the strategic and narrative function of spectacle.

Spectacle

As Producer Barrie Osborne emphasized, spectacle was a central aesthetic strategy. "Throughout, we picked the most spectacular appropriate locations we could find. Rather than letting the difficulty or ease of getting to locations dictate where we filmed, we'd go for what we thought would be most impressive on screen." (Duncan, *Ringmasters*: 101) The use of New Zealand's photogenic and enormously varied landscape was a central component in both the narrative's aesthetics and the marketing and promotion of the film. Shooting locations in both the North and South Islands used some of New Zealand tourism's most famous sites, including the Southern Alps, Queenstown, the Kawerau River, and Skipper's Canyon, Lake Wakatipu and Mount Ruapehu. For two months, a scenic unit headed by Phil Pastuhov, Paul Lasaine, Craig Potton, and famed New Zealand cinematographer Alun Bollinger (*Vigil* [1984], *Heavenly Creatures* [1994]), together with helicopter pilot Alfie Speight photographed mountains, glaciers, volcanoes, and waterfalls as background plates, which later became the core material for subsequent digital manipulation and enhancement. Late in the production of the first film, New Line approved the scenic unit's use of a spacecam, a remotely operated gyrostabilized camera that mounts on helicopters, to improve the stability of its aerial shots. The aerial photography of the fellowship's physical progression through and across difficult landscapes that form narrative impediments became a stylistic leitmotif of the trilogy, and is illustrated by the lighting of the beacon signals in *The Return of the King*. Beginning in Minas Tirith, a sequence of aerial shots of cloud-capped mountains show the relaying of the signals all the way to Rohan in a plea for assistance that Aragorn ultimately sees. Similarly, the urgency of Gandalf and Merry's journey by horse as they ride from Edoras to Minas Tirith is accentuated by helicopter shots of the two tiny figures galloping across the plains, as is the harrying of the Gondorians outside Minas Tirith by the winged Nazgûl.

The unit's still photography also relieved the first and second units from having to spend time shooting establishing and background plates on location. Tiled, duplicated, and projected, these plates would form the basis for three dimensional CG cycloramas in which 360-degree digital camera moves would create the film's striking visualization of narrative place, like the mountains which surround Isengard or the backdrops to Rivendell. Similarly location plates of the Remarkables (a mountain range in the South Island) were sampled and manipulated by matte painters to create the moody Mordor kingdom.

A key aspect of the aesthetics of spectacle was the use of motion-controlled camera movement in combination with the extensive use of 'bigatures' (or big miniatures). Richard Taylor's Weta Workshop built 68 miniatures whose most typical scale was 1/14 – large enough for fine detailing for close camera work, yet small enough to fit inside studio space. "We coined the phrase 'bigatures'," remarked Taylor,

> because a high percentage of these miniatures were bigger than houses [...] The reason for that was Peter's desire to generate the immense scale and size of environments that Tolkien described in his books. These environments allowed a great deal of flexibility in motion control camera moves and big fly-throughs and so on, to create the massive scale of this world (*Ringmasters*, 72).

Jackson agreed, remarking that

> On a location or set, you're locked to the laws of physics: how quickly can you push a dolly along, how quickly can you move a crane through the air, and what can a helicopter do? But on the miniatures, I could be more dramatic with the camera moves, traversing a seemingly huge area, which would have been impossible in reality (*Ringmasters*, 77)

Traditionally motion photography of miniatures is conservative, but Jackson's are so flamboyant, he believes they fool the audience even more. In fact, vertiginous camera movement is a key aesthetic component in the trilogy and becomes a stylistic leitmotif of the director.

Movement

The trilogy's aesthetic use of movement is produced through four principal procedures: 1) aerial helicopter shots 2) vertiginous camera movement 3) digital camera movement (swoop/flythrough) and 4) the falling motions of characters. The first three involved actual or simulated photography of the mise-en-scène. The extensive use of helicopters for both background plates and principal photography emphasized the peril in which characters find themselves, as when we see Frodo and Arwen being chased by Ring Wraiths. Aerial photography was also used for point-of-view shots as with Treebeard's view of the trees and mountains as he and the Ents move toward Isengard. Second, vertiginous camera movement provides a dizzying mode of entry into the narrative as frequent tilts and pans, rapid zooms in and out, and forceful transitions from extreme long shot to close-ups punctuate scenes. Jackson's constantly mobile frame repeatedly shifts between the micro and the macro, alternating extreme close-ups of significant objects such as the Ring, with extreme long shots of characters dwarfed by their physical surroundings. A typical example of this photography occurs in *The Two Towers* and acts to intensify the urgency of the narrative. The three hunters (Aragorn, Legolas and Gimli) are pursuing the Uruk-hai who hold Merry and Pippin captive. An extreme close-up showing us Pippin's brooch (that he has dropped as a clue for Aragorn) is followed by a large Uruk-hai foot stepping on it. After several medium close-ups Jackson shifts to the macro scale through two lengthy aerial shots of the hunters, in which the camera simultaneously zooms out and circles the three to reveal that they are climbing ever higher in their pursuit, as the score gives an orchestral flourish to underscore the spectacle of the landscape. Finally we cut back to micro scale, with a close-up of Aragorn's hand discovering Pippin's brooch. ("Not idly do the leaves of Lórian fall.")

Jackson repeatedly uses digital camera swoops and fly-throughs, usually beginning with extreme high-angle or extreme long shots. Occasional hand offs are used to link miniature photography to digital and to live location shooting in various combinations. Thus enabled by complete or partial digital environment, vertiginous camera movement links characters who are widely separated in space. It also thrusts the spectator through dizzying heights, skimming up or down the sides of the two towers, and often moving rapidly from the micro to macro level or from extreme heights to depths. When the fellowship is on Caradhras Mountain, a forceful zoom-out to an extreme long shot occurs to show the fellowship on the ledge of the mountain. This is followed by a digital fly-through past Saruman on Orthanc Tower. We then cut to a medium long shot (in profile) of the figures on the mountain followed by a sudden tilt up to an extreme long shot of lightning striking the mountain. This dynamic combination of long shots, coupled with digital zooms, pans, or other transitions shows the powerful long-distance effects of Saruman's wizardry on the fellowship's environment.

Another such dynamic fly-through occurs with a long shot of Orthanc Tower, which then dissolves to Saruman inside. A digital fly-through then takes the spectator into his crystal ball, the Palintir "seeing stone" which shows us a vision of Mordor bridge with Uruk-hai troops on it. This is then followed by a camera crane up the Black tower, ending at Sauron's Eye, just as Saruman says "together my lord Sauron, we shall rule this Middle-Earth."

Through rapid digital or live-action camera cranes, zooms, and fly-throughs the spectator is repeatedly interpellated into a vertiginous movement through narrative space. The fourth principal form of movement is that of characters falling. When Gandalf drops off the tower of Isengard, the camera hurtles down with him as he falls onto the back of an owl and flies away. *The Fellowship of the Ring* ends with Gandalf engaged in battle with the giant Balrog ("from the lowest dungeon to the highest peak I fought him") and *The Two Towers* opens with a continuation of the giddying plummet of the two down through the interior of Caradhras mountain. Here are encapsulated a number of stylistic trademarks of Jackson. Beginning with rapidly moving aerial shots circling the Southern Alps, a series of lap dissolves shows us several long shots of the mountains and then takes us into the mountain's interior, where we see a recapitulation of the end of the first film, in which Gandalf falls with the Balrog. In an extremely lengthy sequence the camera then plunges with Gandalf, and after several minutes of close-up battle we cut to an extreme wide-angle long shot of a cave opening at the bottom of Caradhras Mountain, which brightens with red fire as Gandalf and Balrog fall into the frame, still fighting and enveloped in flames.

Massive Software

A key visual element that combines scale, spectacle, and vertiginous movement is Steven Regelous's pioneering software, which was specially developed over five years for the trilogy's crowd and battle sequences. In 1996 Jackson asked Regelous, then working as a technical director on *The Frighteners* (1996) to develop a software program capable of creating vast crowd scenes of hundreds of thousands of warriors for the battle of Helm's Deep. Massive (*M*ultiple *A*gent *S*imulation *S*ystem *I*n *V*irtual *E*nvironment) Software is a 3D animation system that generates extremely large crowd scenes based upon individual characters, called Agents, who are generated as being capable of independent, autonomous action.[2] Rather than multiplying by merely cloning individual characters, Massive endows each Agent with a "digital brain" and gives it the power to act completely on its own. These Agents are then scaled up and interact in autonomous and believable ways.

Regelous chose not to base his software on already existing programs that used particle physics. Dan Koeppel describes particle physics in this way:

> Using basic rules governing attraction and repulsion, designers aimed single points called particles at each other. Each particle represents a different individual, and when a satisfactory mix is achieved to portray the movements

---

[2] Massive has also been used in a SONY Playstation Commercial *Mountain* (Frank Budgen, (aired Oct 30 2003) which featured 126,000 people; Radiohead's music video *Go To Sleep* (Black Dog/RSA, produced by CG Company The Mill); an animated feature *Happy Feet* (George Miller, 2006). It generated thousands of robots in *I Robot* (Alex Proyas, 2004), and has already garnered a series of awards, including a Scientific and Technical Engineering Academy Award (February 2004), a Technological Innovation at the 2nd Annual International 3D Awards (May 2004) and a World Technology Network Award (September 2004).

Space, Spectacle and Movement

of a group or crowd, animation is added: The particle is rendered as a digital human or creature... particle trajectories emulate pool-table-level physics across a two-dimensional space. (Koeppel, *Massive Attack*).

The movement generated is cost-effective but not always visually credible, and when the terrain upon which the scene is set varies, the animation's realism breaks down. Instead, Regelous was influenced by

Images 23, 24: Massive's digital agent, and agents in action at Pelennor Fields (Copyright © Massive Industries)

the work of former MIT researcher Karl Sims whose 1994 article "Evolving Virtual Creatures" suggested the artificial intelligence direction that Regelous ultimately adopted. Sims outlined the problem which earlier special effects techniques had presented in creating unrealistic crowd movement:

> Our perception of characters is very sharp, which makes it all the more difficult to get the subtle details of artificial life forms believable. Human (and humanoid) forms represent the highest order of CG simulation because audiences are trained since birth to track human movement in all its complexity. (*Massive Attack*)

Jackson and Regelous struck a deal whereby Regelous could retain rights to the Massive software code in return for Weta Digital's unlimited use of

Massive into the future, with the result that the software has been used again in Jackson's *King Kong* (2005).

Rather than the traditional binary options of 1's and 0's typical of computer programming, Massive software uses "fuzzy logic" or data values which are a shade of gray or "fuzzy". For example, an archer does not just hit or miss his target, but he adjusts his aim as each arrow follows a slightly different path from the previous one, and the success or failure of the targeting will also vary depending upon the programmed variables of skill, terrain, weather, and so on. Agents are instructed to perform specific actions – to walk, or to fight. Each of these actions is ultimately a blend of more than one characteristic; for example, a walk is combined with uphill movement and a tired manner. Each Agent's brain is made up of a network of rules programmed by the Massive technical director, which include 7000-8000 logic nodes of appropriate responses to environmental stimuli. Physical traits (size, height, weight) and behavioral traits (aggression, fear, strength) are all dimensions of the software's programming. Agents can win and live, or lose and die, can find, identify, and engage enemies, and can see, hear, and even touch within their digital environment.

In particular, Agents have three patented sense functions: 1) vision simulation is created through a scanline rendered image of the scene around the Agent; 2) hearing simulation is constructed through output values that represent sound without the actual sound waves. Agents could transmit these frequencies to each other, and all creatures (Elves, Orcs) had a specific sound; 3) simulated touch was created through collision detection (Agents could respond in real time to other creatures and their environment). These programmed sense functions enable the individual characters to respond in real time to their environmental cues, adjust their gait to the pitch of the terrain, and avoid crashing into each other. For example, all Uruk-hai units emit a specific sound frequency which other Agents can interpret, and this enables them to identify friend from foe. The effect of this autonomous programming creates realistic crowd behavior, as each Agent responds to the unique actions of other Agents.

Thirty prototype models called Master Agents of different races and warrior types were created for *The Fellowship of the Ring* (e.g. Orc

Pikesmen, Uruk-hai Berserker, etc) and a hundred were made for the trilogy. These master Agents were then used to reproduce thousands of individual Agents through a process called "instancing." Randomly assigned variables enabled the production of thousands of *unique* copies, which formed the vast crowds instanced from the scaling and reproduction of master Agents. In the Prologue sequence of *The Fellowship of the Ring*, twelve master Agents were created (such as Elf spear, Orc swordsman), and then these master Agents were reproduced with many variables of height, weight, and arm and leg length, to generate 80,000 instances for the battle scene. A typical Master Agent has 10-30 cycles each for walking, running, climbing and fighting, with each Agent's brain capable of twenty-four actions per second. Each master Agent draws from a set of 200 broad and 350 smaller action cycles each of about a second in duration (e.g. step forward, stab sword). To keep track of all these cycles and movements, Massive designers and animators use a Motion Tree, which is a graphical interface that provides a detailed map of each Agent's characteristics. As with most contemporary computer-generated imagery, the source material for all the Agents' physical actions has an initial basis in reality. Over 200 physical actions or values per master Agent were motion-captured (mo-capped) from live-action stunt performers, and then modified. Mo-cap technology digitizes the motion through space of electronic markers attached to actors and props. As each character's race has different physical characteristics, the live-action actors who were motion-captured had to perform in different physical styles, from the more ponderous movement of the Orcs to the fluid dexterity of the Elves.

    Once the master Agents and instanced "copies" are generated, they are placed into their digital environment by the technical director and left to go into battle. Test simulations allow for adjustments to ensure that the crowds behave in dramatically interesting ways. Because Massive creates autonomously acting Agents, unpredictable behavior is always possible. An example of this unpredictability led to humorous results in one early test simulation. Explained Jackson, "I still get a chuckle […]: we had about 2000 foreground guys desperately trying to kill each other, but in the background about fifty of them had thought the better of it and had turned around to flee the battle. I thought, "Those are the smart guys. It was extraordinarily spooky" (*Ringmasters*, 86). This problem of "cowardly" warriors fleeing the battle scene was caused by the fact that their location in the terrain meant that they could not see any opponents with whom to fight, and so they changed direction to find some, and in so doing created the appearance of their own cowardice. Nonetheless, specific choreography and tool sets enabled the technical directors to massage the action to ensure that the groups of warriors began fighting at particular places in the terrain and that their actions were collectively cohesive. This function, which Massive calls "directability," is done through tool sets called "flow fields" which encode spatial information in specific places in the terrain in which the agents perform. The agents then respond to the flow fields as part of their environmental reactions. The technical directors can also "paint" particular places in the environment as trigger points for particular actions, for instance, a point can be marked, "begin fighting here."

Massive created over 200,000 Agents for a number of key scenes in each of the films of the trilogy (including a number of deleted scenes which reappear in the expanded DVD versions). Many of these crowd scenes featured live-action stars shot in front of a blue screen and then composited into wide-angle shots, filled with thousands of Massive warriors behind them. In the Prologue, in a stunning act of timing, a wave-like group of Elves swings weapons in synchronized response to the Orc's wedge attack, with the thousands of Elves and Orcs all generated by Massive. In *The Two Towers*, the Battle of Helm's Deep featured 12,000 Uruk-hai Agents, charging the Deeping Wall and scaling ladders to enter the fort. Although Massive was designed to place Agents in the middle and background of composited shots, because the Helm's Deep action looked rather sparse to Jackson additional stock Agents were layered into the foreground, running past the camera. Jackson wanted Massive to create a sense of spectatorial immersion "as if the battle were being photographed by CNN". Massive was also used to create thousands of Orcs crawling down the columns in Dwarrowdelf, hundreds of Orc laborers in the mines of Moria, and hundreds of thousands of Uruk-hai at Orthanc Tower, and also to amplify the number of refugees fleeing from

Edoras. Massive Orcs cross the bridge over the river Anduin, when the Mordor army attacks the ruined Gondorian capital of Osgiliath, and even Saruman's crows were a combination of Massive and key-frame animation. The final battle of Pelennor Fields in *The Return of the King* featured over 220,000 Orcs and Uruk-hai, surrounding the walls of Minas Tirith. To handle the rendering of such a large number, Massive consolidated groups of Agents into clumps of 25, which were rendered as single platoons, and thereby gave an economy of scale. The large number of warriors generated by the program offered both spectacle and monumental scale, and because the Agents acted autonomously, also offered a plausible movement that could not be visually distinguished from human actors. In combination with digitized camera movement and composited bigatures, the spectatorial effect is one of complete immersion into the trilogy's fantastic mise-en-scène.

Conclusion

The use of artificial intelligence through Massive software in *I, Robot* (2004), *Elektra* (2005), *The Chronicles of Narnia: The Lion, the Witch and the Wardrobe* (2005) and *King Kong*, and particle physics for the last installments of *Star Wars Episode II: Attack of the Clones* (2002) and *Episode III: Revenge of the Sith* (2005), is a harbinger of the future direction of special effects technology. In 2005 Regelous introduced a new generation of Massive software with Massive 2.0™ and Ready-to-Run-Agents™, which are the first of several planned sets that will form part of the Massive Ready-to Run-Agent Library. Ready-to-Run-Agents are preassembled Agents including skeleton, geometry, and rigid body dynamics, with textures, shading, and choreography controls, and motion pre-provided by Mo-cap. Animators can use them as building blocks to quickly assemble a large crowd. Massive now makes available two ready-to-Run-Agents, LocoGuy™ and LocoGirl,™ agents who can run, walk, sit, and stand, and StadiumGuy,™ an agent who can cheer, clap, and behave like an audience member at a sports event. Interestingly, gender and its anticipated relationship to space and environment already informs the design of these prefabricated agent sets. Massive 2.0 also introduces a memory function into its agents so that they can remember things, and, like humans, base their actions and responses on this experiential memory. Massive Live features a joystick control that allows the animator to control heroes or secondary digital extras and to interact with other Agents to create battle and fight choreography as if the animator were playing a network game. In other words, Massive Live creates 3D animation in real time in the same way a game engine automatically renders play in real time.

Massive's principal industrial advantage is its relative cheap cost; at time of writing the $18,000 license enables a single animator or small effects house to create with speed and flexibility large three-dimensional digital crowds of hundreds of thousands of "actors" in a matter of a few days. In addition, Massive has just announced an even cheaper stripped down license of its software called Massive Jet™ for US $6000. Digital Domain, one of the United States' leading effects houses, has already announced it is officially adopting the software. Training in Massive technology is already offered at the Media Design School in Auckland, New Zealand and the company is in the process of developing educational courses for use internationally. It is evident that Hollywood is rapidly adopting this technology and it is likely that this will continue the trend of special effects blockbusters in which large crowds form an important part of the narrative and mise-en-scène. Further, given the software program's emphasis on stunt action, Massive will likely strengthen the generic dominance of fantasy, epic, disaster, and action films in mainstream commercial cinema, but it may also expand these trends into small- and medium-budget film production.

Massive is an important new visual tool in computer generated special effects which combines the realism of plausible physical behavior with the scale and spectacle which only digitized imagery can cheaply and easily create. Not unlike SIMS, the world's most successful computer game, Massive creates a virtual Petri dish in which elements (human, animal, or fantasy) are collectively "grown" like biological specimens rather than individually created. As Regelous says, "Massive is moving towards creating virtual or artificial ecologies that can evolve and develop on their own" (*Ringmasters*, 85). Like live-action cinema, Massive creates actors who must still be "directed" in their performance, but unlike live-action this direction occurs at an interface level of "tweaking and massaging" rather than at an interpersonal level, with the technical director shaping the unruly digital performance with application adjustments. Performance is changed from an individual, idiosyncratic physical act to a virtual, collectively idiosyncratic action produced in response to environmental cues, and which is "captured" when deemed dramatically satisfactory. As artificial intelligence, Massive's software is rooted in a conceptual understanding that decisions and actions are integral to identity: *that what I do creates who I am*, whether as warrior Orc or StadiumGuy. By extension, agent-based modeling constructs groups that emerge from the collective interaction of these action-based individuals, and as an outgrowth of complexity theory presents unexpected behavior. Ultimately Massive offers the tools to create new stunning spectacles in filmmaking, and further blurs the distinction between pro-diegetic reality and the digital realm. The traditional photography of real actors and props is fast becoming replaced by the digital manufacture of the mise-en-scène, and, like the mo-cap technology used in the creation of Gollum, by the replacement, in whole or in part, of the live actor as a filmmaking staple. "Right now," says artificial life pioneer Karl Sims

> you can still usually tell when something is synthetic. But we'll soon be crossing over into a time where that's not possible. It's going to be a very interesting moment (Koeppel *Massive Attack*, 5).

Morphing Sean Astin: "Playing Fat" in the Age of Digital Animation

Jerry Mosher

> *"I was told I had to gain a lot of weight because hobbits are very portly. Peter Jackson is forever suggesting I have more food. 'A little more shepherd's pie for Mr. Astin.'"*
> – Sean Astin (Forde "Greetings")

When actor Sean Astin auditioned for Peter Jackson and Fran Walsh in the summer of 1999, he had two concerns: he'd read only a smattering of *The Lord of the Rings*, and his main competition for the role of the corpulent hobbit Samwise Gamgee was reportedly a "naturally stout" British actor (Astin *There and Back*, 97). At five feet six inches and 160 pounds, the twenty-eight-year-old Astin was hardly fat. In fact, he was in the best shape of his life and had recently run the Los Angeles Marathon. To show he was capable of "playing fat," Astin had sent Jackson and Walsh a videotape of selected performances when he'd been particularly unfit. But when he walked into the audition looking like "a lean, mean fighting machine" and "almost like a movie star," Astin's fears were confirmed; Jackson visualized Samwise Gamgee as a much softer, rounder figure (123). Jackson knew what hobbits should look like; he would later comment about his search for hobbit extras, "They had to be slightly short and squat and have large eyes and round faces" (Jackson "Commentary").

Despite the significant amount of screen time afforded to Sam, he was not a leading man but rather a supporting character in the truest sense of the word: he was Frodo's unwavering, loyal friend and attendant, a simple gardener who personified the traditional values of the homeland they left behind. As sidekick to the lean, elfin heartthrob Elijah Wood (who had already been cast), the actor playing Sam would have to be particularly "squat" to set him apart and would have to visually embody both a passive hobbit temperament and a working man's physical resiliency.[1] "I enjoyed having cheekbones and a flat stomach," Astin wrote in his autobiography. "It made me feel like I could be a leading man. To Peter, however, such things were distractions, obstacles to overcome in developing a character." After much discussion, Astin convinced Jackson he could look the part: "To secure the role, I vowed to do less running and more eating. By the time I met Elijah, I'd already begun to morph into Sam" (*There and Back*, 124).

Astin gained more than thirty pounds by the time principal photography for *The Lord of the Rings* commenced in October 1999. He maintained the weight throughout a rigorous fourteen-month shooting schedule and then kept it on for another six months to accommodate additional shooting during postproduction. Believing that Samwise Gamgee was the role of a lifetime, Astin displayed a steady sense of commitment and good humor throughout his ordeal. But during a press conference to promote *The Two Towers*, when asked about the difficulty of gaining and losing so much weight, Astin wondered aloud, "If you can make a completely computer-generated character [Sméagol/Gollum], you can find a fat suit for me" (Head "Interview"). Indeed, why would the producers of an epic film series featuring the most extensive special

---

[1] Tolkien explicitly acknowledged that his characterization of Sam was inspired by the working-class Englishmen who sacrificed their lives in the First World War. "My 'Sam Gamgee,'" he said, "is indeed a reflexion of the English soldier, of the privates and batmen I knew in the 1914 war, and recognised as so far superior to myself" (Carpenter *Biography*, 81). It has become a tradition among illustrators and filmmakers to portray Sam as fat (perhaps because he fulfills a subservient role), but he is never described as such by Tolkien, who emphasizes his robustness and physical strength.

effects and costume prosthetics in cinema history ask one actor to gain thirty pounds and maintain it for a year and a half? Why did they shun both fat suits and fat actors when casting the role of Samwise Gamgee? The perceived humanity and physical labor of the Robert De Niro-style weight gain, I shall demonstrate, offers a way to anchor *The Lord of the Rings* fantasy in the corporeality of actors. Among so many computer-generated bodies and sets, Astin's much-publicized and overdetermined weight gain carries the burden of bodily sacrifice that distinguishes these films and their live action from seemingly effortless (and heartless) digital animation.

An Actor's Sacrifice

> *"It can't be good for my heart – I'm aware of all of it.*
> *I know what to do to take it off, but...*
> *I'm literally seeking guidance from all quarters*
> *to try to maintain the weight."*
> – Sean Astin (Head "Interview")

The most famous and iconic instance of an actor gaining weight for a role occurred in 1980, when Robert De Niro made headlines by gaining sixty pounds to play boxer Jake La Motta for Martin Scorsese's *Raging Bull*, in a stunning performance of bodily sacrifice that earned him an Academy Award for Best Actor. Near the film's end, De Niro's lean, muscular physique swelled into a bloated mass, expressing La Motta's decline in a vulgar display of corporeal dissolution. By the time he accepted his award, De Niro had lost the sixty pounds, which some considered a more extraordinary achievement than winning an Oscar. In the wake of De Niro's feat, the tactic of deliberate weight gain remained a relatively isolated phenomenon through the 1980s: Vincent D'Onofrio gained seventy pounds for an impressive breakthrough performance as Private "Gomer Pyle" in *Full Metal Jacket* (1987); Edward James Olmos put on a significant amount of weight to play high school teacher Jaime Escalante in *Stand and Deliver* (1987), for which he received an Academy Award nomination; and De Niro himself gained weight again to play Al Capone in *The Untouchables* (1987).

In the 1990s the practice of gaining weight for a role became so widespread as to be almost commonplace. This could be partially attributed to escalating media reportage of an "obesity epidemic" in the United States, and to the increasing number of films featuring fat characters and fat issues (although the more intelligent of these, such as *Heavy* [1996] and *Real Women Have Curves* [2002], sensibly cast fat actors). A more likely motivation, however, was the critical and professional acclaim awarded to De Niro, D'Onofrio, and Olmos. As a highly visible demonstration of sacrifice for the craft, the weight gain became a proven strategy for fledgling actors looking to get noticed, and for commercially popular actors seeking artistic recognition. In contrast, actors who wear prosthetic "fat suits" (such as Eddie Murphy in *The Nutty Professor* [1996] and Gwyneth Paltrow in *Shallow Hal* [2001]) earn comparatively little professional respect because their physical sacrifice is less risky and they typically appear in comedies, which garner few awards. The comic impersonation of fat people has also come under attack as an insensitive stunt akin to blackface.[2] But actors in dramatic or serio-comic roles who really gain their weight continue to earn admiration rather than condemnation, no matter how quickly they shed their pounds after production. Notable examples of actors gaining weight for roles include Val Kilmer, who put on weight to portray both a burned-out Jim Morrison in *The Doors* (1991) and a plump Philip of Macedon in *Alexander* (2004); Tom Hanks, who gained thirty pounds to play a softball coach in *A League of Their Own* (1992) and then garnered a Best Actor Academy Award after losing even more weight to play a lawyer with AIDS in *Philadelphia* (1993); the relatively unknown actresses Toni

---

[2] Fat suits received considerable media scrutiny after the National Association to Advance Fat Acceptance (NAAFA, founded in 1969) called for a boycott of *Shallow Hal* in November 2001. "Putting thin performers in fat suits is no different than putting white performers in blackface," said NAAFA executive administrator Maryanne Bodolay. "To have these actors become 'fat' and then film them gorging on food and breaking chairs is an insult to the 55 percent of Americans who are deemed 'overweight.'" After presenting a litany of fat jokes, both *Shallow Hal* and *The Nutty Professor* meekly professed that inner beauty is more important than appearance, a tactic condemned by the NAAFA because "the end does not justify the means" (NAAFA "Fat Rights").

Collette and Minnie Driver, who each gained thirty pounds for breakthrough performances as ugly ducklings in *Muriel's Wedding* (1994) and *A Circle of Friends* (1995), respectively; Sylvester Stallone, who put forty pounds of fat on his once-chiseled washboard abs in a failed attempt to gain critics' respect as a small-town sheriff in *Copland* (1997); Benicio Del Toro, who gained forty pounds to play Hunter S. Thompson's attorney sidekick in *Fear and Loathing in Las Vegas* (1998); Ed Harris, who gained thirty pounds to play an aging Jackson Pollock in *Pollock* (2000); Renée Zellweger, who gained more than twenty pounds to play a lovelorn secretary in *Bridget Jones's Diary* (2001) and its 2004 sequel; D'Onofrio, who received far less publicity fifteen years after *Full Metal Jacket* when he gained forty-five pounds to play a sadistic drug dealer in *The Salton Sea* (2002); and former fashion model Charlize Theron, who gained thirty pounds and won a Best Actress Academy Award for her portrayal of serial killer Aileen Wuornos in *Monster* (2003). Theron's award merely confirmed what had already become apparent: beautiful people working in Hollywood films usually have to make themselves fat or ugly to be taken seriously as actors. Their bloated ambition, manifested in body fat and temporary disfigurement, must be worn like a badge until the world takes notice.

The deliberate weight gain is intended to evidence the actor's physical sacrifice and professional commitment, but in an era when fat-suit prosthetics, special-effects cosmetics, and computer graphics imaging make such labor unnecessary, the feat requires advance publicity to assure viewers it is real and thereby secure their admiration. De Niro's addition of sixty pounds prompted so many media inquiries about his food intake that he dryly noted in one interview that he was "answering the question for the six-thousandth time" ("Dialogue," 40). Because Astin was starring in one of the most anticipated film epics in history, his weight gain also received international media attention. His size, diet, and physical regimen were discussed in almost every interview he gave during the films' five-year publicity cycle, which encompassed production, postproduction, theater premieres, festivals, awards shows, press junkets, and DVD releases. Fans became intimately acquainted with the inner workings of Astin's body as he struggled to gain and then lose thirty pounds. "When I stopped weightlifting and kept eating, it's amazing what happens to the metabolism as it slows down and the belly appears," Astin told an interviewer (WENN). In an interview for a fan club magazine, the actor described his physical regimen during the film's production: "I just didn't watch what I ate. I ate anything and everything that I wanted. I did a lot of weightlifting right away, and didn't run a lot. But I stopped weightlifting, because once you have the prosthetic feet and ears on, you don't want to move around too much, because your sweat can loosen the glue, and the feet can come off. So I had fifteen-hour days of sitting still and eating." ("Sam I Am"). To lose the weight, Astin said, "I didn't change my diet at all. Literally, I was like Forrest Gump. I was running and running" (WENN). The publicity confirmed Astin's physical sacrifice and created the desired effect. On one *Lord of the Rings* Internet fan site, in an article titled, "Sean Astin Deserves More Credit," a contributor wrote, "All that Sean Astin's weight gain means is that he is a dedicated actor who is more committed to the art of acting than the superficial celebrity contest of looking like an industry imposed ideal" (Mitchell "Credit").

As a subject of so much media scrutiny, Astin's expanding and contracting body became a point of convergence for multiple discourses – star gossip, film history, public health, and medical pathology – that transformed the reception of his performance. Audiences familiar with the publicity for Astin's physical regimen were more likely to scrutinize his onscreen performance with a scientific gaze, seeking empirical verification of his weight gain. The most common way for filmmakers to visually foreground an actor's weight gain is to offer a quick glimpse of the belly, usually a moment when a shirt is taken off or climbs up to reveal a roll of fat, as happens in *Raging Bull* when viewers are given a low-angle shot of the obese La Motta standing in a Miami phone booth. Sometimes requiring a special shot or break in the narrative flow, this method of foregrounding operates similarly to what Linda Williams has identified in pornography as the "principle of maximum visibility": it is a scientific gaze that privileges close-ups of certain body parts over others; overlights easily hidden body parts, and highlights positions that reveal as much of the body as possible (Williams *Hardcore*, 48-49).

Morphing Sean Astin 307

Image 25, 26: Sean Astin displays his lean physique as star of the 1993 football film *Rudy* (left) and his pot belly after gaining thirty-five pounds to play Samwise Gamgee in *The Lord of the Rings* (right). Courtesy TriStar Pictures (left), New Line Cinema (right).

The principle of maximum visibility seeks knowledge: in pornography, the verification of arousal and ejaculation; and for actors who have gained weight for a role, the assurance that their fat is real. Because Sam and Frodo are fully clothed throughout their journey, *The Lord of Rings* films offered no shots of Astin's bare belly.[3] Many close-ups, however, prominently displayed the fatty jowls that had replaced Astin's formerly tight jaw line, a physical transformation that startled his fans and the actor himself: "I just kept looking at my face and seeing how fat I was, and

---

[3] After *The Lord of the Rings* films were completed, Astin highlighted his return to slimness with his next film role in *50 First Dates* (2004), in which he frequently displayed his naked torso while playing a steroid-abusing amateur bodybuilder obsessed with flexing his muscles. Astin was asked to gain weight – in the form of muscle – for the role. In publicity for the film, the actor summarized his career of shape-shifting: "I put on ten to fifteen pounds for *Rudy*. I took that off when I got married. Then I had to put on thirty-five to forty pounds for *The Lord of the Rings* and then just as I was done taking it off, I got this part and Adam [Sandler] and Peter [Segal] asked if I could put on some weight. I said to my wife, 'here we go again' and headed back to the gym." (50 First Dates Production Notes, 2004)

seeing how many chins I had," Astin said. "It just hurt... It just sucked" (Plume, "Interviews"). Film theorist Béla Balázs noted in 1945 that close-ups encourage the scientific scrutiny of screen bodies, for they reveal "the world of microphysiognomy which could not otherwise be seen with the naked eye or in everyday life" (Balázs *Theory*, 65). In contrast to a cosmetic application of simulated fat (such as that worn by Paltrow in *Shallow Hal*), the real fat on Astin's face might convey fatness more truthfully, because "there are certain regions of the face which are scarcely or not at all under voluntary control and the expression of which is neither deliberate nor conscious" (Balázs, 74). In Astin's corpulent face, there thus lies a second face: "behind the faces we can control, those other faces which we cannot influence because they have already hardened into anatomy" (83-84). Because the close-up exposes previously hidden physiology, Balázs argued that actors, filmmakers, and audiences needed an "education in physiognomics" to properly evaluate and interpret onscreen facial movement (80). Of course, viewers today are unlikely to be confused about whether an actor's fatty second chin is real or prosthetic when so much behind-the-scenes information is made available to them by film producers and the actors themselves.

Astin's weight gain highlighted the fact that a "movie star" is a carefully orchestrated but ultimately unstable cultural construction. The instability lies in the star myth's contradictory demands that stars somehow be at once *ordinary* (anyone can become a star, with a little talent and luck) and *extraordinary* (possessors of charisma and special abilities, they are not like you or me) (Dyer *Stars*, 43). The weight gain reveals the "ordinariness" of the star; at a time when many public health experts claim that more than fifty percent of the adult population in the United States is overweight, obesity is certainly an ordinary condition. But when a thin person – especially a svelte movie star – *chooses* to rapidly put on fat, it becomes an extraordinary condition. (It is not news when stars work out and lift weights for roles, since these self-improvement routines are expected and condoned as healthy.) Publicity trumpeting the fattened star's struggles with weight and diet resonate with many of us ordinary folks who daily fight a "battle of the bulge." The star reveals his or her special abilities, on the other hand, by losing the weight just as quickly as it was gained, an extraordinary achievement considering that millions of perpetual dieters never manage to lose more than a few pounds. De Niro's comments about his gain and loss of sixty pounds during the filming of *Raging Bull*, for example, served to exaggerate how effortless it was for him: "It was very easy. I just had to get up at six-thirty in the morning and eat breakfast at seven in order to digest my food to eat lunch at twelve or one in order to digest my food to eat a nice dinner at seven at night. So it was three square meals a day, that's all. You know, pancakes, milk, beer." And did he have any trouble losing all that weight he gained? "No," the actor replied, somewhat disingenuously, "I just went back to my old eating habits. It was easy" ("Dialogue," 40). At that point in his career, De Niro could afford to be the self-effacing artist; he had already won a Best Supporting Actor Academy Award for *The Godfather Part II* (1974), and after an astonishing performance in *Taxi Driver* (1976) he was considered to be the greatest actor of his generation. Astin, in contrast, had appeared in the popular adolescent film *The Goonies* (1985) and had starred as an unlikely football hero in the sentimental *Rudy* (1993), but he was eager to prove himself as a serious, mature actor. Consequently, his interviews repeatedly called attention to the labors of his physical sacrifice: "I had to agree to be as heavy, as fat, as I've ever been in my life for the year and a half that I was down there. And that was physically painful and emotionally trying, because when I think of myself or when I look in the mirror, I want to see a guy who's in good shape and is sort of a leading man – and for a year and a half, the guy looking back at me in the mirror was this fat, chubby, kind of insecure guy. That was painful" (Plume).

De Niro and Astin may have been at different places in their careers and abilities, but both sought to promote the art of acting and the authenticity of their work in an era when American cinema was perceived to be a director's medium, excessively market-driven, and artistically compromised by juvenile stories and ostentatious special effects. By the time De Niro appeared in *Raging Bull* in 1980, the "New American Cinema," which had infused classical Hollywood film genres with the energies and ambiguities of 1960s European art cinema, was in decline. High-concept blockbuster films aimed at younger audiences, such as the

Star Wars, *Star Trek*, and *Alien* franchises, were in ascendancy and would define the American cinema of the 1980s. Animated creatures, computer-generated backdrops, and quicker cutting took attention away from actors and fragmented their performances. Extratextual publicity thus enabled actors to exert control over the reception of their work, promote their preparation and craft, and remind audiences what actors actually do. Actors who followed the intense preparation routines required by Lee Strasberg's "method" approach were choice subjects for publicity, and, after De Niro's performance in *Raging Bull,* the deliberate weight gain has never failed to generate buzz. Director Martin Scorsese, who claimed he wanted to make *Raging Bull* like "a documentary with actors" (Kelly *Martin Scorsese*, 33), enabled De Niro to take "the method" to extreme lengths.[4] De Niro sparred with boxer Jake La Motta every day for a year before production commenced, and the shooting of the film was stopped for more than a month while De Niro gained sixty pounds.

Despite his sincerity, De Niro's extreme weight gain revealed that corporeal metamorphosis does not guarantee a satisfying or fully integrated performance. Many critics were awed by De Niro's commitment to his craft, and Andrew Sarris, though skeptical of the actor's need to gain so much weight, linked De Niro's techniques to the physical makeovers made famous by Lon Chaney in the 1920s (Sarris "Mean Fighter"). But some critics found De Niro's physical transformation so excessive that it proved distracting. "What De Niro does in this picture isn't acting, exactly," Pauline Kael wrote. "I'm not sure what it is. Though it may at some level be awesome, it definitely isn't pleasurable... what I found myself thinking about wasn't La Motta or the movie but the metamorphosis of De Niro" (Kael "Pulp," 107). De Niro's transformation set the standard for actors gaining weight for a role, but it is a standard of grotesquerie and self-involvement rather than one of

---

[4] The "method" is an adaptation of the Stanislavsky system popularized by actor Lee Strasberg at the Group Theater and Actors Studio in New York City in the 1940s and 1950s. *Raging Bull* is an homage to the quintessential method performance, Marlon Brando as boxer Terry Malloy in *On the Waterfront* (1954), and both films exhibit method hallmarks such as an inarticulate, working-class protagonist; existential angst; and a naturalistic setting. But when the obese De Niro (as La Motta) imitates the young Brando (as Malloy), *Raging Bull* slips into unintentional parody.

subtlety and ensemble acting. The weight gain—like any cosmetic or technological enhancement—is merely one tool among many that actors and filmmakers can use to create compelling characters, narratives, and emotions. It is only when such tools draw too much attention to themselves that audiences become aware of them as "special effects." De Niro used many techniques to personify his character, but the enormity and notoriety of his weight gain overwhelmed his scenes and disrupted the "realism" of the film itself. Astin's weight gain, on the other hand, was less dramatic than that of De Niro, and despite international publicity it did not call attention to itself any more than did Astin's prosthetic feet or spoken dialect. But in De Niro's wake, the weight gain has continued to be viewed as an endorsement of method acting and kitchen-sink realism, standing in sharp contrast to the dreary soundstage work in most blockbuster films that required actors to pretend to interact with animated characters and backdrops.

Two decades after *Raging Bull*, Astin was sacrificing his body, ironically, for a film franchise showcasing the most extensive use of special effects in cinema history. Through his performance Astin was well integrated into a large ensemble cast, but the actor's eagerness to discuss his physical travails – and thus reveal his "ordinariness" and humanity – had been made all the more necessary by the encroachment of computer graphics imaging on the art of acting. At the end of the twentieth century, screen actors were not only confronted with digitally created "synthespians"[5] who required no food, sleep, or money; they were contending with a cybernetic culture that offered the possibility, however fleeting, of escape from the human condition.

---

[5] The term "synthespian," according to media scholar Henry Jenkins, has been used in Hollywood for more than a decade to describe digitally-generated characters. These range from Shrek and the Lion King, stars of computer-animated movies; to Jar Jar Binks and Gollum, cast next to live action performers; to the masses of digital extras filling in scenes in *Gladiator* (2000) and *Gangs of New York* (2003). In some instances the synthespians are completely synthetic, and in others "the initial character template is generated through motion capture and then enhanced in the lab." Actors' fears of losing their jobs to synthespians indistinguishable from humans, Jenkins argues, are unwarranted: "Right now, synthespians are an extremely costly and laborious means of creating extremely wooden performances" and "are used more often to impress us with their creators' virtuosity than to confuse us about the line between reality and fantasy" (Jenkins "Celluloid Heroes").

This Mortal Morph

"I'm like the universe; either expanding or contracting at any given moment."
— Sean Astin (Head "Interview")

An early and popular use of digital morphing, now cliché, displayed the back-and-forth interchangeability of two "opposites"; for instance, cats turn into dogs and back into cats, or whites turn into blacks and back into whites (as in Michael Jackson's "Black or White" music video from 1991). Like this oppositional morph, an actor's deliberate weight gain creates the expectation of palindromic transformation. The actor is expected to lose the weight as quickly as he or she gained it, returning to an original body and persona. A performance by an actor experiencing long-term struggles with obesity, such as Marlon Brando playing Colonel Kurtz in *Apocalypse Now* (1979), does not command the same fascination, for the expectation of return to an earlier form is diminished. Astin, who lost his thirty pounds within six months after postproduction photography ended, fulfilled his palindromic obligation. After the actor returned home and returned to his original form, he wrote an autobiography aptly titled *There and Back Again* (which was J.R.R. Tolkien's original title for the novel now commonly known as *The Hobbit*). Ever conscious of his public image, Astin used interviews as an opportunity to warn the public about the medical dangers of his palindromic morphing, popularly known as "yo-yo dieting."

The temporal reversibility of a digital morph is effortless as it transforms from one pole of opposition to the other. Viewers perceive its uncanniness, but they are also aware that the digital morph is a *quick* change, requiring only the manipulation of binary code. "With its end in its beginning (and vice versa)," Vivian Sobchack notes, "digital morphing transforms the very grounds of a cinematic temporality tethered to – if not completely bound by – gravity: gravity as a value of photographic indexicality to a spatial and material world, to the visibility of particular human and representational labors marked by change in space and time, and to human mortality" (Sobchack *Meta-Morphing*, 137). The deliberate, palindromic weight gain and loss, on the other hand, *foregrounds* its labor; indeed, its labor is its reason for being. Although an actor like De Niro might claim it was easy, audiences are meant to marvel at the sacrifice – and physical risk – undertaken in the actor's struggles with the forces of gravity and the addition and subtraction of flesh. The foregrounding of the actor's physiology, in concert with extratextual publicity, creates a different reception than would a digital enhancement or the cosmetic application of padding to simulate fat. By stating in interviews that yo-yo dieting was detrimental to his health, Astin set in motion a critical apparatus that extended beyond the mere judgment of art and popular culture. The scientific gaze is a disciplinary gaze, situated within the apparatuses of power and knowledge, which serves to evaluate and maintain standards of health and beauty. The labor and duration of Astin's "morph," and the strain it put on his body, made audiences aware of his vulnerability and mortality as a *man*. In contrast, audiences lacked investment in the human and scientific status of the digitally morphing "man" who appears as the liquid-metal T-1000 in *Terminator 2: Judgment Day* (1991), Sobchack notes, because he "was never a man *originally*, and thus his transformation into the tiled floor has no hierarchical value in either form or substance" (137).

Peter Jackson knew that the completely computer-generated character (Gollum) and extensive digital special effects he planned for *The Lord of the Rings* also posed a challenge to sustaining the audience's empathy. The director was undoubtedly aware of the stilted acting and poorly conceived synthespians in George Lucas's *Star Wars Episode I: The Phantom Menace* (1999), which was released just months before Astin was hired and principal photography began on *The Lord of the Rings*. One of its stars, Liam Neeson, was so demoralized by the blue-screen production process and its deadening effect on the actors' performances that he briefly threatened to retire from screen acting.[6] "I'm

---

[6] Blue screen is an in-studio process in which actors perform in front of a large blue screen, which is later replaced with computer-generated special effects. "We all come across as pretty wooden," Liam Neeson said of the actors in *The Phantom Menace* (1999). "But a lot of that was interacting with blue screen, which was difficult and was also a great challenge, you know, to try to make it seem as an everyday thing that [you're with] a winged beast that talks." (Kirkland 2003)

not happy doing it," Neeson said. "Film is a director's medium; it has nothing to do with actors. We are basically puppets, walking around, hitting marks, saying lines" (Wolf "We've Got Male"). Before *The Phantom Menace* appeared, Jackson had already identified in preproduction what he believed were the pitfalls of typical high-budget fantasy films: too many flashy special effects; overdesign; lack of realism; coldness; and wooden acting. To combat these problems, he conceived *The Lord of the Rings* as an historical epic. "I just thought that would be interesting, to treat fantasy as history, as if it had a degree of reality to it," Jackson said. "So everything we did in the movie we tried to make feel real and just tried to avoid an overdesigned sort of film and tried to make it more earthy and organic" (Fischer "Hobbit Man"). Before shooting began in New Zealand, Jackson screened the historical films *Braveheart* (1995) and *The Thin Red Line* (1998) for the cast. According to Astin, the director told them, "This is the tone I want to strike with the *Ring* movies. I want to see the grime on their faces, the dirt on the ground, and I want that level of gritty emotionalism and intensity" (Pearlman "Hard Hobbit"). To enliven the actors' work with the computer-generated Gollum, Jackson hired classically trained Shakespearean stage actor Andy Serkis not only to provide the character's voice but also to stand in for Gollum with the actors during the blue-screen production process. And, to produce that "grime" on the face, that "dirt on the ground," that "gritty emotionalism and intensity," Jackson required that the actor playing Samwise Gamgee, nemesis of the computer-generated character, gain thirty grimy, dirty, intensely emotional pounds.

Astin's weight gain – and the international promotion of it – strategically served to balance public perception of the films' human and digital elements. In Sam's scenes with Gollum, Astin's additional weight functions as an extra body, an appendage that compensates for the digital character's emaciation and hollowness. Indeed, Astin's fattened body was so publicized and overdetermined that it seemed to exist separately from the "normal" actor/celebrity Sean Astin, who claimed that at his heaviest weight he barely recognized himself: "It was uncomfortable. You look in the mirror and say, 'Who is that fat guy?'" (Pearlman) The twenty months during which Astin carried his extra body can thus be seen as a kind of extended pregnancy whose fecundity contributed to Sam's humanity and offset Gollum's sterility. As such, the pairing of the carbon-based Astin and the computer-generated Gollum dramatizes a contemporary dilemma facing humans (and human actors) who interact with digital avatars in electronic environments such as video games, the Internet, and digital cinema: "An organic body just gets in the way" (Morse "Cyborgs," 125). Travelers on the virtual highway, Margaret Morse argues, have at least one body too many – a "largely sedentary carbon-based body... that suffers hunger, corpulence, illness, old age, and death" (125). A silicon-based digital animation, on the other hand, has no need to eat and sleep; it is "jacked into immaterial realms of data" and "is a program capable of enduring endless deaths" (125). To animate is to literally "give life," and in the increasingly mediated and virtual daily experience of industrialized society, "life" no longer separates humans from computer-generated beings. "Our machines are disturbingly lively," Donna Haraway's celebrated observation reminds us, "and we ourselves frighteningly inert" (Haraway "Manifesto," 152). What defines being human now, Morse argues, is our need to eat and eliminate waste. In a technology-driven society that constantly promotes dieting and rewards corporeal "beauty" created by self-starvation and eating disorders, it is not surprising that "body loathing and machine desire" have resulted in the wish to deny hunger and the need for food (126). The excessive eating necessary for an actor's deliberate weight gain is commonly perceived to be a perverse and antisocial act, but it underscores the actor's human contribution to an industry all too willing to valorize its "cutting-edge" digital technology and animation. Astin's weight gain highlights not only his own mortality, but also that of Samwise Gamgee, for it is a love of food that defines what it means to be a mortal hobbit.

Sam and Gollum's bickering and mutual distrust center around their attempts to protect or deceive Frodo, but their differences become manifest in the issue of food. Sam, of course, loves to eat and is skilled in cooking. Their first argument, a lighthearted disagreement over how

Image 27: Sam and Gollum discuss how rabbits ("coneys") should be prepared. In Sam's scenes with Gollum, Astin's additional weight functions as an extra body, an appendage that compensates for the digital character's emaciation and hollowness. Copyright ©New Line Cinema.

rabbits ("coneys") should be prepared, prompts Gollum's now-famous invective, "Stupid, fat hobbit!" Their next squabble over food, however, has dire consequences: in an act that temporarily turns Frodo against Sam, Gollum tosses away their last piece of bread and claims that the fat hobbit is "always stuffing his face when master's not looking." The two scenes are relatively short and economically handled, but extratextual knowledge of Astin's weight gain and vigorous eating regimen enriches them. For the miserable Gollum, who is seen chomping down a horrible-looking worm, food offers little pleasure – it is merely a necessity for survival and an object of exchange. Gollum is only interested in coneys and bread because the hobbits value them and he can use them as tools of manipulation. For the hobbits, on the other hand, the pleasure of eating is one of the greatest pleasures of living. "If more of us valued food and cheer and song above hoarded gold," Tolkien wrote in *The Hobbit*, "it would be a merrier world" (*Hobbit*, 266).

Jackson's films, unfortunately, incorporate little of the hobbits' gustatory pleasures that Tolkien so richly described in his novels. The director's only miscalculation in the original theatrical releases was his privileging of massive battle sequences and hard-bodied action heroics over the hobbits' soft bodies and less spectacular travails. Jackson, who said he strove to match Tolkien's masterful "mixture of the epic and the intimate" (Faraci "Interview"), certainly faced commercial pressure to accentuate the battle scenes in order to compete with other special-effects-driven adventure epics such as *Gladiator* (2000). But many reviewers agreed with critic Roger Ebert's complaint that "the Hobbits themselves have been pushed off center stage. If the books are about brave little creatures who enlist powerful men and wizards to help them in a dangerous crusade, the movie is about powerful men and wizards who embark on a dangerous crusade, and take along the Hobbits" (Ebert "Review"). Many viewers of the theatrical versions were left with the sense that the films were ultimately about Aragorn's heroism, whereas Tolkien, in a 1944 letter to his son Christopher, claimed that the novels were really Sam's tale: "Sam is the most closely drawn character, the successor to Bilbo in the first book, the genuine hobbit. Frodo is not so interesting, because he has to be highminded, and has (as it were) a vocation. The book will prob. end up with Sam. Frodo will naturally become too ennobled and rarefied by the achievement of the great Quest, and will pass West with all the great figures; but S. will settle down to the Shire and gardens and inns" (Carpenter *Letters*, 105). Jackson acknowledged and somewhat rectified the problem by adding many of the hobbits' deleted scenes to the extended versions on DVD. Perhaps sensing that Sam's story had been obscured in the films, the DVD producers included a featurette devoted to "Samwise the Brave" on the *The Return of the King* DVD, in which producer Barrie M. Osborne notes that Sam "started out the film as Frodo's sidekick and by *The Return of the King* he becomes the rock, the guy that drives them forward on their mission and actually takes on heroic proportions." Actor Christopher Lee (Saruman) concurs, stating, "He is, for me, the hero of the stories – the ordinary man." In this light, Astin's weight gain and the extratextual publicity it generated brought the complexity and detail to Sam's character that were lacking in the theatrical releases themselves.

Jackson's insistence on the weight gain, coupled with his digital conception of Gollum, constitutes a prescient take on the forces shaping human mortality in the twenty-first century. The excessive eating that is allegedly killing so many people in the United States is also, paradoxically, making them more human in the technologized landscape. The need to eat and the pleasure of eating are conditions of mortality that carry no meaning for digital creatures. In *The Return of the King* Gollum does suffer a death that is arguably redemptive and emotionally moving, but it is a death only in the narrative sense; the binary code that animates him, Morse argues, "might suffer obsolescence, silica fatigue, and sudden crashes, but not hunger or death" (126). Jackson, who has been called "hobbit-like" due to his round, bearded face, large belly, and penchant for going barefoot, is intimately acquainted with the mortal pleasures of eating.[7] By ordering "a little more shepherd's pie for Mr. Astin," he brought a modicum of humanity to what could have been a cold-hearted fantasy.

---

[7] Ironically, after completing *The Lord of the Rings* films, the portly Jackson went on a diet and lost a considerable amount of weight while working on his next project, *King Kong* (2005).

Gollum and Golem: Special Effects and the Technology of Artificial Bodies

Tom Gunning

A New Order of Celebrities

I must begin, rather uncharacteristically, with a personal anecdote. One of my closest friends, a director of experimental theater, lives in Los Angeles, but cultivates a relative ignorance of the world of celebrity and glamour surrounding him. A few years ago he attended a premiere of a highly-touted Hollywood film because it included, in a key supporting role, a truly extraordinary actor, with whom my friend was developing a project for a one-man performance of Macbeth. At the premiere the actor asked my friend to drive a friend of his, an actor visiting from London, to the post-premiere party. My friend agreed, happy to ferry the affable young man. However, as soon as they emerged from the premiere theater, a horde of paparazzi surrounded them, snapping pictures and calling out, "Hey Andy! Andy, look over here!" My friend told me the story to indicate how out of touch he was with the Hollywood world he lived in, that he had not realized he was chauffeuring Andy Serkis who played Gollum in the highly anticipated and just-about-to-be-released second part of *The Lord of the Rings* trilogy, *The Two Towers*.

I found this story, about my crazy friend in the world of celebrities, amusing to tell my son, then around 14, as we settled down in a Chicago movie theater a few weeks later to watch *The Two Towers*. I had read the Tolkien books to my son years before and we were familiar with Gollum as a character. Now, I have to confess that although I am immersed in the world of movies, I too am sometimes fairly ignorant of the publicity surrounding new films, rarely watching "Entertainment Tonight," or reading the trade magazines (at least those published after 1914!). Imagine my chagrin when Gollum appeared on screen, clearly a product of CGI! Had my friend lost his mind in tinsel town? Had he actually driven a computer-generated character to a Hollywood party? Had LA merged with Toon-town?

When I finally read some of the publicity for the film, especially as a controversy emerged a few weeks later surrounding the possibility of nominating Andy Serkis for an Academy Award as Best Supporting Actor, I learned, of course, that my friend had not been subject to a technologically-induced hallucination. Gollum *was* "played" by the actor who rode in his car after being hailed by paparazzi hungry for a new celebrity. Serkis, of course, not only supplied the voice for Gollum, but had also been filmed along with the principle actors who appear in photographic form in the film. Animation technicians used Serkis's photographed physical actions as one basis for the final character as it appears on the screen. Thus, one could claim Serkis had "appeared" in the film, and had certainly acted in it.

I tell this anecdote because in this essay I intend (again uncharacteristically) not to offer a stylistic discussion of the *Lord of the Rings* trilogy or a discussion of the director (although I am an admirer of Peter Jackson's earlier films, especially *Dead Alive* aka *Braindead* [1992]). *The Lord of the Rings* seems to me to be a film in which directorial voice takes second place to the technology of film. Jackson certainly guided and shaped the work of his collaborators, but I feel that the technicians, and art directors, and – even more – their technical processes deserve the most attention. Have "special effects" transformed cinema, and can traditional film theory offer us any insight into them? My discussion will not really be technical, nor will it be exclusively focused on the "digital." Further, my meditation on "special effects" will run in two directions, on the one hand stressing the way recent film technology seems to raise new issues, while on the other pointing out their continuity throughout film history, back to its origins, and even beyond, lingering deep in the technological imagination of history. Recent special effects encourage us to rethink the nature of cinema throughout its history, and to point out the somewhat narrow field of focus of much traditional film theory.

Serkis's contribution to the character of Gollum raises many of these key issues: How does reference and representation takes place in the movies in an era of special effects? Is cinematic reference passé? As I see it, current thinking about the nature of cinematic representation wanders between two extremes. On one side lies classical film theory which, represented best by André Bazin and Siegfried Kracauer, defined the essence of cinema as deriving from the ontology of the photographic image (see Bazin *What is Cinema?* Vol. 1 and Kracauer *Theory*). This view not only benefits from being expounded by two of the finest minds in the history of cinema but also from having a certain coherence – provided one limits cinema to its photographic aspects, as Kracauer argues we should. On the other side we have the utopian speculation of new media pundits who usually take an antagonistic attitude towards cinema, often seemingly an Oedipal one, anxious to condemn the limitations (and ideals) of photographic cinema to the dustbin of history – the better to envision the effulgence of the media of the future, untrammeled by photographic reference or indexicality. Lev Manovich offers the most compelling articulation of this point of view. Rather than privileging the photographic, Manovich claims that, in the age of new computer-generated images, cinema should be seen as merely a subset of the larger realm of graphic and animated images (Manovich *Language*, 295).

My own theoretical attitude has been evolving in recent years, buffeted by both contemporary practices that I feel traditional film theory may not account for fully, and by my absorption in a history of cinema that refuses to see films exclusively in terms of either their most recent and hyped forms, or by their most dominant traits. I would claim that, while the photographic aspect remains perhaps cinema's dominant legacy, over its century-long history cinema has rarely existed in a form restricted to this legacy, unmixed with other modes of representation. Although the recent cinema of special effects may help one realize this, a strong and catholic sense of film history also reveals its lengthy genealogy.

To give Manovich his due, it has always seemed to me extraordinary – if not scandalous – that most traditional, photography-based film theory simply ignored the realm of animation, as if it were a childish aspect of film, unworthy of serious consideration. The new cinema of special effects forces us to redress this imbalance – less because of an actual transformation in cinema itself than because of the increasingly visible role post-production special effects play in the Hollywood Blockbuster and the amount of critical attention paid to them. I suspect that the referential aspect of these non-photographic modes of cinema has generally been underestimated. Motion Capture, for instance, a technique that has its roots in the very origin of the cinema, makes animation dependent on reference to "real" motion.[1] Finally, the twin narrative poles around which recent special effects tend to cluster – portrayal of ancient forms of magic and the possibilities of new technology – invite us to probe even further back into the cultural roots of cinema's animated images in the Western traditions of magic and technology.

---

[1] Motion Capture (sometimes referred to as "mocap") involves filming an actor wearing a suit studded with dots that will provided reference points for his bodily motion. Fed into a computer, these studded images provide data that can plot motion co-ordinates that are then transferred to a three-dimensional animated figure. Through computer programs this animated figure mimes the motion of the actor filmed in Motion Capture, in effect driven by the actor's movements like a puppet. Rotoscoping, a decades-old animation technique that mapped two-dimensional animated images on the basis of a filmed image was a more technically primitive, labor intensive, and less three-dimensional process achieved without the aid of a computer (basically involving frame-by-frame tracing of a moving image taken from film, so the points I make here need not be restricted to contemporary "digital" special effects.

That's "Gollum" not "Golem" and you're in the wrong FAQ[2]

> *"Hey dude, it's "Gollum.*
> *The golem is the man o' clay of Jewish mythology"*
> – souljerky.com/archives/000077.php

This essay emerges from a homonym that may have been accidental, a case of mistaken identification based on a similarity of sound. But, as we will see, the belief that letters and sounds have a meaning – even a power – plays a key role in creating a Golem. The character that Andrew Serkis performed in the last two films of *The Lord of the Rings* trilogy, and that a variety of CGI and Motion Capture technologies "bring to life" (begging a question) on the screen, originated in one of J.R.R. Tolkien's most vivid creations, Gollum. This name immediately recalls for many people the word *Golem*, originally a somewhat obscure Hebrew word that occurs only once in the Old Testament (Psalm 139:16) and therefore (to use a term from classical philology beloved to the master filmmaker Hollis Frampton) a *hapax legomenon,* a term whose limited use makes ascertaining its original meaning difficult (see Scholem, "Idea," 161, Idel *Golem*, especially 35-36; Goldsmith *Golem Remembered*). *Golem* most likely meant "unformed, amorphous" (or according to Moshe Idel "embryo"), a meaning that becomes fixed in later texts such as the Talmud, which uses it to describe the formless nature of Adam before his final creation by God. This association led to its primary meaning – a man made of clay brought to life by a magical process that repeats or imitates God's primordial creation of Adam.

Gollum (as the web sites cited above hasten to inform the ignorant, over-jealous Kabbalists, or the victims of simple misspelling), rather than referring to a magical restaging of God's act of creation, names a creature that results from a de-evolution from human (or in his case, Hobbit) form into a monstrous and somewhat pathetic being. Originally named Sméagol, Gollum degenerated into a semi-animal, semi-demonic form, a decadence mainly caused by the baleful influence of the Ring. In

---

[2] http://golem.plush.org/faq/

Tolkien's books (Gollum first appears in *The Hobbit*, the predecessor to the Ring trilogy, as the original owner of the Ring; and although the mythology of the Ring transforms and deepens in the later books, his physical appearance and character remain fairly consistent), Gollum's degeneration explains not only his strangely repellent appearance but also his unique voice, a trait skillfully realized by Serkis in the films. As Tolkien describes it when introducing the character in *The Hobbit*, "He made a horrible swallowing noise in his throat. That is how he got his name..." (*Hobbit*, 70). The name, therefore, rather than deriving from Hebrew, likely comes from onomatopoeia; "Gollum" reproduces the strange gurgling that the slimy, mainly subterranean, creature makes deep in his throat.

A scholar of ancient texts and religion like Tolkien may have known the word "Golem" and the lore connected with it. Even without erudition, Tolkien could have been aware of the Golem from its circulation in popular culture in the teens and twenties. In Eastern Europe in particular, a large number of works dealt with the legend. The Czech author of the uncanny, Gustav Meyrink, wrote a popular novel about the Golem in 1915 that had a world-wide audience; H. Leivick in 1921 wrote one of the great plays of the Yiddish theater, based on the legend that during the Middle Ages Rabbi Loew of Prague constructed a Golem to guard the ghetto from persecution; while various versions of the legends and folktales of the Golem were published in this era – not to mention the two German silent films made on the theme, both starring Paul Wegener, in 1914 and 1920 (see Goldsmith). But little in the Gollum recalls the figure of Jewish legend – at least, little did until the conjunction of modern computer and cinematic technology transformed the literary character into a cinematic figure whose very ontology challenges us to rethink the limit between the animate and the inanimate, the human and the synthetic, not only raising issues relevant to the newest technology but invoking the oldest sources of the cinema.

Cinema has been understood as the climax of a long tradition of realistic representation. In his seminal essay, "The Myth of Total Cinema," Bazin claims that behind the invention of the cinema (the essay was originally a review of the first two volumes of Georges Sadoul's

Histoire générale du cinéma and therefore constitutes Bazin's main comment on early cinema) lies a Platonic ideal, a myth, "the recreation of the world in its own image" (Bazin "Myth," 21). Other than the temptation to ahistoricism to which Bazin seems to succumb, approaching cinema in terms of a centuries-long desire to reproduce the world with a detailed sensual accuracy has a great deal of value, provided its historical and cultural mediations are carefully considered. But a complementary tradition, closely related to the ambition to reproduce the world – but with a different center – also supplies some of the complex genealogy of the cinema. This tradition focuses less on the recreation of the world than on reproducing the human figure, the simulacrum of a total human being.

The dream of creating an artificial human reaches at least as far back as the Jewish mystical tradition of the Golem and its magical repetition of the original genesis of Adam. According to Genesis, Adam is created in the image of God, and this complex simile led to a long tradition of interpretations in which the relation between creation and an "image" drew analogies between artistic representations and Biblical creation. The Biblical injunction against the creation of a graven image could be interpreted as not only a condemnation of idolatry but, as in Islam, a stricture against the impious portrayal of the human figure so closely tied to the Divine Image.

The great scholar of Jewish mysticism, Gershom Scholem (whose name – to pick up our theme of similar sounds – Jorge Luis Borges used in his poem, "The Golem" partly because it rhymed with Golem) traced the tradition of the Golem to stories included in the Talmud and traditions connected with the Jewish neo-Pythagorean work of theosophic speculation, the *Sepher Yetzirah* (Book of Creation), both dating from the around the third century CE. The *Sepher Yetzirah* contained a revelation given to Abraham showing that the universe was created through the combination of letters and numbers. In the Middle Ages these traditions merged with the Kabbalistic system of magic and mystical experience. Within these traditions Scholem believes the creation of a Golem appeared first as a ritualistic act, whose sole purpose was "to demonstrate the power of the holy Name" (Scholem "Idea," 190). Scholem's heir (and critic) as dean of the study of Jewish mysticism, Moshe Idel, in his more recent study of the Golem, finds evidence that the tradition may be quite ancient and have a magical as much as a mystical significance. Borges described this magical and linguistic mode of creation in his poem:

> *So composed of consonants and vowels,*
> *There must exist one awe-inspiring word*
> *That God inheres in – that, when spoken, holds*
> *Almightiness in syllables unslurred*
> (Borges "The Golem," 193)

There are three aspects of this tradition that relate to our investigation of the creation of a synthetic figure in *The Lord of the Rings*. First, the creation of a living (or at least animate) human being not only imitates the Godly act of the creation of the first man, Adam, but in effect takes on a Divine power. Secondly, this creation takes place through a technique that involves the manipulation of letters and numbers, understood as the abstract intermediaries by which God effected the first creation. Finally, as Scholem especially stresses, "Golem-making is dangerous" ("Idea," 190). A human taking on the divine power of creation sets up a potentially blasphemous rival to God the creator.

Technology and the Automaton: Artificial Humans

> *Once out of nature I shall never take*
> *My bodily form from any natural thing,*
> *But such a form as Grecian goldsmiths make*
> *Of hammered gold and gold enameling*
> *To keep a drowsy Emperor awake;*
> – W.B. Yeats, "Sailing to Byzantium"

Can ancient and medieval magical practices and traditions help us understand contemporary cinematic techniques? The films of *The Lord of the Rings* trilogy aspire to this confluence of the modern and the magical, the technical and the mystical. But can this ambition be discussed without succumbing to New Age vagaries? Doesn't an unbridgeable historical abyss yawn between medieval Jewish mysticism and the invention of the cinema? A gap between the techniques of magic and those of technology must be acknowledged, a gap that pivots around the collapse of magical systems of belief as the primary way humans manage their environment and survive. Over centuries of cultural transformation, magic gave way to the gradual dominance of science and technology. While dubbing this centuries-long process "The Enlightenment" oversimplifies history, nonetheless the seventeenth- and eighteenth-century ideology of embracing scientific principles and overcoming superstitions provides a convenient rubric for this great separation. Curiously, the creation of an artificial anthropoid became one of the emblematic projects of the Enlightenment, as if the challenge to divine omnipotence implicit in the creation of the Golem became an explicit provocation, a demonstration that with the aid of science and technology, but without Divine aid, human beings could create a being in their own image.

The eighteenth-century creation of a mechanical automaton in human form that could perform a number of human functions demonstrated the new materialist view of man as essentially a machine, a conceit exemplified in extreme form by Julien Offroy de La Mettrie's book *L'Homme machine* published in 1747. The actual creation of automata took several forms and served more than one purpose. Automata provided pedagogic demonstration and were designed to illustrate new philosophical ideas about the nature of the body and human consciousness, attitudes associated with Cartesian systems. But all eighteenth-century automata were also intended to entertain, and, as the latest innovations in show business, were put on display for profit. Hence the apparent oxymoron coined to describe them, "Philosophical Toys." Jacques Vaucanson produced the most famous of these devices, which Gaby Wood describes as "emblems of the Enlightenment" (Wood *Edison's Eve*, 17). His Flute Player, exhibited in 1738, was made of wood and clockwork, stood five and half feet high, and could play twelve different tunes. Designed partly as a demonstration of the human respiratory system, this automaton could be opened to display its complex mechanical innards. Mechanically controlled pneumatics allowed the automaton (or *androide*, as the *Encyclopédie* of Diderot named the machine-man, defined as "an automaton in human form which by means of certain well positioned springs etc. performs certain functions which resemble those of man" [quoted in Wood, 21-22]) to breathe into its instrument, while an intricate mechanism controlled the fingering of the flute to produce the tunes. In order to perfectly block the stops of the flute, Vaucanson had the automaton's hands dressed in glove-like coverings made of skin (whether human or animal is not clear).

The automata manufactured by the father-and-son team of machinists Pierre and Henri Jaquet-Droz of Geneva likewise performed complex but single tasks: a female figure played the harpsichord, while a youth wrote a fine hand, often inscribing this enigmatic reflection on Descartes's dictum: "I do not think ... do I therefore not exist?" (see Wood *Edison's Eve*, 8). Wolfgang von Kempelen in the 1770s perfected a speaking machine which, through manipulation of a keyboard and bellows, could utter clearly a number of words and sentences (Wood, 124-127; see also Standage *Turk*, 76-81). As entertaining marvels, automata were often subject to a degree of conjurer-like deception. The working process of Vaucason's famous "Shitting Duck" (which swallowed bits of corn, supposedly digested them, and then expelled the "waste"), while designed to demonstrate theories of digestion, was actually a faked mechanism with no relation between intake and product (Wood, 27-33). The most famous of such deceptive marvels was the Turk, a chess-playing automaton designed by Kempelen that had a long exhibition life, in spite of several exposés that theorized correctly that a chess-playing human being was concealed within the mechanism.[3]

The eighteenth- and nineteenth-century exhibition history of automata as devices of wonder that oscillated between scientific demonstration and show-biz legerdemain shows their many affinities with those late nineteenth-century mechanical wonders, the phonograph and the cinema. Indeed, Georges Méliès first approached the Lumière brothers about buying a Cinématographe in the 1890s in order to have an entr'acte attraction that could buy time in between the elaborate magic spectacles he was staging at the Théâtre Robert-Houdin – a role previously performed by audience visits to a lobby display of the

---

[3] The most complete account of the chess playing Turk is Standage.

automata of the theater's previous owner, renowned magician Jean-Eugène Robert-Houdin, which now seemed a bit old-fashioned next to the marvels of motion pictures (on Méliès and the Robert-Houdin automata, see Fechner "Théâtre," 72-114). In their first receptions, the phonograph and the cinema seemed to offer improved versions of the previous attempts at presenting the human voice and figure through mechanical means. P.T. Barnum had exhibited a device operated by a Herr Faber similar to Kempelen's talking machine at his Museum, creating a voice that issued from an effigy head of a woman whose lips and eyes moved. Barnum exhibited such a talking machine into the 1870s with an announcement that offered ten thousand dollars to any one who could equal its effects, an offering quickly rescinded when he heard rumors of Edison's new "Talking Machine" (Kunhardt, Kunhardt, and Kunhardt *Barnum*, 63).

We might find a radical difference between the imitation of the behavior (and possibly the consciousness) of human beings in these automata and modern recordings of the human voice or figure through phonography or motion pictures. But at the end of the nineteenth century this difference was not so obvious.[4] The extraordinary work of Symbolist science fiction, Villiers de l'Îsle Adam's *Eve Futur* from 1886, portrayed a fictional Thomas Edison creating an android of a perfect woman aided by the devices of the phonograph (which supplied an endless recording of profound statements that the android would seem to utter) and motion pictures (which, in fact, Edison had not yet invented, but Villiers cannily predicted)(1982). In modern automata, recording of data and the possibility of playback replaced the magical process of combinations of letters and numbers. As the French anthropologist of technology, Phillippe Breton, has pointed out, in the twentieth century the principal heir of the creation of a humanoid has been the computer, which not only seems to mime human consciousness (and can play chess without concealed human collaborators) but also threatens to become the mode through which scientists understand and explain the human mind (*Image*). In 1965, Scholem himself dedicated the first computer at the Weitzman

---

[4] I owe a debt to James Lastra's insightful discussion of the relation between devices of sound recording (and photography) and the tradition of automata (*Sound Technology*, 16-60).

Institute of Science at Rehovot and christened it Golem Aleph. Finding many parallels between the man of clay and the rather new technology, Scholem slyly stresses one in particular:

> The old Golem was based on a mystical combination of the twenty-two letters of the Hebrew alphabet, which are the elements and building blocks of the world. The new Golem is based on a simpler, and at the same time more intricate, system. Instead of twenty-two elements, it knows only two, the two numbers 0 and 1, constituting the binary system of representation. Everything can be translated or transported into these two basic signs, and what cannot be so expressed cannot be fed as information to the Golem. I dare say the old Kabbalists would have been glad to learn of this simplification of their own system. This is progress (Scholem *Golem of Prague*, 339).

Motion Capture, Tracing the Human Body

"I will reproduce this woman exactly,
I will duplicate her, with the sublime assistance of Light!"
– Edison in Villiers de l'Îsle Adam, *L'Eve futur*

As heir to the centuries-long pursuit of the recreation of the human image, artificial intelligence abandoned the simulacrum of the human body as unimportant (Villiers *Eve*, 47). As I have discussed elsewhere, at the end of the nineteenth century a human voice emerging from a machine that had no resemblance to a human body seems to have affected some hearers as uncanny (Gunning, "Eye/Ear"). Edison may have addressed this anxiety by his marketing of dolls containing miniature record players, like Lilliputian versions of Villiers's Future Eve (Baldwin *Edison*, 195-197). But the motion pictures devices introduced at the end of the nineteenth century proposed a new way of fulfilling the dream of a moving human simulacrum. In Villiers's novel, Edison's preparation for creating the perfect woman includes something he calls "the cylinder of gestures" which first captures the gestures of the woman that Edison wants to recreate in a "perfect" version. This becomes the apparatus for the motion pictures Edison projects of a dancing woman, the prototype for his android. While motion pictures serve in this narrative principally as a model for a fully realized android, motion pictures of the human body, supplemented by the phonograph (as Edison actually planned, and as Villiers predicted), fulfill the dream of an artificial human – more supple, more realistic than any android – albeit virtual and made of light.

Edison's kinetoscope derived from the motion study chronophotography of Eadweard Muybridge and Etienne-Jules Marey (Baldwin *Edison*, 211-212). The primary purpose and the principle subject of the chronophotography of these two men was the motion of the bodies of animals and humans.[5] Although Muybridge began with a concentration on horses and in his later encyclopedic work at the University of Pennsylvania included an exotic range of animal species, the bulk of the later work recorded the human body in motion. Likewise, although Marey began his photographic work by recording the flight of birds, later added records of animals and insects, and ended up filming such inanimate, yet mobile, subjects as waves and air currents, his primary focus remained on the human (in his case predominantly male) body.

Lumière's Cinématographe derived from both Edison's kinetoscope and the devices of Marey, but projected, as I have claimed elsewhere, a very different world (Gunning, "New Thresholds"). Derived from the travel views and domestic scenes of amateur photography, the films shot by the Lumière Company primarily presented a world of deep space, recording familiar or exotic sites. For the most part, Edison's films look very different. While a few exterior views and scenes were filmed (*The Empire Express*, *Feeding the Doves*, *The Burning Stable*), Edison's "Black Maria" studio was designed to capture the human body in motion, eliminating any extraneous background (see Musser, *Edison Motion Pictures* 40-43). Edison's kinetoscope films, shot in the studio, devised a black background against which sharply lit human bodies performed, whether strong men, acrobats, knock-about comedians, sharpshooters, or skirt dancers. Charles Musser relates this elimination of the extraneous visual material to the sound-dampened space of the phonographic

---

[5] The most reliable and insightful treatment of Marey is Marta Braun's (*Picturing*); no such definitive work exist for Muybridge, although a recent catalogue by Phillip Prodger (*Time*) and the curious California-centered biography by Rebecca Solnit (*River*) provide new insights and information.

recording studio Edison had pioneered (Musser, *Emergence* 78). Edison himself undoubtedly associated it with the dark backgrounds found in the work of Muybridge and Marey. Phillippe-Alain Michaud describes Edison's first films as "based on a system of relationships that proceeded from the figures alone, independently of the place in which they were filmed, as if the latter were purely and simply annulled" (*Warburg*, 51). These strange claustrophobic images make it clear that Edison's subject was the human body in motion, but in place of the analysis into discreet poses sought by the scientific recorders of motion study his kinetoscope presented tiny human figures that capered against a dark background, as if alive.

As has frequently been pointed out, techniques of digital Motion Capture very closely resemble Marey's chronophotography. Unlike Muybridge, who was trained in photography (specifically in landscape photography), Marey was a physiologist, a rigorous scientist who, after seeing Muybridge's work, decided photography could be used as a scientific tool in recording and analyzing motion (see Braun *Picturing*). But the iconic aspects of the photographic image, so important to Muybridge, posed an encumbrance to Marey's more strictly scientific eye; photographs carried too much information, a sort of visual "noise" that interfered with the essential plotting of motion that Marey intended. Thus Marey's chief assistant, Georges Demenÿ, donned a black body suit on which buttons prinked out essential joints while thin strips of white cloth traced major limbs. Filmed against a dark background this draped body disappeared, as in the "black box" magic of the contemporary magic theaters (like Méliès's Théâtre Robert-Houdin), rendering the image a sort of automatic graft of human motion.[6] Thus we should keep in mind not only that, especially in the case of Marey, motion pictures (or pictures conveying motion) were focused on the body nearly exclusively, but that photography provided a means of processing the body into data.

Not only visually and technically similar to Marey's processes, but derived primarily from medical photography, the Motion Capture process used with Andy Serkis as he enacted Gollum required him to wear "a

---

[6] On Black Box Magic, or "the Black Art," see Hopkins *Magic*, 64-67.

specially designed black suit covered in highly reflective referencing dots, positioned by means of Velcro at strategic points, wherever your body bends or has extremities" (Serkis *Gollum*, 35). Likewise Serkis's face was graphed by Special Effects Master Bay Raitt ("Bay drew lines all over my face, breaking it up into muscle groups"), then scanned into a computer after he made a series of expressions (*Gollum*, 38). Although the purposes of these processes are entirely different (Marey achieving motion analysis as an end in itself; Serkis being processed though Motion Capture as one preliminary stage in the creation of a synthetic creature), they both involve technology intervening on the human body in action and breaking it down into visual units. The creation of Gollum thus returns to the goal of the automata: the creation of an artificial mobile human figure.

It must be emphasized how synthetic the creation of Gollum on the screen was, drawing as it did on a range of techniques. Motion Capture served as the basis of a computer-generated range of bodily motion (allowing the actual physical movements made by Serkis to "drive" the motions of a computer-generated virtual figure of the character). Serkis was also filmed interacting with the other actors, yielding shots from which his figure would later be digitally removed to be replaced by the virtual figure of Gollum. Many sequences relied on a variety of frame-by-frame animation techniques independent of actual Motion Capture (although often using moving images of Serkis as a reference that could be adhered to, or radically departed from). Gollum was built up, often frame by frame, using a variety of intermeshing techniques including some that were directly dependent on data derived from Serkis's performance while others had varying degrees of dependence or autonomy in relation to recordings of Serkis's body motions.

In addition, the voice of Gollum was married to the animated image through ADR (automatic dialogue replacement). With the visual eclipse of Serkis from the final film (other than the sense of Serkis "driving" his animated image), his voice came to represent the authenticity of physical presence. Publicity for the film stresses that Gollum's voice came entirely from Serkis. Sound recordist Mike Hopkins has been quoted as saying, "People find it hard to believe there is no electronic processing applied to the original vocal track to enhance either the texture or the timbre of Gollum's voice, and even other sound editors have difficulty believing that the magic is a hundred percent Andy." To describe this as "a hundred per cent Andy" begs a question, given that even conventional sound recording always involves some process of electronic transformation. In traditional filmmaking sound recording has always been the most synthetic of filmic processes, yet, ironically, it often carries the authority of presence. Audiences tend to be less aware of auditory manipulations than they are of visual ones. Serkis's vocal performance therefore fulfills contradictory demands: Gollum's strange gurgling intonations certainly seem inhuman (recalling for me a cross between Peter Lorre and Donald Duck with a slight West End accent). Yet one senses (or publicity for the film cues us to notice) the physical tremors, bodily textures, and careful emotional intonations Serkis as a human actor manages to bring to Gollum's voice. Serkis's performance therefore provides a human texture and even a degree of physical presence to an inhuman creature more effectively than sounds smacking of mechanical or electronic generation could. Serkis stressed his need to act with his whole body when recording Gollum's voice ("There was no way I could stand up to do the voice – the physical and the vocal were all inextricably linked, and I had to be hunched and on all fours to make the voice work" [*Gollum*, 40]).

The voice of Gollum possesses an apparent degree of authenticity and physically embodied presence while the animated image, although tethered frequently to the Motion Capture of Serkis, shows a greater independence. The vivifying nature of the spoken word recalls creation myths in which the inert body of a human creature must be brought to life through an infusion of Divine breath. In Biblical tradition God breathes life into Adam. This breath constitutes the soul of the creature, the borrowed breath that will be delivered up at death in a last gasp. Breath, (as Allen S. Weiss emphasizes in an analysis of the desire to record the voice [*Breathless*]), also carries the voice and speech. And it is language, specifically its expression as letters, which magically brings the Golem to life. This permutation of letters described by the *Sepher Yetzirah* parallels the modern manipulation of data, as Scholem observed, setting up an uncanny similarity to the technical transformation of Serkis's actual body into data that will be rearranged through a computer program to create the synthetic image of Gollum. (Serkis claims he said to himself, "Your body will vanish into thin air and be replaced by digital ones and zeros, so get your head around that" [*Gollum*, 19].)

Image 28: "It's the only way. Go in... or go back." The body of the Andy Serkis/CGI creation, Gollum. Digital frame enlargement. Copyright ©New Line Cinema.

However, as much as technology and magical processes bear formal similarities, the differences in assumptions and effects remain equally essential. In spite of their similarity in sound, Golem and Gollum differ not only in the processes of their creation but in their very nature. An inability to speak, an essential, material muteness constitutes the primary sign of the inferior, non-Divine nature of the Golem[7] (as Borges put it "Perhaps the sacred name had been misspelled/or in uttering been jumbled or too weak./The potent sorcery never took effect:/man's apprentice never learned to speak" [Borges "The Golem,"195]). In contrast to the primitive Golem, the decadent Gollum seems too highly developed. Not only does he possess a voice, but in the film's conception of him as a schizoid creature split between residual Hobbit (Sméagol) and progressively demonic (Gollum) parts, he actually possess two voices – "Sméagol has a high, more nasal tone and speaks more briskly than

---

[7] Scholem "Idea," 192-93. Although muteness characterizes the dominant strain of Golem accounts, it does not appear in all traditions, as Idel shows in detail.

Gollum, whose tone is lower, slower and more guttural" explains Serkis (*Gollum*, 43) – and, in climactic moments, the creature actually conducts conversations with himself.

The combination of Motion Capture, voice recording, animation techniques (as well as the final digital compositing and ADR editing that combines them all seamlessly) seems to mark Gollum as a climax in the dream of the technological creation of an artificial human being, the figural counterpart of Bazin's "Myth of Total Cinema." But far from a material, mechanical, or magical entity, Gollum remains only a trace on celluloid, the result of data gathered and combined through extremely sophisticated technology, the latest advance in the technique of artificial motion, cinematic animation.

Creation and Destruction of the Golem/Gollum

> *"The entire box was filled, to a depth of about seven inches, with a fine powder, pigeon-gray and opalescent, that Joe recognized at once from boyhood excursions as the silty bed of the Moldau. He had scraped it from his shoes a thousand times and brushed it from the seat of his trousers. The speculations of those who feared that the Golem, removed from the shores of the river that mothered it, might degrade had been proved correct."*
> Michael Chabon, *The Amazing Adventures of Kavalier and Clay*

Rituals for creating a Golem also specify the means for undoing the magic, for destroying of the artificial human. As Scholem stressed, the creation of a Golem carries dangers for all involved. Most myths of animating the inanimate carry a freight of anxiety that, once brought to life, the creature might become independent and ignore the command of its maker. Tales of the tool that turns on its master, most often identified with the Frankenstein monster (the principle modern Goyishe form of the Golem legend), became, in the twentieth century, the dominant allegory of man's relation to technology (see, for instance, Baldrick *Shadow*). One thinks particularly of Kubrick's versions of this nightmare of technology exceeding human command, from *Dr. Strangelove*'s Doomsday Machine (1964), triggered by the errant bomber (the falcon that cannot hear the falconer, to paraphrase Yeats), as well as HAL 9000, the human simulacrum as paranoid computer in *2001: A Space Odyssey* (1968). In fact, Disney's animated fable "The Sorcerer's Apprentice" from *Fantasia* (1940), in which magic and technology blur in their uncontrollable effects, dramatizes a folktale one of whose forms originally described a Golem manically bringing water from a well, rather than a pail-bearing broom.[8]

As opposed to the stitching together of dead bodies, the Golem is animated by letters and numbers, primal elements of data. Rituals of Golem-destruction also involved the manipulation of letters. As Idel points out, there were two basic traditions for returning the Golem back to the mud from which it came. One involved an inversion of the linguistic processes, reversing the combination of letters that created it. The other involved erasing a significant letter that had been inscribed on the Golem, usually on the creature's forehead. In this tradition the Hebrew word that animated the clay man is *Emeth* (Truth). He can be reduced to clay (or ashes) by simply erasing the first letter of the word, aleph, leaving the word *Meth* (Dead).

Scholem provides some vivid scenarios of this mode of destruction.[9] One version involves a Golem that continues to grow to a gigantic and threatening size from the power of the word inscribed upon, or attached to, his forehead. The creature becomes so huge its maker can no longer reach its forehead. Cunningly, the rabbi commands the Golem to remove his boots. Bending over, the Golem brings its forehead into reach and the rabbi removes the animating letter. In some versions the resulting collapse of earth and clay buries the rabbi.[10] Scholem found the richest account of the destruction of a Golem in a thirteenth-century Kabbalistic commentary. In this version the prophet Jeremiah and his son Sira create a Golem after studying the *Sepher Yetzirah* for three years and

---

[8] As "The Golem as Water Carrier" this tale can be found in Bloch (*Golem*, 70-71). Goethe's retelling of this served as the basis of "The Sorcerer's Apprentice."

[9] In the 1920 film *The Golem and How He Came into the World*, the word *aemeth* (written on parchment and placed within a sort of amulet) endows the man of clay with life. His destruction comes when children almost playfully remove the amulet, and the figure falls over with a thud, like an Energizer Bunny deprived of its battery.

[10] A version similar to this was recorded by Jakob Grimm (one of the Brothers) in his *Journal for Hermits* in 1808. See Scholem, "Idea," 159

then combining the letters. The result was a human creature on whose forehead stood the inscription YHWH ELOHIM EMETH (God is the Lord of Truth). But the creature also held a knife in his hand with which he himself erased the aleph, the first letter of Emeth, converting the magical inscription into the blasphemy, "God is Dead." Horrified by this impiety, Jeremiah listened as the Golem explained that to create a man means to compare oneself to God and even to aspire to replace him. Jeremiah then asked how to undo this unintentionally sinful act and was told to write the letters backward. "Only do not meditate in the sense of building up, but the other way around." As they followed his instructions, father and son watched as the Golem returned to dust and ashes (Scholem "Idea," 180).

On the occasion of christening the computer/Golem of Rehovot, Scholem declared, "It is indeed significant that Nietzsche's famous cry 'God is dead!' should have gone up first in a Kabbalistic text warning against the making of a Golem and linking the death of God to the realization of the idea of the Golem" (*Golem of Prague* 338). Conservative political philosopher Erich Voegelin has stressed the modern implications of this parable, by carefully reading its relation to Nietzsche's parable from *The Gay Science* (Voegelin *Science*, 279-284; Nietzsche "Madman," 181-182). For Nietzsche the murder of God presages the appearance of a new man, the superman. But the parable of Golem, Voegelin claims, shows the blasphemy involved in this modern ambition. "Man cannot transform himself into a superman; the attempt to create a superman is an attempt to murder man. Historically the murder of God is not followed by the superman, but by the murder of man" (284). In what sense could this vision of a perfected man entail the destruction of the human, and does it have anything to do with the simple technological animation of a figure in an entertaining film?

One might explore the relevance to Gollum of such dire consequences of the modern and technological creation of human simulacra by the gathering and re-combination of data, through a more proximate parable, the 1957 novel *The Glass Bees* by German writer and theorist of technology Ernst Junger. Junger describes a postwar industrial and technological mogul, Giacomo Zapparoni, a figure recalling the sorcerers of E.T.A. Hoffman and, as Bruce Sterling points out in his Introduction, Walt Disney and Bill Gates, combined (Junger, ix). The Zapparoni Works produces robots for every conceivable purpose, specializing in Lilliputian insect-like robots that perform tasks essential not only to industry but also to the housewife (such as the eponymous glass bees which buzz through the air performing surveillance on employees, anticipations of the Pentagon's airborne drones). But besides these useful machines, Zapparoni also delights in a sideline to his main industry, the cinema, which "he had brought to an almost fabulous perfection with his robots and automatons" (Junger *Bees*, 28).

Rather than simply an expensive and capricious hobby, the novel's narrator, an unemployed former cavalry officer seeking a job at the Zapparoni Works, sees this new form of cinema as the essence of Zapparoni's project: "Zapparoni's ambition was to recreate the automaton in the old sense... he wanted to create artificial people, life-sized figures which looked exactly like human beings" (99). But Zapparoni's ambition extends beyond the human figure:

> The figures, it is true, still differed slightly from the human actors we are used to seeing, but they differed pleasantly: the faces were more brilliant, more flawless; their eyes of a larger cut, like precious stones, the movements slower, more elegant, and in moments of excitement, even more violent and sudden than anything in our experience... Thus one could say that these figures did not simply imitate the human form but carried it beyond its possibilities and dimensions. (100)

Zapparoni's films excelled in presenting fantastic and legendary creatures: Caliban, Goliath, Tom Thumb, or the angel of Annunciation. One could imagine this cast of characters including both the Golem and Gollum.

Like Nietzsche's superman, this perfection or exceeding of the human figure may be only an opening move in a game between humans and technology. As the narrator observes, Zapparoni's automata constitute a passage to even greater transformations where "mechanics would become refined to a degree that would no longer require any crude embodiment. Lights, words, yes even thoughts, would be sufficient. Clearly the Zapparoni films had nearly realized such a future" (28-29).

But after exploring Zapparoni's realm of enchantment for some time, the former riding master reacts in horror at Zapparoni's dissecting mentality and the drive toward technical perfection his Works embody. The perfect image of the human actually announces the inhuman: "Human perfection and technical perfection are incompatible... Technical perfection strives towards the calculable, human perfection toward the incalculable" (112-113).[11] The synthetic image of man results not only from calculation but from an abstraction and dissection of a sort that destroys, as it replaces, "the image of the free and intact man." Man becomes reduced to a combinatoire, product of an archive of units of data with various programs for assembly. The former horseman claims, Zapparoni's project "intended to rely on man power in the same way that it had relied on horsepower. It wanted units to be equal and divisible, and for that purpose man had to be destroyed as the horse had already been destroyed" (141).

The danger of creating a Golem, Scholem profoundly underscores, comes not simply from the unleashing of the power of the creature itself, as in the Frankenstein myth. In spite of the threat inherent in the titanic growth or irrational, mechanically repetitive actions of a Golem, for Scholem (like Voegelin and Junger's narrator) the true danger lies elsewhere: "The danger is not that the Golem, become autonomous, will develop overwhelming powers; it lies in the tension which the creative process arouses in the creator himself" (Scholem "Idea," 191). It is less the monster than the overeacher Dr. Frankenstein that constitutes the threat, less any specific aspect of technology than the Will-to-Power it announces.

In *The Return of the King* the destruction of Gollum parallels and accompanies the final destruction of his "precious," the Ring itself. As a post-technical fable projecting contemporary anxieties onto a synthetic mythical past, the film often seems to posit the Ring as an allegory for the

---

[11] Marcus Bullock (*Eye*, 143-144) points out that the German text, "*Menschliche Vollkommenheit und technische Perfektion sind nicht zu verinbaren*" which he translates as "The accomplishment of mankind and the perfection of technology may not be reconciled," involves a strong contrast between *Volkommenheit* and *Perfektion* which the English translators of the novel translate with the same word. In normal use the words are synonymous, but Marcus claims Junger draws out etymological connotations, a contrast between an organic growth and fulfillment and a perfection corresponding to an outside ideal.

ultimate in technological control (equating magic with previously unseen degrees of technological development, as did Arthur C. Clarke, author of *2001* [Clarke "Hazards"]). The dissolving of the Ring in the crucible of boiling magma that forms the climax of the trilogy offers a parallel to the magic-in-reverse for the dissolution of a Golem, just as the Ring's effect of irresistible megalomania infecting Gollum and threatening Frodo recalls the dangerous tension within the creator of a Golem that Scholem describes. Symmetrically, Gollum becomes dissolved in the same bath of fire that destroys his "precious" – both are reduced to elements and ashes.

But my comparison has not been between the process of creating a Golem and any aspect of the diegetic world of *The Lord of the Rings* trilogy. I have been interested instead in the films' technology: the processes of ADR, Motion Capture, and animation that created the image of Gollum. Should one find in the complex technology that brought this entertaining epic into being the same sort of danger Scholem, Voegelin, and Junger warned us about? Is the creation of Gollum innocent entertainment, or does it participate in a technological Will-to-Power whose ultimate end will be the destruction of "the image of the free and intact man?" Is *The Lord of the Rings*, with its invocation of a pre-technical mythic world of magic and even its putative anti-technological allegory, simply another example of the tendency of the Hollywood Blockbuster to produce anti-technological narratives while using the most complex and cutting edge technology available?[12] While the imperial ideology of an inevitable military confrontation between the forces of Good and Evil in the trilogy may seem to support (intentionally or not) the most dubious aspects of current U.S. Global policy of destroying the "axis of evil," may its true threat not perhaps lie not in the story, but in processes of constructing myths, images and legendary creatures in a technological age?

---

[12] I thank Julie Turnock for this observation that the most technologically sophisticated Hollywood blockbusters often offer anti-technological narratives.

Animation and the Imaginary Body

> *"Thus we would enter into a whole new pictorial world, as into a magic forest, and come to the realm of the truly kinetic, the optical lyric... perhaps one day it could gain a great importance and open up new beauty for humanity. That is finally the goal of every art, and thus the cinema would gain its own unique aesthetic realm."*
> – Paul Wegener, "Die kunsterlichen Moglichkeiten des films" 1916

Although I take the questions I just raised seriously, I believe that taking them too seriously – or perhaps I should say too simply—involves a serious misunderstanding. In this essay I have tried to indicate my strong belief that film technology holds a key place in a culture of modernity and in issues of representation that are central to Western culture. However, I also feel it would be less than serious (or, at least, I could not take it seriously) to claim a film work like *The Lord of the Rings* bears responsibility for the most horrific aspects of our technological age. I also feel that film critics who assume that an ideological critique of popular films contributes in some vital way to changing our world are most likely guilty of bad faith.

My point is not that popular films do not raise critical and disturbing issues, but rather that we cannot assume that as critics and historians we occupy a lofty position of judgment outside of these critical areas. It seems to me the value (rather than the fault) of many popular films lies precisely in the way they help us investigate the dangers and deceptions of our culture, dangers and deceptions we – and the films – also participate in. Certainly the critique of culture aims at clarifying alternatives to the horrors in which modern technology and instrumental reason involve us. But this remains a difficult project, and a self-congratulatory and moralistic sense of political correctness seems to me an obstacle to significant critical thinking and action.

My jeremiad aims at stressing the ambivalence of cultural texts, claiming that *understanding* them, even in their complicity with the horrors that surround us, may be more urgent and more difficult than condemning them. Further, my critique of technological thinking has no illusion that profound aspects of our modern history could be transformed by simply decrying them. I also feel that Luddite opposition to technology or longings for a pre-technical age, while rich as utopian fantasies or expressions of unfilled longings, ultimately remain reactionary formations. As Siegfried Kracauer claimed in his early essay on "The Mass Ornament," the way to a powerful critique lies through confronting these manifestations of an abstracting, calculating Will-to-Power, not avoiding them (Kracauer *Ornament*, 86).

Even the most profound opponent to the project of technological progress, Martin Heidegger, declares that "it is precisely in this extreme danger that the innermost indestructible belongingness of man within granting may come to light, provided that we, for our part, begin to pay heed to the coming to presence of technology" (Heidegger *Question*, 32). The full implications of Heidegger's statement lie beyond the limits of this essay. But the questions that we must direct towards technology–and that technology itself poses for us – already surround us in our daily life: in our work, in our entertainment, and in the ways we envision the future and even imagine a mythical past. I feel that the presentation of technology as spectacle found in recent Hollywood blockbusters, such as *The Lord of the Rings*, while fully complicit in the ambivalent penetration of the technological into the process of representation, nonetheless (or perhaps *for that very reason*) performs a vital function in bringing us close to this intertwining of mythopoeisis and modern technology, allowing us to experience, through all our senses, the fantasies, narrative, and sensual imagery both invoke.

The creation of Gollum occurs within a long genealogy of fascination with the technical and magical creation of a figure that possesses the essential elements of the human. If the Enlightenment automaton performed some aspects of human motion and seemed to possibly possess consciousness, its most obvious achievement was a mimicking of the appearance of a living human being. In the twentieth century the triumph of data recording and cybernetic programs could eschew such "crude embodiment" and rely on more rarified means of realization–essentially light and electrical impulses – to effect a simulacrum of consciousness, or create on film the perfection of the moving image of the human being.

But we must not lose sight of our object of investigation: this pathetic, misshapen figure with its uncanny voice, this degenerate former Hobbit, Gollum/Sméagol (the furthest thing from a superman). This technological reproduction of the human body aims less at miming the classical human body than at the creation – as in Zapparoni's films – of a fantastic body, a creature of legend and fiction, of imagination. Gollum's ineluctable difference from humans, his distance even from the more nearly humanoid (within Tolkien's mythology of Middle Earth) Dwarves, Elves, and Hobbits, demanded the creation of a figure through animation techniques, rather than the pro-filmic resources of make-up, prosthetics, and careful framing of shots that suffices for the most part in the trilogy to create characters belonging to these other species. The art direction that conceived of Gollum's physical appearance quite brilliantly conceived of a figure that has moved away from the qualities of a mature human adult. His physiognomy recalls simultaneously an infant, an aged person, a fetus, and a corpse. Besides possessing a body that seems in turn too immature (almost fetus-like at points) or too deathly, Gollum also shows affinities with a range of animal species: a creature that bounds on four feet like a rabbit, carries things in its mouth like a dog, and has the sharpened teeth and ability to spring upon its victims of a predator; while his pale, slimy skin, huge eyes, ridge-like spine, and abilities to navigate in water and creep through rocky crevices evoke a fish or reptile.

Enlightenment mechanics sought to create a man in the image of a machine, in terms of regularity and predictability of motion, but with a hyperrealism of appearance (with some nods towards exoticism in the both the chess player and the Talking Turk). Although much of contemporary CGI and digital manipulation blends imperceptibly into familiar realities, spectacular special effects films primarily visualize the fantastic. Ironically, in such work, methods of gathering photographic data about the human body that have their origins in the physiology of Marey and further development in contemporary medical practices, provide the basis for non-existent bodies.

The extraordinary teams of technicians assembled for *The Lord of the Rings* realized fantastic physiologies to match Tolkien's rich mythopoetic imagination of a cosmos populated by widely varied creatures. The highly imaginative end products of this collaborative process make visible and audible bodies never seen before, although resonant in our imagination. The creatures of the trilogy recall figures from our dreams and nightmares, as well as combining disparate elements from a variety of human and animal bodies we know from our waking life, as creatures of fancy are supposed to do.

As Paul Wegener, the actor who twice portrayed the Golem, commented in 1916, the filmic creations of new and fantastic bodies derive from the origins of cinema in the trick film. They possess a long and rich history (on which *The Lord of the Rings* frequently draws), which includes the creatures of Méliès and the fantastic creatures of Weimar cinema (created primarily through make-up and masterful performance), such as Conrad Veidt's Cesare, Max Schreck's Nosferatu, and Wegener's Golem. The cinema did not need to wait for CGI to embrace this popular romantic tradition. Thus this new assembly of techniques can be seen as a climax of a long tradition, rather than a transformation – or even violation – of the essential nature of film.

The essential nature of film: as if there were such a thing! I often claim that rather than *a nature* cinema possesses *a history*. That history includes a wholesale cannibalizing of other media, matched by a polemical differentiation and claim to uniqueness. Cinema appropriated a long heritage of imagery, stories, and attractions, as well as a constant desire to bring something new to the table, a technological ambition that involves a continuous process of research and development and an engagement with ideological and utopian fantasies. This desire finally entails a hybridity of natures inherent in a variety of practices.

Without entirely endorsing Lev Manovich's folding of cinema into a larger graphic tradition of animation, I welcome the broadening of horizons of film's identity that the new attention to "special effects" entails. Animation deals with line, form, and colors in motion, including both abstract and representational scenarios. However, even abstract animation often involves a literal invocation of the animate, the living, that essence endowed with soul, *anima*. Animation, as Eisenstein claimed in his extraordinary writings on Disney, allows the creation of a "plasmatic" body, one that certainly refers to and addresses our own corporeal sense but exceeds our actual physical limitations in its ability to change its contours. Film animation invokes not only the *anima*, since movement gives the impression of being alive, but also the mythic *animism* in which all objects potentially possess souls. For Eisenstein, Disney and the animated cartoon penetrated into the sources of the folktale by imagining a body not limited by its form but constantly changing shape and identity, constantly in process. This fairytale world, rather than the realm of the ideal superman, dominates the animated film, the realm of little animal helpers, of the comic grotesque body, and of creatures like Gollum.[13]

Rather than absolutely shuffling (and perhaps discarding) traditional concepts of cinema, recent technological innovations in special effects allow us to overcome the dualities created by theories focused on the uniquely photographic essence of cinema. An alternative view would emphasize the common roots of photographic cinema *and* animation in what Eisenstein calls the attraction of the plasmatic, the moving transforming body (Eisenstein *Disney*, 21). The creation of Gollum shows the pragmatic transgression of the boundary between theoretically distinct modes in its combination of photographic and animation effects. The very concept of Motion Capture, in which the recording of a living actor drives the motion of an animated figure through complex logorhythmic programs, embodies this interdependence. Animation enables a departure from any reference to reality, but in the creation of Gollum animation often took its cue from the recorded motions of Serkis. Providing animation with a reference to reality demonstrates a desire (and perhaps an anxiety) to found fantasy within a realm of realistic (indeed, in Peirce's sense, indexical) observation and recording (see Buchler *Peirce*, 107-111). "We couldn't afford to have it look artificial," said Peter Jackson, "it had to look totally real" (quoted in Serkis, 85).

---

[13] See Eisenstein (*Disney*). I also want to signal my debt to two fine commentaries on Eisenstein discussion of Disney, Moore (*Savage Theory*) and Hansen ("Mice," x).

I believe we distort our experience of films if we try to assign the effect of realism – or even the sensation of physical presence – exclusively to the photographic or confine the artificial to "special effects." The hybridity of photographic and various other forms of remediation evident in one form or another throughout the history of film undercuts such a simple identification. For example, as is well known, André Bazin's discussion of Susan Alexander's suicide attempt in *Citizen Kane*, perhaps his most extensive discussion of the effect of deep-focus photography and its ability to preserve the dramatic unity of space and time, is describing what was actually a process shot, in which the large glass and spoon in the foreground were matted into a long shot of the dimly lit Susan lying unconscious in bed (Bazin *Welles*, 77-81). But I would not claim this fact invalidates his analysis; it only destroys a naïve identification of the dramatic effect he is describing with the "realism " of the photographic. Serkis describes director Peter Jackson's insistence that the sequence of Gollum's monologue (or dialogue with himself) that provides the hook to the end of *The Two Towers* be shot in a single continuous three-minute take, giving a Bazinian effect of duration to a scene enacted by an animated figure (Serkis *Gollum*, 66).

Describing the animation of Gollum's face (done entirely by key frame animation after experiments in Motion Capture did not yield the results desired), lead facial animator Bay Raitt praises Randy Cook, the animation director, by saying the suggestions he gave made "the whole thing buzz with presence" (Serkis *Gollum*, 81). When Bazin claimed, "It is no longer as certain as it was that there is no middle ground between absence and presence," he referred to his theory of the special ontology of the photographic image (*What is Cinema?*, I: 97). But we might wonder whether a sense of presence needs to depend entirely on the photographic, when cinema has always had a larger bag of tricks than a putative photographic ontology to convince us that we are watching living beings.

In contrast to the film theory of the seventies that saw cinema as a linchpin in a totalizing system of controlling and positioning institutions and practices, cinema presents an amalgam of fantasies and ambitions of both control and escape with both sinister or libratory implications. The fantasy of creating images of living bodies that both recall and exceed the bodies we know possesses this depth of ambiguity as an incitement to new theory and discussion. In this fantasy, photography and animation intertwine, as exemplified by the process of creating the Gollum. Thus, without denying important formal differences, animation and motion photography share the project of portraying bodies and forms in motion, of animating images, creating both new fantasies and renewing ancient ones.

I feel that at their best the new techniques of digital effects do more than simply reproduce the familiar human body; they offer not only fantastic variations on the human form that relate it to the animal and mineral kingdoms, but also a vision of matter itself as animate. One early theory of cinematic specificity, the discussion in France in the twenties of *photogénie*, often described this aspect of cinema as dependent less on the resources of photography per se than on the animating effect of the new medium, its ability to endow matter with an inner life, a sense of soul. Jean Epstein claimed, "It is hardly surprising that [cinema] should endow the objects it is called upon to depict with such intense life" (quoted in Abel *French Film Theory*, 316). Antonin Artaud described the essential sorcery of cinema in terms of revealing the secret life of matter (Artaud "Witchcraft," 65). Junger also found this animism in Zapparoni's cinema, claiming, "Here a principle operative in dreams – namely, that matter thinks – seemed to be realized" (Junger *Bees*, 29). The work of modern animators, whether using traditional or computer aided means – Jan Svankmajer, the Brothers Quay, and Peter Jackson, with the extraordinary climactic scenes of *Braindead* (1992) – seem to capture this transformation of things and matter, bodies and viscera, life and death, as if literally fulfilling Eisenstein's and Artaud's sense of cinema.

Scholem theorized that the dark side of the Golem derived from his earthly energy, his tellurian nature. As I noted before, one of the contrasts that the cinematic Gollum poses to the Golem lies in his immateriality, his existence not as a material entity but as information and programs stored in a computer, and as a flickering image of light moving on a screen. But Mosche Idel disputes Scholem's interpretation of the Kabbalistic text in question, claiming it actually attributes the Golem's energy to a supernal light. If the animating force of the Golem comes from a heavenly beam of light, the two figures of Golem and Gollum may converge. The combination of letters and numbers that create the Golem and whose reversal causes his dissolution recall not only computer data and programs but the runes inscribed on the Ring itself. At the climax of *The Return of the King*, the Ring floats on the lava that has just engulfed Gollum and, before it too melts away, the runes within it illuminate and spill out a brilliant light. Magic, codes, projected light. At the moment of dissolution, images appear of the film's own conditions of possibility.

But why should an epic of heroism and magic culminate in the destruction of the most powerful magic its mythic world possesses? Why do technically sophisticated Hollywood blockbusters primarily express paranoia about technology and suspicion of machines? Why do rituals of the Golem include essential instruction for his destruction? Do these queries simply double back on themselves, posing an inescapable ring of ideology and illusion? Or do they express an essential ambivalence that forces us to confront the complexities of our relations to our modern environment with its promise as well as its deceptions? Heidegger ends his essay on the question of technology with this quote from the poet Hölderlin's "Patmos":

Wo aber Gefahr ist, wächst
Das Rettende auch

(But where danger is, grows
The saving power also.)

We might end with the ironic and skeptical last stanzas of Borges's poem, "The Golem," in which the rabbi who created the Golem questions his action, followed by a nearly cinematic switch in point of view:

"What made me supplement the endless series
of symbols with one more? Why add in vain
to the knotty skein always unraveling
another cause and effect, with not one gain?"

In his hour of anguish and uncertain light,
Upon his Golem his eyes would come to rest.
Who is to say what God must have been feeling,
Looking down and seeing His rabbi so distressed?

The Laddy Vanishes

Murray Pomerance

*"We're a bit suspicious round here of anything out of the way –
uncanny, if you understand me;
and we don't take to it all of a sudden."*
(*Fellowship*, 214)

Spectacle

Writing about the far from lavish use of lanterns for the production of street illumination and public safety in nights without moonlight that preceded the nineteenth century, Wolfgang Schivelbusch makes a curious observation: It is something of a mystery how the eighteenth-century eye saw night-time Paris, with its scattered patches of light, as a brightly lit city. Perhaps two different levels of perception overlapped here, so that *symbolic* light was seen as *actual* light. (*Night*, 95)

The luminosity of a single lantern, he conjectures, may have been seen as having produced a luminous culture, even when lanterns were placed so far apart on city streets that the effects of their power were sorely reduced in cumulative effect. It was the marvel of the lantern itself, the *idea* of the light that it could shed (through its artful design for maximizing reflection), that entered the public consciousness as "city light."

Something of the same "overlapping" of perception – the public adoption of symbol as actuality – may be said to have occured in the gallery with the exhibition of the long-perspective landscape. While the economy of the gallery required the cramming of walls with numerous framed pictures, often hung above and below one another on a single wall, the perspective in a framed landscape could convey to the viewer a sense of expansive space, tranquil remove, meditative access, and capacious possibility even when other paintings jostled for attention nearby. So it is that the nineteenth century could have been considered an age of perspectives and vistas, an age of possibility, because of the representation achieved in a single canvas, say the bucolic "View of Salisbury" by John Constable – exactly such a view, indeed, as is realized in Grant Major's design of Hobbiton and the Shire in one film that will concern me here, *The Lord of the Rings: The Fellowship of the Ring*. The experience of viewing a Constable landscape in the gallery setting was at the same time anything but expansive and liberating, since each of his canvases competed for attention with others all around. (In much the same way, the "expansive" vistas of Jackson's film competed in December 2001 with helicopter perspectives of bombed-out Mogadishu in Ridley Scott's *Black Hawk Down* [2001], the kids of Hogwarts playing Quidditch in *Harry Potter and the Sorcerer's Stone* [2001]), and the bizarre family portraits in *The Royal Tenenbaums* [2001].) Just as the streets of Paris were in fact far from brilliant in the late eighteenth century, but could be thought so because of the brilliance of the devices that were being used to light them; so the space of the gallery was far from voluminous, and indeed the space of nineteenth century art far from capacious and all-embracing, although a single landscape could present a contradictory, and deceptive, impression. Interestingly, the same sense of vast space can be felt by audiences to permeate cinematic spectaculars like *The Fellowship of the Ring*, owing to the effect of a limited number of exquisitely composed long perspective vista shots by Andrew Lesnie. It may turn out that when we consider its view of human (and Hobbit) affairs, political relations, or struggling for progress against the retrenching forces of darkness, the landscape of *The Lord of the Rings* onscreen is hardly as vast or as all-embracing as the panorama shots suggest.

Nevertheless, in both cases – the street lanterns of Paris and other great European cities, and the landscapes of the nineteenth century – a central feature is the capacity of a technology to open, for what had heretofore been a relatively confined bourgeois consciousness, a view: to make available a spectacle. Illumination is thus intrinsically related to scape, our ability to see linked to our sense that we are seeing *an extent*, a thrilling sight. To this day, we take delight in watching the spread-out lights of a great city from an isolated vantage and thus pleasuring ourselves with the image of the incandescent metropolis – see for example any night shot made from Mulholland Drive looking over Los Angeles, or the sweeping opening perspective on Champion City by night in Kinka Usher's *Mystery Men* (1999), or the intoxicating, if also hideous, views of the grimy, virtually nocturnal Isengard that dot all three *Lord of the Rings* films – and we thrill, watching movies in the dark theater, to see cinematographic replications of the landscapes which used to thrill viewers only in the cramped rooms of the gallery. Because we are able to see, we think of what we see as being especially worth seeing. When our ability is spiked, by special effects, by the long lens, by the dramatically choreographed construction, so is our estimation of our vision. We inhabit a culture in which the encapsulation of experience as a sighting or a prospect has been exploited economically to vast profit and in the name of panoptical social control (the nocturnal lighting of Paris was a police function). Indeed, the empowering – and simultaneously disempowering – gaze described by Mulvey (*Pleasures*) is possible only when experience is magnified through being seen, through being filtered by an imagination cultured, and therefore limited, as "perspective." When sight and illumination are relatively unimportant, it matters little who is looking at whom.

The making available of spectacle, suddenly, uncannily, from a bizarre and engaging perspective, is surely one of the central preoccupations of the drama of the cinematic invisible hero, from James Whale's "invisible man" (1933) to James Bond (Pierce Brosnan) in his invisible car in *Die Another Day* (2002) or Praetor Shinzon (Tom Hardy) in his invisible spaceship in *Star Trek: Nemesis* (2002), all creatures who are intriguing at least partly because, shifting strikingly in and out of our sight, they manage to exist onscreen alternatively as what the psychoanalytic theorists of vision would call phallus and lack. Certain features of male invisibility are made especially emphatic, however, when the protagonist who vanishes is not a man but a boy. This is the character who captures my attention here as he shows himself – or fails to – in a number of interesting films, but principally *The Lord of the Rings* where he appears as the sometimes disappearing Frodo Baggins, a particularly fascinating challenge to the moviegoer's imagination. If in the cinematic universe luminosity, perspective, and magnitude of vision are the foundations of the viewer's engagement and yield mechanically, to those who pay for the privilege of renting it, a position in the safe darkness from which to feel the power of the all-seeing eye (even, perhaps, Sauron's all-seeing eye), it is precisely this all-seeing eye the invisible boy seems to possess in his own way, and this haven of darkness he seems particularly to need, since there is a particular vision that comes to him only, or especially, when he is invisible, it being a curious feature of his experience that he cannot see so very well when others can see him seeing. One recalls John Berger's observation in *Ways of Seeing* that Western art and pornography have succeeded in representing female beauty as an object of exploitation by turning the line of the model's eyesight away, so that the painter (and the admiring males he stands in for) cannot be seen by her seeing her. This is how the male viewer, notably in his invisibility, comes to possess what he sees. But in order for me to explore Frodo here, from my own metadiegetic position of extreme invisibility – an invisibility that swallows all cinematic invisibilities that I write about, while I am writing about them – I must seem to detour, as that young man does, indeed, on his great adventure, through some adjacent territory.

And the subject I promise to return to is precisely the Frodo we cannot see, at the apotheosis of his quest for purity, dignity, honor, love, sanctity, and truth, the Frodo who, about to toss the Ring into the swallowing abyss, standing at the precipice, with Samwise Gamgee wailing behind him, "Throw it! What are you waiting for!?," finds himself stunned by the thing that is dangling from a chain in his hand, stunned and changed and hungry. In a macro-close shot, Peter Jackson shows us Frodo's face all smeared with dirt, his long hair disheveled and diabolic, the Ring swaying like a hypnotist's talisman. His glaucque eyes are frozen open and huge, flooded with hot white light, and the light is literally dripping from them. Frodo turns to Sam now, his face lowered lustfully, his lips pouting with hunger: "The Ring is mine!" He puts it on and becomes invisible, and as Sauron's fiery eye swings over to the mountain cave to search for him we see his footprints in the dirt of the outcropping, stepping away from the edge, step, step, step, step. The hideous Gollum jumps into the air and lands on his invisible back. Looking down from high above we see Gollum struggling in an air dance on the invisible boy's back, and then in a close shot the massive sharp-toothed Gollum mouth opens to take a bite. The ring finger is severed. Frodo drops, visible again, to the ground, howling in pain. Gollum leaps up and down in ecstasy, his "precious" now safe in his hand, but Frodo rises, leaps upon him, and throws him over with the Ring, so that both fall into the magma which will erase them forever. Frodo, hanging at the precipice, is, for now, saved.

View

The display of the world as bounded, retrievable, objective, and possessable is a central fixation in the history of technological and social development since the advent of capitalism, and one which has led to alienation even as it has inspired and satisfied those who have been privileged to look. A passage in Forster's *A Room With a View,* originally published in 1908, nicely illustrates how the late nineteenth century *perception of the Other* could be a delightful, while also an exploitative and categorical, social operation:

> "I had got an idea – I dare say wrongly – that you feel more at home with me in a room."
> "A room?" she echoed, hopelessly bewildered.

"Yes. Or, at the most, in a garden, or on a road. Never in the real country like this."
"Oh, Cecil, what ever do you mean? I have never felt anything of the sort. You talk as if I was a kind of poetess sort of person."
"I don't know that you aren't. I connect you with a view – a certain type of view. Why shouldn't you connect me with a room?" (*Room*, 125)

Succinctly merged here are three ways of seeing Lucy Honeychurch as a "person *with* a view": first, she can be imagined to be a "kind of poetess sort of person," that is, a scanner with taste and perspective, a meditator upon distances. She voyages to Italy to see pretty landscapes the way I voyage to the cinematic Hobbiton to see the rolling hills and pretty gardens or to Rivendell to see the glorious waterfalls. Like any moviegoer, she can be taken to understand the cultural construction of beauty. Secondly, she has a view of Cecil viewing her, specifically the view that his view makes no sense at all: in this regard she is anything but a disempowered object of vision herself and something of a connoisseur of viewers. Having been looked at all her life, she knows what it is to be looked at by people of discernment; she is a discerner of discerners. Thirdly, people can take a view *of her,* just as Cecil does, even while she is busy looking, even at them. She is an object of examination. It is evident throughout this novel, certainly, that Cecil Vyse "connects" her with a view precisely because, in his unremitting way, he takes a view *of* her; measures, evaluates, places, and credits her; and is doing so now, indeed, in his act of description. Does he not think her unaware of his moves, indeed? The figure of Lucy as the object of Cecil's evaluation proceeds in two directions. Her being "connected" with his view is perhaps a paramount example in contemporary literature of a beautiful girl converted to an object of vision, though, as I say, not an ignorant one, and also an example of the male's calculated vision being linked not just with formal beauty but with sexuality and power. Cecil is clearly both sexually excited and repressed. He later finds a passage in a book, to the effect that "men fall into two classes – those who forget views and those who remember them" (*Room*, 178).

Mulvey's formulation of a division between men, who have the power to look, and women, who experience to-be-looked-at-ness (*Pleasures*, 19-26) vaguely covers Lucy and Cecil, but only vaguely.

Robert Samuels reflects that feminist film critiques are centrally flawed in their interpretation of the Lacanian gaze. For these theorists, he laments, "the 'gaze' is considered to be equivalent to the (masculine) control of the visual field. On its most basic level, these theories argue that men control women by making them the object of their visual intent" (*Bi-Textuality*, 109). For Jacques Lacan, on the contrary, the gaze is a perceptual lack, structured by the sometime looker who is looked at:

> When Lacan states that I see from one point, but I am looked at from all sides, he is indicating that there is an inverse relation between the one who is looking and the one who is looked at. Furthermore, he places the subject that is looked at in the position of the object (a) in the form of the gaze. (*Bi-Textuality*, 110)

This is a somewhat clearer illumination of Cecil Vyse's contention that Lucy, for him, is connected with a gaze. Although he persists in seeing her and defining her, in taking a view, she represents for him the locus of a gaze that can be coming his way. When Frodo meets Galadriel the Queen of the Elves we have a reprise of this hungry look that is met by an oncoming gaze (in both directions), though Galadriel and Frodo are beyond sexuality. Bachelard, too, writes of this mutuality of the gaze, when he says that "Tout ce qui brille voit" ("Everything that casts a light sees") and goes on to reflect, "The lonely dreamer who sees himself being watched begins to watch his watcher" (1971, in Schivelbusch *Night*, 96).

The male who looks is seen by feminist critics to derive his power from his perspective, and to be as invisible in the act of looking as his object is notably visible. But his "invisibility" is tenuous, because this watcher is watching from only one point; from all around, others can gaze at him while his watching locks and bounds him. This tenuousness is at the heart of the discussion of the gazing screen in Wheeler Winston Dixon's alarming and wonderful *It Looks At You*, in which he works to argue that "perhaps film subjectivity is possible" (93) – film subjectivity, note, not subjectivity *in* film. Watching – and defining – women through his look, contemporary man is himself the object of other people's critical gaze, is seen seeing by a gaze that has its own subjectivity and social valence. The critic sees the seer, for one; but so do other men, who estimate his merit on the basis of what it can be seen that he has seen.

After looking, one shows one's captured prize to others who gaze and understand one by looking at it. Looking and seeing for men in competitive, male-dominated society is something of a performance. How desirable, then, perhaps how profitable, to be able to look without being seen!

A character called The Invisible Boy (Kel Mitchell) in *Mystery Men* has his own politically inflected reasons for wanting to vanish, a feat of which he is capable only when no one is looking at him. His friends must turn aside, indeed, and the camera follow them instead of him, in order for him to become what his name suggests he is. He is an African American of about eighteen years, who says of himself, "All my life I've been ignored by people – and finally, after years of being overlooked, I found I had the power to disappear." This is nothing if not self-consciously ironic on his part, of course; he is reflecting the "invisibility" of the African American presence in racist white society. When at the turning point of the story he heroically manages to disappear, he squeals with delight, as his clothing drops to the floor, "I am like Saran Wrap!"

The Dramaturgy of the "Invisible Moment"

It is only *apparently* that we are incapable of seeing the invisible hero. In fact, the dramaturgy of the "invisible moment" onscreen requires a great deal more from the audience than acceptance of the protagonist as simply invisible. The pleasure of experiencing *invisibility* in a cinematic frame requires that like other aspects of the frame open to enjoyment, invisibility itself be made visible, and pleasurably so. Since on the screen everything that exists, exists to be seen, invisibility itself must be staged. As the promotional material for *The Invisible Maniac* (1990) urges, the film "is a shocker you've just got to *not* see to believe!" – the *not-seeing* being a carefully produced possibility. Typically, the trick of staging the unseen (and unseeable) resides with those two extradiegetic factota that linger nearest the screen, the invisible orchestra and the camera. A musical cue will associate itself with the key "invisible agent" inside the frame, and through its variation in timbre, melody, tempo, and harmony, changes in the state of that agent will be made accessible to listening viewers. Further, the camera will usually fixate, from a locked position, upon a space in which we take the invisible agent to be standing and glide through a space in which we take the invisible agent to be moving, thereby signaling us, by its own motion or fixity, of a movement or stance we "see" without actually seeing.

Oddly, it is also the case that we cannot see the motion of the camera, although we do see – and this is the basis of our great delight in cinema altogether – the residuum of that motion, a fluid construction of the screen space. In the case of screen invisibility, then, a hidden camera motion will signal by its residuum a hidden dramatic motion; an orchestral sound the source of which is hidden will signal the experience of a hidden character. When we can believe that we see, with all the assiduity and passion of a *flâneur*, the quality, the character, the motion, and the expression of such a being as the camera and the orchestra denote (not alone, but with the aid of the activities of others who present themselves to our eyes and "interact" with the mute invisible One), we can be pleasured by invisibility. To love it, we must "see" it. Normally, then – although, as we shall soon see, *not* in *The Lord of the Rings* – we are convinced we can detect the unseen presence. In a startling moment in John Carpenter's *Memoirs of an Invisible Man* (1992), when the vanished Chevy Chase is caught in a rainstorm as he scurries down a street, the water reflecting off his form gives it an outline, *but only the outline we already believe is present in the frame*. In *Forbidden Planet* (1956), the outline of a hidden monster is suddenly revealed as it is bombarded by laserfire, and this outline is far less easily discernable than Chase's, resembling, as it does, both an animated cartoon (the monster was produced by Disney) and an unspeakable blob.

It should not be surprising to find the theme of the invisible male coupled with the popular *Bildungsroman,* in short, the tale of the boy coming of age exactly through negotiation with his own unseen-ness. Such a story can dramatically assert that the power of seeing the world while being "invisible" oneself is not only properly male, but also part of the natural process of growing up and becoming whole, as though being seen and recognized in adulthood depends in a vital way on having been able to spy on people undetected earlier in life. The invisible boy tends to see what he never thought he could—a world suddenly, inexplicably, enchantingly, alarmingly, profoundly, esoterically made visible *just for him*. His sight, indeed, is what specializes him. While the theme of the invisible protagonist dates back to the early days of cinema – *The Invisible Dog* (1909), for example – and has been a persistent theme since the sound age, when the antics of adult characters who could not be seen could often eerily be heard,[1] there has been a recent surge of interest in these unseen protagonists who have not yet grown up. Following from Herman Hoffman's *The Invisible Boy* (1957) and more recently Avery Crounse's *The Invisible Kid* (1988) have been the strange "invisible" adventures of the extended adolescent Sebastian Caine in Paul Verhoeven's *Hollow Man* (2000), the escapades of the title character in Chris Columbus's *Harry Potter and the Sorcerer's Stone* or *Harry Potter and the Chamber of Secrets* (2002), and Alfonso Cuarón's *Harry Potter and the Prisoner of Azkaban* (2004), or the visions of Frodo Baggins in *The Lord of the Rings*, all of which moments have offered spectacular opportunities for audience identification with notably immature optical empowerment.

The fantasy on display in these films is surely voyeurism (seeing without being subjected to a gaze), but not only that: there are also what we might refer to as puppetry (the ability to cause action from a distance) and, for the viewer invisibly watching all this onscreen, an ability to predict the future. In *The Fellowship of the Ring*, voyeurism can be seen when at Weathertop, as he is threatened by the fierce Ring Wraiths (the Nazgûl) Frodo disappears and watches them from the safety of his invisible envelope; and in *Harry Potter and the Sorcerer's Stone* when Harry (Daniel Radcliffe), covered by the cloak of invisibility he has received as a Christmas present, spies upon a conversation between two teachers without being detected. The voyeurism of the invisible boy is

---

[1] In, for example, *The Invisible Man* (1933); *Topper* (Norman Z. McLeod, 1937), *The Invisible Menace* (John Farrow, 1938), *Topper Takes a Trip* (Norman Z. McLeod, 1939), *The Invisible Man Returns* (Joe May, 1940), *Invisible Woman* (A. Edward Sutherland, 1941), *Invisible Agent* (Edwin L. Marin, 1942), *The Invisible Man's Revenge* (Ford Beebe, 1944), *Harvey* (Henry Koster, 1950), *Abbott and Costello Meet the Invisible Man* (Charles Lamont, 1951), *Invisible Invaders* (Edward L. Cahn, 1959), *The Invisible Maniac*, and *Memoirs of an Invisible Man*.

more generally and expansively that of the film viewer: uneducated, in that we do not know the story, we too cannot be detected in the midst of our detection. The invisibility of a boy hero is thus a technique for solidifying irresponsible audience engagement in a narrative. Sometimes, as when Luke Skywalker dons an Imperial trooper's white suit in masquerade, the invisibility is openly staged; sometimes, as when the camera follows "invisible Harry Potter" disappearing through a doorway by panning across to the door and showing the door open and then close, it is not. But we can "enter" the drama by recognizing the bond we share with the boy who is watching but not being watched. In *The Lord of the Rings*, Frodo's invisible moments are lynchpins for the audience's deepest commitment to the tale.

The invisible boy's capacity is often dramatically stunted in his voyeurism, as though he has awakened into a hideous dream in which he can have no effect, exactly because he cannot be seen. In *Harry Potter and the Chamber of Secrets*, Harry's principal moment of invisibility occurs when he travels fifty years back into the past by means of a magical transporting diary. In the "historical" sequence, the film is shot in tinted black-and-white with only Harry's scarlet cable-knit sweater in color (through frame-by-frame computer enhancement, such as was used in *Schindler's List* [1993]); when he tries to get the attention of the characters they pay him no heed; when he calls out he is not heard. Watching this sequence one is reminded boldly of the observational paralysis that strikes us when we are captivated by a view; and also of the dream moment when, crying out, we realize no sound is coming from our body. Alfred Hitchcock, of course, took care to dramatize this "optical paralysis of invisibility" often, most notably in *Rear Window* (1954).

Puppetry is beautifully evident in *Memoirs of an Invisible Man* in a scene where Nick Halloway (Chase), invisible onscreen, is chewing gum and smoking. The wad of gum is seen jiggling and being chomped out of shape in what we take to be a "mouth," though only the wad of gum is visible onscreen. Filling what may well be an "oral cavity," then descending into the "bronchial tubes," only the smoke is to be seen. We take the gum and the smoke to be animated by some offscreen presence, in this case invisible Nick who is mouthing them. The action of puppetry neatly symbolizes the routine procedures through which an unseen power structure shapes and controls everyday action in society: we are all, in some sense, puppeted by what Joanne Naiman calls "unseen, abstract forces over which we have little or no control" (*Societies*, 111). In *The Invisible Killer* (1939), murder is commited long distance through sound waves. In *The Invisible Boy*, a soup spoon rises out of, and falls back into, a bowl while slurping indicates consumption. In *Hollow Man* a cabinet is opened, a tv set programmed to show a video loop, a detection system evaded, clothing seen to come away from bodies.

    The trope of invisibility also sets viewers up for the pleasure of prediction. Heroes typically interact onscreen with a bevy of accomplices and supporters, even as they align themselves against foes. In dramas of visibility, viewers can adopt the perspective of the supporting characters in following the exploits of the hero – can join the crusade – but in dramas of invisibility the bond between viewers and these friendly others is severed since the conceit of the story is that the others cannot see the hero, and imaginatively at least viewers can – this because he is flagged for their attention. There is almost always to be found a scene, often comedic, in which the hero "invisibly" plays a joke on an accomplice who cannot find him in the same diegetic space (the joke working because we *can*). As the joke is developed, we usually see where it is going well before the climax; and in this way, the invisibility of the hero makes possible for us the thrill of seeing a predictable future event approach stage by stage until it unfolds on cue in front of our eyes. Something of a variation on this theme is played in *The Invisible Boy* when Timmy Merrinoe (Robert Eyer), rendered invisible through ingesting a potion donated by his friend Robby the Robot, sneaks into his parents' bedroom to tease them as they are preparing for bed. Giggling while they neck amicably in what they believe is privacy, jumping away (we imagine) from his father's futile lunges, turning on the alarm clock on the bedside table, Timmy is finally "tackled," then "turned" onto his father's knee and "spanked." The father even goes so far as to notice that Timmy has his "pajama bottoms on backwards." We are able to predict most of what happens in this scene, with the reversed pajama bottoms being a kind of writer's and director's joke on our involvement. This trick of dramaturgy, which need not be comical, is not used in *The Lord of the Rings*, either when Frodo goes invisible or when Bilbo does, disappearing from the hobbits' feast, except in one spot: in the conclusion, Frodo's donning of the ring predictably attracts the eye of Sauron, thus turning the tide of the ultimate battle.

Invisibility in *The Lord of the Rings*

But aside from this brief episode, the moments of invisibility in *The Fellowship of the Ring* work quite differently and do not include the mechanism of prediction, since the conceit of the narrative is that we become invisible with Frodo (as we do with Harry Potter), disappearing at his side into the private scape of his secret visions; that is, losing the normal world.

The visions of Frodo are central to the story of *The Lord of the Rings*, and it is crucial that they weigh properly. Consider that *The Fellowship of the Rings* is produced as the first of a trio of spectacular films filled with vast panoramas of natural beauty spread out receptively before our eyes, part of what *The New York Times* calls "the greatest movie gamble of all time"; and that huge sums – nearly $300 million – were publicly spent to marshall sophisticated special effects "over a grueling 15-month period in New Zealand" (Cooper) – in short, that it is in every respect, apparently, a *big film* (nestled, needless to say, against other very big films on the not-so-very-big screens of our cramped multiplexes). In danger of being utterly lost within its "spacious" diegesis, then, is a central feature of invisibility given by J.R.R. Tolkien in the books from which it is adapted, namely the fact that when he vanishes, what is opened to the protagonist is an exceptional vision, a spectacle. Since all visions in *The Lord of the Rings* seem to be spectacles, those of the invisible Frodo are reduced to being only some among many. Frodo's invisible visions may be electric, or they may be perilous, but they are never other in kind than the visions Peter Jackson is spreading out before us *all through these films*. Consider, for example, the visual eeriness of Tolkien's description of Bilbo Baggins's "invisible" experience on Gollum's slimy island in *The Hobbit*

> But now the light in Gollum's eyes had become a green fire, and it was coming swiftly nearer... The hiss was close behind him. He turned now and saw Gollum's eyes like small green lamps coming up the slope. Terrified he tried to run faster, but suddenly he struck his toes on a snag in the floor, and fell flat with his little sword under him. (*Hobbit*, 80)

after which, soon enough, Bilbo figures out the riddle. "It seemed that the ring he had was a magic ring: it made you invisible!" (81). Almost every scene in the film mundanely exhibits this kind of visual excitement. Or note what Frodo Baggins sees on Weathertop in *Fellowship*, threatened under moonlight by the ominous Nazgûl:

> Immediately, though everything else remained as before, dim and dark, the shapes became terribly clear. He was able to see beneath their black wrappings. There were five tall figures: two standing on the lip of the dell, three advancing. In their white faces burned keen and merciless eyes; under their mantles were long grey robes; upon their grey hairs were helms of silver; in their haggard hands were swords of steel. Their eyes fell on him and pierced him, as they rushed towards him. Desperate, he drew his own sword, and it seemed to him that it flickered red, as if it was a firebrand. Two of the figures halted. The third was taller than the others: his hair was long and gleaming and on his helm was a crown. In one hand he held a long sword, and in the other a knife; both the knife and the hand that held it glowed with a pale light. (*Fellowship*, 258)

This text suggests, with its jumping perspective and repetition, with its tremulous uncertainty – the shapes became *terribly* clear; it *seemed to* him that his sword flickered red – a frantic, even panting, subjectivity on Frodo's part. The ring has made him dreamy and panicky at once. The action described, and witnessed by Frodo, is subjugated to this feeling, not to his powers of observation and description.

But film is always a medium in which description is at once effortless and relentlessly precise. What can be done onscreen here, then, to mark the specialness of the vision that falls to him in Frodo's moments of invisibility? To be more practical: how can the "invisible" vision, a kind of play within the play, be differentiated onscreen so that it doesn't look as though Frodo, having slipped the magic ring onto his finger, has

The Laddy Vanishes

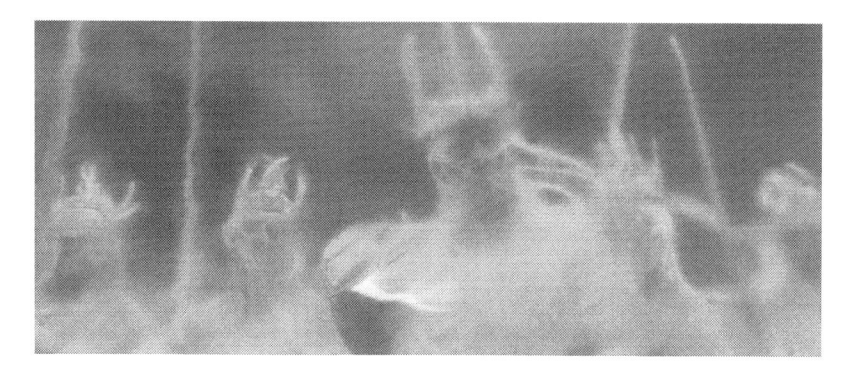

Images 29, 30: In *The Fellowship of the Rings* we see the Witch King through *Frodo's* invisibility...

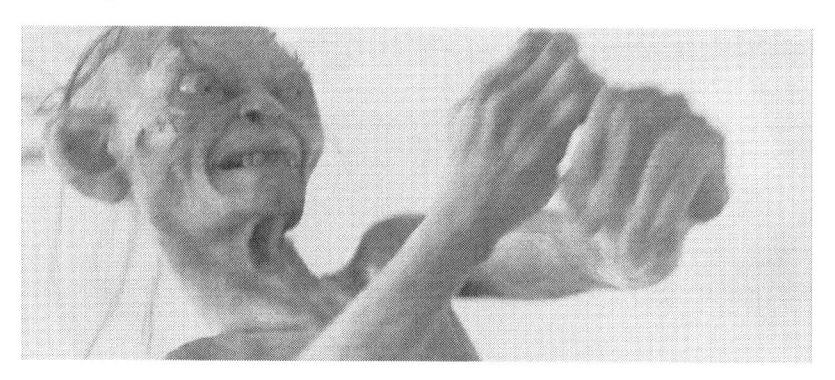

... but at the climax of *The Return of the King*, when Frodo is in the grasp of Gollum, the screen is filled with *our* vision of the invisible "boy." Digital frame enlargements. (Copyright © New Line Cinema)

simply gone off to a Peter Jackson movie? That we may identify with him, the secret visions must precisely seem like a film, of course; yet they must somehow also seem more; and Jackson has raised the ante by making the film that contains them so intoxicating throughout.

    The answer, I think, is that rather than seeing the world in a straightforward way, Frodo experiences a kind of plastic dream-transformation, an oneiric, almost druggy, shift. While his actual moment of disappearance may be accented, acknowledged, and verified by others who gape at the empty space he leaves behind, once he has vanished we find him having left these others outside the special hallucinatory world of his Ring-vision. Chanting choirs (recorded with reverberation, and singing dissonant chords) fill the space of "invisibility" with unresolved sound. Wide-angle lenses are used to spread the elements of the vision across the screen in distortion, exploding outward from a central node which is the focal point of his sight. The camera is over-cranked so that there is a slight slow-motion effect. Animation superimposed on straight film footage gives a chilling see-through effect to the white apparitions of the Nazgûl. In all, the emphasis in the Ring-vision is on the displacements, expansions, and permeabilities of what Frodo can see; not (as in *Harry Potter* and other dramas of invisibility) on the grounding centrality of the fact that he cannot be seen seeing it. And rather than identifying with his position (as we do with Harry's), we are removed to a safe view at his shoulder, made invisible, indeed, in a way that even Frodo is not. Frodo's invisibility, then, is a *special effect* inside the story, even though it is produced with special effects as well.

Earlier, in the tavern of the Prancing Pony, the young Hobbit first had occasion to disappear. In the book, this is an event of the starkest simplicity: "He simply vanished, as if he had gone slap through the floor without leaving a hole!" (*Fellowship*, 212). Moments later, "Not knowing what else to do, he crawled away under the tables to the dark corner..." (212). The film, however, takes advantage of the disappearance to introduce viewers to the diegetic power associated with the marquee object of the narrative project – The Ring – by elaborating a fantastic hallucinatory scenario. Frodo is transplanted to an extra-dimensional space of lambent darkness, where with shrieking and howling noises in the background he sees the Nazgûl riding hellbent through the night, gathering around him, looming. Shots of the Nazgûl are intercut with a gigantic flaming orifice, the (vaginal) eye of Sauron, that seems to suck at Frodo even as it fronts for an immense all-seeing invisibility, an invisibility-within-the-invisibility. In the way that its shapes seem to grow out of one another with a graphic rather than rational continuity, the sequence suggests dream integration and dream process.

The Ring-vision sequences in the film thus stand out as unique moments against a background of florid, exceptional spectacles composed of wild and strangely colored and formed landscapes, magnificent period costumes, and virtually incessant magical – that is noteworthy – effects. Because the film is so visually elaborate, in order to make the Ring transforms appear significant in themselves it has been necessary to play them as dream sequences, Frodo as something of a tripper. Frodo's ring-wearing, instead of focusing on the "reality" of his invisibility, repeatedly suggests he has fallen into an "unreal" trance. Typically in the *Ring* books, when Frodo emerges from his trance he seems to retreat into ordinariness, becoming in a flash one of those people Forster's Cecil read about, "who forget views."

In his specific moments of magical invisibility the onscreen Frodo is unlike all other invisible boys of the screen in that he becomes a dreamer instead of a controlling but hidden presence. Yet if we look at his presence in the film as a whole we see him very much as controlling and hidden. What, after all, could be more dominantly unobtrusive than the relatively insignificant bearer of a central cherished object, the unexamined container of an item of paramount narrative interest? His presence comes to indicate not itself but the presence of the Ring, because after he gains possession of it, Frodo comes to *re-present* the Ring as its servile bearer and he becomes what Jean-Paul Sartre calls "the proper end of the existence of the object" ("Meaning," 143). Armies form around him, line up to antagonize him, not because of what he is in himself but because of what he possesses. His existence is displaced into that of the Object. And as to the precious Ring itself, while it is in fact material chattel, appertaining to Gollum ("My birthday-present!" he whispered to himself [*Hobbit*, 77]), and then to Bilbo Baggins, and finally to Frodo, and in that respect a distinctive and unitary object (the result, we may imagine, of craft production); it quickly becomes associated, for Frodo and for viewers, with a more generalized climate of magical liberation and horizonless possibility, of wealth and puissance, of willfulness and profound intoxication. The Ring, then, both decorates and enchants. Like the lanterns of Paris, it is an actuality that is taken for a symbol, an entity that is understood as a principle. And so, too – because he carries it so faithfully – is Frodo. He is a single "boy"[2] displaced as, and blown into, all brave heroism everywhere.[3] This simple young Hobbit who is, in himself, invisible to human concerns is able, because of what he carries upon his person, to mobilize the action of thousands, inspire cataclysms, and cause the earth to open and towers to loom, forces to be displayed, wraiths to materialize, monsters to threaten, heroes to die. It is only the Hollywood publicity machine, utilizing the exceptionally beautiful, alabastrine face of Elijah Wood in its poster imagery, that drives Frodo home to us as significant in his own right; the story makes clear from the beginning that he is a humble and decent sort upon whom greatness has been thrust but whose actions never indicate a hunger for the dramatic moment.

Being an Invisible Boy

The invisible boy is not quite an invisible man, Mulvey's male figure who "according to the principles of the ruling ideology and the psychical structures that back it up" is unable to "bear the burden of sexual objectification" (*Pleasures*, 20) or else Lacan's "one who is looked at" in gazing. As yet immature, and unable to shape the material of the world through his recursive, self-reflective, narcissistic optical configurations, the invisible boy's greatest thrill, superceding even seeing what he should not see, is not having to imagine himself being seen seeing it, knowing with certainty that he cannot be calibrated, measured, positioned, choreographed, or understood. His pleasure in seeing denies the Other, emphasizes the self, and is often – although explicitly *not* in *The Lord of the Rings* – undertaken in a context that is sexual.

In many ways Frodo is the opposite of Sebastian Caine (Kevin Bacon), the brilliant and boyish scientist hero of *Hollow Man*. Sebastian

---

[2] Frodo is not defined in the books as a "boy" Hobbit, but only as small. Yet the casting of Elijah Wood is salient evidence of Jackson's intent to make *The Lord of the Rings* a film about boyhood as much as it is a film about adventure and the redemption of Good.
[3] Christopher Lee, who plays Saruman, appears in a National Geographic television documentary about Tolkien and the films; bemoaning the fact that there are so many wars being fought on earth at the present time he wonders aloud, "Who will be the ring bearer?"

has invented a procedure for rendering organic creatures invisible and has tested it on himself, with the help of his research team of good-looking young men and women, among the latter his brilliantly scientific ex-girlfriend Linda McKay (Elizabeth Shue). Invisible, he cannot restrain himself from frolicking around his lab like a randy adolescent (as the narrative would have it, indeed, like the randy adolescent he truly is, under the artificial surface of maturity and control he wears like all other men). Donning special goggles, one of the assistants catches him sidling up to two of the women, his "invisible" body manifested as orange and green heat waves, his "invisible" penis bobbing to the merry accompaniment of the "invisible" grin on his face. One of the women on the team is dozing at some computer controls: "invisibly" he unbuttons her sweater, withdraws a breast, and suckles it. Finally he discovers Linda and gives her the chance to taste his "invisible" organ, which she pronounces "familiar." Eventually he escapes from the lab and invisibly rapes one of his neighbors. Contemporized and extrematized for the early twenty-first century, *Hollow Man* is an in-the-face thematic reflection of the earlier, tamer "invisible" male sexuality of *The Invisible Boy,* where, we may remember, "undetectable" little Timmy Merrinoe took to spying on his parents as they made out in their bedroom.

Cinematic invisibility seems frequently to make possible a coupling of sexuality and innocence, an exploitative sensualism for which no responsibility need be taken since no perpetrator can be seen. The "invisible boy" is thus the perfectly manipulative, yet also unblamable, mate for the female who is the object of prurient vision (see also Pomerance "Girl"). But hairy-toed little Frodo Baggins is quite beyond the sexual impulse, even if we are to understand him as being besotted by attraction to greater forces. Carrying the One Ring from Hobbiton to Rivendell, Frodo in his invisibility has no sexual impulse that need be hidden from the world – no strange and prominent *ding-an-sich,* whose sudden and significant excitements have long been for boys the supreme embarrassment that makes invisibility seem a panacea. The great forces with which he comes into contact in his invisible moments are instead military and industrial, strategic, political. *The Lord of the Rings* thus suggests not only that the boy protagonist is truly an adult warrior hiding invisibly in boy's clothing (just as Sebastian Caine is a boy hiding out in the garb of a man), but also that arms, arguments, profitability, domination, and imperial aggression are the true constituent parts of the Nature to which, in his invisible purity, he responds. Frodo's sex become merely one more utensil in a grand array, indeed a utensil for which he has no earthly need: he is the prototype for a bold new vision of the boy, a stealthy soldier who operates from a distance. When he is invisible he has military, not sexual, fantasies. If once he has been rendered invisible by chemistry Dionysiac Sebastian Caine's testosterone is liberated (so that in the end he must die), Apollonian Frodo Baggins, rendered invisible by the One Ring, can escape his own sexuality even as he escapes the threats of his enemies and live to fight bravely in a war where no man's passion survives.

The nexus of illumination, vision, and landscape can reside in sexuality – the city at night as a forum for escapades, the landscape as a space for dance – but in the case of Frodo it does not. He is the dreamer who, unseen, uses light to identify an enemy, who imagines landscape as a haven for danger. What he sees when others cannot see him is monstrously rational.

Moral Eyes

Monstrously rational, and often fearsome – except, and this is an important exception – at the precipice. Here, the screen is essentially filled with *our* vision of the invisible "boy," a vision guided, targeted, focused, and cued by the moves of Gollum in his leaping, pouncing, riding, biting, and celebrating frenzy. The only subjective shot we are given in this climactic sequence is of Frodo's footsteps in the sand. As Sam is present, now in despair, the shots of glowing Gollum, gulping his visions of power by looking through the golden Ring, are entirely readable as his depressed sightings. And they certainly belong to us, as beneficiaries of the third-person narrative position of the camera. Whereas earlier in the trilogy, Frodo not only became invisible when he put on the Ring but also had alarming and sharply-focused visions, and whereas here he does not have these visions, we must ask what can have happened to account for the change.

And the answer, I think, is that for a moment on this precipice, he has lost sight of his own goodness. In this sequence, when Frodo wears the Ring, he is as though blind, this in the specific sense that no visions come to him beyond those of his own self as it moves through space. The power of vision, then, is augmented by invisibility in *The Lord of the Rings* when the seer is good, and is darkened and limited when the seer is not. What this implies to me is the fascinating idea that beauty, our optical expansion of an object of view, depends not only on our not being seen seeing it but on our moral state when we look. But if it is possible to take this equation to mean that the invisible gazer who devotes himself to a purity of intent – an innocence, say, such as is available to the boy perhaps more than to the man – is apt to discover the beauties of the world (a Ruskinian view, to be sure); it may be possible, too, to reverse it: by constructing a view of the world congruent with principles of "beauty," we can in fact appropriate to our own invisible selves a cloak of moral superiority. The display of bourgeois taste is a way of achieving moral status. Whichever way we choose to interpret this relation between moral stance and the spectacular vision, it is clear that in *The Lord of the Rings* we are being treated to clear display of both.

And now, imagining our way back to the nineteenth century gallery, we can see not only that the canvases displayed vistas but also that denying the mercantile arrangement of paintings and the political economy of public display was a way of producing at once a certain aesthetic illusion and a vision of the self as grand and noble. To be blinded to the beauty of the canvas, locked in the confines of a debased economic perspective, was to be low; to enter the canvas proper and see the capacious beauty of its world, was to be elevated. Similarly elevating was the perception of Paris not as a political battleground in which resources were battled for, and social inequality of access to those resources everywhere, but as a sweeping and enthralling panorama of light. Middle Earth, too, is a prospect of darkness, ugliness, hopelessness, and rot when, invisibly, we gaze upon it without an "uplifting" moral vision, which is to say, a vision that seeks not for reality but for the good.

It is the search for good that has moved Frodo and his friends; it is the search for good alone that makes Frodo's view of the world magnificent; and it is also the focus upon magnificence, even in the face of horror, that raises Frodo up. A vision less abstracted, less self-indulgent, less flattering, would have revealed a different story: Frodo and his band freeing the pathetic Orcs from their abysm of slavery, perhaps. But would we, in our own invisibility, and now cut off from the possibility of self-aggrandizement in our seeing, have wanted to read or watch?

Works Cited and Consulted

(non academic web site only materials are listed separately at the end)

Abel, Richard, ed., *French Film Theory and Criticism 1907-1939* Vol. I, Princeton: Princeton University Press, 1995.
Altman, Rick, ed. *Sound Theory Sound Practice*, New York: Routledge, 1992.
Anonymous. "One Film to Rule Them All," *The Times* (9 December 2003).
Artaud, Antonin. "Witchcraft in the Cinema," in *Collected Works* Vol. III, London: Caldor, 1974, 65-67.
Astin, Sean, with Joe Layden. *There and Back Again: An Actor's Tale*. New York: St. Martin's Press, 2004.
Attallah, Paul. "The Audience." In Paul Attallah and Leslie Regan Shade, eds., *Mediascapes: New Patterns in Canadian Communication*, Scarborough, ON: Nelson, 2002, 90-106.
Auden, Wystan Hugh. "The Fellowship of the Ring," *New York Times Book Review* (31 October 1954). Retrieved August 10, 2005 from http://www.nytimes.com/1954/10/31/books/tolkien-fellowship.html
Austin, Thomas. *Hollywood Hype and Audiences*, Manchester: Manchester University Press, 2002.
Bachelard, Gaston. *The Poetics of Space*, trans. Maria Jolas, Boston: Beacon Press, 1969.
----------. *The Poetics of Reverie*, Boston: Beacon Press, 1971.
Badiou, Alain. *Ethics: An Essay in the Understanding of Evil*, trans. Peter Hallward, London and New York: Verso, 2001.
Baillie, Roger "One Film to Rule Them All," *The Times* (12 December 2003).
Baird, Vanessa. "Review of Roland Jacquard, *In the Name of Osama bin Laden: Global Terrorism and the bin Laden Brotherhood*," *New Internationalist* (July 2002), 31.

Balázs, Béla. *Theory of the Film: Character and Growth of a New Art*. Trans. Edith Bone. New York: Dover, 1970. [Reprint; originally published London: Dennis Dobson, Ltd., 1952

Baldrick, Chris. *In Frankenstein's Shadow*, New York: Oxford University Press, 1987.

Baldwin, Neil. *Edison: Inventing the Century*, New York: Hyperion, 1995.

Barker, Martin. "News, Reviews, Clues, Interviews, and Other Ancillary Materials--A Critique and Research Proposal." *Scope, An Online Journal of Film Studies*, accessed February 2004, retrieved February 2004 from (http://www.nottingham.ac.uk/film/journal/articles/news-reviews.htm).

Barron, W. R. J. *English Medieval Romance*, London: Longman, 1987.

Barthes Roland. *Mythologies*, trans. and ed. Annette Lavers, New York: Hill and Wang, 1972.

Bassham, Gregory and Eric Bronson. *The Lord of the Rings and Philosophy: One Book to Rule Them All*, Chicago: Open Court, 2003.

Baudrillard, Jean. "L'Esprit du Terrorisme," *South Atlantic Quarterly* 101 (2002), 403-415.

Bazin, André. "An Aesthetic of Reality: Neorealism (Cinematic Realism and the Italian School of the Liberation)." In *What is Cinema?* Vol. 2, ed. and trans. Hugh Graym Berkeley: University of California Press, 1971, 16-40.

----------. "The Ontology of the Photographic Image," In *What is Cinema?* Vol. I, Berkeley: University of California Press, 1967, 9-16.

----------. "The Myth of Total Cinema" in *What is Cinema*? Vol. I, Berkeley: University of California Press, 1967, 17-22.

----------. *Orson Welles*, New York: Harper and Row, 1978.

Beatie, Bruce A. "The Tolkien Phenomenon: 1954-1968," *Journal of Popular Culture* 3: 4 (1970), 689-703.

Bell-Metereau, Rebecca. "Searching for Blobby Fissures: Slime, Sexuality, and the Grotesque," in Murray Pomerance, ed., *BAD: Infamy, Darkness, Evil, and Slime on Screen*, Albany: State University of New York Press, 2004, 287-299.

Benjamin, Walter, "The Work of Art in the Age of Mechanical Reproduction." In Hannah Arendt, ed., *Illuminations*, New York: Schocken Books, 1968, 217-251.

----------. *The Origins of German Tragic Drama*, London: New Left Books, 1977.

Bennett, Tony and Joan Woollacott. *Bond and Beyond: the Political Career of a Popular Hero*, New York: Methuen, 1987.

Berger, John. *Ways of Seeing*, London: British Broadcasting Corporation/Penguin, 1981.

Biltereyst, Daniel and Philippe Meers. "The Distribution of *The Lord of the Rings* and the Hype around its Release." In Ernest Mathijs, ed., *The Lord *of the Rings: Popular Culture and Commercial Context*, London: Wallflower Press, 2006.

Bettelheim, Bruno. *The Uses of Enchantment: The Meaning and Importance of Fairy Tales*, New York: Alfred A. Knopf, 1976

Blake, Andrew. *J. R. R. Tolkien: A Beginner's Guide*, London: Hodder & Stoughton, 2002.

Bick, Ilsa, J. "The Look Back in *E.T.*," *Cinema Journal* 31: 4 (1992), 25-41.

Birzer, Bradley. "Tolkien: Man Behind the Myth," *Christian History* 78 (Spring 2003), 10-17.

Bloch, Chayim. *The Golem: Mystical Tales from the Ghetto of Prague*, Blauvelt: Steiner Books, 1972.

Booth, Michael R. *English Melodrama*, London: Herbert Jenkins, 1965.

----------. "Soldiers of the Queen: Drury Lane Imperialism." In Michael Hays and Anastasia Nikolopoulou, eds., *Melodrama: The Cultural Emergence of a Genre*, New York: St. Martin's Press, 1996, 3-20.

Bordwell, David. *Making Meaning: Inference and Rhetoric in the Interpretation of Cinema*, Cambridge MA: Harvard University Press, 1989.

Borges, Jorge Luis. "The Golem." In *Selected Poems* ed. Alexander Coleman, New York: Penguin Books, 1999, 193-197.

Botting, Fred. "Horror." In Marie Mulvey-Roberts, ed., *The Handbook of Gothic Literature*, London: Macmillan, 1998.

Braun, Marta. *Picturing Time: Etienne-Jules Marey*, Chicago: University of Chicago Press, 1992.

Breton, Philippe. *A l'image de l'Homme du Golem aux creatures virtuelles*, Paris: Editions du Seuil, 1995.

Brewer, Derek. "*The The Lord of the Rings* as Romance." In Mary Salu and Robert T. Farrell, eds., *J. R. R. Tolkien: Scholar and Storyteller: Essays in Memoriam*, Ithaca: Cornell University Press, 249-264.

Brodie, Ian. *The Lord of the Rings Location Guidebook*. Auckland: HarperCollins, 2002.

Brooks, Chris. *The Gothic Revival*, London: Phaidon Press, 1999.

Brooks, Peter. *Melodramatic Imagination: Balzac, Henry James, Melodrama and the Mode of Excess*, New York: Columbia University Press, 1985.

Bruno, Giuliana. *Atlas of Emotion: Journeys in Art, Architecture, and Film*, London: Verso, 2002.

Buchler, Justus, ed. *Philosophical Writings of Peirce*, New York: Dover, 1955.

Buck-Morss, Susan. *Thinking Past Terror: Islamism and Critical Theory on the Left*, London and New York: Verso, 2003.

Buhler, James. "*Star Wars*, Music and Myth." In James Buhler, Caryl Flinn and David Neumeyer, eds., *Music and Cinema*, Hannover and London: Wesleyan University Press, 2000, 33-57.

Bullock, Marcus Paul. *The Violent Eye*, Detroit: Wayne State University Press, 1992.

Calhoun, John. "Hobbit Forming," *Entertainment Design* 35: 12 (Dec. 2001), 16-24.

Campbell, Duncan. "24 reasons to be afraid in Los Angeles," *The Age* (22nd February 2003), 2.

Campbell, Joseph. *The Hero With a Thousand Faces*, New York: Meridian, 1956.

Cantor, Norman F. *Inventing the Middle Ages: The Lives, Works, and Ideas of the Great Medievalists of the Twentieth Century*, New York: William Morrow and Co., Inc., 1991.

Carpenter, Humphrey. *J.R.R. Tolkien: A Biography*, London and Boston: Houghton Mifflin Co, 1977.

Carpenter, Humphrey, ed. *The Letters of J.R.R. Tolkien*, Boston: Houghton Mifflin Company, 1981.

Carter, Lin. *Tolkien: A Look Behind The Lord of the Rings*, London: Gollancz, 2003 [1969].

Chance, Jane. *Lord of the Rings: The Mythology of Power*, Lexington, Kentucky: The University Press of Kentucky, 2001.

----------. "Is There a Text in this Hobbit? Peter Jackson's *Fellowship of the Ring*," *Literature/Film Quarterly* 30: 2 (2002), 79-85.

Chin, Bertha and Jonathan Gray. "'One Ring To Rule Them All': Pre-viewers and Pre-texts of *The Lord of the Rings*," *Intensities: Journal of Cult Media* 2 (2001), retrieved October 15, 2005 from http://www.cultmedia.com/issue2/Achingray.htm.

Chion, Michel. *Audio-Vision: Sound on Screen*, trans. Claudia Gorbman, New York: Columbia University Press, 1994.

----------. *The Voice in the Cinema*, trans. Claudia Gorbman, New York: Columbia University Press, 1999.

Clark, George and Timmons, Daniel, eds. *J. R. R. Tolkien and His Literary Resonances: Views of Middle Earth*, Westport CT: Greenwood Press, 2000.

Clark, Nigel. "The Demon-Seed: Bioinvasion as the Unsettling of Environmental Cosmopolitanism," *Theory Culture and Society* 19: 1-2 (2002), 101-25.

Clarke, Arthur C. "Hazards of Prophecy: The Failure of Imagination." In *Profiles of the Future*, New York: Harper and Row, 1962, 36.

Conley, Tom. *The Self-Made Map: Cartographic Writing in Early Modern France*, Minneapolis: University of Minnesota Press, 1996.

Conrich, Ian. "Seducing the Subject: Freddy Krueger, Popular Culture and the Nightmare on Elm Street Films." In Deborah Cartmell, I.Q. Hunter, Heidi Kaye, and Imelda Whelehan, eds., *Trash Aesthetics: Popular Culture and its Audience*. London: Pluto, 1997, 118-131.

Cooper, Rand Richards. "Simulsequeling," *The New York Times Magazine* (December 15, 2002), 120-121.

Creed, Barbara. *The Monstrous Feminine: Film, Feminism and Psychoanalysis*, London and New York: Routledge, 1993.

Cubitt, Sean. "The Art of Partition: Globalisation, Diaspora and Ecological Aesthetics." In Bryan Biggs, Angela Dimitrakaki and Juginder Lamba, eds., *Independent Practices*, Liverpool: Bluecoat, 2001, 60-71.

----------. "*Delicatessen* or Eco-Apocalypse." In Ziauddin Sardar and Sean Cubitt, eds., *Aliens R Us: Postcolonialism and Science Fiction*, London: Pluto Press, 2002, 18-33.

Dainville, Père François de. *Le Langage des géographes*. Paris: Picard, 1964.

Davis, Mike. "The Flames of New York," *New Left Review* 12 (2001), 14-50.

Davis, Mike. *Ecology of Fear: Los Angeles and the Imagination of Disaster*, London: Picador, 1998.

Delano-Smith, Catherine. *Maps in Bibles*, Geneva: Droz, 1992.

Deleuze, Gilles. *Cinéma 1: L'Image-mouvement*, Paris: Editions de Minuit, 1983.

Dery, Mark. "Downsizing the Future: Beyond *Blade Runner* with Mike Davis," *Escape Velocity*, 2001, retrieved October 15, 2005 from http://www.levity.com/markdery/ESCAPE/VELOCITY/author/davis/html

"Dialogue on Film: Robert De Niro." *American Film* 6:5 (March 1981), 39-48.

Dixon, Wheeler Winston. *It Looks At You: The Returned Gaze of Cinema*, Albany: State University of New York Press.

Dufournet, Jean, ed. *La Chanson de Roland*, Paris: Garnier/Flammarion, 1993, 200-209 (*laisses* 135-140).

Jody Duncan, "Ringmasters," *Cinefex* 89 (April 2002): 64-131.

Dyer, Richard. *Stars*. 2nd ed. London: British Film Institute, 1998.

Ebert, Roger. "Shiny 'Ring' Isn't Quite Flawless," *Chicago Sun-Times* (*December* 19, 2001), 49.

"Edoras: The Rohan Capital." *The Lord of the Rings: The Two Towers*. Dir. Peter Jackson. 2002. DVD. New Line. 2003.

Edson, Evelyn. *Mapping Time and Space: How Medieval Mapmakers Viewed their World*, The British Library Studies in Map History 1, London: The British Library, 1997.

Eisenstein, Sergei. *Eisenstein on Disney* ed. Jay Leyda, London: Methuen, 1988.

Epstein, Jason. "Leviathan," *The New York Review of Books* (1 May 2003), 13-14.
Epstein, Jean. "On Certain Characteristics of *Photogénie.*" In Richard Abel, ed., *French Film Theory and Criticism 1907-1939* Vol. I, Princeton: Princeton University Press, 1995, 314-320.
Fanon, Frantz. *Black Skin, White Masks*, trans. Charles Lam Markmann, New York: Grove Press, 1967.
Faraci, Devin. "Lord of the Rings: Peter Jackson Interview." *CHUD: Cinematic Happenings Under Development*, retrieved December 19, 2002 from http://www.chud.com/news/dec02/dec19jackson.php3.
Christian Fechner, "Le Théâtre Robert-Houdin de Jean-Eugène Robert-Houdin à Georges Méliès," In Jacques Malthête and Laurent Mannoni, eds. *Méliès magie et cinéma* (Paris, Espace Edf Electra, 2002), pp. 72-114.
50 First Dates Production Notes (2004), retrieved October 15, 2005 from http://www.sonypictures.com/movies/50firstdates/index.html.
Finé, Oronce. Single cordiform world-map (1534), illustrated in Rodney Shirley, *The Mapping of the World: Early Printed World Maps, 1472-1700*, London: Holland Press, 1987, frontispiece.
Fischer, Paul. "'Hobbit Man' Talks Tolkien." *Film Inside Out* (December 2001), retrieved October 15, 2005 from http://www.iofilm.co.uk/feats/interviews/p/peter_jackson.shtml.
Forde, John. "Greetings from Hobbiton." *E! Online* (February 1, 2000), retrieved October 15, 2005 from http://www.eonline.com/Features/Specials/Lordrings/Word/000201.html.
Forster, E. M. *A Room With a View*, Harmondsworth: Penguin, 1987 © 1908.
Foster, Hal. "In New York," *London Review of Books* (20 March 2003), 16-17.
Foucault, Michel. *Les Mots et les choses*, Paris: Gallimard, 1966.
Freud, Sigmund. "A Disturbance in Memory on the Acropolis" (1937). *Character and Culture*. Ed. Philip Rieff. New York: Collier Books, 1963. 311-320.
Fuller, Graham. "Kingdom Come," *Film Comment* (Jan/Feb 2004), 24-29.
Garnham, Trevor. *Oxford Museum: Deane and Woodward*. London: Phaidon Press, 1992.
George, Susan. *The Debt Boomerang: How Third World Debt Harms Us All*, London: Pluto, 1992.
Gillam, James H. *Treasures From the Misty Mountain: A Collector's Guide to J.R.R. Tolkien*, Burlington ON: Collector's Guide Publishing, 2001, 182-194.
Gledhill, Christine. "The Melodramatic Field: An Investigation." In *Home is Where the Heart Is*, London: BFI, 1987.

Gillespie, Angus Kress. *Twin Towers: The Life of New York City's World Trade Centre*, Piscataway, NJ: Rutgers University Press, 2002.

Goldmann, Lucien. *The Hidden God: A Struggle of Tragic Vision in the Pensees of Pascal and the Tragedies of Racine*, London: Routledge, Kegan & Paul, 1964.

Goldsmith, Arnold L. *The Golem Remembered: Variations of a Jewish Legend*. Detroit: Wayne State University Press, 1981.

Goodkind, Terry. *The Pillars of Creation*, London: Gollancz, 2001.

Grant, Barry Keith. *A Cultural Assault: The New Zealand Films of Peter Jackson*, Nottingham: Kakapo Books, 1999.

Gray, Jonathan. "Those Rings; the End of Close Reading?" Email posted on the CULTSTUD-L discussion list (Posted 16 December 2003), archived at http://mailman.acomp.usf.edu/mailman/private/cultstud-l/.

---------. "Bonus Material: The DVD Layering of *Two Towers*," in Ernest Mathijs, ed., *The Lord of the Rings: Popular Culture and Commercial Context*. London: Wallflower Press, 2006.

Greydanus, Steven. "Peter Jackson's *The Lord of the Rings* Film Trilogy: Will it be true to Tolkien?" (2001), retrieved August 4, 2005 from http://www.decentfilms.com/commentary/tolkien.html.

Gunning, Tom. "Doing for the Eye What the Phonograph Does for the Ear." In Rick Altman and Richard Abel, eds., *The Sounds of Early Cinema*, Bloomington: University of Indiana Press, 2001, 13-31.

----------. "New Thresholds of Vision: Instantaneous Photography and the Early Cinema of the Lumière Company." In Terry Smith, ed., *Impossible Presence: Surface and Screen in the Photogénie Era*, Sidney: Powers Publications, 2001, 71-100.

Hadley, Elaine. *Melodramatic Tactics: Theatricalized Dissent in the English Market place, 1800-1885*, Stanford, CA: Stanford U P, 1995.

Hansen, Miriam. "Of Mice and Ducks . . .," *South Atlantic Quarterly* 92: 1 (Winter 1993), 27-61.

Hanson, Rob. "THEN: Rob Hansen's history-in-progress of British science fiction fandom." (1994), retrieved August 4, 2005 from http://www.dcs.gla.ac.uk/SF-Archives/Then/then_3-1.html.

Haraway, Donna. "A Cyborg Manifesto: Science, Technology, and Socialist-Feminism in the Late Twentieth Century." In *Simians, Cyborgs and Women: The Reinvention of Nature*, 149-181. New York: Routledge, 1991.

Hart, Steven. "Who's Sauron--bin Laden or Bush?," *Salon* (February 28, 2004), retrieved October 15, 2005 from http://www.salon.com/ent/feature/2004/02/28/lord/.

Hartley, Jenny. *Reading Groups*, Oxford: Oxford University Press, 2001.

Head, Steve. "An Interview with Sean Astin," *FilmForce* (December 18, 2002), retrieved October 15, 2005 from http://filmforce.ign.com/articles/380/380756p1.html.

Hegel, G.W.F. *The Science of Logic*, trans A.V. Miller, New York: Humanities Press, 1969.

Heidegger, Martin. *The Question Concerning Technology and Other Essays*, trans. William Lovitt, New York: Harper & Row, 1977.

Hills, Matt. "Interview with Henry Jenkins," *Intensities: The Journal of Cult Studies* 2 (Autumn/Winter 2001), retrieved August 12, 2005 from http://www.cult-media.com/issue2/CMRjenk.htm.

Hiro, Dilip. *War Without End: The Rise of Islamist Terrorism and Global Response*. London and New York: Routledge, 2002.

"The Hobbit Habit," *Time* 88: 3 (July 15, 1966), retrieved August 10, 2005 from http://www.time.com/time/magazine/0,9263,7601660715,00.html.

Hoberman, J. "Final Fantasy," *Village Voice* (15 December, 2003), Accessed December 1, 2004 http:www.villagevoice.com/issues/0351.hoberman.php

Hobsbawm, Eric. *Age of Extremes: The Short Twentieth Century 1914 - 1991*, London: Abacus, 1994.

Hopkins, Albert, ed. *Magic: Stage Illusions, Special Effects and Trick Photography*, New York: Dover, reprint 1976, originally 1898.

Hoxter, Julian. "Taking Possession: Cult Learning in *The Exorcist*," in Xavier Mendik and G. Harper, eds., *Unruly Pleasures; the Cult Film and its Critics*, Guilford: FABPress, 2000, 173-185.

Hughes, H. Stuart. *Consciousness and Society*, New York: Transaction Publishers, 2002.

Idel, Moshe. *Golem: Jewish Magical and Mystical Traditions on the Artificial Anthropoid*, Albany: SUNY Press, 1990.

Isaacs, Neil D and Rose A Zimbardo, eds. *Tolkien and the Critics: Essays on J. R. R. Tolkien's The Lord of the Rings*, Notre Dame: University of Notre Dame Press, 1969.

Jackson, Peter. "A Passage to Middle Earth." *The Lord of the Rings: The Fellowship of the Rings*. 2001. DVD. New Line. 2002.

----------. Audio commentary, *The Lord of the Rings: The Fellowship of the Ring* DVD (extended version). New Line Home Entertainment, 2002.

Jackson, Rosemary. *Fantasy, The Literature of Subversion*, London: Methuen, 1981.

Jacob, Christian. *L'Empire des cartes: Approche théorique de la cartographie à travers l'histoire*, Paris: Albin Michel, 1992.

Jameson, Fredric. "The Dialectics of Disaster," *South Atlantic Quarterly* 101 (2002), 297-304.

----------. *The Political Unconscious*, Ithaca, New York: Cornell University Press, 1981.

Jenkins, Henry. *Textual Poachers: Television Fans and Participatory Culture*, New York: Routledge, 1992.
----------. "Celluloid Heroes Evolve," *Technology Review* (April 4, 2003), retrieved October 15, 2005 from http://www.technologyreview.com/articles/03/04/wo_jenkins040403.asp?p=1.
Jones, Leslie Ellen. *Myth and Middle Earth: Exploring the Medieval Legends behind J.R.R. Tolkien's Lord of the Rings*. Cold Spring Harbor, NY: Cold Spring Press, 2002.
Jourde, Pierre. *Géographies imaginaires de quelques inventeurs de mondes au XXe siècle. Gracq, Borges, Michaux, Tolkien*, Paris, José Corti, 1991.
Junger, Ernst. *The Glass Bees*, introduction by Bruce Sterling, New York: New York Review Books, 2000.
Kael, Pauline. *The Citizen Kane Book: Raising Kane*. London: Secker and Warburg, 1971.
----------. "Religious Pulp, or The Incredible Hulk." In *Taking It All In*. New York: Holt, Rinehart and Winston, 1984, 106-112.
Kampmark, Binoy. "The Spectre of bin Laden in the Age of Terrorism," *CTheory* (April 11, 2002), retrieved October 15, 2005 from http://www.ctheory.net/text_file?pick=355.
Kant, Immanuel. *The Critique of Judgement*, trans James Creed Meredith, Oxford: Oxford University Press, 1952.
Kellner, Douglas. *Herbert Marcuse and the Crisis of Marxism*, Berkeley: University of California Press and London: Macmillan Press, 1984.
----------. *Critical Theory, Marxism, and Modernity*, Cambridge UK: Polity Press and Baltimore: John Hopkins University Press, 1989.
----------. *Media Culture,* London and New York: Routledge, 1995.
----------. *Grand Theft 2000*, Lanham, MD.: Rowman and Littlefield, 2001.
----------. *Media Spectacle*, London and New York: Routledge, 2003.
----------. *From September 11 to Terror War: The Dangers of the Bush Legacy*, Lanham, MD: Rowman and Littlefield, 2003.
----------. *Media Spectacle and the Crisis of Democracy*, Boulder CO: Paradigm Press, 2005.
Kellner, Douglas and Michael Ryan. *Camera Politica: The Politics and Ideology of Contemporary Hollywood Film*, Bloomington IN: Indiana University Press, 1988.
Kelly, Mary Pat. *Martin Scorsese: The First Decade*. Pleasantville, New York: Redgrave, 1980.
Kepel, Gilles. *Jihad: The Trial of Political Islam*, trans. Anthony F. Roberts, London and New York: I.B. Tauris 2002.
Kilgarriff, Michael. *The Golden Age of Melodrama: Twelve 19th Century Melodramas*, London: Wolfe Publishing, 1974.

Kim, Sue. "Beyond Black and White: Race and Postmodernism in the *Lord of the Rings* Films," *Modern Fiction Studies* 50: 4 (2004), 875-907.
Kirkland, Bruce. "Shine Off *Star Wars* for Liam Neeson." *Toronto Sun*, October 11, 2003, 36.
Klein, Naomi. "Signs of the Times." In Phil Scraton, ed., *Beyond September 11: An Anthology of Dissent*, London: Pluto Press, 2002, 146-147.
Klinger, Barbara. "Digressions at the cinema: reception and mass culture," *Cinema Journal* 28: 4 (1989), 3-18.
Koeppel, Dan. "Massive Attack," Popular Science online (November 27, 2002), retrieved August 2, 2004 from http://www.popsci.com/popsci/science/article/0,12543,390918,00.html.
Kolker, Robert. "The Film Text and Film Form," in John Hill and Pamela Church Gibson, eds., *The Oxford Guide to Film Studies*, Oxford: Oxford University Press, 1998, 13-15.
Kozloff, Sarah. *Overhearing film Dialogue*, Berkeley: University of California Press, 2000.
Kracauer, Siegfried. *Theory of Film: The Redemption of Physical Reality*. New York: Oxford University Press, 1960.
----------. *The Mass Ornament: Weimar Essays*, Cambridge: Harvard University Press, 1995.
Kunhardt, Philip B. Jr., Philip B. Kunhardt III, and Peter W. Kunhardt. *P. T. Barnum, America's Greatest Showman*, New York: Alfred A. Knopf, 1995.
Landro, Laura. "The Power of Synergy," *The Wall Street Journal Europe* (March 2000), vi.
----------. "Hobbits in Cyberspace," *The Wall Street Journal Europe* (March 2000), vi.
Lash, Scott. *Critique of Information*, London: Sage, 2002.
Lastra, James. *Sound Techology and the American Cinema*, New York: Columbia University Press, 2000.
Lawrence, John and Robert Jewett. *The Myth of the American Superhero*, Grand Rapids MI: William B. Eerdmans Publishing Company, 2002.
Lee, Alan. *J.R.R. Tolkien. The Lord of the Rings*. Centenary edition. Ill. Alan Lee. Boston: Houghton Mifflin Company, 1991.
Lewis, C.S. "Letter to Fr. Peter Milward." In W.H. Lewis, ed., *The Letters of C.S. Lewis*, New York: Harcourt Brace, 1956.
Lewis, Michael J. *The Gothic Revival*. London and New York: Thames and Hudson, 2002.
Lyman, Rick. "Sites give Tolkien fans their fix," *New York Times* (January 17, 2001), retrieved August 8, 2005 from http://www.tolkien-movies.com/words/2001/01-17-01c.shtml.

Lyotard, Jean-François. *The Postmodern Condition: A Report on Knowledge*, trans Geoff Bennington and Brian Massumi, Manchester: Manchester University Press, 1984.

----------. *Lessons on the Analytic of the Sublime*, trans Elizabeth Rottenberg, Palo Alto: Stanford University Press, 1994.

Maas, John-Michael. "Back to the Future," *Publishers Weekly* (19 August 2002), retrieved October 15, 2005 from http://www.publishersweekly.com.

Machor, James L. and Philip Goldstein. *Reception Study: from Literary Theory to Cultural Studies*, New York: Routledge, 2001.

Magid, Ron. "Imagining Middle Earth," *American Cinematographer* 82:12 (December 2001), 60-69.

Manovich, Lev. *The Language of New Media*, Cambridge: MIT Press, 2001.

Marcuse, Herbert. *Der deutsche Kunstlerroman, Schriften* 1, Frankfurt: Suhrkamp, 1978 (1922).

Mathews, Richard. *Fantasy: The Liberation of the Imagination*, London and New York: Routledge, 2002.

Mathijs, Ernest. "'The Wonderfully Scary Monster' and the International Reception of Horror; Ridley Scott's *Hannibal*," *Kinoeye* 2: 19 (2002), retrieved October 15, 2005 from http://www.kinoeye.org/02/19/mathijs19.php.

----------. "AIDS References in the Critical Reception of David Cronenberg: It May Not Be Such a Bad Disease after All," *Cinema Journal* 42: 4 (2003), 29-45.

Mathijs, Ernest and Xavier Mendik, eds. *The Cult Film Reader*. London: Open University Press, 2006.

McGuigan, Cathleen. "A Tale of Two Towers," *Newsweek* (10 February 2003), 62.

McQuail, Dennis. *Mass Communications Theory: An Introduction*, 2nd edition, London: Sage Publications, 1997.

Mellor, Adrian. "Science Fiction and the Crisis of the Educated Middle Class," in Christopher Pawling, ed., *Popular Fiction and Social Change*, London: MacMillan 1984, 20-49.

Meskys, ed. "Tolkien Fandom," *The View from Entropy Hall* 12 (May 31, 1997), retrieved August 4, 2005 from http://www.worldpath.net/~bullsfan/entropy/issues/12.html

Michaud, Phillippe-Alain. *Aby Warburg and the Image in Motion*, New York: Zone Books, 2004.

Miller, Toby, Nitin Govil, John McMurria, and Richard Maxwell. *Global Hollywood*, London: BFI, 2001.

Mitchell, Rebecca. "Sean Astin Deserves More Credit." *Bit of Earth*, http://humans.bitofearth.net/sean/rebcredit.html, 2004.

Mooney, Chris. "Kicking the Hobbit," *The American Prospect* 12:10 (June 4, 2001).

----------. "Tolkien picks up a few more bits of cultural baggage," *Tolkien Online: The One Ring*, 2003, retrieved October 15, 2005 from http://www.tolkienonline.com/docs/8639.html.

Moore, Rachel O. *Savage Theory: Cinema as Modern Magic*, Duke University Press, 1999.

Morse, Margaret. "What Do Cyborgs Eat? Oral Logic in an Information Society." In *Virtualities: Television, Media Art, and Cyberculture*, 125-151. Bloomington: Indiana University Press, 1998.

Mulvey, Laura. *Visual and Other Pleasures,* Bloomington: Indiana University Press, 1989.

Mumford, Lewis. *Technics and Civilization*, London: Routledge and Kegan Paul, 1934.

Muschamp, Herbert. "The New Arcadia. Why Art Nouveau is Suddenly Fashionable." *The New York Times Style Magazine*. Fall 2004. 224.

Musser, Charles. *Edison Motion Pictures 1890-1900: An Annotated Filmography,* Washington D. C.: Smithsonian Institution Press, 1997.

----------. *The Emergence of Cinema: The American Screen to 1907*, New York: Scribners and Sons, 1990.

Naiman, Joanne. *How Societies Work,* 2nd ed, Toronto: Irwin, 2000.

National Association to Advance Fat Acceptance. "Fat Rights Organization Boycotts *Shallow Hal*" (press release, November 7, 2001), retrieved October 15, 2005 from http://www.naafa.org/news/shallow.html.

"Nethien." "I was Wrong" (December 31, 2004), retrieved October 15, 2005 from http://www.lotrfanfiction.com/viewstory.php?sid=3980.

New Lion Press Release. "New Line Cinema verifies approximately 1.7 million downloads of exclusive 'The Lord of the Rings' preview during 1st day of operation" (April 10, 2000), retrieved August 5, 2005 from http://www.xenite.org/faqs/lotr_movie/download-press-release.html.

----------. "New Line Cinema Begins One Year Countdown to Release of 'The Lord of the Rings' - First Theatrical Trailer to Debut on January 12, 2001; Studio Announces Relaunch of Web Site" (December 19, 2000), retrieved August 5, 2005 from http://www.theonering.net/perl/newsview/2/977279827.

Newman, James. *Videogames*, New York: Routledge, 2004.

Nietzsche, Friedrich. "The Madman," in *The Gay Science* trans. and ed. Walter Kaufmann, New York: Vintage, 1972, 181-182.

O'Brien, Suzie and Imre Szeman. *Popular Culture: A User's Guide*, Scarborough, ON: Nelson, 2004.

Ockman, Joan. "Architecture in a Mode of Distraction: Eight Takes on Jacques Tati's *Playtime*." In *Architecture and Film*, ed. Mark Lamster, New York: Princeton Architectural Press, 2000, 170-195.

Ong, Walter J., S. J. *Ramism and the Decay of Dialogue*, Cambridge: Harvard University Press, 1984.

Overington, Caroline. "Glass spire of liberty chosen as twin towers memorial," *Age* (28 February 2003), 12.

Panofsky, Erwin. *Perspective as Symbolic Form*. Trans. Christopher S. Wood. New York: Zone Books, 1991.

Partridge, Brenda. "No Sex Please--We're Hobbits: The Construction of Female Sexuality in *The Lord of the Rings*." In Robert Giddings, ed. *J.R.R. Tolkien: This Far Land*, London: Vision Press, 1983, 179-197.

Paul, Robert A. "The Eyes Outnumber the Nose Two to One," *The Psychoanalytic Review* 64: 3 (Fall 1977), 381-390.

Pearlman, Cindy. "It's a hard Hobbit to break, as Sean Astin finds." *Chicago Sun-Times*, February 8, 2004, 11.

Peloff, Richard M. "The Third-Person Effect." In J. Bryant & D Zillman, eds., *Media Effects: Advances in Theory and Research*, Mahwah, NJ: Lawrence Erlbaum, 2002, 489-506.

"Peter Jackson Bio." *Bad Taste*. Dir Peter Jackson. 1987. DVD. Anchor Bay Entertainment, 2001.

Plume, Kenneth. "IGN Interviews Sean Astin." *FilmForce* (December 22, 2003), retrieved October 15, 2005 from http://filmforce.ign.com/articles/446/446990p1.html.

Pomerance, Murray. "'Don't understand, my own darling': The Girl Grows Up in *Shadow of a Doubt*." In Frances Gateward and Murray Pomerance, eds., *Sugar, Spice, and Everything Nice: Cinemas of Girlhood*, Detroit: Wayne State University Press, 2002, 39-53.

Prodger. Phillip. *Time Stands Still: Muybridge and the Instantaneous Photography Movement*, Oxford University Press, 2003.

Pryor, Ian. *Peter Jackson: From Prince of Splatter to Lord of the Rings*. New York: St. Martin's Press, 2004.

Radway, Janice. *Reading The Romance: Women, Patriarchy and Popular Literature*, London: Verso, 1986.

Romney, Jonathan. "A Critic's Diary." In John Boorman and Walter Donahue, eds., *Projections 8*, London: Faber & Faber, 1998, 64-86.

----------. "OK Peter, Message Received," *The Independent on Sunday* (21 December 2003), 8.

Rose, Jacqueline. *States of Fantasy*, Oxford: Clarendon Press, 1996.

Rosebury, Brian. *Tolkien; A Cultural Phenomenon*. London: Palgrave-MacMillan, 2003.

Rosenbaum, Jonathan, ed. *This is Orson Welles: Orson Welles and Peter Bogdanovich*. London: Harper Collins, 1993.

"ROTK Production Notes." *TheOneRing.net* (20 November 2003), retrived December 20, 2004 from http://www.theonering.net/perl/newsview/8/1069353525.

Rousse, Michel, ed. *Yvain ou Le Chevalier au lion*, Paris: Garnier/Flammarion, 1999, 281-292 (ll. 5100-5360).

Russell, Gary. *The Art of The Fellowship of the Ring*. Boston and New York: Houghton Mifflin Co., 2002.

Said, Edward. *Covering Islam*, New York: Vintage, 1997.

"Sam I Am: An Interview With Sean Astin." *The Lord of the Rings Fan Club Official Movie Magazine* 1 (February/March 2002), 34-43.

Samuels, Robert. *Hitchcock's Bi-Textuality: Lacan, Feminisms, and Queer Theory,* Albany: State University of New York Press, 1998.

Sandler, Kevin and Gaylyn Studlar, eds. *Titanic: Anatomy of a Blockbuster*. New Brunswick: Rutgers University Press, 1999.

Santner, Eric L. *On the Psychotheology of Everyday Life: Reflections on Freud and Rosenzweig*, London and Chicago: University of Chicago Press, 2001.

Sarris, Andrew. "Mean Fighter from Mean Streets." *The Village Voice* (November 19, 1980), 55.

Sartre, Jean-Paul. "The Meaning of 'To Make' and 'To Have': Possession." In Clark E. Moustakas, ed., *The Self: Explorations in Personal Growth*, New York: Harper & Row, 1956, 140-146.

Schivelbusch, Wolfgang. *Disenchanted Night: The Industrialization of Light in the Nineteenth Century*, Berkeley: University of California Press, 1995.

Scholem, Gershom. "The Idea of the Golem," In *On the Kabbalah and Its Symbolism*, New York: Schocken Books, 1965, 158-204.

----------. "The Golem of Prague and the Golem of Rehovot." In *The Mystical Idea in Judaism*, New York: Schocken Books, 1971, 335-340.

Schorow, Stephanie. "Beloved Tolkien Trilogy Sets Cash Registers Ringing," *The Boston Herald* (October 23, 2004), 25.

Schrøder, Kim. "Audience Semiotics, Interpretive Communities and the 'Ethnographic Turn' in Media Research," *Media, Culture & Society* 16 (1994), 337-47.

Scott, Danny. "Relative Values," *The Sunday Times Magazine* (25 November 2001), 13.

Scruton, Roger. *The West and the Rest: Globalisation and the Terrorist Threat*, London: ISI Books, 2002.

Serkis, Andy. *Gollum: How We Made Movie Magic*, Boston: Houghton Mifflin, 2003.

Sharpe, Ella Freeman. *Dream Analysis*, New York: Brunner/Mazel, Inc., 1937.
Shippey, Tom. *J.R.R. Tolkien: Author of the Century*, London: HarperCollins, 2001.
Sibley, Brian. *The Lord of the Rings: The Making of the Movie Trilogy.* Boston: Houghton Mifflin, 2002.
Silverman, Kaja. *The Acoustic Mirror: The Female Voice in Psychoanalysis and Cinema.* Bloomington: Indiana University Press, 1988.
Simpson, Paul, Helen Rodiss, and Michaela Bushell, eds. *The Rough Guide to The Lord of the Rings*, London: Rough Guides and Haymarket Customer Publishing, 2003.
Singer, Ben. *Melodrama and Modernity: Early Sensational Cinema and Its Contexts*, New York: Columbia Univerity Press, 2001.
Sobchack, Vivian. "'At the Still Point of the Turning World': Meta-Morphing and Meta-Stasis." In *Meta-Morphing: Visual Transformation and the Culture of Quick-Change*, ed. Vivian Sobchack, 131-158. Minneapolis: University of Minnesota Press, 2000.
Solnit, Rebecca. *River of Shadows: Eadweard Muybridge and the Technological Wild West*, New York: Viking Penguin, 2003.
Speake, Tracie. "The Power of the Ring: JRR Tolkien and American Popular Culture," *Sextant* 1: 1 (2003), 71-85, retrieved October 15, 2005 from http://www.history-journals.de/articles/hjg-eartic-j00298.html.
"Spengler." "The 'Ring' and the remnants of the West," *Asia Times Online* (January 11, 2003), , retrieved October 15, 2005 from http://www.atimes.com/atimes/Front_Page/EA11Aa02.html
Stagnaro, Carlo. "Tolkien's Lesson for September 11," *LewRockwell.com* (2002), retrieved October 15, 2005 from http://www.lewrockwell.com/orig2/stagnaro3.html.
Standage, Tom. *The Turk: The Life and Times of the Famous Eighteenth Century Chess-playing Machine*, New York: Walker and Company, 2002.
Steinberg, Marc W. *Fighting Words: Working-Class Formation, Collective Action, and Discourse in Early Nineteenth Century England.* Cornell University Press, 1999.
Sudjik, Deyan. "Towering Ambition," *Sunday Age* (16 March 2003), 16.
Taussig, Michael. *The Nervous System*, London and New York: Routledge, 1998.
Taylor, A. B. *An Introduction to Medieval Romance*, London: Heath Cranton, 1930.
Theweleit, Klaus. *Male Fantasies Volume 1: Women, Floods, Bodies, History*, Minneapolis MN: University of Minnesota Press, 1987.
----------. *Male Fantasies Volume 2: Male Bodies, Psychoanalyzing the White Terror*, Minneapolis: University of Minnesota Press, 1989.

Thompson, E. P. *The Making of the English Working Class*, London: Gollancz, 1963.
Todorov, Tzvetan. *Hope and Memory: Lessons from the Twentieth Century* trans. David Bellos, London: Atlantic Books, 2003.
Tolkien, J.R.R "Foreword." In *The Lord of the Rings,* London: Harper Collins, 1999 [1954/1966].
----------. *The Silmarillion*, London: HarperCollins, 1999.
----------. *The Hobbit, or There and Back Again*, London: HarperCollins, 1999.
----------. *The Fellowship of the Ring*, London: HarperCollins, 1999.
----------. *The Two Towers*, London: HarperCollins, 1999.
----------. *The Return of the King*, London: HarperCollins, 1999.
Tolkien, J.R.R. "Beowulf: The Monsters and the Critics," Sir Israel Gollanez Memorial Lecture, Proceedings of the British Academy (1936) pp. 245-295. Reprinted in *Beowulf: A Verse Translation*. Trans. Seamus Heaney. Ed. Daniel Donoghue. New York and London: W.W. Norton & Company, 2002. 103-130.
Tönnies, Friedrich. *Community and Civil Society*, Cambridge: Cambridge University Press, 2001.
Tookey, Chris. "Long Live the King of the Rings," *Daily Mail* (12 December 2003), 52-53.
Trinh T Minh-ha. *Woman, Native, Other: Writing Postcoloniality and Feminism*, Bloomington: Indiana University Press, 1989.
Turner, Jenny. "Reasons for Liking Tolkien," *London Review of Books* (15 November 2001), 15-24.
Venturi, Robert. *Learning From Las Vegas: The Forgotten Symbolism of Architectural Form*, Cambridge, Mass.: MIT Press, 1977.
Vidler, Anthony. "The Explosion of Space: Architecture and the Filmic Imaginary." In *Film Architecture from Metropolis to Blade Runner*, ed. Dietrich Neumann, Munich, London and New York: Prestel, 1996, 13-25.
Villiers de l'Isle-Adam, Auguste, comte de. *Tomorrow's Eve*, Champaign/Urbana: University of Illinois Press, 1982.
Viollet-le-Duc, Eugene. *The Architectural Theory of Viollet-le-Duc: Readings and Commentary*, ed. M. F. Hearn, Cambridge, Mass: MIT Press, 1990.
Voegelin, Erich. *Science, Politics and Gnosticism* Vol. 5 of *The Collected Works of Eric Voegelin*, Columbia: University of Missouri Press, 2000.
Voll, John O. "Bin Laden and the new age of global terrorism," *Middle East Policy* 8 (2001), 3-8.
Wald, Gayle. *Crossing the Line: Racial Passing in Twentieth-Century U.S. Literature and Culture*, Durham NC: Duke University Press, 2000.

Walmsley, Nigel. "Tolkien and the '60's." In *J. R. R. Tolkien, This Far Land*, ed. Robert Giddings, London and Tatawa, N.J.: Barnes & Noble Books, 1984, 73-85.
Wasko, Janet. *Hollywood in the Information Age: Beyond the Silver Screen*, Cambridge: Polity Press, 1994.
----------. *How Hollywood Works*, London: Sage, 2003.
Weber, Max. *Essays in Sociology*, trans. and ed. by H. H. Gerth and C. Wright Mills, New York: Oxford University Press, 1946.
Webster, Leslie. "Archaeology and Beowulf." In *Beowulf: An Edition*, ed. Bruce Mitchell and Fred C. Robinson, Oxford: Blackwell, 1998, 183-194. Reprinted in *Beowulf. A Verse Translation*, trans. Seamus Heaney, ed. Daniel Donoghue, New York and London: W. W. Norton & Co., 2002, 212-236.
Weiss, Allen S. *Breathless*, Middleton: Wesleyan University Press, 2002.
WENN Celebrity News. "Astin Pigs Out for LOTR" (November 23, 2001), , retrieved October 15, 2005 from http://www.imdb.com/news/wenn/2001-11-23.
Westbrook, Bruce. "Ward of the Rings" (Rev. of *The Two Towers*, dir Peter Jackson), *Houston Chronicle* (18 Dec. 2002), Star ed.: Houston, 1. LexisNexis Academic. Clemson University Library. 13 Dec. 2004.
White, Michael. *Tolkien: a Biography*, London: Little, Brown and Company, 2001
Williams, Linda. *Hardcore: Power, Pleasure, and the "Frenzy of the Visible,"* Berkeley: University of California Press, 1989.
----------. "Melodrama Revised." In Nick Browne, ed., *Refiguring American Film Genres*, Berkeley: University of California Press, 1998, 42-88.
Wolf, Jeanne. "We've Got Male: Liam Neeson," *Redbook* 193: 1 (June 1999), 88.
Wolf, Naomi. *The Beauty Myth*, New York: Vintage, 1991.
Wood, Gaby. *Edison's Eve: A Magical History of the Quest for Mechanical Life*, New York: Random House, 2003.
Wood, Robin. "An Introduction to the American Horror Film." In Robin Wood and Richard Lippe, eds., *American Nightmare: Essays on the Horror Film*, Toronto: Festival of Festivals, 1979, 7-28.
Woodward, David. "Roger Bacon's Terrestrial Coordinate System," *Annals of the Association of American Geographers* 80: 1 (March 1990), 109-22.
Wright, Andrea. "Selling the Fantastic: The Marketing and Merchandising of the British Fairy Tale Film in the 1980s," *Journal of British Cinema and Television* 4 (2005, forthcoming).
Wyatt, Justin. "The Formation of the 'Major Independent': Miramax, New Line and the New Hollywood." In Steve Neale and Murray Smith, eds., *Contemporary Hollywood Cinema*, London: Routledge, 1998, 74-90.

Yerovi, Luis. "Free Trade and the Ring of Power" (August 14, 2004), , retrieved October 15, 2005 from http://www.goecuador.com/magazine/editorials/ringofpower.html.
Zizek, Slavoj. "Welcome to the Desert of the Real," *South Atlantic Quarterly* 101 (2002), 385-389.

Web Sites

Baggins, Megan "A Hobbit in the Hand...is Worth Two in the Brush!," *Library of Moria* (July 11, 2005), retrieved October 15, 2005 from www.libraryofmoria.com/frodolegolas/ahobbitinthehand.txt.
Cassandra Claire, "Aragon's Journal," *The Very Secret Diaries* (2005), retrieved October 15, 2005 from http://www.ealasaid.com/misc/vsd/.
Dean, Roger, "Roger Dean: Architecture" (2004), retrieved December 15, 2004 from www.rogerdean.com/architecture/index.htm.
Devereaux, Cat. "Lord of the Rings Costume," *Alley Cat Scratch* (September 24, 2005), retrieved March 3, 2005 from http://www.alleycatscratch.com/lotr/.
Grayson, Donna "Lord of the Rings – Gifts and More," *Donna Grayson's Home Page*, retrieved October 15, 2005 from http://www.donnagrayson.com/movies/lordoftheringsgifts.html.
Jackson, Kate (Communications Advisor New Zealand Post) "New Zealand Post Sends Greetings From Middle-Earth," *New Zealand Post* (November 3, 2003), retrieved March 3, 2005 from http://www.nzpost.co.nz/Cultures/en-NZ/AboutUs/MediaCentre/MediaReleases/.
Jensen, Steuard. *Tolkien Meta-FAQ*, retrieved October 15, 2005 from http://tolkien.slimy.com/.
L., Sophie "A Few Replies," *Tolkien Movies Forum* (August 15, 2001), retrieved October 15, 2005 from http://www.tolkien-movies.com/forum/2001/08-15-01.shtml
Miller, Kim and Michelle Miguelez, "Burger King Restaurants Capture the Magic of *The Lord of the Rings: The Fellowship of the Ring* With Unique Collectibles," *Media-File.Net* (November 15, 2001), retrieved October 15, 2005 from http://www.media-file.net/various/lr/lordoftheringsrelease.htm.
Wynn. *Feed You With a Kiss; the Merry/Pippin Slash Archive* (June 20, 2005), retrieved October 15, 2005 from http://crickhollow.net/kiss/welcome.htm.

(No author available) "The Characters of Middle Earth," *Official Lord of the Rings Web Site*. New Line Cinema (December 1, 2004), retrieved October 15, 2005 from http://www.lordoftherings.net/legend/characters/.

(No author available) "Lord of the Rings Merchandise Shop," *Lord of the Rings Fanatics Shop*, etrieved October 15, 2005 from http://www.lotrfanshop.com.

(No author available) "Lord of the Rings Merchandise," *Starstore Online Catalogue* (2004), retrieved October 15, 2005 from http://www.starstore.com/acatalog/Starstore_Catalogue_LORD_OF_THE_RINGS_MERCHANDISE_14.html.

(No author available) "Lord of the Rings Movie Trilogy – Peter Jackson: Merchandise," *The Tolkienshop* (July 12, 2005), retrieved October 15, 2005 from http://www.xs4all.nl/~rossnbrg/movies.htm.

(No author available) "Lord of the Rings Toys," *Toybiz* (2005), retrieved October 15, 2005 from http://www.toybiz.com.

(No author available) "Burger King: Lord of the Rings Merchandise Shop," *Raving Toy Maniac* (September 5, 2003), retrieved October 15, 2005 from http://www.toymania.com/features/bklotr/index.shtml.

(No author available) "Lord of the Onion Rings?," *TolkienMovies.com* (June 19, 2001), retrieved October 15, 2005 from http://www.tolkien-movies.com/words/2001/06-19-01.shtml.

(No author available) "The Lord of the Rings: The Two Towers Assortment One," *Raving Toy Maniac* (2005), retrieved October 15, 2005 from http://www.toymania.com/columns/spotlight/twotowersasst1.shtml.

(No author available) "Lord of the Rings Costumes," *Costume Shopper*, retrieved October 15, 2005 from http://www.costumeshopper.com/lord-of-the-rings-costumes.htm.

(No author available) "Arwen Dress Costumes," *Costume Craze*, retrieved March 3, 2005 from http://www.costumecraze.com/index-lotr-arwen.html.

(No author available) "The Lord of the Rings Swords and Arms," *Blades By Brown*, retrieved March 3, 2005 from http://www.bladesbybrown.com/lotr.html.

(No author available) "Lord of the Rings Coins," *New Zealand Post* (November 3, 2003), retrived March 3, 2005 from https://secure.nzpost.co.nz/cgi-bin/nzstamps/.

(No author available) "PM Strikes First The Lord of the Rings' Coin," *Scoop Independent News* (July 17, 2003), retrieved March 3, 2005 from http://www.scoop.co.nz/stories/BU0307/S00174.htm.

(No author available) "Surge In Us Tourists Proof Positive Of Power Of The Ring," *Scoop Independent News* (January 24, 2003), retrieved March 3, 2005 from http://www.scoop.co.nz/stories/CU0301/S00068.htm.

(No author available) "All-Time Worldwide Box Office," *The Internet Movie Database*, retrieved October 15, 2005 from http://imdb.com/boxoffice/alltimegross?region=world-wide.

(No author available) "Can't We Just Buy You An IPod?," *Fandom_Wank, JournalFen* (August 10, 2005), retrieved October 15, 2005 from http://www.journalfen.net/community/fandom_wank/776590.html?thread=74794894#t74794894.

(No author available) *LASFS – Los Angeles Science Fiction Society*, retrieved October 15, 2005 from http://www.lasfs.org/.

(No author available) *Least Expected*, retrieved October 15, 2005 from http://www.femgeeks.net/tolkien/ (currently offline).

(No author available) *Lord of the Rings Fanatics Network*, Retrieved October 15, 2005 from http://www.lordotrings.com/

(No author available) "Thread: How did You Become A Fanatic?," *Lord of the Rings Fanatics Forum*, retrieved October 15, 2005 from http://www.lotrplaza.com/forum/display_topic_threads.asp?ForumID=50&TopicID=184933&PagePosition=1.

(No author available) "The Lord of the Rings Motion Picture Exhibition," *Museum of New Zealand Te Papa Tongarewa*, retrieved October 15, 2005 from http://www.tepapa.govt.nz/rings/default.htm.

(No author available), *Mythopoeic Society*, retrieved October 15, 2005 from http://www.mythsoc.org/.

(No author available), *The One Ring*, retrieved October 15, 2005 from http://www.theonering.net/.

Index

A320 Airbus, 135
Abyss, The (James Cameron, 1989), 71
Academy Awards (Oscars), 129, 213, 284, 303, 304, 309, 320
Ace Books, 95
Acropolis, 206
Adam, Villiers de l'Isle, 329, 330, 331
Afghanistan, 33, 107
AIDS, 304
Air New Zealand, 66, 135
al Qaeda, 25, 105
Alexander (Oliver Stone, 2004), 304
Alien, films, 310
Aliens, (James Cameron, 1986), 276
Alighieri, Dante, 278
Alps, Southern, New Zealand, 288, 291
American Cinematographer, 164
Angels in America (2003), 272
Aotearoa (New Zealand), 65, 66, 67, 69, 74, 76
Apocalypse Now (Francis Ford Coppola, 1979), 312
Apple Macintosh, 91
"Architect's Dream, The" (Thomas Cole), 206
Aristotle, 13
Art Nouveau, 185, 199, 202
Artaud, Antonin, 348
Asia Times Online, 108
Asia, 65, 66, 201
Astin, Sean, 13, 301, 302, 303, 305-309, 311-318
Atlantic Ocean, 215

Auckland, New Zealand, 298
Austin Powers films, (1997-2002), 121
Austin Powers: International Man of Mystery (Jay Roach, 1997), 122
Austin Powers: The Spy Who Shagged Me (Jay Roach, 1999),125
Austin, Jane, 28
Austin, Thomas, 44
Australia, 69, 110, 116, 218

Bachelard, Gaston, 357
Bacon, Kevin, 368
Bad Taste (Peter Jackson, 1987), 2, 191, 192
Badiou, Alain, 113
Baggins, Megan, 151
Bakshi, Ralph, 83, 119, 127, 141
Balázs, Béla, 308
Ballantine Books, 106
Barker, Judith, 82
Barnum, Phineas T., 329
Bassham, Gregory, 48
Batman, films (1989-2005), 17
Baudelaire, Charles, 216
Baudrillard, Jean, 114, 115
Bazin, André, 321, 325, 336, 347
BBC, 83, 85, 98
Bean, Sean, 23, 143, 169
Beatie, Bruce, 91
Ben-Hur (William Wyler, 1959), 47, 56
Benjamin, Walter, 3, 6, 46, 210
Bennett, Jeremy, 202
Bennett, Tony, 45

Benson Medal, 139
Beowulf, 157, 205, 211
Berger, John, 354
Bettelheim, Bruno, 270, 278
Beverly Hills Cop films (1984-1994), 121
Bible, The, 59, 217
Bick, Ilsa J., 279
Big Kids Meals, 123
Birmingham, England, 199, 201
Birth of a Nation, The (D.W. Griffith, 1915), 47
Birzer, Bradley, 93
Black Hawk Down (Ridley Scott, 2001), 352
"Black or White" (Michael Jackson), 312
Blade (Stephen Norrington, 1998), 127
Blade Runner (Ridley Scott, 1982), 191
Blair, Tony, 33, 116
Blake, Andrew, 92
Bloom, Orlando, 1, 147
Boeing 747, 135
Boeing 767, 135
Bollinger, Alun, 288
Booth, Michael, 170, 172
Bordwell, David, 81
Borges, Jorge Luis, 325, 335, 349
Boucicault, Dion, 156
Boyens, Philippa, 30, 159
Braindead (Peter Jackson, 1992), 2, 348
Brando, Marlon, 312
Braveheart (Mel Gibson, 1995), 314
Breton, Phillippe, 329
Brewer, Derek, 155, 171
Bridget Jones's Diary (Sharon Maguire, 2001), 305
British Royal Mint, 134
Bronson, Eric, 48
Brood, The (David Cronenberg, 1979), 183
Brooks, Peter, 156, 172
Brosnan, Pierce, 353
Brueghel, Pieter, 205
Brunelleschi, Filippo, 205
Bruno, Giuliana, 195
Burger King, 123-126

Burlingame, California, 106
Burne-Jones, Edward, 202
Bush, George Walker, 8, 18, 25, 29, 33, 35, 103, 106, 107, 116
Byzantium, Ancient, 205

Cabinet of Dr. Caligari (Robert Wiene, 1920), 191
Campbell, Joseph, 18, 270
Cannes Festival, 60
Cantor, Norman, 212
Capone, Al, 304
Caribbean Sea, 215
Carter, Lin, 5, 6
Cassini, Giovanni Domenico, 220
Castle of Otranto (Horace Walpole), 211
Celtic languages, 78
Center for Libertarian Studies, 106
"Chalky and Co" (Rudyard Kipling), 76
Chance, Jane, 112, 163, 168
Chaney, Lon, 310
Chase, Chevy, 361
Chelsin, Ken, 139
Chicago, 320
Christ, allegory, 70
Christchurch, New Zealand, 192
Chronicles of Narnia: The Lion, the Witch and the Wardrobe, The (Andrew Adamson, 2005), 297
Circle of Friends, A (Pat O'Connor, 1995), 305
Citizen Kane (Orson Welles, 1941), 43, 347
City of Lost Children, The (Jean-Pierre Jeunet and Marc Caro, 1995), 70
Civil Rights, movements, 92, 96
Claire, Cassandra, 149
Clark, Helen, 135
Clarke, Arthur C., 341
Clouser, Chris, 125
Coalition of the Willing, 36
Cold War, 22
Cole, Thomas, 206
Collette, Toni, 304-305
Conan, films (1982-1984), 17
Connery, Sean, 142
Constable, John, 352

Index

Cook, Randy, 347
Crounse, Avery, 360

D'Onofrio, Vincent, 303-305
Daily Mail, The, 3, 59
Dainville, Francois de, 220
Dali, Salvador, 194
Das Blaue Licht (Leni Riefenstahl, 1932), 26
Davis, Mike, 102, 103, 106, 115
De Niro, Robert, 303, 304, 305, 309, 310, 311, 313
Dead Alive (Peter Jackson, 1992), 192, 320
Dean, Roger, 201, 202
Deane, Thomas, 204
Decline of the West, The, (Oswald Spengler), 108
Del Ray, 106
Del Toro, Benicio, 305
Delicatessen (Jean-Pierre Jeunet and Marc Cano, 1991), 70
Demeny, Georges, 332
Denmark, 205
Derrida, Jacques, 78
Dery, Mark, 103
Descartes, René, 328
Dick, Philip K., 104
Diderot, Denis, 327
Die Another Day (Lee Tamahori, 2002), 353
Digital Domain, 298
Disney, Walt, 337, 339, 346, 359
Distant Drums (Raoul Walsh, 1951), 215, 216, 229
Dixon, Wheeler Winston, 357
Doors, The (Oliver Stone, 1991), 304
Dr. Strangelove (Stanley Kubrick, 1964), 191, 336
Dresden, 72
Driver, Minnie, 305
Dungeons and Dragons, 91
Dürer, Albrecht, 225

E.T. the Extra-Terrestrial (Steven Spielberg, 1982), 279
eBay.com, 122, 124, 149

Ebert, Roger, 317
Ecclesiological Movement, 211
Edison, Thomas, 329-332
Eisenstein, Sergei, 346, 348
Electronic Arts, 144
Elektra (Rob Bowman, 2005), 297
Eliot, Thomas Stearns, 211
Enclave, 106
Encyclopédie (Denis Diderot), 327
England, 19, 21, 155, 156, 157, 211
"Entertainment Tonight" (1981), 320
Enya, 146
Star Wars Episode III: Revenge of the Sith (George Lucas, 2005), 297
Epstein, Jason, 102
Epstein, Jean, 348
Europe, 31, 202, 212
Eve Futur (Villiers de l'Isle Adam), 329
Everglades, Florida, 215
Exorcist, The (William Friedkin, 1973), 44, 174
Eyer, Robert, 362

Faber, Herr, 329
Fact of Blackness, The (Frantz Fanon), 260
Faeries (Alan Lee, Brian Froud), 193
Fanon, Frantz, 252, 260
Fantasia (James Algar, Samuel Armstrong, 1940), 337
Far Left, 98
Fear and Loathing in Las Vegas (Terry Gilliam, 1998), 305
Feed You with a Kiss, website, 150
Fellowship of the Ring, The, fan club, 139
Fifth Element, The, (Luc Besson, 1998), 70
Film Comment, 168
Film New Zealand, 120, 132
Finding Nemo (Andrew Stanton, 2003), 121
Florida, 215, 229
"Flute Player" (Gaby Wood), 327
Fly, The (David Cronenberg, 1986), 43
Forbidden Planet (Fred Wilcox, 1956), 359

Forster, Edward Morgan, 355, 367
Foucault, Michel, 112, 178
France, 156, 348
Francombe, Mr., 82
Free Internet, movements, 91
French May Events, 95
French Revolution, 156
Freud, Sigmund, 110, 206, 268, 279
Frighteners, The (Peter Jackson, 1996), 292
Full Metal Jacket (Stanley Kubrick, 1987), 303, 305
Fuller, Graham, 168

Gadamer, Georg, 68
Games Workshop, 128
Garland, Judy, 279
Gates, Bill, 339
Genesis, 325
Geneva, 328
Geographia (Ptolemy), 217
George, Susan, 72
Germany, 79, 123, 155, 156, 205; expressionist cinema, 195; languages, 78
Gillam, James H., 126
Gish, Lillian, 163
Gladiator (Ridley Scott, 2000), 317
Glass Bees, The (Ernst Junger), 338
Gledhill, Christine, 159
Godfather, Part II, The (Francis Ford Coppola, 1974), 309
Godfather, The films (1972, 1974, 1990), 56, 59
Golden Age, The, 68
Goldmann, Lucien, 96, 97
Goldstein, James, 88
Gondwanaland, 69
Gone with the Wind (Victor Fleming, 1939), 47
Goonies, The (Richard Donner, 1993), 309
Gothic Revival, 211
Gray, Jonathan, 45, 46, 61
Greed (Erich von Stroheim, 1924), 43
Griffith, David Llewelyn Wark, 163
Guernica, Spain, 72

Gygax, Gary, 91

Hadley, Elaine, 157
Hanks, Tom, 304
Hannibal (Ridley Scott, 2001), 45
Haraway, Donna, 256, 315
Hardy, Tom, 353
Harper, Clay, 106
HarperCollins, 106
Harrington Brewery, 133
Harrington, Craig, 133
Harris, Ed, 305
Harry Potter and the Chamber of Secrets (Chris Columbus, 2002), 360, 361
Harry Potter and the Prisoner of Azkaban (Alfonso Cuaron, 2004), 360
Harry Potter and the Sorcerer's Stone (Chris Columbus, 2001), 352, 360
Harry Potter films (2001-), 119
Harryhausen, Ray, 228, 285
Hartley, Jenny, 87
Heavenly Creatures (Peter Jackson, 1994), 192, 288
Heavy (James Mangold, 1995), 304
Hebrew, 324, 337
Hegel, Georg Wilhelm Friedrich, 79
Heidegger, Martin, 67, 78, 79, 80, 343
Heinlein, Robert, 95
Hickey, Jim, 133
Hidden God, The (Lucien Goldmann), 96
High Treason (Maurice Elvey, 1928), 73
Hiro, Dilip, 111
Hiroshima, 72
Hitchens, Christopher, 112
Hitler, Adolf, 26, 29, 31
"Hobbit, The" (1977), 141
Hobbit, The (J.R.R. Tolkien), 4, 63, 173, 242, 243, 312, 316
Hoberman, J., 272
Hoffmann, Ernst Theodor Amadeus, 339
Holcroft, Thomas, 156
Holderlin, Johann Friedrich, 349
Hollow Man (Paul Verhoeven, 2000), 360, 362, 368, 369

Holy Land, 217
Homer, 56
Homme machine, L' (Julien Offroy de la Mettrie), 327
Hopkins, Mike, 333
Houghton Mifflin Company, 106, 193, 213
Howard, John, 116
Howe, John, 193
Howell, John, 286
Hugo, Victor, 211, 212
Hulk (Ang Lee, 2003), 17
Hunchback of Nôtre-Dame (Victor Hugo), 211
Huntington, Samuel, 116
Hussein, Saddam, 31, 33

I, Robot (Alex Proyas, 2004), 297
Iceland National Museum, 200-201
Iceland, 200
Idel, Moshe, 323, 326, 337, 348
Imitation of Life (Douglas Sirk, 1959), 156
Incredible Shrinking Man, The (Jack Arnold, 1957), 277
Incredibles, The (Brad Bird, 2004), 121
Independent, The, 59
Indiana Jones films (1981-1989), 121
Industrial Light and Magic, 2
International Fantasy Award, 139
International House (A. Edward Sutherland, 1932), 73
International Ideal Home Exhibition, 1982, 201
"Into the West" (Annie Lennox), 248
Invisible Boy, The (Herman Hoffman, 1960), 360, 362, 369
Invisible Dog, The (1909), 360
Invisible Kid, The (Avery Crounse, 1988), 360
Invisible Killer, The (Sam Newfield, 1939), 362
Invisible Man, The (James Whale, 1933), 353
Invisible Maniac, The (Adam Rifkin, 1990), 358
I-PALATIR, 139

Iran, 35
Iraq, 33, 35, 106, 111
Islam, 117, 325
Italy, 206

J'Accuse (Abel Gance, 1919), 36
Jackson, Michael, 312
Jackson, Peter, 1, and acting style, 168, 169, 301-302, 313, 317-318; and allegory, 75; and architecture and set design, 190-193, 195-198, 206, 210, 213; and Army of the Dead, 36; and casting choices, 163, 301-302, 317-318; and DVD commentary, 30, 31, 254, 261; and extended DVD version, 45, 53, 179, 254; and fandom, 138, 142-147, 152; and globalization, 75; and Gollum, 254, 261, 346-348; and homoeroticism, 271-272, 277, 279; and ideology, 175; the legend of, 59; and maps, 220; and Middle Earth, 164, 220; and monstrosity, 179, 254; and music, 243, 246; and New Zealand, 76, 120, 133; and *palantír*, 72; and psychoanalysis, 269; and realism, 346, 347, 348; and "The Real Middle Earth", 133; and reception, 190; and Samwise Gamgee, 301-302, 313, 314, 317-318; and the screenplay, 159, 161; and sexuality, 271-272, 273, 276, 277, 279, 281; and special effects, 283, 289-295, 313, 314, 346-348; and Tolkien books, 2, 21, 170, 171;
Jackson, Rosemary, 179
Jacob, Christian, 225
Jacquard, Roland, 105
Jacquet-Droz, Pierre, 328
James Bond films (1969-), 45, 115, 191
James, Henry, 28
Jameson, Fredric, 111
Jaquet-Droz, Henri, 328
Jason and the Argonauts (Don Chaffey, 1963), 228, 285
Jenkins, Henry, 92
Jens Hensen Jewellers, 133

Johnstone, Ted, 139
Jordan, Robert, 111
Junger, Ernst, 340, 341, 348
Jurassic Park (Michael Crichton), 211

Kael, Pauline, 310
"Kalevala" (Elias Lonnerot), 118
Kampmark, Binoy, 105
Kant, Immanuel, 70, 79, 98
Kawerau River, New Zealand, 288
Kempelen, Wolfgang von, 328, 329
Kepel, Gilles, 116
Kids Meals, 123
Kilmer, Val, 304
Kim, Sue, 255
Kinder Egg, 123, 136
King Kong (Merian C. Cooper and Ernest B. Schoedsack, 1933), 2, 192
King Kong (Peter Jackson, 2005), 2, 294, 297
King Lear (William Shakespeare), 60
King of the Ring, 125
King, Stephen, 114
Kipling, Rudyard, 76
Klein, Naomi, 108
Klinger, Barbara, 43, 44
Knickerbocker Toys, 127
Koeppel, Dan, 292
Kolker, Robert, 43
Konigsberg, Russia, 79
Kracauer, Siegfried, 195, 321, 343

La Motta, Jake, 303, 306, 310
Lacan, Jacques, 368
Laden, Osama bin, 25, 31, 33, 105, 106, 107, 112, 115, 118
Lahr, Bert, 279
Lanza, Mario, 192
Lasaine, Paul, 288
Lash, Scott, 75
League of Their Own, A (Penny Marshall, 1992), 304
Learning from Las Vegas, (Robert Venturi, Steven Izenour, Denise Scott Brown), 182
Least Expected, website, 150

Lee, Alan, 45, 10, 193, 197, 198, 199, 201, 202, 205, 206, 210, 213, 317
Leivick, Halper, 324
Lennox, Annie, 146, 248
Lesnie, Andrew, 352
Levinas, Emmanuel, 113
Lewis, Bernard, 116
Lewis, Clive Staples, 5, 6, 70
Library of Moria, The, website, 150
Liverpool, 98
Loew, Rabbi, 324
London, 319
Lord of the Rings: and architecture, 189-214; and ecology, 65-80; figurines, 123-127; and invisibility, 351-372; and maps, 215-229; merchandise, 119-136; prestige collectibles, 127-131; and production software, 283-299; reception of, 41-63, 81-99, 137-153, 190; and special effects, 319-349; and terrorism, 101-118
Lord of the Rings (musical, 2006), 147
Lord of the Rings, The, (Ralph Bakshi, 1978), 141
Lorre, Peter, 334
Los Angeles Marathon, 301
Los Angeles Science Fantasy Society, 139
Los Angeles, 103, 319, 320, 353
Lost Horizon (Frank Capra, 1937), 191
Lumière, Auguste and Louis, 328, 331
Lynskey, Melanie, 192

Mabinogion, The (Anonymous), 193
Macbeth (William Shakespeare), 29, 319
Macedon, Philip of, 304
Machor, James, 88
Magnificent Ambersons, The (Orson Welles, 1942), 43
Major, Grant, 192, 195, 208, 213, 352
Manovich, Lev, 321, 322, 345
Maori culture, 69
Marceau, Sophie, 142
Marey, Étienne-Jules, 331, 332, 344
Marvel Comics, 92
Marvel Enterprises, 126
Marx, Karl, 98, 177

Massachusetts Institute of Technology, 293
Massive 2.0, 297, 298
Massive software (Multiple Agent Simulation System In Virtual Environment), 283, 292-299
Matamata, New Zealand, 135
Mathews, Richard, 111
Matrix series (1999-2003), 71, 196
Matrix, The (Andy Wachowski, Larry Wachowski, 1999), 114
Max, Peter, 194
McKellen, Ian, 1, 143, 271
Media Design School, 298
Meet the Feebles (Peter Jackson, 1989), 192
Méliès, Georges, 328, 332, 345
Mellor, Adrian, 96, 97
Melville, Herman, 102
Memoirs of an Invisible Man (John Carpenter, 1992), 359, 361
Mercator, Gerardus, 217
Metal Hurlant (Valerio Evangelisti), 70
Metropolis (Franz Lang, 1927), 191
Mettrie, Julien Offroy de La, 327
Mexico, Gulf of, 215
Meyrink, Gustav, 324
Miami, 306
Middle Ages, 156, 205, 211, 217
Miller, Toby, 66
Minority Report, (Steven Spielberg, 2002), 104
Miramax, 20
Mitchell, Elvis, 3
Mitchell, Kel, 358
MLA database, 88
Moby Dick, (Herman Melville), 102
Mo-Cap, 295, 297
Mogadishu, 352
Montreal, Quebec, 146
Monty Python, 191
Mooney, Chris, 107
Morrison, Jim, 304
Morse, Margaret, 315, 318
Mortensen, Viggo, 143, 146, 147, 169
Motion Tree, 295

Moulin Rouge! (Baz Luhrmann, 2001), 164
Mulholland Drive, Los Angeles, 353
Mulvey, Laura, 353, 356, 368
Mumford, Lewis, 68
Munsterberg, Hugo, 195
Muriel's Wedding (Paul John Hogan, 1994), 305
Murphy, Eddie, 304
Murray, Sean, 136
Muschamp, Herbert, 203
Musser, Charles, 331
Muybridge, Eadweard, 331, 332
Myirony.com, 103, 115
Mystery Men (Kinka Usher, 1999), 353, 358
Mythopoeic Society, The, 139

Nation, The, 108
National Geographic, 3, 61, 118
NATO, 79
Natural Law, 79
Nazgul's Bane, 139
Nazis, 23, 67
Neeson, Liam, 313, 314
Nelson, New Zealand, 133
New International Division of Labor, 74
New Left Review, 102
New Line Cinema Films, 81, 121, 142, 143, 158, 231, 235, 288
New Line Entertainment, 219
New York Times, The, 3, 140, 363
New Zealand, 2, 7, 8, 9, 20, 65, 66, 67, 69, 74, 76, 77, 109, 110, 111, 119, 120, 122, 131, 132, 134, 135, 136, 143, 191, 193, 198, 288, 298, 314, 363; army, 133; Nomad Safaris, 135; Museum of, 146; Reserve Bank of, 134
"New Zealand – Home of Middle Earth," stamp set, 134
New Zealand Post, 134
Nibelungen cycle, 21, 108
Nietzsche, Friedrich, 338, 339
Night of the Living Dead (George Romero, 1968), 191

Nightmare of Elm Street, A films (1984-1991), 120
Nightmare of Elm Street, A, (Wes Craven, 1984), 121
Norman invasion of 1066, 212
Norman, John, 95
Northumbria, 205
Nôtre Dame Cathedral, 212
Now, Voyager (Irving Rapper, 1942), 156
Nuremberg, 31
Nutty Professor, The (Tom Shadyac, 1996), 304

Okeechobee, Lake, Florida, 215
Old Testament, 323
Oliver Twist, (Charles Dickens), 160
Olmos, Edward James, 303, 304
Ong, Walter J., 219
Ortelius, Abraham, 217
Osborne, Barrie O., 288, 317
Otto, Miranda, 169
Oxford: Museum of Natural History, 204; University, 5, 78, 109, 112, 157, 211

Pacific Ocean, 135
Pakeha settlers, 69
Paltrow, Gwyneth, 304, 308
Panofsky, Erwin, 195
Paramount Pictures, 121
Paris, 212, 351, 352, 353, 367, 371
Partridge, Brenda, 271
Pascal, Blaise, 96
Pastuhov, Phil, 288
"Patmos" (Friedrich Hölderlin), 349
Peloff, Richard M., 81
Pentagon, 339
Perry, Michael, 125, 128
Philadelphia (Jonathan Demme, 1993), 304
Pilote, 70
Pixar, 121
Pixerecourt, René-Charles Guilbert, 156
Play Station, 144
Playtime (Jacques Tati, 1967), 210
Pollock (Ed Harris, 2000), 305

Pollock, Jackson, 305
Poltz, Richard, 139
Popelinière, Lancelot de la, 218
Porras, Rick, 254
Potton, Craig, 288
Prague, 324
Psycho (Alfred Hitchcock, 1960), 174
Ptolemy, 217
Publisher's Weekly, 106
Pugin, Augustus Welby Northmore 211
Pullman, Philip, 112, 116
Purgatory, 36

Quay, Brothers, 348
Queenstown, New Zealand, 288

Racine, Jean, 96
Radcliffe, Daniel, 360
Radway, Janice, 87
Raging Bull (Martin Scorsese, 1980), 303, 306, 309, 310, 311
Raitt, Bay, 333, 347
Rasputin, Grigori, 22
Reading Groups (Jenny Hartley), 87
"Real Middle Earth, The" (2004), 133, 136
Rear Window (Alfred Hitchcock, 1954), 210, 361
Rebel Without a Cause (Nicholas Ray, 1955), 156
Red Carpet Tours, 135
Red Desert, The (Michelangelo Antonioni, 1964), 210
Reeve, Simon, 116
Regelous, Steven, 283, 292, 293, 297, 298
Rehovot, Israel 330, 338
Renaissance, 205, 206
"Return of the King, The" (1980), 141
Richmond, New Zealand, 133
Ricoeur, Paul, 68
Rings Scenic Tours, 135
Robert-Houdin, Jean-Eugène, 329
Robert-Houdin, Théâtre, 328, 332
Rome, Ancient, 205
Romney, Duncan, 62
Romney, Jonathan, 59, 61

Index

Room With a View, A (Edward Morgan Forster), 355
Roosevelt, Franklin Delano, 3, 61
Rose, Jacqueline, 110
Rosebury, Brian, 48
Royal Doulton, 127
Royal Society of Literature, 139
Royal Tenenbaums, The (Wes Anderson, 2001), 352
Ruapehu, Mount, New Zealand, 288
Rudy (David Anspaugh, 1993), 309
Ruskin, John, 211

Sadoul, Georges, 324
Safari of the Rings, 135
Said, Edward, 116
"Saint Jerome in his Study" (Albrecht Dürer), 225
Salton Sea, The (D.J. Caruso, 2002), 305
Samuels, Robert, 357
San Lorenzo, Italy, 206
Sarris, Andrew, 310
Sartre, Jean-Paul, 367
Savigny, Christofle de, 219
Schindler's List (Steven Spielberg, 1993), 361
Schivelbusch, Wolfgang, 351
Scholem, Gershom, 325, 326, 329, 330, 336, 337, 338, 340, 341, 348
Schreck, Max, 345
Schroder, Kim, 87
Schwarzenegger, Arnold, 182
Scott, Sir Walter, 211
Scripture, 217
Scruton, Roger, 116
Sepher Yetzirah, 325, 334, 337
Serkis, Andrew, 12, 314, 319, 320, 321, 323, 332, 333, 334, 335, 336, 346, 347
Seventh Voyage of Sinbad, The (Nathan Juran, 1958), 285
Shakespeare, William, 59, 170, 201
Shallow Hal (Bobby Farrelly, Peter Farrelly, 2001), 304, 308
Sharpe, Ella Freeman, 269
Sherman's March, 72
Shippey, Tom, 112, 113

Shire, Talia, 56
"Shitting Duck" (Jacques Vaucanson), 328
Shore, Howard, 144, 146, 245, 286,
Shue, Elizabeth, 369
Siena, Italy, 206
Silence of the Lambs (Jonathan Demme, 1991), 45
Silmarillion, The (J.R.R. Tolkien), 63, 236
Simplicity, 129
Sims, Karl, 293, 299
SIMS, The, 298
Sir Gawain and the Green Knight, 157
Skipper's Canyon, New Zealand, 288
Smith, Duncan, 61
Sobchack, Vivian, 312, 313
South Island, New Zealand, 289
Soylent Green (Richard Fleischer, 1973), 70
Spain, 155
Spanish Civil War, 72
Speake, Tracie, 92, 93
Speight, Alfie, 288
Spengler, Oswald, 108
Spider-Man (Sam Raimi, 2002), 121
Spider-Man 2 (Sam Raimi, 2004), 121
Spirited Away (Hayao Miyazaki, 2002), 196
Stagnaro, Carlo, 106, 107
Stallone, Sylvester, 182, 305
Stand and Deliver (Ramon Menendez, 1987), 303
Star Trek films (1979-2002), 121, 310
Star Trek: Nemesis (Stuart Baird, 2002), 354
Star Wars films, 17, 119, 123, 310
Star Wars [*Star Wars Episode IV: A New Hope*] (George Lucas, 1977), 59
Star Wars Episode I: The Phantom Menace (George Lucas, 1999), 313, 314
Star Wars Episode II: Attack of the Clones (George Lucas, 2002), 121, 297
Star Wars: Episode III: Revenge of the Sith (George Lucas, 2005), 121

States of Fantasy (Jacqueline Rose), 110
Stella Dallas (King Vidor, 1937), 156
Sterling, Bruce, 339
Stetson, Mark, 191
Stowe, Harriet Beecher, 162
Stranger in a Strange Land, (Robert Heinlein), 95
Strasberg, Lee, 310
Subway (Luc Besson, 1985), 70
Superman films (1978-2006), 17
Svankmajer, Jan, 348
Syria, 35

Tableux parisiens (Charles Baudelaire), 216
Talmud, 323
Tasman, Abel, 65
Taussig, Michael, 109, 111, 112
Taxi Driver (Martin Scorsese, 1976), 309
Taylor, Richard, 75, 125, 192, 255, 285, 289
Taylor, Zachary, 215
Technicolor, 215
Teenage Mutant Ninja Turtles (Steve Barron, 1991), 122
Teenage Mutant Ninja Turtles films (1990-1993), 121
Terminator 2: Judgment Day (James Cameron, 1991), 313
Terror War, 33, 38
TheOneRing.net, 142
There and Back Again (Sean Astin, Joe Layden), 312
Theron, Charlize, 305
Thin Red Line, The (Terrence Malick, 1998), 314
Thomas, Dylan, 74
Thomas, Henry, 279
Thompson, Hunter S., 305
Time Warner, 20
Time, 139
Timeline (Michael Crichton), 211
Times, The, 59, 60
Titanic (James Cameron, 1997), 43, 71
Tolkien Society of America, The, 139
Tolkien Society, 89

Tolkien, Christopher, 111, 317
Tolkien, John Ronald Reuel (1891-1973): admirers of, 5; and aesthetics, 4, 5; and allegory, 4, 5, 75, 105; architecture, experience of, 212; and *Beowulf*, 213; books admired by Peter Jackson, 2; calligraphy, 235; childhood in Sarehole, 199; and children, 115; and Celtic, 78; death of, 152; and ecology, 29, 74, 92; and Elven languages and songs, 108, 118, 140, 166, 233, 236; epic scale of his writing, 21; fandom, *see readership and reader response*; and fascism, 31, 38, 112; and gustatory pleasure, 316; and Heidegger, 78-80; and industrialism, 207; influenced by World War II, 4; interpretive communities and, 8, 32, 175; and the Kalevala, 118; and Kant, 79; letter to Christopher Tolkien, 1944, 317; male-centeredness of, 171; and mapmaking, 220ff; medieval sources of, 169; and modernity, 113, 189, 234; movie rights, 189; music and, 11, 108, 231-248; and Nordic architecture, 200-201, 212; and Oxford, 5, 109, 157, 204, 211; and palantír, 73; popularity, 93; and psychedelia, 195, 201; publishers, 10, 1936; purpose, 161; readership and reader response, 17ff, 81-99, 137-153, 194; sexuality in his text, 28; sexuality of, 271; and technology, 27, 76, 118, 190, 245; and Wagner, 108; and the war on terrorism, 107; writing speed, 284; writing as vision, 21, 26, 345; youth, 75, 163
Tolkien-Movies.com, 142, 147
Tongarewa, Te Papa, 146
Toronto, Ontario, 147
Tory, 61
Tourism New Zealand, 134
Tourism Research Council, 136
"Tower of Babel" (Pieter Brueghel), 205

Index

Toy Biz, 122, 123, 126
Toynbee, Philip, 91
Treasure Island (Robert Louis Stevenson), 225
Trelleborg, Denmark, 204
Trinh T. Minh-ha, 258
Trois Mondes, Les (Lancelot de la Popelinière), 218
Troy (Wolgang Petersen, 2004), 127
Troyes, Chretien de, 171, 228
Turner, Jenny, 116
2001: A Space Odyssey (Stanley Kubrick, 1968), 337
Tyler, Liv, 1

United Kingdom, 130, 139, 190
United States of America, 19, 25, 31, 33, 72, 95, 102-104, 106, 108, 109, 125, 139, 140, 144, 298, 308, 318
Untouchables, The (Brian De Palma, 1987), 304
Uriah Heep, 201
Usher, Kinka, 353

Vaucanson, Jacques, 327, 328
Veidt, Conrad, 345
"Very Secret Diaries, The," Internet satire series, 149
Vienna, 110
Vietnam, 72
Vietnam, anti-war movements, 96
Vietnam, war, 85
"View of Salisbury" (John Constable), 352
Vigil (Vincent Ward, 1984), 288
Viollet-le-Duc, Eugène, 204, 212
Voegelin, Eric, 338, 340, 341

Waco, Texas, 106
Wagner, Richard, 21, 108
Waitangi, Treaty of, 66
Wakatipu, Lake, New Zealand, 288
Wald, Gayle, 259
Walmsley, Nigel, 194
Walpole, Horace, 211
Walsh, Fran, 30, 159, 301
War in the Air (H.G. Wells), 102

War on Terror, 188
Warner Bros., 215
Washington Post, The, 107
Watergate age, 93
Waterloo (Sergei Bondarchuk, 1970), 192
Ways of Seeing (John Berger), 354
Weaver, Sigourney, 276
Weber, Max, 110, 233
Wegener, Paul, 324, 345
Weimar, cinema, 345
Weiss, Allen S., 334
Weitzman Institute of Science, 329-330
Wells, Herbert George, 102
Wenham, David, 169
Westworld (Michael Crichton, '73), 211
Weta Digital, 284, 293
Weta Workshop, 2, 74, 75, 192, 202, 255, 284, 285, 289
Wheel of Time, The (Robert Jordan), 111
White, Michael, 109, 118
Whopper sandwich Value Meal, 125
Williams, Linda, 157, 158, 162, 167, 171
Wilson, Colin, 118
Wilson, Edmund, 91
Wingnut Productions, 235
Winslet, Kate, 192
Wizard of Oz, The (Victor Fleming, 1939), 13, 279
Wood, Elijah, 1, 143, 147, 163, 169, 281, 368
Wood, Gaby, 327
Wood, Robin, 178
Woodward, Benjamin, 204
Woodward, David, 220
Woollacott, Joan, 45
World Science Fiction Convention, 139
World War I, 4, 36, 105, 196, 212
World War II, 4, 30, 35, 105, 188
Wyatt, Justin, 121

Yes, 201
Yvain, Le Chevalier au lion (Chretien de Troyes), 228

Zellweger, Renee, 305
Zizek, Slavoj, 114, 115